Violence and Public Anxiety

Social and Economic Studies No. 47
Institute of Social and Economic Research
Memorial University of Newfoundland

Violence and Public Anxiety

A Canadian Case

Elliott Leyton, William O'Grady, and James Overton

ISER

**Institute of Social and
Economic Research**

Published by the
Institute of Social and Economic Research
Memorial University of Newfoundland
St. John's, Newfoundland
Canada
ISBN 0-919666-65-5

Printed on paper
containing over 50%
recycled paper including
10% post-consumer fibre.

∞

Printed on acid-free paper

Canadian Cataloguing in Publication Data

Leyton, Elliott, 1939-

    Violence and public anxiety

    (Social and economic studies, ISSN 0847-0898 ;
no. 47)

    Includes bibliographical references.
    ISBN 0-919666-65-5
1. Violent crimes -- Newfoundland -- Public opinion.
2. Public opinion -- Newfoundland. I. O'Grady,
William, 1959- II. Overton, James, 1943-
III. Memorial University of Newfoundland. Institute
of Social and Economic Research. IV. Title.
V. Series: Social and economic studies (St. John's,
Nfld.) ; no. 47.

HV6809.N5L49 1992 364.1'09718 C92-098595-5

Contents

Tables

Part II

Acknowledgements

In the course of our research we accumulated many debts. Without the cooperation of the police, parts of this study could not have been conducted. We are grateful to Don Randell, past Chief of the Royal Newfoundland Constabulary, and to Dale Henry, the former Chief Superintendent of the Royal Canadian Mounted Police, for the enlightened manner in which they encouraged and authorized our examination of police files. Help was also provided by Lt. Gary Browne of the Royal Newfoundland Constabulary's Crime Prevention Unit and by the following people in the records department of the Royal Newfoundland Constabulary: Dale Alcock, Linda Bowering, Everett Bryant, Leonard Clowe, Michelle Furlong, Margaret Hall, Shirley Jones, Kathy Kirby, Doloris Miller, Doug Tilley, Dave Underhay, Eric Wiseman. Jerry O'Grady and the records staff of RCMP "B" Division also provided assistance.

Marvin McNutt of Adult Corrections, Ron Penny of the Department of Justice, Richard Fuchs, Craig McKie of Statistics Canada and Ron Day of Newfoundland Department of Social Services also provided wise counsel.

The staffs of the Public Records Office in London, England, the Public Archives of Newfoundland and Labrador, the Newfoundland Division of the Provincial Reference and Resource Library and Memorial University's Queen Elizabeth II Library all provided valuable aid, particularly during the difficult and often tedious process of piecing together the events of the 1920s and 1930s.

Many thanks also to Peter Neary, Nigel Rapport, Jeff Webb, Susan Hoddinott and Grace Ollerhead for valuable assistance, stimulating discussion and support. ISER and the SSHRCC generously funded the project. Susan Nichol did a fine job of editing the manuscript. Her work and Jeanette Gleeson's painstaking preparation of the manusctipt are very much appreciated.

Our project on violence in Newfoundland took a relatively calm and uneventful course—so much so that fully two-thirds of the research team were neither arrested, charged, nor convicted on charges of obstructing the police during the course of the research.

This book has been published with the help of a grant from the Social Science Federation of Canada, using funds provided by the Social Sciences and Humanities Research Council of Canada.

Elliott Leyton, Bill O'Grady, Jim Overton
St. John's, 1992

Preface

In the early 1980s the popular belief that Newfoundland was experiencing a significant change in its pattern of crime and violence led Elliott Leyton to initiate a project examining aspects of violence in the province. In 1983 his initial idea was to examine the significant shift in the extent and severity of violent behaviour which appeared to have taken place since the late 1960s. The main thrust of Leyton's initial proposal was to examine changing patterns of violent behaviour through participant observation research in both urban and rural areas.

Early in 1984 when James Overton became involved in discussions with Elliott Leyton, the focus of research attention began to shift away from ethnography and what eventually became the "Violence in Newfoundland" project started to take shape. The need for a statistical analysis of patterns of crime was recognized and a historical dimension was added to the project.

In 1984 funding was made available by the Institute of Social and Economic Research at Memorial University. Nigel Rapport (as an ISER post-doctoral research fellow) and William O'Grady (as an ISER pre-doctoral fellow) joined the project and began full-time investigation. Rapport was to use participant observation techniques to examine patterns of aggression in both urban and rural areas and O'Grady intended to plot changes in patterns of violence using official statistics and information compiled from police records. Leyton planned to investigate homicide in order to uncover "zones of stress" in modern Newfoundland society, while Overton decided to use archival and other information to discuss collective violence in Newfoundland during the 1930s and 1940s. At this stage it was clearly acknowledged that the various research projects were associated but *not* "integrated."

By the fall of 1984, the focus of the project had changed. The main area of research attention had already been identified as that of whether or not Newfoundland was becoming increasingly violent. It was now decided to try to understand the process which generated concern about violence in the province. O'Grady decided to focus on questions of how violence is defined and measured, by examining how official statistics are compiled and used in order to provide a critical analysis of their "strengths and limitations as indicators of the incidence of violence in Newfoundland." Rapport planned to investigate "current concern with violence" using participant observation in St. John's. He was to look at how individuals use the idea of an increase in violence as part of their world view. Overton planned to scrutinize the complex relationship between state policy, collective violence and economic circumstances in the 1930s and 1940s. This would provide examples of specific circumstances in which Newfoundlanders had been prepared to break the law and engage in violence. Leyton was to study homicide in Newfoundland because it is the violent crime which is the focus of most public concern. He also aimed to uncover assumed shifts in patterns of homicide and to understand the social, economic and cultural factors shaping these changes.

However, during 1985 the project was redefined. Nigel Rapport's ethnography became a separate study and was published by ISER in 1987 under the title *Talking Violence*. Elliott Leyton began to investigate in detail the role played by the press and by various interest groups in creating and shaping public and official concern over violence. He decided to concentrate on the mechanisms by which concern over violence has been manufactured in the period since the mid-1970s. The other two researchers continued their work as already outlined, although Overton came to focus specifically on the 1930s and on the *meaning* of violence in a particular context. The manuscript was completed in the fall of 1986 and has since been revised but not updated.

Introduction

FEAR AND DANGER, CRIME AND VIOLENCE

Fear of crime and violence has become a worldwide phenomenon since the 1960s. In Britain much has been made of the "crime wave" in the popular press, and the question of law and order was a key political issue for the Conservatives under Margaret Thatcher in 1979.[1] The promise of a strong stand on crime is given as one of the factors which led to the Conservative's election in that year. Over the last decade, official statistics in Britain record an increase in crime in general and violent crime in particular and together with the publicity given to the size of the so-called "dark figure" of unrecorded crime, this has provided support for those who argue that a crisis exists. Whether or not there actually is a "crime wave" occurring in Britain, it is clear that *fear* of crime has become a major problem, in some ways just as major a problem as crime itself.

The recent obsession with the crime issue in the United States is examined by Wright (1985). He documents the breadth and depth of the fear that "crime is becoming quantitatively and qualitatively worse." Related to this he argues that "fear of crime appears to be gnawing away at the very fabric of our culture," causing people to alter their patterns of behaviour in response to what anthropologist Marvin Harris calls "terror in the streets" (1981).[2] It is true that those most fearful of crime are least likely to become victims (women over sixty, for instance), but this may in part be due to the fact that certain groups take precautions to "protect" themselves from crime and violence, for example, by exercising caution in their movements.

The images presented by those concerned with crime and violence are powerful and disturbing. Once peaceful communities are held to be experiencing social breakdown, many people are paralysed by fear of attack and forced to live stunted and anxious lives. Neighbourhood watch programs proliferate and in some areas vigilante groups are formed. The calls go out for more policing and for tougher justice. Women organize to "take back the night" and people like Bernhard Goetz become heroes.[3]

While perhaps not as intense or as common as in Britain and the United States, fear of crime is a major problem in Canada. This fear is to be found in urban areas, but also in relatively non-urban provinces such as Newfoundland. According to Ian Taylor, Canadians willingly believe that they are in the midst of a decades long increase in crime (1983). By the early 1980s "fear of crime" had become so pronounced that the Ministry of Justice conducted a survey to measure the extent of this "fearful attitude." Not only do Canadians think that the incidence of violent crime is increasing, but they also think that the character of crime is changing. Many people think that Canada's "peaceable kingdom" is threatened by a type of violence that was thought to be characteristic of life south of the border (Torrance 1986). Thus, on 15 November 1986, the host of CBC's *Cross-Country Check Up* asserted that there was a rise in violent crime in Canada and posed the question "How far would you go to protect your property?" The idea that Canada was in the midst of a crime wave was supported by a representative of Victims of Violence when he was allowed, without question, to state that violent crime in Canada is rising at an "astronomical rate." Significantly, the question posed by *Cross-Country Check Up* was stimulated by the killing of armed robbers by the owners of small stores in Quebec and Manitoba.

The striking thing about the feeling that crime and violence are increasing and that violence is becoming more dangerous, is its all-pervasive nature. From the United States and Britain to Canada, from New York and Toronto to St. John's, Newfoundland, the perception is the same. From the sober statements of statistical agencies to the imaginative articles of journalists, the message is the same: We live in an increasingly threatening and dangerous world.

Taking Canada's easternmost province of Newfoundland as a case in point, this book addresses some of the complex issues involved in the notion that we are currently experiencing an escalation in the incidence of crime and violence, and that the character of this violence is changing. We hope to shed some light on the question of whether this perception is accurate or not, and to examine some of the social processes by which the issues of crime and violence and law and order have been generated *as issues.*

VIOLENCE IN NEWFOUNDLAND: IMAGES OF FEAR AND DANGER

> There's a killer on the loose right now. . . .A stranger. You may pass
> him on the street and not know it. You may brush gently up against
> him in the supermarket while reaching for the fresh cut steak. . .
> You never know. . . .In the dark, hollow soul of the killer, you may
> form the perfect picture of a victim. You may die, screaming in
> tearful fear as life is torn from you (*Metro* 29 June 1986).

This statement from an article entitled "A killer will kill *you*," both expresses and reinforces the widespread belief that the danger of becoming the victim of a violent criminal act has very much increased in recent years in Newfoundland. Four out of every ten residents of St. John's reported in a 1982 crime victimization survey that they were afraid to venture out at night.[4] In a myriad of ways, the message that a once peaceful place is now becoming more dangerous and violent is conveyed to those who live in Newfoundland. If we were to believe all that we read in the local press we would be convinced that since the mid-1970s the province has been in the grip of vandals, armed robbers, and child abusers.[5] The impression is created that strange forces have seized hold of a normally quiescent and law-abiding population in recent years and the province is being led down the path of moral decay.

The concern about crime and violence was already well developed in the mid-1970s. It focused particularly on the problem of vandalism and led to calls for curfews for young people in 1977 and 1978. It brought about the establishment of a *Task Force on Vandalism* in St. John's in 1979.[6] Since then there has been successive waves of concern about such problems as shoplifting, armed robbery and child abuse.

By the early 1980s the perception that crime and violence in the province were increasing in frequency and changing in nature at an alarming rate was finding widespread expression in the local media, casual conversation and in the statements of those in positions of responsibility. According to McGahan, the police in St. John's were of the firm opinion that there was an increase in the level and sophistication of criminal violence in the province's capital (1984).

Anxiety about crime was boosted in this period by the belief expressed by the police and other groups that oil development in Newfoundland would bring an increase in crime and violence.[7] The police feared that the disruption and prosperity associated with oil would cause problems. For a variety of other people, however, the factors in the worsening of the crime situation were unemployment and hard economic times.[8] Not only did the present seem to be more dangerous than the past, but the future did not bode well either.

These concerns were reinforced by official statistics. Levels of recorded violence (traditionally low by Canadian standards) were reported to have increased by 39 percent between 1974 and 1983.[9] This seemed to confirm that Newfoundlanders should be anxious about the crime situation in the province.

Given that crime rates have been often used as indicators of the relative health of societies, it is perhaps not surprising that the apparent change in the pattern of crime should be taken as evidence of a "rent in the social fabric" in Newfoundland (Leyton 1986). In fact, most statements of concern about increasing crime and violence contain some explanation of why this is taking place. One very common account sees crime and violence as the products of the complex set of social and economic changes which have taken place in Newfoundland since World War II and confederation with Canada in 1949. Thus, long-time probation officer Pat Kavanagh explains the "continual downward spiral to more serious and even brutal crime" as the product of increased permissiveness, especially among young people. The decline of the "old values" and the weakening of the controls traditionally exercised by police and clergy has led to the decay of society (*Evening Telegram* 4 October 1975). Michael A. Butler claims that since the 1940s there has been a loss of pride and independence in Newfoundland. He argues that together with the "bad effect" of the media, this has led to the "permissive age" with its materialism, rejection of the law of God, and increased violence:

> Now sad to say that Newfoundland is even experiencing shootings and murders here on her own soil and dear little innocent babies are being killed before they are born to satisfy 'liberated women' who think nothing of the sin they are committing. We had 4,230 babies killed in Newfoundland from 1975 to 1984 (Butler 1986).

The idea that modern life leads to social disorganization, increased estrangement, and even crime and violence is a well established one in Newfoundland. It is a central theme in Farley Mowat's book *A Whale for the Killing*, and it runs through Felt's (1987) work on domestic violence.[10] The argument rests on the belief that Newfoundland has traditionally been a non-violent society. Conflict avoidance mechanisms and strong community control have, it is suggested, prevented high levels of interpersonal violence in Newfoundland. An egalitarian ethos and lack of strong class divisions also limited social tensions in rural areas. It is the forces of modernization (urbanization in particular) which have weakened traditional social controls and led to increased violence, especially in St. John's. The further weakening of social control mechanisms by oil development and/or unemployment threaten to bring even more serious problems in the future.

INVESTIGATING VIOLENCE AND ANXIETY

Much has been written about rising crime and violence and public anxiety in recent years. Rather than give an exhaustive review of all that has been done in this area, we will focus on studies which we have found particularly useful.

If crime and violence are unequivocally on the increase, it would be reasonable to assume that current fears reflect this increase in a fairly unproblematic way. Our study started out by looking at the question of whether or not crime and violence have increased in recent years in Newfoundland. The obvious starting point was a thorough and critical examination of the statistical evidence.

Many students of crime and violence within "administrative criminology" do accept in a relatively unproblematic way the idea that official statistics provide a reasonably accurate indication of a substantial upward shift in the incidence of violence in recent decades (Matthews and Young 1986). When these statistics are treated with caution it is most often because they are thought to underestimate levels of crime and violence. Greater accuracy is then obtained by means of victimization surveys. For those operating within this perspective, explaining fear of crime is relatively easy: People are afraid of crime because it is on the increase. Common explanations for the rise in crime include higher levels of relative deprivation in many countries in the 1970s and 1980s.

Although rejecting many of the central assumptions of "administrative criminology," a school of "left realists" also accepts the fact that crime is on the increase.[11] However, unlike the "administrative criminologists," they are centrally concerned with the victims of crime and with social justice issues. In Britain, the "left realists" developed their ideas as a specific critique of the economic and social policies of the Thatcher government. Young, a major figure of the left realist perspective, both accepts the idea that crime is rising and argues that the "central tenet of left realism is to reflect the reality of crime, that is in its origins, nature and impact" (Matthews and Young 1986). This approach emphatically rejects tendencies to "romanticize crime or to pathologize it. . .to underestimate crime or to exaggerate it." However, besides the quest for theoretical development based on an accurate victimology, Phipps, another adherent of the left realist position, is concerned with developing a criminology which confronts the realities of crime by focusing on practical implications "for justice and against socially generated harms of which criminal harms are a part" (Phipps 1986).

However, there has been sufficient criticism of the accuracy and significance of official crime statistics for us to be cautious about accepting these figures at face value. Do official statistics accurately measure shifts in criminal behaviour? How much value can be placed in the reports of crime increases? Or can changes in recorded levels of crime be explained by changes in police practices and public attitudes? The answers to these questions are important determinants of crime rates.[12] Also, unless it can be clearly shown that crime is increasing, the argument that anxiety is the simple and 'natural' response to this increase breaks down. And if this argument breaks down, we then have to look for other explanations as to why public anxiety about crime is currently so high.

Even if we could be reasonably sure that certain kinds of crime and violence were increasing, it would still be important to try to determine how closely waves of public anxiety are related to these increases. The exact timing and intensity of waves of anxiety about particular types of crime or violence would have to directly correspond with the level and frequency of crime for us to suspect that a causal connection between the two phenomena exists. Even a reasonably close correspondence does not necessarily tell us much about the causal mechanisms involved in this relationship between anxiety and crime. Heightened fear of crime might be caused by an increase in recorded crime rather than as a result of more criminal activity.

What we are taking as problematic is the relationship between what is often thought of as the 'real' amount of crime and violence in society, its measurement by various statistics, and public anxiety. In exploring the nature of this relationship we have drawn upon work which has claimed that much recent popular anxiety about crime and violence can be understood using the concept of "moral panic" (Cohen 1972, Hall *et al.* 1978).

The broad "moral panic" approach is centrally concerned with the social meaning of violence and the mechanisms by which public anxiety about crime and violence or a disease such as AIDS is socially constructed.[13] This approach looks at the role of the media and of various social agencies in shaping concern about crime in general and problems such as mugging, vandalism, and armed robberies in particular. Central to the moral panic approach is the idea that responses to problems are out of proportion to, or even unrelated to, the actual occurrences and real threats. Researchers such as Cohen and Hall *et al.* have tended to focus on how powerful groups in society use the powerless as scapegoats, particularly during hard economic times. They look at the heightened attention focused on offenders and how they are often subjected to severe measures to maintain order. Cohen's early work on the Mods and Rockers in Britain is now the classic moral panic text. More recent work by Hall *et al.* develops and refines Cohen's perspective by analysing concern about mugging in Britain in the early 1970s. Adopting a broadly similar perspective, Fishman in his study of purse snatchings in New York suggests that societal responses to crime do not necessarily correspond to its frequency and severity (Fishman 1978). A similar point has been made by Box and his associates (1983). They argue that the rising incarceration rates in Britain in recent years do not result from an increase in crime, but that they come about because judges are now sending people to prison who would not have been incarcerated in the past. The argument is that heightened anxiety about unemployment and youth in the hard economic times of the 1970s and 1980s led judges to try to stem what they saw as a rising tide of crime by more severe punishment. Although most of this research has focused on the recent past, there is a growing body of work which shows that there is a long history of panics about crime and violence. Pearson's *Hooliganism: A History of Respectable Fears* (1983) is particularly important here.

INVESTIGATING VIOLENCE IN NEWFOUNDLAND

The central question posed in this book is that of whether or not Newfoundland is becoming more violent. The aim is not to provide a simple resolution to this question, but rather to use it as a focus of attention and a point of departure for investigating various dimensions of the current concern with crime and violence in the province. It was for this reason that we decided not to employ a restrictive definition of violence. Rather we have examined the social meaning of this term by (1) a critical analysis of official statistics; (2) an investigation of the media's role in shaping and sustaining the idea that Newfoundland is in the midst of a wave of crime and violence; and (3) a historical case study which examines the complex relationships between violence, questions of public order, and economic and political conditions in Newfoundland in the 1930s.

*Criminal Statistics and Stereotypes: The Social Construction of
Violence in Newfoundland*

In part one of this book William O'Grady addresses the question of
whether an examination of official crime statistics can help provide
a clear picture of changes in the incidence and character of violent
crime in Newfoundland.

Recent statements which use statistics to support the notion
that Newfoundland is becoming more violent are examined in some
detail, together with the kinds of commonsense theories used to
explain the worsening crime situation. Representatives of a variety
of a social groups in Newfoundland have, in recent years, expressed
concern about the growing crime problem in general and about
vandalism, armed robbery, rape, and other violent crimes in particular. The statements have come from business organizations and
trade unionists, from lawyers and judges and from academics. Many
of these groups and individuals base their observations, at least in
part, on official statistics, although the perception that Newfoundland is becoming more violent does *not* seem to depend on a coherent
and thorough examination of statistics. A variety of theories are also
put forward to explain this disquieting situation. An increase in
crime and violence is said to be typical of a population in turmoil or
of a breakdown in traditional modes of social control. It has been
linked with rising unemployment and economic hardship on the one
hand and with the tensions and permissiveness associated with
urbanization and modernity on the other.

Many organized groups have attempted to get government action
to deal with what they regard as an intolerable situation. Statistics
have been used quite extensively to support these calls for assistance. However, does existing statistical evidence show that
Newfoundland is becoming more violent? An examination of the
"violent crime rate" and official statistics reveals that there is *no
concrete evidence* of any significant shift in either the pattern or
incidence of violent crime in Newfoundland since the late 1960s.
There have, however, been increases in *recorded* crime—at least for
some types of offenses. The best evidence suggests that changes in
levels of crime recorded can be explained by shifts in the way certain
offenses have been dealt with by the police and translated into
statistics. Improved police methods, greater citizen involvement in
policing, changes in reporting practices, and a greater willingness
to see certain types of incidents as criminal offenses may also have
played an important role in increasing the amount of crime recorded.
At the same time, a detailed investigation of police files reveals that

many crimes which are classified by the police as non-violent do involve levels of violence which are as great as crimes which are classed as violent. In all, the conclusion is that the "violent crime rate" is not a reliable guide to the level of violence in a particular jurisdiction, and the use of crime rates over time is of doubtful validity as an indicator of changes in levels of violence.

O'Grady's examination of the production and use of statistics shows that at best some conclusions can be drawn if the figures are employed with extreme caution. His work supports the observation made by Farington and Dowds that official criminal statistics *cannot* be interpreted unless police practices in relation to criminal behaviour and the production of statistics are "disentangled" (1985: 41–72). This observation came out of a study which demonstrated that the different methods used by county police forces in Britain accounted for up to a 75 percent variation in recorded crime rates.

An apparently simple problem of examining figures in order to determine recent changes in patterns of violence in Newfoundland, turned into a rather complex attempt to understand something of the social processes by which statistics are made and used.[14] Such an understanding of where statistics come from does not make the problems associated with their use go away. It does not make the drawing of concrete conclusions about crime patterns any easier. But it can, hopefully, save us from making any unwarranted statements about what is happening in Newfoundland at the present time. Unfortunately, official statistics cannot provide a simple and satisfying resolution to the key question of the violence project.

This conclusion may not be very comforting for those who like to think of statistics as rather solid social facts which can be used to indicate the health of the social organism. It also suggests that the widespread obsession with the use of official statistics as "social indicators" is a rather dangerous trend, not least because many of those using such figures show no awareness of the nature of the data they are using. What seems to happen is that various social groups and individuals use statistics in a totally uncritical way to simply support an argument. Explanation, for the most part, proceeds and precludes observation.

If the observation that Newfoundland is becoming more violent is *not* supported by a body of statistical evidence, then why do so many people embrace the notion that we are experiencing a crime wave? O'Grady concludes that we need to begin to raise questions about the ways in which crime and violence, *as issues*, are socially constructed and explained. What is the conventional wisdom about the causes of crime and violence? How do popular theories shape perception? Is it possible that the widespread belief that social breakdown leads to crime and violence creates a situation where, in periods of economic crisis and social disruption, people expect crime and violence to increase? Is the current concern about violence an expression of collective social anxiety? If so, why do we project our fears in this direction?

Finally, it is important to note that while crime and violence do not appear to be increasing in Newfoundland at the present time, it can be shown that the problems of many crime victims are not being voiced in the public domain and are not subject to social censure.

The Theatre of Public Crisis

This section examines the question of the social meaning of violence. It investigates the perception that Newfoundland in the 1970s and 1980s is a more violent place than in the past, even if the levels of crime have not yet reached those found in Toronto and Detroit. Why is this? What is the source of the idea that Newfoundland is becoming more violent?

Much of the concern about violence appears in the media, particularly in the press. For this reason it was decided to conduct a detailed investigation of the reporting of crime and violence in the St. John's *Evening Telegram* from the mid-1970s until the mid-1980s.

Past research has shown that the media can play a powerful role in manipulating the public's fear of violence to sell more papers. However, a detailed investigation of the *Evening Telegram's* coverage of violence and its announcements of crime waves produced few lurid headlines and few exploitation stories. It was found, though, that in the 1970s, dozens of special interest groups, political groups, and pressure groups all realized—consciously or otherwise—that linking their arguments to concern about rising violence was the most potent and useful single card to play in accomplishing their political aims. From that time onward, violence quickly became the symbol of everything that was wrong with our society and why we must chart a particular course; it became the ammunition for the justification of any political position; the language of discourse and the *lingua franca* for any social matter; the proof of any argument; and the necessary factor which legitimised the expansionist aims of any pressure group or profession. A very partial list of those individuals and associations that had announced the explosion of violent crime includes the Director of Justice Statistics from Statistics Canada, the Newfoundland Department of Rural and Northern

Development, the Minister of Social Services (arguing for an expansion of his staff), the Alcohol and Drug Dependency Commission, the Atlantic Institute of Criminology (arguing for more funding), labour and church groups (arguing against increasing unemployment), the Board of Trade (justifying repressive measures against shoplifting), many judges in court (justifying their savage sentences), the Association of Chiefs of Police, the Vice President of the Status of Women's Council, the President of the Citizen's Coalition Against Pornography, the Community Services Council, the Newfoundland Teachers' Association (who wished to expand their staff to deal with this violence problem), the Janeway Children's Hospital (ditto), and Elliott Leyton himself, politicking for a study of violence in Newfoundland. As for the newspaper, except when pursuing its own ideological arguments for capital punishment or providing wildly exaggerated accounts of labour violence, which equated picket line scuffles with revolution, it merely soberly reported the announcements of all these special interest groups. As each announcement was made, the newspaper provided further ammunition for other groups—each special interest reinforcing the other, and each announcement confirming the public in its fear and certain knowledge of an explosion of violent crime.

And what of the police role in all this? It might be expected that the police would be one of the prime offenders in creating the impression that violence was increasing, and that they would announce crime waves in order to expand their own domain. This did not prove to be the case. In fact, the police had periodically assured the public that there was not an explosion of violent crime. The police officers' union had, however, made much of increased crime in an effort to justify their demand for weapons in St. John's.

The conclusion reached by this section of the study is that a variety of otherwise responsible individuals and groups have played a role in generating fear of violence through the release of unanalyzed statistics, by overstating their arguments in order to draw attention to a problem, by uncritically accepting each others' statements, and by not thinking through the consequences of announcements about crime and violence.[15] Widespread fear of crime has resulted from this systematic use of very powerful arguments about violence to add weight to the political demands of pressure groups. The press has been but a medium for these arguments to be presented.

*Riots, Raids and Relief; Police, Prison and Parsimony: The Political
Economy of Public Order in Newfoundland in the 1930s*

What can a historical study of collective violence related to public
relief, unemployment, and public order contribute to an understanding of the current concern with crime and violence in
Newfoundland?

All statements of concern about current violence in Newfoundland implicitly or explicitly rest on the assumption that in the past
the country/province was a peaceful and law abiding place. For the
most part, Newfoundland's golden era of non-violence and order is
presented as a self-evident truth. Occasionally it is backed up by
personal observation, anecdotal information, quotations from turn-
of-the-century observers or the research of social scientists in the
1960s and 1970s. The assumption of a non-violent past is a central
element in explanations which see the current crime wave in terms
of modernization and/or the weakening of traditional patterns of
social control associated with outport Newfoundland.

If the work of William O'Grady and Elliott Leyton makes us
cautious about the validity of present-day announcements of crime
waves, it should also make us very wary about the myth of the
non-violent past in Newfoundland. In fact there has been little
historical research on the patterns of crime and violence in Newfoundland, and there is very little basis for making any *systematic*
comparison between past and present. The detailed account
provided here of violence connected with public relief and unemployment in the 1930s provides a simple antidote to the belief that in
the past Newfoundlanders were unwilling to break the law and
engage in violent acts. But the aim of this section is not to explode
the myth of the non-violent past in Newfoundland in order to
undermine current statements about crime waves; rather, the aim
is to help create an awareness of the great complexity of the issue
of violence by examining particular forms of violence in their historical, political, and economic context.

The 1930s were a decade which saw a major economic and
political upheaval in Newfoundland, with the political crisis cul-
minating in the loss of Responsible Government in 1934. In the early
1930s, in particular, several serious riots took place in the country,
and there were many raids on merchants' stores in order to obtain
relief supplies. The whole decade was one in which the threat of
violence hung in the air; the problem of law and order worried the
authorities right up to the outbreak of World War II. In response to
outbreaks of collective violence early in the 1930s the police force of

the country was more than doubled, but, even so, those responsible for maintaining law and order remained acutely aware of their vulnerability to mass action.

This part of the book traces the complex relationship which existed in the 1930s between state policy regarding public relief and unemployment on one hand and public protest and collective violence on the other. It also examines the relationship between relief policy and the issue of law and order during a period of acute economic crisis and political instability. As in the other sections, much is made of the meaning of violence, particularly for those responsible for law and order.

What the study shows is that changes which occurred in relief and policing policies in Newfoundland in the 1930s were intimately associated with the story of civil disturbance and, in particular, with the organized efforts of the unemployed to improve or prevent the erosion of their standard of life. All policy decisions of the government, however, were strongly influenced by the events of the Depression, the fragile economic structure of Newfoundland, the distribution of political power and the perceived limits to state action. The state attempted to cut relief support to save money and to ensure that the need to work for whatever could be earned was not undermined. Public resistance set the limits to which they were able to cut relief without risking major unrest, which they would not be able to control with the forces available. Organized resistance did not arise spontaneously, but occurred in greatest strength in St. John's and Conception Bay where the unemployed/working class were most concentrated. In the final analysis, the level of support provided to the unemployed was determined by what they were able to squeeze out of the government by protests, political means, raids and riots. In this situation the issue of law and order was loaded in class terms and the police became a means of trying to enforce unpopular decisions onto a starving population.

What can this study add to an appreciation of the current concern with violence in Newfoundland? One answer is that we should be very suspicious of simple, all-embracing explanations for the occurrence of violence. Does unemployment lead to violence? Do political crisis and breakdown lead to violence? Does the breakdown of the social fabric, as in the case of one-third of the population being on public relief in the 1930s, lead to violence? The evidence suggests that the question of the causes of violence is much more complex than is often recognized.

We need to carefully examine the *meaning* of violence, by studying the popular theories within which violent acts, whether they be

xxvi   *Violence and Public Anxiety*

riots or armed robberies, are understood. The evidence of the 1930s
suggests that this meaning shifts, depending upon a variety of
factors of a broad political and economic nature. A population's
sense of vulnerability can be a key factor in influencing interpretation of and reactions to violence. Theories about the causes of
violence, even when they are wrong, can have very real consequences. They can shape patterns of policing and call forth measures to
deal with perceived threats.

Notes

1. The situation in Britain is reviewed by Jones (1985). The importance
   of the issue is also conveyed in Lea and Young (1984), and Kinsey
   (1986). See also "There's nothing to fear but fear itself," *The Guardian*,
   13 June 1989.

2. A good critique of the myth of "Canada as the peaceable Kingdom" is
   provided by Torrance (1986, passim).

3. In the wake of the Goetz incident in New York in 1984 a great deal of
   attention was focused on the "fear of crime." See, for example, "Images
   of Fear," *Harper's Magazine*, 270(1620), May 1985, pp. 39–47.

4. A criminal victimization survey of seven major urban centres in
   Canada was conducted in 1982 by the Ministry of the Solicitor General
   with the assistance of Statistics Canada. This survey included St.
   John's.

5. Any number of examples of this line of argument can be culled from
   the pages of the St. John's *Evening Telegram*. According to Bob
   Nutbeam, "we have our own terrorists" in Newfoundland (*Evening
   Telegram* 13 July 1985). Here Nutbeam is focusing the fear of terrorism
   on domestic problems such as armed robbery, vandalism, wife beating, and "boozed up bums." Thus "anything capable of striking terror
   into a human heart is a terrorist act." This writer also used his pen to
   conjure up images of "anarchy" in connection with the strike of the
   Newfoundland Association of Public Employees: see "Strikers are
   being incited," (*Evening Telegram* 20 September 1986). On the same
   page of the *Telegram*, philosopher Lin Jackson accused Fraser March
   of "fascistic machinations" in the strike. He had led his followers into
   "the wasteland of civil disobedience" and had produced a "mini-rebel-
   lion against the state." These arguments were consistent with the
   Telegram editor's view of the strike. He argued that taking seriously
   the strikers' argument that they should be treated "fairly" is "like
   saying cancer cells are part of your body and shouldn't be destroyed,"
   (*Evening Telegram* 27 September 1986). In such writing there is clearly
   a tendency to equate picket line scuffles and any evidence of lack of
   quiescence on the part of organized labour with anarchy and civil
   disorder.

6. Concerned Immigrant, "In favour of a curfew," (*Evening Telegram* 14 September 1977); A nervous resident of St. Brides, "Too much vandalism on Cape Shore," (*Evening Telegram* 27 May 1978); "Vandalism Task Force to decide priorities," (*Evening Telegram* 7 May 1979).

7. See Powell (1981); "Randell expects prosperity will bring boost in crime," (*Evening Telegram* 7 September 1985); and Leyton (1986).

8. "Unemployment, hard economic times blamed for increase in shoplifting," (*Evening Telegram* 7 February 1985). Much of the material which links unemployment with a wide variety of social pathologies is reviewed in Overton (1986).

9. These statistics were obtained by Elliott Leyton from Statistics Canada and used to support his early proposal for a study of increasing violence.

10. See Overton (1987). The idea that traditionally Newfoundland was a non-violent place was supported by the observations made by social anthropologists in the 1960s and 1970s. See, for example, the work of Cohen (1975); Firestone (1967); Szwed (1966); and Leyton (1975).

11. The classic "left realist" text is perhaps Lea and Young (1984).

12. For a review of this literature see the O'Grady essay in this book.

13. A body of work also exists on the construction of public problems and issues. See Gusfield (1981) and Nelson (1984).

14. The outcome was not surprising. It conforms to the conclusions reached by many who have examined statistics. Box (1981:210) writes that official data "is not a valid indicator of a country's 'real' extent or pattern of criminal activity." He suggests that the "formation and variation" of such data is "determined by organizational, legal and social pressures" and that while the study of these pressures and the process by which the data are produced is valid in its own right, the data are "irrelevant for the purpose of developing and testing etiological accounts of criminal behaviour."

15. Overton (1986) offers a parallel analysis of the way that various groups have presented the problem of unemployment in an effort to stimulate government action.

Part I

Criminal Statistics and Stereotypes

The Social Construction of Violence in Newfoundland

William O'Grady

Historically, Newfoundland society has been viewed as non-violent and relatively crime free. Social researchers who have worked on the island of Newfoundland have consistently emphasized the peacefulness of the people and the absence of criminally violent behaviour. Fairfield (1912), for instance, noted that crimes of violence were seldom heard of and murder startled the entire population. The people as a whole were described as being "so peaceloving." The Newfoundland character has also been described as being based on a dominant ethic of general goodwill, cooperation, intimacy, camaraderie, friendliness, trust, tolerance, stoicism, harmony, respect for others, and good manners. The maintenance of personal relationships, non-hostility and conflict avoidance were considered other important characteristics (Firestone 1967:111–127). Indeed A.P. Herbert, one of a parliamentary committee of three sent over to the island by the British Government in 1943 to report on the status of Newfoundland because the issue of Confederation with Canada was coming up, made these observations about the people:

> They are the best-tempered, best mannered people walking. I do not believe I ever heard a Newfoundlander swear. . . .They are gay, good-humoured and generous; tolerant, temperate, tough, God-fearing, Sabbath-keeping and law-abiding (Herbert 1987:17).

And, as Szwed has written, Newfoundland communities are places where one "smiles and nods 'no'" (1966:84).

Within recent years, however, this image has changed. Many people have formed the impression that the *incidence* and *character* of crime and violence in Newfoundland are changing, and that the days of the "non-violent" Newfoundland are over. Representatives of a variety of groups in Newfoundland society (business people, politicians, police, feminists, academics, teachers, lawyers, judges, trade unionists, community groups, and others) have voiced their concerns and anxieties about the "growing crime problem"—much of which has been described as *violent*. Further, according to popular sentiment, the situation is expected to worsen once offshore oil development begins off the Grand Banks, and thousands of young males move to the province in search of work. The idea that crime is increasing in Newfoundland—particularly in urban areas— is reflected in results obtained by the Canadian Victimization Survey. In 1981, 40 percent of those randomly surveyed in St. John's reported that they were afraid to walk the streets after dark (the percentage of women and the elderly who were afraid to walk out of doors was in fact greater than 40 percent). This level of "fear," according to the survey, is similar to that registered in other 'mainland' areas in the country such as Montreal, Edmonton and Vancouver.

On this basis, many have argued that something has to be done in order to curb or ultimately eliminate this 'new' and disturbing problem manifested by rising crime rates. In fact, in 1984, Statistics Canada reported that the violent crime rate in Newfoundland had increased by 39 percent from 1974 to 1983—one of the greatest increases recorded for any province in Canada during this period. As a response to this growing 'problem,' many individuals and groups have lobbied for various types of *action* in order to control effectively this recent surge of mayhem: measures such as arming the Royal Newfoundland Constabulary, demands for stiffer senten- ces, and/or more police foot patrols in downtown St. John's—and some of this lobbying has been successful.

Not only has this situation elevated the level of fear and anxiety about crime and violence, but it has also motivated several people to examine what they feel are the reasons or *causes* of the changes in crime and violence in Newfoundland in recent years. In this way, a 'theory' seems to have emerged which attributes this disquieting situation (typically based on the use of official crime statistics) to a breakdown in social control. Implicit in this 'theory' is the general association which many people have made between rising crime and breakdowns which are believed to have taken place in traditional forms of social control such as the family, religion, community, etc.

These forms of social control were thought to have functioned to keep crime rates low in Newfoundland. Others have suggested that recent changes in the level and character of crime in Newfoundland are related to the breakdown of social control in quite another way. Statements made by academics, trade unionists, community activists and others have attributed Newfoundland's high rate of unemployment (especially among the young) as being directly responsible for rising rates of crime and violence. The main assumption of this view is that people who are without work and who are poor are more likely to become involved in crime and violent behaviour (as well as other pathological behaviours such as alcoholism) than people who have jobs and are not poor.

This essay will begin by reviewing statements made by various groups and individuals who have in some fashion used official crime statistics to suggest that Newfoundland has become a more violent society. Along with this, we will also present the 'theories' which people have used to explain the causes of this recent breakdown of law and order. This will be followed by a critical examination of the evidence which is most often used to support the statements that there is a "crime problem" in Newfoundland; that is, the official crime statistics as well as information we gathered directly from the police files of the Royal Canadian Mounted Police (RCMP) and the Royal Newfoundland Constabulary (RNC). The detailed investigation will clearly demonstrate that crime and violence in Newfoundland (as they are commonly characterized), have *not* generally been increasing in recent years, nor have they radically changed character to become more heinous—as many people have come to believe. We will show that although the recent statistical increases in violent crime in Newfoundland have been widely accepted as reflecting 'real' increases in the level of criminal behaviour, these changes result from revised procedures and improvements in police record keeping policies, the dubious and careless use of statistics by certain interest groups, and other factors. In this way, we will demonstrate that the *statistical* increases in crime and violence in Newfoundland are not, in fact, due to a radical shift in criminal behaviour.

The next section of the analysis will raise some serious questions regarding the ways in which crime and violence have been socially constructed and explained in Newfoundland—which we will demonstrate may also be the case in other societies—and the consequences which this conventional wisdom has had in terms of stereotyping and perhaps punishing the unemployed and the poor. Furthermore, a set of alternative insights will be presented as a means of challenging these extremely prevalent, socially dangerous and virtually unquestioned conventional or orthodox accounts of the causes of crime and violence.

CRIME STATISTICS AND CRIME TALK: A SURVEY OF CONVENTIONAL WISDOM

First we will be concerned with attempting to answer the question: Is Newfoundland becoming more violent? This is an extremely difficult question to answer. Many people have developed the impression that the level and character of violence in Newfoundland is changing. It is believed to be approximating the situation elsewhere.

According to official statistics—the measure used most often to support statements of changing levels of crime and violence—the situation elsewhere is indeed disquieting. In the United States, England and in Canada generally, over the past quarter century not only have rising levels of minor offenses been reported, but official statistics indicate that levels of violent crime have increased enormously as well.

In the United States the violent crime rate in 1960 was 161 per 100,000 population, while in 1980 the figure had jumped to 581 per 100,000 population, an increase of 260 percent. In Canada, based on official figures published by Statistics Canada, Brantingham *et al.* note:

> . . .violent crime increased in Canada from the early part of the 1960s until the mid-1970s. From 1962 to 1975, the murder rate increased 460 percent; the wounding and assault rate went up 185 percent. The rape rate increased in number by 161 percent, and the robbery rate increased by 252 percent. The rates for all of these crimes leveled, and declined slightly, in the mid-1970s. But the rates for rape, robbery, and wounding and assault began to rise at the end of the 1970s. The 1980 rates for these crimes were the highest ever recorded (1984:132).

Increases in rates of violent crime in England and Wales are generally similar to those registered in the United States and in Canada in that violence against the person increased from 38.9 per 100,000 population to 193 per 100,000 population between 1961 and 1979, an increase of 395 percent.

Although official criminal statistics are the most widely used source of data relied upon to answer the question of whether or not rates of crime are increasing, social scientists have for years questioned the use of these measures as accurate indicators of the 'real' level of crime and violence in society. Thus to conclude that there have been *real* or *significant* changes in patterns of crime, certain factors must be taken into account. That is, there are serious problems in the gathering and processing of information which is used to calculate the level of crime and violence in any society. These problems may arise from the following factors:

(a) *Legal Definitions*: The legal definition of crime has varied over time and space. Legislative changes and technical adjustments in the wording of the law may cause *new* behaviours to be subjected to legal censure and, therefore, be added to the criminal statistics. Similarly, changes in legislation may remove certain behaviours from criminal statistics.

(b) *Police Discretion*: Police do not lay charges in all cases, even when they have a suspect they feel may be convicted. That is, they may drop a lesser charge for something more serious and in such a situation the smaller crime is not included in the official statistics (Sewell 1985:40). Furthermore, police may not lay a charge if they feel that, from the standpoint of a court, there is weak evidence to warrant a conviction. Another type of discretion is involved in those crimes where the discovery of the offense depends on police initiative. With respect to so-called 'victimless crimes' (i.e., prostitution, narcotic trafficking, etc.), the resources that the police are willing and able to commit to detection can be an important determinant of the "crimes known."

(c) *The Dark Figure of Criminality*: For various reasons, many crimes are not reported or detected by the police. Some crimes may not be reported because the offender may be a friend or relative of the victim; or the behaviour may be not perceived as criminal; a person may not know that a crime has been committed against them; or the victim may feel the incident is too trivial to report to the police (cf. McCabe and Sutcliffe 1978 and Farrington and Dowds 1985).

(d) *Level of Policing*: The proportion of police per persons in an area may be related to the number of crimes which are detected by, or reported to police. In areas where there is high police visibility, people may be more inclined to use them to solve their disputes. On the other hand, in areas where police visibility is low, people may be more likely to employ more informal means for dispute resolution. Also, in areas where police presence is high, more crimes may actually be detected by police (McDonald 1976).

(e) *Public Attitudes*: Public attitudes towards crime and policing affect the numbers of crimes which are reported to police. For example, in jurisdictions where there are crime prevention programs in place (i.e., Neighbourhood Watch, Block Parents, etc.) people may learn to be 'on the look out' for criminal activity which previously may have gone unrecognized or unnoticed. Moreover, some groups may be less tolerant than others in their attitudes toward crime. For example, if certain members of a community had a 'zero tolerance towards' drugs, they could be much more willing to report the activities of drug dealers to police than a group which was more tolerant towards such activities.

(f) *Police Record Keeping*: Different police administrations have different standards and priorities for collecting and interpreting crime statistics. Therefore, police forces with a very effective record management system would be more likely to produce accurate criminal statistics (crimes which are reported to or detected by police) than administrations where such measures are not a priority. Moreover, the quality of a police jurisdiction's system will change over time, as improvements in record keeping continue to be made.

Although the deficiencies of official crime data have been known about for sometime now within the social science community, criminal statistics have nevertheless been used to construct theories of criminal behaviour.[1] However, other researchers have come to view criminal statistics and their limitations primarily in terms of the information they reveal about social control agencies (Kitsuse and Cicourel 1963; Black 1970). For these researchers, studying the process by which crime statistics are produced is much more important than using them as a measure of crime in society. In fact Bottomley and Pease (1986) have gone as far as saying that the currently fashionable view about criminal statistics is that they are "meaningless" in terms of what they tell us about the level and nature of crime in society.

This is not to say, however, that all contemporary researchers treat criminal statistics quite as cynically as this. Young (1987:341) suggests that the debate continues between those researchers who regard changes in crime rates as the result of increased sensitivity to deviance plus a stronger administrative reaction to crime, (Pepinsky 1980, Pearson 1983) and those who see a rise in criminal behaviour itself [Kinsey *et al.* 1986].

Indeed the question of what criminal statistics *can* and *cannot* tell us about the level and nature of crime and its control in society has yet to be resolved. For instance, it is has recently been recognized that the "necessity of reliance on official police statistics to examine crime trends. . .has obvious limitations, the many factors likely to produce unreliability in these statistics are exerted reasonably consistently over the years" (Chappell 1983:12). Continuing along these lines, Scalon writes:

> Despite the limitations attendant on the use of police reports to determine levels of crime, there is reason to believe that official crime data do reflect, in a relative way, changes over time in actual crime levels, especially at the national level (cited in Chappell 1983:12).

Similarly, in recent years critical criminologists working within a "left realist" perspective have also been willing to accept official statistics in a similar light. In an attempt to expose the theoretical contradictions and oversimplified practice of what is identified as the left idealist position (which is said to attribute social anxieties about crime to "media generated moral panics set in place by the over-reaction of the propertied middle classes" [Kinsey *et al.* 1986[]) the left realist position has accepted the notion that crime has increased in *real* terms in western societies since World War II. For example, in Britain recent increases in crime and violence and a breakdown in law and order have been linked to the period following the 1979 election of the Conservative Government under Margaret Thatcher. Kinsey, Lea and Young (1986), major proponents of the left realist perspective, argue strongly that there has been a "crisis of rising crime" in Britain over this period and that these statistical increases in England and Wales — a 40 percent increase from 1979 to 1984 — reflect real changes in law and order because rates of crime have risen faster than increases in police numbers.[2]

Reflecting upon the Canadian context following the economic recession of the early 1980s, Taylor, also sympathetic to the left realist position, points out:

> The increase in crimes of violence, as we indicated earlier, is frequently dismissed in liberal accounts but it did result in 110,616 assaults, 20,899 robberies, 754 attempted murders and 626 homicides in 1979 (nearly twice the numbers of 1969) and it is a particularly powerful expression of this sense of desperate individualism, especially amongst working-class youth (1983:50).

Taylor further states:

> The really key lesson for socialists in Canada, would seem twofold — first, socialists must obviously take popular anxieties about crime seriously and distinguish socialist explanations of crime quite clearly from those advanced by liberals. The increases in violence revealed by the criminal statistics are real. They are not merely an artifact of increasing labelling or an increase in the size of the police and social control apparatus in general (1983:51).

Despite the fact that some researchers who take a left realist approach to the study of crime—as well as some liberal and conservative social scientists—are willing to accept that crime (as it is officially defined) *really* is increasing, the approach to official statistics we will use in this analysis is similar to that of Bottomley and Coleman (1981) and Bottomley and Pease (1986). What is at issue is the notion that official crime statistics should be treated as problematic, and constitute a major object of study in their own right. The central idea of this approach is not to engage in a 'technical audit' of police work in the production of statistics in terms of any concept of accuracy. We shall also avoid evaluating the appropriateness of the decisions and organizational procedures involved in the final official records, as measured against some external yardstick. Our view does not accept the assumption that there is some specific number of crimes which occur in a particular jurisdiction over a particular period of time which can be represented by 'n.' As a result our attempt to explain violent crime in Newfoundland will neither begin with an outright dismissal of crime statistics, nor will it be an attempt to find the 'true facts' of the contemporary crime scene. Indeed, we will approach them as have Bottomley and Pease, that is, "critically and with great caution, recognizing them as the proper starting point of any systematic analysis of crime in society" (1986:2).

According to official statistics there is evidence that violence may in fact be increasing in Newfoundland in recent years. Publications produced by Statistics Canada have regularly been used by the press in Newfoundland as a source of information to be commented upon as an indicator of the province's moral health. For example, between 1 January 1975 and 31 December 1986 there were over 300 references made to the 'fact' that crime and/or violence had been increasing in Newfoundland generally or in St. John's.[3] A great many of these references were either 'backed up' by the use of official statistics or were made with the impression that violence was 'empirically' increasing.

Even more convincing are comments which were made by Dr. Gaylon Duncan, then the executive director of the Canadian Centre for Justice Statistics. Speaking to the Rotary club of St. John's in 1984, Duncan said that "detailed data showed that violent crime rates are increasing in Newfoundland" (*Evening Telegram* 16 December 1984). In fact, according to this "detailed data," the violent crime rate in Newfoundland increased by 39 percent between 1974 and 1983. Consequently, over this ten year period Newfoundland had one of the greatest percentage increases in violent crime in the entire country and in 1983, it had, in fact, become the most "violent" province in Atlantic Canada. This 39 percent increase is 16 percent greater than the national average over this period.

Duncan had no explanation for the increased number of violent crimes in Newfoundland over this period; however, he did put forward one "theory" which might explain this increase. According to Duncan, violent crime was related to a population in "turmoil" — or a large amount of migration in and out of society. Duncan added that these increases might be explained in two other ways. Firstly, the violent crime rate was said to be in close relationship to the rate of people between the ages of 17 and 25, thus if Newfoundland had a growing number of young people, that might explain the higher number of violent crimes. A second explanation, Duncan suggested, might be found in the way police recorded spousal assaults. According to Duncan, such had been the case in Manitoba when the assault rate in that province jumped considerably from one year to the next. The reason for this sudden change was that incidents connected with domestic assaults were recorded by police as violent crimes in the latter year.

Statistics presented in the study *Persistence and Change* (1983) by the Department of Rural, Agricultural and Northern Development of the Government of Newfoundland and Labrador, suggested that violent crime may be increasing in the province, particularly in urban areas. Before the study began to analyze changes in crime rates between 1974 and 1980, the authors were careful to point out the limitations of the data used:

> Crime statistics are notoriously unreliable for identifying or in-dicating the volume of law violation which takes place in a society. Records of criminal incidents are extremely variable in their reliability because of the differential amounts of effort which police agencies devote to crime detection, changes in police record keep-ing procedures and variations in the public's disposition to report certain kinds of crimes (Newfoundland Department of Rural, Agricultural and Northern Development 1983:173).

Moreover, before any attempt was made to compare time se-quence developments in the patterns of criminality between urban and rural communities in Newfoundland and Labrador, the study mentioned that additional factors must be considered such as, "The police are much more visible in urban centres where the provincial and regional headquarters of the Royal Newfoundland Constabulary and the Royal Canadian Mounted Police are located." People in urban areas may then report more crimes to police than those in rural areas. Also, people in urban areas may be under closer surveillance by police than those in the lesser populated areas of the province. Consequently, the authors of the study noted that, "The conclusions that can be drawn from the criminal statistics without benefit of a detailed knowledge of changes in police administration, records maintenance and organization are, at best, tentative and indeterminate" (Newfoundland Department of Rural, Agricultural and Northern Development 1983:174).

Nevertheless, the authors continued in their analysis by comparing rural and urban crime rates over time in Newfoundland from 1974 to 1980 and found that whereas in rural areas violent crime had in fact decreased by 3 percent, the reverse pattern occurred for urban areas. They wrote:

> Our cities (St. John's, Corner Brook and Labrador City/Wabush) have become more dangerous places to live. In fact they were 50 percent more dangerous to personal safety in 1980 than they were in 1974 (Newfoundland Department of Rural, Agricultural and Northern Development 1983:175).

The authors found that the resulting rate for violent crime was very high and consequently they felt that this pattern of change over time "reflects a real change in behaviour." They concluded that "While Newfoundland and Labrador's cities have low rates of violent crime compared to other Canadian urban areas, they are clearly more dangerous places to be in the 1980s than they were in the early 1970s". In an attempt to explain these findings, the authors noted that, "The popular conception that rural areas are safer places to live, where the security of one's property and person are unlikely to be challenged, is supported by the crime rates which exist for the province" (Newfoundland Department of Rural, Agricultural and Northern Development 1983:176).

It is also important to point out that the authors of *Persistence and Change* were somewhat surprised that despite the fact that rural areas in Newfoundland have higher rates of unemployment and lower average incomes compared to urban areas in the province, rural crime rates actually decreased over this period and other offenses and violations (except for drug related offenses and violations of government statutes) increased only moderately.

In 1984, Kaill and Smith of the Atlantic Institute of Criminology published a paper on crime statistics in Atlantic Canada in which they too discovered that some crimes were increasing in Newfoundland. According to the authors of the study, their "crime profile" had two primary purposes. Firstly, it was to serve as a "preliminary survey of the character and extent of criminal behaviour in the Atlantic Region" where such information was hoped to be of value to "policy makers, criminal justice personnel and the general public" (Kaill and Smith 1984:2). The second purpose was to "identify crime pattern anomalies in the Atlantic Region as a basis for research and investigation."

Kaill and Smith, however, clearly emphasized that the data analysis in the paper was intended as commentary, "*rather than providing definitive conclusions or explanations of particular phenomena*" (1984:2). Following this general caution, these authors outlined some of the "factors" which impair such data, for example: the failure to detect or report crimes; selective investigation and/or recording of offenses by police, and the exercise of discretion at most levels of this process. Kaill and Smith also observed that it was very "dangerous to make statements based on data for a limited time period" (1984:3). It was for this last reason that these authors used five-year averages in their study.

After the problems (as they perceived them to be) of data collection were outlined by Kaill and Smith, they proceeded to examine official crime statistics for Atlantic Canada. Their initial examination of these data, confirmed the "traditional opinion" that:

> with the exception of violations of provincial statutes, crime rates in Eastern Canada fall consistently below national averages [and that] with respect to all other general categories—all crimes, criminal code offenses, violations of municipal ordinances, crimes of violence and property offenses, each Atlantic Province has a lower offense rate per 100,000 population than the remainder of the country (Kaill and Smith 1984:4).

Kaill and Smith suggest that the low rate of criminal code violations in the Atlantic Region are due to "population stability." According to these authors, the region was "settled and politically stable" while the rest of Canada was being opened up by pioneers (and was thus unstable). A sense of rootedness in the "more staid" part of Canada contributes to "more conformist, less deviant behaviour patterns" than in the rest of the country. The two authors use this kind of analysis to predict that the Atlantic Region will experience an increase in crime in the near future as the "traditional social and cultural stability" of the area is eroded by in-migration and cuts in social services (Kaill and Smith 1984:14–15).

A closer reading of the paper also reveals that the violent crime rates in Newfoundland are said to be characterized by a relatively high level of "serious" offenses when compared with violent crime rates in the other Atlantic provinces (Prince Edward Island, Nova Scotia and New Brunswick). For the period 1977–1980, the types of violent crime which appeared to be particularly high in Newfoundland were assaults and sexual offenses. In fact, because Kaill and Smith recognized that these rates were so relatively high, they felt that a further investigation into this "anomaly" was warranted.

Although the authors did not attempt to theorize specifically about the empirical 'fact' that Newfoundland was a somewhat more violent province compared to other Atlantic provinces, the explanation they did use to generally explain crime in Atlantic Canada could easily be applied in order to explain the apparent situation in Newfoundland. Perhaps Newfoundland is losing its "staid" character, thus people are becoming less conformist and are expressing more deviant behaviour patterns as traditional forms of social control are breaking down, particularly those which are most often associated with "ruralness." Consequently, Newfoundland may be becoming more violent as values which are associated with "urbanism" and modernity are replacing traditional and staid values of the past.

In 1983, an anthropology professor at Memorial University was interviewed in a St. John's newspaper about violence in Newfoundland. Dr. Elliott Leyton said that although the province is one of the least violent places in the world and has a low murder rate, Newfoundland society is becoming more violent.[4]

During the past couple of years Leyton had noticed that there had been three "sex-murders" and one "family annihilation," crimes usually associated with "mainland North America." Leyton expected more of these mainland style acts of violence to take place in Newfoundland in the future as the "fabric of Newfoundland society begins to disintegrate under pressures of outside influences" (*Evening Telegram* 12 February 1983:4).

These "outside" or "mainland" influences which Leyton referred to in the interview were films and television programs primarily coming from the United States which promote "American style violence." Yet most frightening of all, according to Leyton, "was the hardcore porno book industry which has made its way to Newfoundland. . .not the Playboy-Penthouse magazines, but the real hardcore stuff" which he believed were "manuals on how to torture and mutilate women" (*Evening Telegram* 12 February 1983:4).

With respect to the level and character of homicide in Newfoundland, Leyton thought it was low because of a set of cultural and social mechanisms which until recently operated to almost entirely eliminate murder. These conflict avoidance mechanisms, frequently commented upon in the Newfoundland anthropological literature (e.g., Firestone 1967 and Szwed 1966), were perceived to be "incredibly complex" and unique to the island of Newfoundland;

their function in the majority of situations was to rule out violent behaviour. According to Leyton, "a man is a man" in Newfoundland if he possesses "stoic gentility" and "courage"—a situation he believes to be completely unlike the "John Wayne" image of men which pervades in the United States of America (*Evening Telegram* 12 February 1983:4).

Leyton also mentioned class issues in his explanation of the changing character of social relations in Newfoundland and he felt this change would produce more violent interpersonal behaviour. This 'prediction' is rooted in an historical explanation of the changing class structure which he considered had taken place in Newfoundland over the past forty years. Because traditional Newfoundland society was made up of a small merchant class and a large class of poor fisherman, almost everyone was equal in terms of income, according to Leyton. But since Confederation in 1949, there had been the growth of a much more profound inequality which was, said Leyton, "pitting people against one another and destroying the social fabric." This new set of social relations is "utterly different" from the system that existed before Newfoundland became part of Canada—society in Newfoundland is now based on "hierarchy" and "inequality." (The "oil boom" would only accentuate the differences as it would mean "big money" for a few, but very little or nothing for the rest of the population.) Leyton spoke of the destruction of "traditional and structural phenomena" which have in the past, "worked to keep violent crime rates down" (*Evening Telgram* 12 February 1983:4).

***

There has been a widespread assumption in recent years that some crimes in particular are developing into serious problems in Newfoundland. For instance, armed robbery in Newfoundland—particularly in the St. John's area—is believed by many groups and individuals to constitute a *new* type of crime taking place in this once staid and non-violent society.

Considerable concern about the incidence of armed robbery has been coming from judges. A judge who passed an eleven year sentence on an eighteen-year-old at an armed robbery trial in 1985, described this crime as being "one of the most heinous crimes that society is aware of." The judge stated that "there is great public concern about the incidence of this type of crime," and said that it was "one of the most frightening things that can happen to an individual" (*Evening Telegram* 6 December 1985). He added that "the incidence of armed robbery in the city [St. John's] and area, as well as in other areas of the province, is increasing and that the sentences being handed down haven't been increasing, and the need for substantial sentences is apparent if the public is to be protected."[5] In the words of a Supreme Court Judge in Newfoundland:

> This Court has consistently stated that armed robbery must attract substantial sentences. The public must be protected and the offenders and like minded people must be deterred. The only way to accomplish these aims is to incarcerate offenders for lengthy terms. Armed robberies with the use of firearms are the most serious of all. They pose the most serious threats to the lives of others (*Evening Telegram* 5 October 1983).

The idea that armed robbery is increasing at an alarming rate has been fostered by the press and the electronic media. Terms like "rash" to describe the number of robberies have been used and in recent years considerable space in the news has been devoted to the issue of armed robbery. For instance, in the wake of an incident which took place in Gander, Newfoundland in October 1985, when a twenty-two-year-old convenience store clerk was killed during an armed robbery (in fact, the first of this type of homicide to have taken place in Newfoundland), the *Evening Telegram* conducted a survey (who, how and where?) of employees and owners of convenience stores and gas bars on the subject of armed robbery. The newspaper reported that "the consensus is that the courts are too soft on armed robbers," or, as one gas bar manager put it "I'm really a believer in capital punishment for those who kill in these robberies. Being nice to these punks is not good" (*Evening Telegram* 29 October 1985).

A few years previous to this, the chief of the Royal Newfoundland Constabulary (RNC) was forced to give a press conference to correct the impression fostered by a local tabloid, the *Daily News*, that St. John's was becoming another "Detroit." During the week in question there had been one armed robbery and a member of the Provincial House of Assembly called for an inquiry into the problem (*Daily News* 11 November 1978). Although RNC management and other Ministry of Justice officials have on occasions made comments in the press attempting to 'calm things down' regarding the sensationalization of crime in the press, these assurances that the police have things under control, however, are not necessarily representative of police *rank and file*. As one member of the RNC put it:

> Ten years ago armed robbery was a big thing, a major crime. But now, it's getting to be an every day occurrence. . .there has been a large increase in armed robbery in the whole city the last few years (McGahan 1984:193).

In 1985, as a response to the concerns of the St. John's business community that armed robbery—as well as other crimes against merchants—was developing into a serious problem, the St. John's Board of Trade published "A Case Study of Retail Crime in St. John's." This included shoplifting, break and enter, and robbery at retail locations. Using statistical information from the Canadian Centre for Justice Statistics and the Royal Newfoundland Constabulary 1977–1983 Annual Statistical Reports, the study argued that "retail crime" (especially with regard to shoplifting) had reached "epidemic proportions" and that it must be controlled by a joint public and government effort. According to the official statistics used in the study, between 1977 and 1983 shoplifting increased by 73 percent, break and enter increased by 97 percent and the robbery total rose by 26 percent. Although the increase in robbery was not as great as were increases in other retail crimes, it was considered "significant" because of the "seriousness and degree of violence involved" (St. John's Board of Trade 1985:4).

The study concluded with a call for more severe punishments for those convicted of retail crimes in St. John's. Heavier fines and tougher prison terms were seen to be the only measures which would act as a deterrent to the others. The study was presented to the Provincial and Federal Ministers of Justice in order to increase sentencing: immediate action was called for in an attempt to stop the problem. Urgent action was seen to be necessary especially during the current economic climate: "In times of recession, when crime tends to rise, it makes it more difficult for recovery in the city's economy" (St. John's Board of Trade 1985:16). This connection was only *assumed*, as no attempt was made to empirically associate increases in "retail crime" with increases in unemployment, etc.

Therefore, robbery is considered by many as a serious crime because of the threat of or use of violence. The robberies which have received the most attention have been those which have taken place in retail locations, as they are the offenses which have popularly been displayed as being most likely to involve victim injury.

***

In the mid-1970s, considerable public attention was given to the 'problem' of vandalism and other 'juvenile' crime in Newfoundland—particularly in St. John's. In 1975, the problem seemed to have reached such a crisis that there was public debate on whether or not to initiate a curfew on youth. More police foot patrols and stiffer sentences were also called for at the time. Certainly other measures

seemed to have failed. An editorial in the *Evening Telegram* which
was headlined, *It's curfew time* illustrates this concern:

> The curfew is a form of restraint aimed at keeping the civilian
> population indoors and out of mischief during the hours of the
> night. . . .Some cities and towns in the United States and on the
> mainland have experimented this year with the curfew as a means
> of controlling the kind of vandalism that comes from the juvenile
> members of society. Now it looks as if St. John's is going to try its
> hand at imposing a curfew on the younger age groups. Considering
> the number of complaints and the large number of youngsters who
> might be doing their share of destruction, the curfew may possibly
> be a useful way to limit the number of children at night as potential
> vandals (*Evening Telegram* 19 September 1975).

The proposed curfew was not in fact implemented in St. John's,
as the public and police both opposed the measure. The chief of the
RNC said that he was not in favour of the establishment of a curfew
because "it is the parents' responsibility to tell their children when
it is time to go home. . .why should the police enforce a curfew when
people are just shirking their responsibilities." The chief added that
he would not be in favour of a curfew because "it would be detrimental to the image of the Constabulary" (*Evening Telegram* 17 October
1975).

Following these statements by the chief, the idea of a curfew did
not appeal to a group of concerned citizens who attended a open
public meeting on vandalism in St. John's. Rather than beginning
a curfew in the city, the group suggested that in order to control the
problem there must be more parental control, increased surveillance
by police, stiffer penalties, and increased education. And, according
to the newly elected mayor, these types of measures would have to
be implemented because "vandals have a psychological problem to
some degree" and the "increases in the number of police which would
be needed to enforce the curfew would involve too much cost"
(*Evening Telegram* 28 October 1975).

Different groups in the city of St. John's (as well as in other
places in the province such as Corner Brook, Placentia and Harbour
Grace) complained to the authorities about the increasing frequency
of attacks on their property and these complaints—as well as
suggestions on what was thought would best control the "problem"—often appeared in the local media. One letter to the editor in
the *Evening Telegram* had this to say:

> People in St. John's increasingly are becoming fed-up with the
> growing vandalism and wanton destruction of public and private
> property. The trend in this sort of behaviour seems to be downward.

Things are getting worse rather than better. One hears rumours of a demoralized police force. One can easily understand this, when after many hours of patience on the part of the police, the criminal is apprehended and brought before the court, only to find that the individual is given a suspended sentence or a sentence which does not measure up to the gravity of the crime. It is difficult to know how one can try to persuade courts to be tougher on criminals. . . I would suggest [that] what we need now is an organization to protect the rights of law-abiding citizens (*Evening Telegram* 24 April 1975).

Another reader of the *Evening Telegram* who lived in the Conception Bay town of Harbour Grace wrote this letter to the editor:

Today, in this island, we are witnessing a developing state of anarchy well documented in your issues of April 4 and 5 concerning vandalism and its concomitants in St. John's. I could add some personal evidence regarding property in Harbour Grace where lawless louts are busy dissecting it piecemeal. How can people protect themselves from this uncivil outrage of person and property? For the once I would prescribe a flick of the 'cat' or the crack of a .410 but that puts you in an adversary position and pre-empts the law (*Evening Telegram* 17 April 1975).

In fact, during the month of April 1975, the mayor of St. John's vowed to close the "library, garage and erect a fence around city hall." She made a call for city employees working in the building to be given "danger pay" as a response to an act of vandalism in which rocks were hurled at windows of the city hall. When the mayor was asked to comment on the root of the problem and ways in which to stop it, she said, "the whole problem centres around the freedom of society with responsibility" and that "this freedom is being used by people without responsibility" (*Evening Telegram* 12 April 1975).

Shortly after these comments were made by the mayor, the "problem" again surfaced in the political realm when the Liberal provincial opposition leader attempted to call a debate on vandalism in the House of Assembly. Such drastic action was needed because he felt government, and particularly the Minister of Justice, had failed to "take appropriate action and implement moves to deal with the increase in vandalism that has occurred in the province in the past three years" (*Evening Telegram* 17 April 1975).

As a response to the "increasing problem of vandalism," the Premier urged the House that "stern measures" would have to be taken "to cut down on the violence which has hit the province recently." The Premier said that there were two means of containing this "growing problem." Firstly, he stated that "police surveillance has to be stepped up," and, secondly, "the courts in the province have to begin handing out sentences which are in line with the seriousness of the crime." These measures were said to be urgently needed as the problem of "vandalism" and other "violent crimes" were becoming "very serious." The days of 'easy-going' Newfoundland were coming to an end, and if the present "crime wave" was to be halted, according to the Tory Premier, "the courts and the police will have to act" (*Evening Telegram* 2 May 1975).

During this barrage of public, political and business concerns about the "problem of vandalism" in the province (especially in St. John's) some "professionals'" comments appeared in the media attempting to point out the "causes" of vandalism and general lack of responsibility by "today's youth" toward authority and property. According to a probation officer who had spent twenty-four years in the business, "The kind of crime we're seeing in adolescents today [vandalism] suggests a continual downward spiral to more serious and even brutal crime," and that "It's getting more serious and that's why I say in a few years you're going to have some serious brutality . . .we can expect more brutality from children in the future" (*Evening Telegram* 11 October 1975). Commenting on the causes of this increased lawlessness amongst today's youth, the probation officer had this to say:

> I think there's a lot more danger today when there's too much permissiveness. It was better when a father was too strict and even sometimes wrong. It's a different code altogether. We fail to realize it ourselves. We are on the way down. The old values aren't there anymore. The police and clergy are no longer respected. I'm firmly convinced the pulpit is the informal conscience of the country. That's where we get our values. Now, with the decline of the importance of the Church, the moral code is left entirely to the family. . . .Man's basic nature is his search for good but nature calls out for pleasure. We're too pleasure seeking now and when this attitude is adopted on a mass scale, you've got decay (*Evening Telegram* 11 October).

In an attempt to answer questions about whether or not this "decay" would develop into a "crime wave" similar to that believed to exist in other metropolitan areas in Canada, Fuchs and Shrimpton (1977) wrote a rather lengthy article on the topic which was published in the weekend edition of the *Evening Telegram*. Essentially, these authors addressed two questions: Is the crime rate in St. John's increasing? Do downtown residents have reason to fear the security of their property? Before these questions were addressed, the authors wrote:

The answers to these questions are by no means simple. Indeed, in attempting to provide answers it would be wise to exercise some caution and discretion. Police records of reported crimes, while they are our only source of statistical information, are subject to variations that need not have much to do with the actual frequency of criminally defined behaviour. . . .There exists no reliable basis on which to describe and explain the frequency and nature of criminal activity in the city (*Evening Telegram* 29 October 1977).

It was also noted, however, that there were "factors at work in the city that might increase the likelihood of offenses against property in St. John's." In other words, without knowing what the 'empirical reality' of the vandalism situation was (who was doing it, where they came from, how old were they, how much damage was incurred, etc.) Fuchs and Shrimpton seem to have an *a priori* theory which could have powerful explanatory power if there were in fact increases in this type of crime. The analysis is, therefore, essentially speculative. Variables such as the economy, demographic attributes of the population and social characteristics were all used in some fashion in the analysis. With respect to the ways in which the economy in St. John's may partly be to blame for increases in crime, Fuchs and Shrimpton write: "The economic situation for a large proportion of the population can be described, at best as insecure and unstable. . .St. John's has the dubious distinction of having the highest proportion of 'low income families' of any metropolitan area in Canada" (*Evening Telegram* 29 October 1977). The authors argue that consequently, St. John's has a relatively large "dangerous class" of people who are under a lot of strain because they are economically deprived and hence may have the potential to commit property crime.

Although Fuchs and Shrimpton are careful not to make a direct causal connection between crime and economic instability in St. John's, they do note that "widespread economic instability is a precondition for increased crime when it is combined with other social factors." The most relevant "social factor" these authors see operating in conjunction with "economic instability" which would 'cause' vandalism and other property crimes is propertylessness. They write:

> People who are without jobs, who perhaps don't own property are less likely to be successfully socialized to the values of private ownership and acceptance of institutional means of economic opportunity. This is especially true when large numbers of them realize that they have very little access to a stable economic future (*Evening Telegram* 29 October 1977).

In this way vandalism (and property offenses in general) are seen as an expression of resentment and hostility towards a social and economic system that does not provide opportunities to people in accordance with life's expectations.

Another factor which Fuchs and Shrimpton suggest might be included in solving the property crime problem in St. John's—especially vandalism—would be population movement. Using population data from the 1971 census, the authors demonstrate that since the early 1970s the downtown and surrounding area of St. John's experienced a population loss of roughly 25 percent. This may have had the effect, they say, of weakening traditional and effective methods of social control in these communities. That is, deviant behaviour might have been prevented because of "Mrs. Batterby, looking out her window, elbows crossed on a pillow. . .[and] kids on the street know full well that Mrs. Batterby's eyes are upon them and that one way or another their parents are going to receive a full report on their days activities." Mrs. Batterby, as community population shifts take place, will "no longer recognize new children on the street, nor does she know their parents" (*Evening Telegram* 29 October 1977). Hence, the result of this *neighbourhood breakdown*, according to Fuchs and Shrimpton is that, "in the absence of informal social controls, people need to resort to official controls such as police with greater frequency."

A demographic variable which Fuchs and Shrimpton considered as another relevant explanation of increasing property crime in St. John's (especially when coupled with increasing economic instability) was the number of people in the population who fell between the ages of fifteen and thirty, "the age grouping at which individuals are most likely to get involved in crime against property." And as most of the "baby boomers" now fell somewhere within this age range, and since a great many people in this age bracket were unemployed, they state that, "it seems plausible to conclude that vandalism and crimes against property may be likely to increase." The study concludes with these words:

> If it can be identified that there has been an increase in crime and vandalism in the city then government policy might be wise to look for economic and social solutions to the problem (*Evening Telegram* 29 October 1977).

Although these authors comments were not based on the empirical fact that vandalism was increasing in St. John's, their explanation of the problem, if it really were to be taking place, certainly fits the notion that "social breakdown" may be responsible for the growing crime problem in St. John's and in Newfoundland more generally.

Although the mid-1970s was the peak of the vandalism 'crisis' in Newfoundland and in St. John's in particular, the issue did not vanish from the public domain. For example, in July 1986, thirteen students were "sworn in" at the Royal Newfoundland Constabulary headquarters in St. John's for "summer duty" as park and playground patrols in the St. John's area. One of the duties of the patrollers was to report any acts of property destruction to police via their walkie-talkies:

> Eight students will patrol major parks, Monday to Friday, from 2 p.m. to 10 p.m. and report any suspicious activities to police over two-way radios. Another five students will patrol Mount Pearl walkways and playgrounds every day of the week from 4 p.m. to midnight (*Evening Telegram* 4 July 1986).

The reason for the "patrols" stemmed from concern that certain public buildings in these areas were being damaged by vandals and in order to stop this, increased surveillance was considered necessary.

***

The impression that violence was increasing in the province was also shared by law enforcement agencies. The Royal Newfoundland Constabulary Police Association, representing the police rank and file, has lobbied for some time to have the right to carry sidearms while on patrol. The RNC, in operation for over 100 years, is the only police force in Canada whose officers do not bear arms during regular duty. According to the president of the RNC association, "One of the major arguments used by public and politicians against arming the RNC has been that if the RNC arms itself, criminals will do the same." (*Evening Telegram* 28 August 1984). The president believed, however, that this argument was no longer valid, because many criminals in the St. John's area were carrying firearms to commit such offenses as armed robberies and break and enters. Because of this, he felt that "so far Constabulary members have been fortunate" and that "the public might change its opinion about the issue if it was aware of some of the situations the officers encounter" (*Evening Telegram* 28 August 1984).

In addition to RNC members being open to situations where they may be confronted by criminals carrying weapons during the commission of armed robberies, the president also felt that constabulary members were unprotected in situations where they may be targets "for people who want revenge." These comments surfaced in the press in St. John's shortly after two police officers in Toronto were murdered while performing their duties in August 1985. The president said that the same thing could happen in St. John's because constabulary members were performing the same duties as other Canadian police forces. "It's a little discouraging thinking that we have police officers in uniform who are a great target for people who want to take revenge" (*Evening Telegram* 22 August 1985).

In October, 1984 the vast majority of RNC association members voted in favour of the RNC becoming an armed force—out of 306 eligible voters, 25 were opposed to being armed, 204 in favour, while 77 failed to vote (*Evening Telegram* 11 October 1984).

This view is also found in a book examining constabulary members' images of the city of St. John's. McGahan notes that police officers in St. John's perceive an increase in the sophistication and frequency of criminal violence and that calls for the services of the police more than tripled between 1979 and 1982 (1984:7). According to one of the police officers interviewed by McGahan:

> It's definitely becoming more mainland in its characteristics. . .I would say we're turning into a big city. We're turning into a big city way of life. Where we used to shop at the corner store, now we shop at supermarkets. I would go so far as to say, as regards our traffic, we used to drive on two-lane roads, now we got four lanes. Now we got a super highway coming through. Crime is increased. Different types of crime from what we were used to: armed robberies, hookers, drugs. It's becoming a metropolis (1984:191–192).

Here are some additional comments which McGahan captured from an officer:

> I feel there is a big increase in violence over the past fourteen years.

> It seems that crime is getting more and more sophisticated, more serious type of crime. There's a fair bit of violence.

> The biggest change I've noticed is in the people. Because one time you go out on a call the first year on the job, I had a baton that was under the front seat of my car and was never taken out of there. That was under the front seat of my own car. I go to work and never bother to take the baton. If you went on a call, there was a fight on in the street, you got there and pull the people apart. They fight with their fists. But you go down there now, you get a call on a fight there, I wouldn't go down without my baton. Because you go now and the first thing a couple of people get into a fight, it's the knife. This is where I see a big change. You're getting into more violence now. One time it was just a fight. The best fellow wins, that sort of thing. But the first thing now, it's the knife. Fellows getting assaulted by stabbing. . . .We're getting a lot more violence, with your

assaults on the street, your domestics. . . .A lot more violence in domestic calls than we got one time (1984:193).

In fact, because the constabulary is an unarmed police force (although arms are available if they should need them) the force has considered using mace as a substitute for sidearms. An RNC inspector said that the chemical repellent could be useful for officers in his organization, "particularly as they are not armed while carrying on their duties" (*Evening Telegram* 22 May 1985). Officers in other jurisdictions who permit their members to carry mace are taught to use it in appropriate situations such as when "they are being attacked or if they must restrain someone who is extremely violent." For example, "if an officer is up against someone brandishing a broken bottle, tire iron, or knife, mace can be used" (*Evening Telegram* 22 May 1985).

The Government of Newfoundland and Labrador, the chief of the RNC, and the local press have been the major stumbling blocks to the police association in the attempt to arm its members in the normal course of their duties.

The Deputy Minister of Justice in the province has said that all members of the force have been highly trained in the use of firearms and they have access to them when they are required.

> The reason why constabulary members don't carry sidearms, he said, is based on the force's history. He said it was modelled on police forces in the United Kingdom where even today in a city as large as London, England, the Bobbies or constables don't carry sidearms (*Evening Telegram* 29 August 1984).

A similar argument was also voiced by the chief of the Royal Newfoundland Constabulary. In September 1985, the chief responded to suggestions from the RNC brotherhood that the force should be armed by saying that:

> As long as I am chief of police, I will be retiring from an unarmed police force [and that] at the present time there is absolutely no reason for me to suggest to government that members of the force should be armed. . .[as the] old English approach still exists (*Evening Telegram* 7 September 1985).

The local press has also been a strong voice in the community wanting the RNC to remain an unarmed police force. A 1985 editorial had this to say about the issue:

> The RNC is the only police force in Canada whose men do not bear arms during regular duties, and as we have said on many occasions in the past, we see no reason why that should change (*Evening Telegram* 10 September 1985).

More recently, the same paper had this to say in its editorial:

> There are no valid reasons why the RNC should be armed while on regular patrols. Men and women of the force are fully trained in the use of weapons and weapons are readily available should the need arise (*Evening Telegram* 11 March 1986).

Although in the past and in the present, the police brotherhood's pressure to have its members armed has not been successful, they may indeed be armed in the future as most people feel the expected prosperity from oil development will bring a boost in the crime rate. According to one member of the constabulary:

> I would think [the oil will bring change]. I think when the thing gets on full beam, you're going to get an influx of people, all elements of society. It's gotta make a difference. . . .With an increase of population, of course, your crime rate's gotta rise (McGahan 1984:196).

McGahan has also recorded a police view regarding what types of crimes will parallel offshore oil production:

> And now since our oil has come off our coast, we're getting a different kind of crime. . . .We got bookies now. . .organized prostitution. . .down the road you're going to see heroin. You're going to see addicts, because there's a lot of money to be made. . .

> We have people from Montreal, I think it is pretty well known, and they have set up prostitution. . . . And then I think you'll get bank robberies. . .I think you're going to find us like Alberta now. So I think they're going to have a sharp increase in armed robberies. . .

> If the time ever comes when Newfoundland gets the benefit of the oil, that's been talked about right now, I feel you're going to see an influx of harder type drugs—your heroin and cocaine—and that's going to be a brand new scene for this area because we don't have. . . .I can see if the oil comes and it's like we expect. . .I think you're going to see a massive increase in crime (1984:196–197).

The police brotherhood's prediction that the RNC will be an armed force in the 1990s may be a credible foretelling if the groups of people who have been against arming the police also see the expected oil boom as a time when the constabulary will need to carry sidearms to maintain law and order. A 1986 editorial in the *Evening Telegram* had this to say about the future of guns and the constabulary:

> We dread the day that our police officers would have to patrol the streets and highways in its jurisdiction armed to the teeth. The longer that day is postponed, the better it is for everyone. There are predictions that day may arrive with the advent of production from oil fields on the Grand Banks. The fear is that the multi-billion dollar development will mean the arrival of many unsavoury char-

acters to this province. Calgary is the example most frequently used where an oil boom created an increase in crime and police are now equipped with shot guns (*Evening Telegram* 11 March 1986).

The chief of police has also made similar comments on this issue:

> I am confident that we are heading in the direction of being a have-province, one with prosperity. . . . Our senior police person- nel should be aware that what's happening in the rest of Canada could be happening in Newfoundland in a couple of years. . .with more people around with more money, chances are there will be an increase in crime (*Evening Telegram* 7 September 1985).

The RNC and the local press, however, are not alone in thinking that an "oil boom" will lead to an increase in crime and violence and other social problems in Newfoundland. The RCMP in the province expect that the disruption associated with rapid economic develop- ment from offshore oil is likely to lead to rising levels of criminal behaviour. In 1981, an RCMP superintendent wrote a report en- titled, *The Impact of Offshore Oil and Gas Development on Policing Requirements in Newfoundland.* In this report he argued that the increased level of affluence of a sector of the population will create problems in terms of increasing criminal activity. According to the superintendent, large numbers of transient rig and supply vessel workers passing through St. John's, could well give rise to a consid- erable amount of drinking and to incidents resulting from rivalries between oil and non-oil workers (Leyton 1986:84–85). The superin- tendent continued by hypothesizing that the increased affluence and greater amount of money in circulation would generate resent- ment among people who were denied a "share" of the affluence— consequently producing an increase in the level of crime.

As has been pointed out, a considerable amount of public interest has centred upon the potential problems which are expected to accompany offshore oil development in Newfoundland. Law en- forcement agencies, the press, the Alcohol and Drug Dependency Commission and the Department of Social Services generally expect various social problems to escalate when outset oil production begins on the Grand Banks.

As an exercise to "identify the strengths and weaknesses in current knowledge surrounding this popular issue" and the conven- tional wisdom concerning it, the Government of Newfoundland's Petroleum Directorate produced a report which reviewed the avail- able information on changes in the "social problems" experienced in resource development areas in other western democratic societies (Norway, Scotland, United States and Western Canada). According to the report, the existing scientific information on social problems which accompany energy development, and offshore development, in particular, were found to be incomplete, but nonetheless the study concluded with these words:

> available information suggests that crime, alcohol abuse, family problems, mental health and welfare dependency have increased in some energy development regions (Cake 1986:29).

What this seems to imply is that although the "scientific" evidence cannot lead the Petroleum Directorate to conclude that energy development leads to social problems, they do not in any way dismiss the idea. Commonsense seems to be informing people that social problems *must* increase once oil development begins in Newfoundland.

***

While not addressing the issue directly, organized labour and some community groups in Newfoundland have reason to believe that crime and violence are increasing in the province. In addressing the problem of unemployment in Newfoundland, these groups have on a number of occasions made attempts to show that one of the most serious *costs* of large scale unemployment is an increasing frequency and severity of crime and violence. Generally, these groups are under the impression that as unemployment increases so does a host of other social problems, crime of course being one of them.

The tendency to link increasing unemployment with crime and other social problems can be found in a study entitled *The Meaning of Work and the Reality of Unemployment in the Newfoundland Context* (Hill 1983). The research, undertaken in the early 1980s, was a response to the Economic Council of Canada's study of Newfoundland published in 1980, and its primary goal was essentially to examine the human costs of unemployment. This specific approach was taken because it was felt by the author and others in the social scientific community that the Economic Council of Canada's study failed to pay adequate attention to the social and psychological costs of unemployment. Although the overall provincial empirical relationship between crime and unemployment was not made all that clear by the findings in the 1983 study, there was felt to be a fairly distinct relationship between these social problems for urban areas of the province. According to comments made by Overton on this study, the evidence came from:

> statements of professionals involved in crime (police and probation officers) and the fact that those found in correctional institutions are mostly unemployed. This was also true of those on probation.

Based on this data it was concluded that there 'is a fairly strong relationship between unemployment and crime' and that criminal behaviour is one of the high costs of unemployment (1986:32).

Statements made to the Newfoundland and Labrador Federation of Labour's unemployment conference in 1983, also made the connection between rising levels of unemployment and criminal behaviour and other social problems in the province. Some of the costs of unemployment being: increased family conflict; divorce and violence between family members; psychological stress and mental depression; and *increasing crime*. With respect to unemployment producing increasing levels of crime, the group stated:

> As a result of frustration, economic desperation or simply boredom, some of the unemployed will resort to behaviour that is against the law. Higher unemployment increases crime of many kinds—from minor offenses such as shoplifting, vandalism, alcohol related offenses and poaching to major crimes of violence, arson and homicide (Newfoundland and Labrador Federation of Labour 1983:12).

In this same vein E.J. Malwaka has written about the "price of unemployment" in a Newfoundland community service publication. He says that because government and the private sector maintain a policy of keeping a significant sector of the population from "meaningful employment," particularly youth, the future will be characterized by:

> anomie, frustration, despair and social disorder(s). If we are concerned about the INCREASES in incidence of crime, spousal abuse, vandalism, disrespect for tradition, and all the other social ills characterizing our troubled times, out failure to address the problems of today's unemployed will increase our difficulties in dealing with what will certainly become crises in our civilization tomorrow (Malwaka 1983:2).

As part of the Canadian Labour Congress's campaign to point out the social costs of high unemployment throughout Canada, the People's Commission on Unemployment was created to hold public hearings on the issue of unemployment in Newfoundland. The Newfoundland and Labrador Federation of Labour published the report of the commission in 1978 entitled, "Now That We've Burned Our Boats. . ." The report attempted to go beyond the unemployment statistics in Newfoundland and to show the public the real problems facing the unemployed in the province. It found "communities in crisis, characterized by economic depression, family breakdown, social dislocation" and an array of other problems which should not be ignored (cited in Overton 1986:3). Unemployment, then, was identified as a major cause of a number of social problems including crime—especially with respect to unemployed youth. A brief submitted to the commission by the Labrador Resources Advisory Council had this to say:

> In a town that has a high level of unemployment, the atmosphere of that community can undergo a change. Where there was once a thriving developing town, high unemployment can create mistrust and tension. Young people seem to become more restless, vandalism becomes more pronounced. People begin to lock their doors at night (Newfoundland Federation of Labour, cited in Overton 1986:35).

A clergyman, presenting another brief to the commission, said:

> There are a fair number of young people who have finished school and have not been able to get into trades school or simply not been able to find gainful employment. That being the case, the young person still has a fair amount of energy, and that energy is sometimes used in a destructive manner. Hence, you will sometimes find in many communities that there is an increase in vandalism. I fear for the summer, unless something happens in this community; in the winter the cold temperatures can keep a lot of things down. Certainly when weather improves and becomes warmer in the spring and summer, things tend to become rather critical (Overton 1986:40).

Considering these briefs, as well as others which were also reported to the commission, the following are summary comments made by the commissioners with respect to high levels of unemployment leading to crime and other social problems:

> The legacy of unemployment is one of insecurity and isolation. When we read in the newspapers about vandalism, crime and other social problems we should not be surprised (Overton 1986:40).

Unemployment threatens everyone in society when it reaches epidemic proportions and the report concludes that jobs are urgently needed because productive work is a "necessity for mental and social health" (Overton 1986:17).

No doubt those who have attempted to publicize the social costs of unemployment have relied heavily on the purported connection between worklessness and criminal behaviour. In doing so, these groups have also made it public that in recent years, as rates of unemployment in the province continue to escalate and remain at the highest level compared to any other province in the country, there are increasing numbers of Newfoundlanders who are physically and mentally unhealthy, suicidal, dishonest and violent.

***

There has also been a considerable amount of evidence suggesting that child sexual violence—or child sexual assault—is on the increase in Newfoundland.[6] A press release in the *Evening Telegram* by the Community Services Council suggested that the reported incidents of child sexual abuse in Newfoundland had increased rapidly since statistics were first recorded by the Department of Social Services in 1974 to a record high in 1984 (only in 1979 was there a dip in these figures). According to these official statistics, the sharpest increase was recorded in 1980 and the figures have been climbing ever since. New reports of sexual abuse now outnumber physical abuse, and are increasing at a greater rate, especially in the St. John's area from which most reports came (*Evening Telegram* 26 April 1986).

In addition to reports of increasing sexual abuse in the province, "the number of prosecutions of child sexual abuse in the St. John's area is also increasing." Moreover, the increased reporting of child sexual abuse "is a national phenomenon as sharp increases in the number of cases brought to the attention of protection agencies are being experienced in every province" (*Evening Telegram* 26 April 1986).

In 1986, stressing the importance of this matter, a St. John's crown prosecutor and former social worker who specialized in child sexual assault cases, gave a talk to a women's workshop on child sexual abuse. In her presentation she used official statistics to point to the "urgency of the situation" as she noted that, "so far this year [March 1986] there have been as many incidents reported as there were for 12 months of 1985 (St. John's Status of Women's Council 1986).

Additional concern about the incidence of child abuse in Newfoundland has been coming from teachers. The Newfoundland Teachers' Association recently accepted a policy statement on child abuse which was researched by the association's "Women's Issues Special Interest Council" and then prepared by a special subcommittee of the association's Political Action Committee. Using statistics produced by the Department of Social Services, the researchers found that "100 cases of child abuse had been reported in the province in 1985, compared with 25 in 1974." Although the association did not feel these statistics actually reflected a "real" increase in the problem because of reporting differences, they did make the claim, however, that "the percentage of sexual assault cases in those child abuse cases, have increased" and it was felt that "this is a big problem in society" (St. John's Status of Women's Council 1986). In an attempt to deal with this "big problem" the committee suggested to the association delegates ways to make teachers more aware of the problem and to recognize the "symptoms" of abuse. In this way, teachers may "spot" abused children and then report the parents to the necessary authorities.

As a response to the report of the *Badgley Committee on Sexual Offenses Against Children and Youth*, the Community Services Council published *A Blueprint for Action* (1986)—the report of the working group on child sexual abuse. The publication was said to have come as a result of a "unanimous request" from a variety of community groups and government representatives in Newfoundland to form a committee to develop a plan to improve services for sexually abused children in the province. Concern about this issue was also a response to provincial government statistics which indicated that reports of sexual abuse were now outnumbering reports of physical abuse and were increasing at a greater rate (Community Services Council 1986).

The committee was divided into five subcommittees with members from various disciplines, such as: social workers, community researchers, lawyers, psychiatrists, psychologists, school guidance counsellors, teachers and a rape crisis worker; members from the Human Rights Association, John Howard Society, Big Brothers and Big Sisters Organization; and women representing the St. John's Status of Women's Council and the Provincial Advisory Council on the Status of Women, Newfoundland and Labrador.

In an attempt to document the extent of the problem of child abuse in Newfoundland, the report compared the number of reports of child sexual assault which came to the attention of the authorities between 1974 and 1975 with what they felt to be a more accurate measure of the extent of the problem. In fact, by using figures which were produced by the nation-wide retrospective research report in which adults recounted their victimization as children—which the *Badgley Report* used to estimate the 'real' incidence of the problem in the country—the *Blueprint for Action* estimated that "24,897 persons [were] at risk of sexual victimization at some point in their lives, *predominantly* before reaching their 21st birthday" and the figure which was arrived at for Newfoundland was 94,800 (Community Services Council 1986: Appendix 3, 4–5). In terms of how these estimates compared with the number of cases of child sexual assault which come to the attention of the authorities the report stated:

Provincially, the official figures represent about one-half of one percent (0.457 percent) of actual occurrence if the figures contained in the Badgley report accurately reflect incidence rates (Community Services Council 1986:5).

The situation appears to become more grim if we accept one of the recommendations put forward by the Education Subcommittee concerning a proposed public information campaign in which:

> The key to this campaign should be a saturation of the public with the knowledge that the problem does exist, that it will not go away, *that it is increasing daily*, and that it is the responsibility of every individual to recognize the problem and assist in its eradication (Community Services Council 1986: Appendix 2, 2).

Along with these sections of the report where it explicitly states that the incidence of child sexual assault is on the increase, other sections implicitly infer that this is indeed the case. Also, despite the report's failure to address the causes of this problem in any systematic and direct fashion, reference to the etiology of this "deviant sexual behaviour" is made several times throughout the *Blueprint for Action* in documents prepared for public consumption by various concerned groups.

For instance, in the report entitled, *The Child: everybody's responsibility—message to the school principal and teacher*, which was produced by the Newfoundland Department of Social Services, the following reasons were given why a person would wish to sexually abuse a child—especially a child of their own: financial problems; physical and mental illness, including drug or alcohol abuse; isolation; inadequate housing and recreational facilities; and lack of know-how about parenting (Community Services Council 1986: Appendix 8, 2). In other words, the document points out that many of the troubles, conflicts and difficulties which the unemployed (or indeed others who are living on or below the poverty line) face on a regular basis are linked to child sexual assault. Considering the fact that there are more unemployed people living in Newfoundland in the 1980s than was the case in the past, it should come as no surprise that increases in child sexual assault have paralleled "hard times."

In a somewhat similar context, the Big Brothers/Big Sisters Association also submitted a report which was published as a background paper for the *Blueprint for Action*. In a *Program for the Prevention of Child Sexual Abuse* they observed:

> Recent studies suggest that the incidence of all forms of child sexual abuse has increased substantially in recent years, with a variety of rationales offered including:

- our more permissive society
- greater societal pressures
- reduced 'closeness' of the family
- expansion of pornography and other forms of eroticism
- media attention to the subject
(Community Services Council 1986: Appendix 3, 18).

In fact, the only document in the report which seemed to vary from the conventional wisdom of some sort of 'social breakdown' being responsible for increasing levels of child sexual assault was the piece which was produced by women from the St. John's Rape Crisis Centre. What this report failed to address seems to be rather significant as no mention was made regarding the 'social breakdown' (particularly economic) factors which other groups in the handbook associated with increases in child sexual assault. Rather, what we see in this document contradicts much of what was said by other groups who have accepted the conventional wisdom (which will be described in greater detail later in this text). According to the Rape Crisis Centre, offenders come from all levels of society, that is, not only those who are burdened with financial and other related economic problems. This group also states that "offenders are not usually psychotic nor do they have social or legal problems." The reason for these differing attitudes to the problem no doubt lies within the feminist philosophy motivating these women:

> The Rape Crisis Centre operates from a feminist philosophy which views child sexual assault not as unfortunate, isolated instances, but as a symptom of a society which condones ownership and power over its weaker individuals. The Centre believes that all adults are accountable for their actions toward children (Community Services Council 1986, Background Paper, Services Subcommittee Report:21).

In this way, some feminists are not so quick to point out that this problem is increasing, since what they perceive as "causing" this type of behaviour has been dominant in our society for many years: that is, patriarchal domination.

With respect to violence against women, the statistical picture is indeed disquieting. For instance, in 1986 an interview with two women associated with the St. John's Rape Crisis Centre appeared in the local press regarding the problem of sexual assault in Newfoundland. The article opened with:

> Nobody likes to consider the thought—being brutally attacked by a stranger, friend or relative—but we should. One woman in four will be raped sometime in her lifetime; one woman is raped every 17 minutes in Canada. . .(*Newfoundland Herald* 1986 vol. 43:3).

Although these statistics were intended to reflect the level of sexual assault on a national level, there was little in the article to suggest that the situation is any different for women living in Newfoundland. When the official statistics are examined, it appears that this phenomenon has indeed been increasing in recent years.

As indicated by Figure 1, the incidence of rape in St. John's began to increase dramatically during the late 1970s and, with the exception of a drop in 1980, the rate has remained relatively constant since then. The establishment of Newfoundland's first Rape Crisis Centre may be seen as a response to the increasing levels of sexual violence toward women.[7]

There is little doubt according to these statistics, that the incidence of sexual violence against women is on the increase—not only in other parts of the country, but in Newfoundland as well. And, in terms of what is commonly perceived to be the causes of these crimes, these increases should not come as a surprise as the proliferation of "pornographic" cultural materials and other entertainment (strip clubs) are believed to have grown considerably in Newfoundland in recent years.[8]

A longstanding and outspoken Christian peace activist in St. John's voiced his concerns in the press over the "recent increases in sexual violence in the province" (which he added was the "worst kind of violence"): this was due to the growing level and changing character of sexually explicitly material, such as "video cassettes and television in particular" (*Evening Telegram* 30 April 1986). The author of this letter to the editor was convinced that "there is a relationship between viewing violence and violent behaviour" and as a method to put an end to sexual violence, he called upon the Canadian Radio and Television Commission (CRTC) to hold public hearings (responding to an application for a new television licence made by the Canadian Inter-Faith Network) on the need for controls to reduce the level and explicitness of sexual violence. In doing so, he made a call for all those who were in favour of "controlling sexual violence on all television stations" to "turn up to the meetings of the CRTC and let them know that we are concerned" or else "write our members of parliament" (*Evening Telegram* 30 April 1986).

Some women's groups also believe that pornography actually incites individuals to violence. According to the Vice President of the Canadian Advisory Council on the Status of Women, who was speaking to a group of Newfoundland women:

> There is proof from studies that violence against women increases with the amount of pornographic material read or viewed on videos.
> . . .This is rather frightening, because of the excess of this material

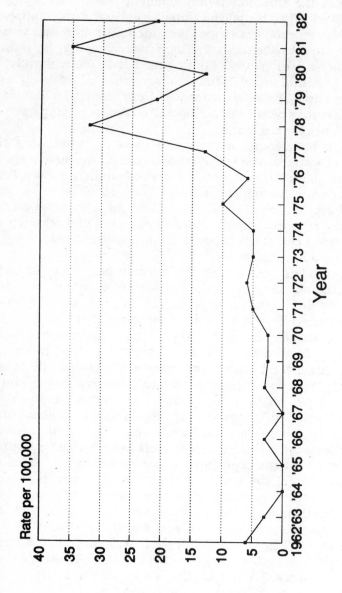

Figure 1: Rape Incident Rates in St. John's, 1962–1982

Rate per 100,000

Year

— Series 1

Source: Compiled from Royal Newfoundland Constabulary Annual Statistical Reports, 1962–1982.

that enters from the US and the promotion being done in corner stores where this is accessible (*Evening Telegram* 14 April 1986).

As a response to the "frightening" situation, this particular women's group was in favour of censoring material which they felt was pornographic and which consequently was regarded as generating violence against women in society.

Although both these sorts of feminist and religious concerns about pornography are rooted in different philosophical orientations (e.g., operational definitions of pornography/erotica), both believe that increases in sexual violence (particularly against women) are reflections of real changes in violent behaviour. The relatively uncontrolled proliferation of pornographic material in society is seen as the reason for the increasing statistics and effective censorship is held to be the only way to control or ultimately eliminate these types of crimes.[9]

In addition to concern about increasing levels of sexual violence against women, mounting concern has been expressed in recent years regarding the issue of wife battering and other 'non-sexual' forms of violence against women. In fact, the number of distress calls which battered women's shelters in the province have received in recent years has significantly increased. For instance in 1981, 114 calls were made by women in the province looking for safe shelter for themselves (and very often their children), while in 1985, the number had increased to over 1,000 distress calls.

Although not all women in Newfoundland who are working with battered women claim that there is actually more battering taking place in the 1980s than was the case in the past—an issue which we will return to later—some do believe that this is indeed the case. For instance, a social worker and counsellor employed at St. John's Family Crisis Centre stated that "more cases of abuse are being reported now [1986] than was previously the case," on account of "the growing factors that contribute to breakdowns of the family units" such as "unemployment and relocation" (*Metro* 29 June 1986). In this way, then, some see the increasing tensions which unemployment is felt to bring to many Newfoundland families as the cause of family breakdown which results in the battering of women.

Certain changes have taken place in policing and punishment over the years which could be interpreted as reflecting the popular or conventional perception that the level and character of crime and violence in Newfoundland have increased and become more violent. A popular notion could be occurring in Newfoundland—increasing crime and violence lead to more people being sent to jail which subsequently creates a demand for more policing. For example,

according to information in Figure 2, the numbers of police (including civilians working as "support staff" in record departments and
secretarial offices in police detachments) substantially increased
from 1962–1984. In fact, in 1962 there were 513 police personnel
employed full-time in the province, which works out to be one police
employee for every 1,000 people in the province. In 1984, this
number had increased to 1,112 police personnel, that is, 2/1,000
population—an increase of 100 percent. In other words, Newfoundlanders are twice as policed in the 1980s as they were in the
early 1960s.

A similar pattern also seems to have emerged with regard to
sentencing patterns in Newfoundland. When sentencing patterns
are examined it could appear that crime and violence have recently
developed into serious problems as more people are being sent to
prison than in the past, and convictions for certain crimes are
carrying longer sentences. Figure 3, shows that from 1971 to 1984,
the number of admissions to Newfoundland correctional facilities
has increased from 806 in 1971 to 2,591 in 1984—an increase of
221 percent.[10]

Not only are more people being sent to jail in Newfoundland in
recent years (usually explained as a result of more crime) as sentencing patterns suggest, but the character of crime may be
changing as well—becoming more 'mainland like.' According to the
1984–1985 Annual Report of the Adult Corrections Division of
Newfoundland:

> The most disturbing aspect of the data is that the "offenses vs. the
> person" category now comprises 8 percent of the admissions when,
> in 1983–1984, the rate was only 4 percent. Since this change
> cannot be explained by a change in the method of data collection
> or a change in definitions, it is fairly obvious that the rate of
> admissions for offenses (murder, sexual assaults and armed rob-
> bery) in which there was a confrontation between victim and
> offender did increase significantly (Newfoundland Department of
> Justice 1984–1985:29).

The report continues by stating:

> [there is] a slight shift towards longer prison terms being issued by
> the courts. For example, whereas in FY [fiscal year] 1983–1984,
> 52.5 percent of admissions were sentenced to terms less than one
> month, only 48.6 percent received such a sentence in 1984–1985.
> This could be a function of the increase in violent offenses. . . .
> (Newfoundland Department of Justice 1984–1985:29).

This trend toward longer sentences for violent offenses seems to
have more than a one year history—at least for certain offenses.

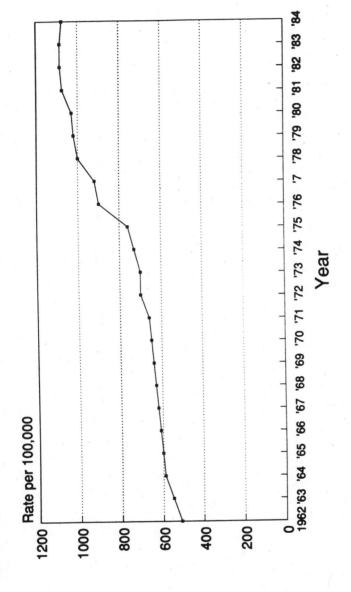

Figure 2: Total Full-Time Police Personnel in Newfoundland, 1962–1984

Rate per 100,000

Year

— Series 1

Source: Compiled from Statistics Canada, Canadian Crime Statistics, 1962–1984.

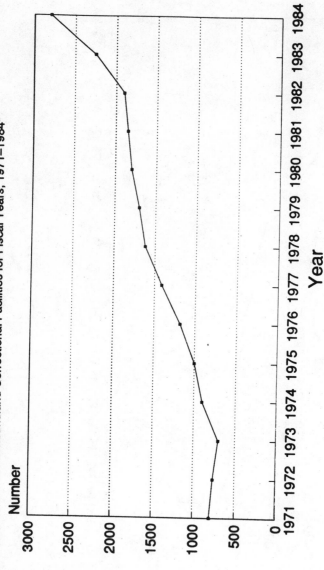

Figure 3: Total Admissions to Newfoundland Correctional Facilities for Fiscal Years, 1971–1984*

Number

Year

— Series 1

*Includes inmates sentenced in Newfoundland to terms of two years and over; this includes transfers to federal penitentiaries. There are no federal prisons in Newfoundland.

Source: Compiled from Department of Adult Corrections, Annual Reports, Newfoundland Department of Justice, 1971–1984.

Table 1 displays a shift which has taken place, for example, in sentencing patterns for robbery with violence between 1950 and 1984. The table clearly shows that the average disposition has increased consistently over the period for those convicted of this particular crime. Although the most recent period only accounts for four years, there is no evidence to suggest that the sentences which judges are issuing for "armed robbers" are getting any shorter, since in December 1985 an eighteen-year-old man was sentenced to eleven years in prison for a series of armed robberies in which very little money was taken and no one was injured.

Table 1

Average (Mean) Length and Range of Prison Sentences for Those Convicted of Robbery in Newfoundland, 1950–1984

	1950–1959	1960–1969	1970–1979	1980–1984
Mean	16.7 mos.	16 mos.	26.2 mos.	33 mos.
Range	1–48 mos.	3–48 mos.	3–78 mos.	1–168 mos.

Source: Compiled from criminal record files, Royal Newfoundland Constabulary, Records Department, St. John's, Newfoundland.

According to information in Table 2, a similar pattern seems to have developed with regard to those who have been convicted of assault in Newfoundland.

Table 2

Average (Mean) Length and Range of Prison Sentences for Those Convicted of Common Assault in Newfoundland, 1960–1983

	1960–1964	1965–1969	1970–1974	1975–1979	1980–1983
Mean	54 days	45 days	90 days	85 days	93 days
Range	14–150 days	14–60 days	30–180 days	3–180 days	3–540 days

Source: Compiled from criminal record files, Royal Newfoundland Constabulary, Records Department, St. John's, Newfoundland.

It is clear from these tables, therefore, that the changing trends which have occurred in the level of policing and the punishing of criminals in Newfoundland are indeed consistent with many of the demands made to the authorities by those 'committed' to eradicating the recent surge of lawlessness and violence.

To summarize the above, many statements have been made regarding the perception that Newfoundland is becoming more violent, and that future oil development will give rise to a crime wave. Furthermore, in order to curb these increasing levels of mayhem, many groups and individuals have called for stricter punishments for those who are responsible for the breakdown in law and order. Despite the fact that some commentators (particularly academics and some professionals) have recognized that official statistics are often deficient and may not always accurately measure the real incidence of crime, they have nonetheless accepted them as essentially being useful in terms of their ability to reflect *increases* or *decreases* in the real level of crime and have consequently used them as data to theorize about what factors have caused these changes. These words perhaps best describe the process:

> It is one of the less important paradoxes of our time that many discussions of criminal statistics begin with the expression of grave doubts about the reliability of the official figures, and then present these statistics in various combinations as if they faithfully portrayed the real world. Apparently no serious student of criminology is happy about the state of criminal statistics, but few. . .are willing to forgo the temptation to use them as a basis for generalizing about the amounts and types of crime and the characteristics of criminals (Giffen 1976:66).

Many generalizations have been based on the assumption (either explicitly or implicitly) that growing rates of crime are linked with changes which have taken place in the social fabric of Newfoundland society. That is, business groups, academics, various members of the criminal justice system, community groups, trade unionists, and others have all more or less taken up the argument that traditional, and, at one time, effective means of social control, have eroded in recent years in Newfoundland, and hence are responsible for the rise in crime and violence. In particular, unprecedented levels of unemployment are linked to increases in many forms of crime and violence, and to increases in other social pathologies such as mental and physical illness. The basic premise of this view (which is in fact shared by those of the political right and left) is that the loss of control associated with being poor and unemployed leads to crime and violence. At a glance, the evidence indicating that this is indeed the case seems impressive. For instance, since the recession of 1982, Newfoundland has had an official rate of unemployment of over 20 percent. Furthermore, rates of unemployment for those under the age of 25 have been calculated to be close to the 40 percent level. In fact, the Pearson correlation coefficient of the official unemployment rate and the violent crime rate between 1974 and 1984 is .88 (r2 = .77). A statistical relationship such as this suggests that a strong level of association exists between these two variables.

In addition to economic explanations being responsible for growing crime and violence, we have also demonstrated that others have linked the growing crime problem to the breakdown of social control which has occurred in the province since confederation with Canada in 1949. In other words, urbanization and modernity are generally thought to have fostered a state of "permissiveness" in Newfoundland society which has caused many forms of crime to increase.

How accurate is this scenario? Is Newfoundland on the brink of chaos? Have unemployment and the other social costs of the current economic crisis (coupled with the drawbacks many have associated with modernity) caused a rupture in the province's social fabric which is manifested by burgeoning crime rates? The next section of this analysis will be concerned specifically with these important matters. We will critically evaluate the statistical information which many have used to suggest that crime and violence have recently been increasing in Newfoundland as well as becoming more 'mainland like.' This will be followed by a critical examination of the 'theories' which many have used to explain these increases and determine what effects these 'theories' may be having.

A CRITICAL EVALUATION OF THE 'EVIDENCE'

In order to conclude that there have been *real* or *significant* changes in patterns of violent crime in Newfoundland, the factors we identified earlier in the chapter must be taken into account. To review, common deficiencies of official crime data concern:

(1) Legal definitions
(2) Police discretion
(3) The dark figure of criminality
(4) Level of policing
(5) Public attitudes
(6) Police record keeping

Let us begin with an examination of the meaning of the "violent crime rate" as this phrase frequently occurs when changes in the level of crime and violence in Newfoundland are discussed. Though the phrase has in fact been referred to a great deal—especially in the media—it is rarely defined, and its meaning is not described in any detail. What precisely does the violent crime rate measure? What crimes of violence are included in these statistics? How is the violent crime rate arrived at in definitional and statistical terms?

According to Statistics Canada, the crimes used to compute the violent crime rate are: homicide (including murder, manslaughter and infanticide), attempted murder, assaults (including sexual assaults), abductions and robberies. Measured in this way, the types of crimes which comprise the violent crime rate would probably not be surprising to the lay person and therefore, fall within the parameters of the conventional images of interpersonal violence which have been the topic of public anxiety. What may be surprising, however, are the types of interpersonal violence which are most often reported to, or detected by police. This may be explained more clearly if, as illustration, the violent crime rate in Newfoundland is compared with the violent crime rate in Quebec for the year 1983. A province with a homicide rate three times greater than Newfoundland's and a robbery rate twelve times greater, nevertheless has a *considerably lower violent crime rate.* These differences seem to be at variance with conventional wisdom, as the crimes of murder and armed robbery are the types of crimes people most often associate with the term violence. However, these puzzling differences in the violent crime rates of Newfoundland and Quebec are essentially the result of variance in the two provinces' assault rates. In 1983, for example, Quebec had an assault rate of 288/100,000 population, while in the same year Newfoundland recorded an assault rate of 574/100,000 population—almost double the rate in Quebec. In this way, the proportion of assaults registered in the Newfoundland violent crime rate in 1983 was much greater than it was in Quebec. In Newfoundland, 88 percent of all violent crimes were simple assaults in 1983, while in Quebec the statistical category of assault was accountable for 60 percent of the number of violent crimes registered by police in that year—these differences have also generally remained constant in the past.

In addition to this, the proportion of assaults which comprise the overall violent crime rate has also been increasing over time. In Figure 4, "The Statistical Composition of Violent Crime in Newfoundland," we see that if we break up the period between 1953–1982 into three parts, (1953–1962, 1963–1972 and 1973–1982), the number of assaults which comprise the violent crime rate has substantially risen over this time from 82 percent in the first period, to 84 percent in the second, to almost 88 percent in the third.

These differences over time are significant as they illustrate that assault (the type of crime we are probably *least* likely to associate with violence) does not only comprise the majority of the crimes of violence which are reported to police, but also has increased the greatest in terms of proportionality over this thirty year period. On

Figure 4: Statistical Composition (percent) of Violent Crime in Newfoundland, 1953–1982

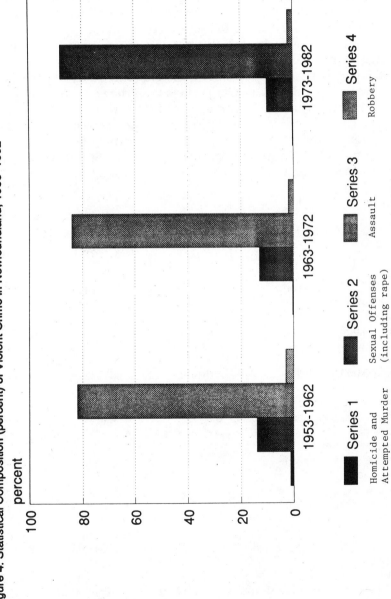

Source: Compiled from Statistics Canada, Canadian Crime Statistics, 1953–1982.

the other hand, the other more disturbing crimes of violence have remained relatively constant, or have in fact *decreased proportionately* over these three periods (as was the case with sexual assault—including rape). This is not to say that crimes other than assault have not increased over time according to official statistics, but rather that they are not increasing at a level which would come anywhere close to the levels of increase of assault.

Somewhat similarly, the information in Table 3, "Percentage change in rates of violent crime in Newfoundland from 1953 to 1982," shows that the percentage increases in violent crime have been more significant in earlier periods than they have been in more recent years. The percentage increase in the rate of violent crime for the most recent period—the period where people seem to be most concerned about the incidence of violent crime—is *substantially lower* than it was for earlier periods. The years 1963 to 1972 show the greatest percentage increase in violent crime.

Table 3

Percentage Change in Rates of Violent Crime in Newfoundland, 1953–1982

	1953–1962	1963–1972	1973–1982
All Crimes of Violence			
Rate/100,000 population	58–137	135–401	426–581
% Change	+135	+196%	+36%
Robbery			
Rate/100,000 population	1.7–1.9	7.4–7.7	7.0–9.4
% Change	+10%	+4%	+34%
Assault			
Rate/100,000 population	51–95	94–349	376–529
% Change	+87%	+271%	+40%
Sexual Crimes			
Rate/100,000 population	6.5–40.2	31.4–42.4	41–45
% Change	+518%	+34%	+9.7%
Attempted Murder			
Rate/100,000 population	NA	.21–.6	.7–1.0
% Change	NA	+185%	+43%
Homicide			
Rate/100,000 population	1-0	.6–.6	.7–1
% Change	-100%	0%	+43%

Source: Compiled from Statistics Canada, Canadian Crime and Traffic Statistics, 1953–1982

Moreover, according to information in Table 4, it is not true that rates of violent crime in Newfoundland, compared to the country as a whole, are growing at an alarming rate. Although this may seem to be the case for the years 1982 and 1983, this does not appear to be a *trend* as Newfoundland's national ranking has consistently fluctuated over this period and *remains statistically as one of the least violent provinces in Canada.*

Table 4

Rates of Violent Crime/100,000 Population for Newfoundland and Canada, 1974–1983

Year	Newfoundland	Canada
1974	434 (9)*	562
1975	428 (10)	594
1976	441 (9)	593
1977	440 (10)	582
1978	459 (9)	592
1979	443 (11)	623
1980	450 (11)	652
1981	474 (10)	671
1982	581 (8)	685
1983	603 (8)	692

*The numbers in brackets denote national ranking e.g., in 1983 Newfoundland ranked eighth in rate of violent crime in Canada.

Source: Compiled from Statistics Canada, Canadian Crime and Traffic Statistics, 1974–1983

It is clear that it is problematic indeed when we use the violent crime rate as an indicator of the 'real' level of violence in society, that is, the forms of violence which most people typically associate with the term violence—such as murder. Consequently, we must be very careful in the way we interpret Statistics Canada's data which indicate that violent crime in Newfoundland increased by 39 percent between 1974 and 1983.

When this violent crime rate in Newfoundland is examined on a yearly basis over the ten year period, we discover that the greatest increase took place between 1981 and 1982. The violent crime rate in 1981 was 474/100,000 population, while in 1982 the rate had jumped to 581/100,000 population—an increase of 23 percent, by far the greatest annual increase over this ten year period. We may examine these changes in greater detail in the following table.

The data in Table 5 show that when the violent crime rate is examined on a yearly basis, 1982 stands out as being a period when dramatic change took place. Keeping in mind the fact that the majority of violent crime in Newfoundland which is recorded in police statistics stems from the category of assault, we will take a closer look at changes which took place in the assault rate in Newfoundland between 1981–1982 as a first step to account for the changes in the overall violent crime rate.

Table 5

Annual Percentage Changes in the Newfoundland Violent Crime Rate, 1974–1984

1974–1975	(-)	1.4%
1975–1976	(+)	3.0%
1976–1977	(-)	.2%
1977–1978	(+)	4.3%
1978–1979	(-)	3.0%
1979–1980	(+)	1.4%
1980–1981	(+)	5.0%
1981–1982	(+)	23.0%
1982–1983	(+)	2.0%
1983–1984	(+)	.5%

Source: Compiled from Statistics Canada, Canadian Crime and Traffic Statistics, 1974–1984

In Figure 5 we see the very similar paths that the assault and violent crime rates have taken as both of these measures increased markedly in 1982. In this way, we can explain the sudden increase in the violent crime rate by a similar increase recorded in the assault rate, as approximately 88 percent of violent crimes in Newfoundland are assaults. In fact, the assault rate increased from 422/100,000 population in 1981 to 530/100,000 population in 1982 — an increase of 25 percent. As with the violent crime rate, the assault rate failed to register any significant changes either *prior to* or *following* the sudden change which was recorded in 1982. In terms of explaining why the assault rate rose at such an alarming rate in 1982, consideration needs to be given to the way in which police began to deal with "domestics" in the province. In 1982, police were encouraged by the Newfoundland Department of Justice to lay charges against assault suspects in "domestic disturbances." In fact, in 1983 Manitoba experienced a similar increase in its violent crime rate which was also directly related to a recording reclassification of domestic disputes by police.

The violent crime rate in Newfoundland has been shown to be a very problematic measure of what is popularly perceived to be "violence." Because the violent crime rate is so closely linked to the

Figure 5: Violent Crime and Assault Incident Rates in Newfoundland, 1974–1982

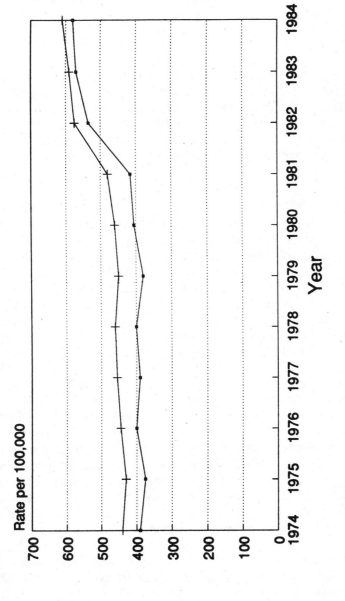

Source: Compiled from Statistics Canada, Canadian Crime Statistics, 1974–1982.

assault rate, the measure is almost meaningless for understanding the level of the more 'serious' crimes of violence such as homicide, attempted murder, robbery and rape—or what is now referred to as sexual assault.

We will now turn to a closer examination of these more 'serious' violent crimes in order to determine if they have increased in recent years.

In so far as we wish to present the best impression of what has been recorded in terms of "serious violent crime" historically in Newfoundland, we will examine not only crimes of violence for Newfoundland in general, but attention will also be paid to the metropolitan St. John's area—the major urban centre of the province which currently has approximately 30 percent of the total number of inhabitants living in the province.

The Incidence and Character of Homicide in Newfoundland

Historically, homicide has been a relatively infrequent phenomenon in Newfoundland society, and according to official statistics, its low level remains relatively the same today as it did in the past. Since 1933, the homicide rate in Newfoundland has fluctuated between 0 to 1.6/100,000 population with no clear pattern or trend. Although the number of homicides has increased in *frequency*, the *rates* of this phenomenon have in fact remained quite stable. Figure 6 displays the yearly totals and rates of homicide offenses in Newfoundland between 1933 and 1984. Unlike the general trend in Canada, where homicide rates have increased over this period (although they have by no means done so in a strictly linear fashion, and they have been prone to considerable fluctuation), there is no indication from these data that homicide offenses in Newfoundland have increased over this period. In fact, these data indicate that homicide rates per 100,000 people have not increased in Newfoundland over the past half century—although the frequency of the phenomenon has increased when population growth is not taken into consideration. Therefore, although homicides and attempted murders do in fact occur in Newfoundland in the 1980s, the *rates* of these offenses have not been changing.

In this section we will deal with the character of homicide in Newfoundland, that is, the types and circumstances of homicidal violence which have taken place in the province in the past. Our intent is to determine whether or not the character of homicide has been changing in Newfoundland. Are we, for example, experiencing

Figure 6: Homicide Incident Rates in Newfoundland, 1933–1984

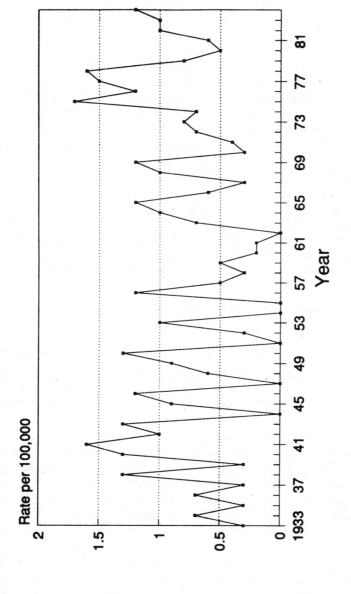

Rate per 100,000

Year

— Series 1

Source: Compiled from Annual Statistical Reports, Royal Newfoundland Constabulary, St. John's.

more 'stranger' types of homicides in Newfoundland in recent years compared to the past as many people seem to think is the case?

To answer these questions in a definitive fashion would be impossible, as the information which would be necessary to undertake such an investigation is simply not available. In other words, it was impossible to achieve access to *all* homicide and attempted murder files which the police have handled in the province during this period. However, it was possible to attain a considerable amount of information which is quite representative of the incidents which have come to the attention of the Royal Newfoundland Constabulary and the Royal Canadian Mounted Police between 1953 and 1984. Why the number of incidents we will be examining in detail here do not match up with the totals one would find in Statistics Canada publications is due to a number of factors which include the following: Firstly, we were not given permission to access files which were under investigation. Therefore, *some* of the more recent slayings and attempted murders which have taken place in the province will not appear in our data set. Secondly, some files were being used by the RCMP and the RNC for training and other police purposes. Finally, we are using in our data set *incidents* of homicide and attempted murder since according to Statistics Canada (and we concur):

> The numbers of rates of murder incidents provide a better measure of changes in the amount of homicide, because these measures are not so affected by the fluctuations abused by multiple-victim murders as are offence based murders (Statistics Canada 1976:8).

Consequently, we have gathered together 126 homicide and attempted murder files from both the RCMP and the RNC (there have been approximately 165 victims of either homicide or attempted murder during this period). In general terms, we have gathered together approximately 80 percent of all the homicide and attempted murder incidents which have taken place in Newfoundland between 1953 and 1984. Although this 80 percent is not a random sample, we feel that under the circumstances it will serve as a fairly representative data base for trying to understand the essential qualities of homicide and attempted murder in Newfoundland.

Out of 124 homicide incidents (there was incomplete information in two of these files) we examined in Newfoundland during this period, 109 or 88 percent involved male offenders or suspects (we will use the term offender throughout the analysis), while female offenders accounted for 12 percent of the total. The majority of incidents involved offenders between the ages of 21 and 40—with 35 percent between 21 and 30, and 35 percent between 31 and 40.

This distribution in age generally applies for offenders of both sexes. The only marked difference is at the young end of the spectrum (16–20 years) where only one woman was charged with a homicide (an infanticide). On the other hand, 17 males within this age group were charged with homicides.

According to information in Tables 6 and 7, there is more variation in the age and sex differences in victims of homicide and attempted murder than is the case for offenders. In fact, in 56 percent of the cases, men were victims, while in 46 percent of the cases females were victims. With respect to differences in sex therefore, we see a lot more homogeneity in the victim category than was evident in the offender category. In other words, men out-kill women by a ratio of about 9/1, but in terms of victimization, men and women are equally represented.

Table 6

Age and Sex of Homicide and Attempted Murder Offenders in Newfoundland

AGE	MALE		FEMALE		TOTAL	
16–20	17	(15%)	1	(1%)		
21–30	37	(31%)	4	(4%)		
31–40	33	(29%)	7	(6%)		
41–50	8	(7%)	2	(2%)		
51–55	2	(2%)	0			
56+	3	(3%)	0			
TOTAL	100	(87%)	14	(13%)	114	(100%)

Table 7

Age and Sex of Homicide and Attempted Murder Victims in Newfoundland

AGE	MALE		FEMALE		TOTAL	
15	9	(9%)	1	(1%)		
16–20	4	(4%)	7	(7%)		
21–30	13	(12%)	21	(19%)		
31–40	15	(14%)	4	(4%)		
41–50	6	(6%)	4	(4%)		
51–55	2	(2%)	3	(3%)		
56+	7	(7%)	8	(8%)		
TOTAL	56	(54%)	48	(46%)	104	(100%)

Note: Figures in both tables may be slightly inaccurate due to rounding.

Source: Compiled from all available police homicide incidents on file in the record departments of the Royal Canadian Mounted Police, "B" Division, and the Royal Newfoundland Constabulary, St. John's, Newfoundland.

With regard to age differences, women victims generally fall into
the same age bracket as do men, as the majority of men and women
who were murdered — as is indeed the case with those who murder —
were between the ages of 21 and 40 with the average age about 30
years (mean).

According to the information in Table 7, the only obvious difference existing between the sexes is in terms of victims who are
under the age of 15, since boys are much more likely to be victims
of a slaying (or attempted slaying) than are girls.

From 1953–1984 the largest proportion of homicides and attempted murder incidents in Newfoundland took place in the
context of a prior relationship between the victim and the offender.
In fact, in over 85 percent of the incidents the offender and victim
knew each other. Incidents taking place within the nuclear family
comprise 55 percent of all available police files involving homicide
and attempted murder in Newfoundland over this period. The data
in Table 8 examine in more detail the victim/offender relationships.

Table 8

Victim-Offender Relationships in Homicide and Attempted Murder Incidents in
Newfoundland, 1953–1984 (percentages)

	%
Husbands vs. wives	27
Wives vs. Husbands	09
Other Immediate Family	19
Other Kinship Ties	08
Unmarried Lovers	17
Close Acquaintances	03
Casual Acquaintances	03
Strangers	07
During a robbery involving strangers (not including Gander robbery/murder)	04
During a robbery where victim knew offender	01
Slaying of police	02
Total n = 93	100

Note: Percentages may be inaccurate due to rounding.

Source: Compiled from all available police homicide incidents on file in the record
departments of the Royal Canadian Mounted Police, "B" Division, St. John's,
Newfoundland and the Royal Newfoundland Constabulary, St. John's, Newfoundland.

A better understanding of the character of murder can be achieved by an examination of homicidal motives. According to the police files, in 87 percent of the incidents which led to a husband killing his wife, the contributing factor which lead to the violent act was sexual jealousy. Not only was this 'motive' a major element in these types of slayings and attempted slayings, but it was also important in incidents which involved intimate couples who were not married or living together. It is important to note however, that we did not come across any files in which a woman killed a man where the motive for the act was described as the result of sexual jealousy—this motive only appeared in files where men killed, or attempted to kill, women. Here are a few vignettes:

Case 1: Attempted murder.

A man entered a local bar with a shotgun and shot a woman patron in the face. A couple of days prior to the incident the man had sexual relations with the woman and, upon finding out that she was with another man after this encounter, he became enraged and wanted to kill the woman whom police described as a casual acquaintance and whom the offender referred to as a "slut" and a "whore."

Case 2: Murder/suicide.

A man came home one evening in an intoxicated state and accused his wife of being unfaithful. A fight between the two ensued and the man killed his wife with a 30/30 and then put the gun to himself and was killed instantly.

Case 3: Attempted murder.

A woman's ex-boyfriend tried to kill her and her new lover with a shotgun. The offender "ambushed" the couple as they were entering the woman's home one evening and shot and wounded the woman.

Case 4: Manslaughter.

A husband killed his wife (by beating her) in the kitchen of their home. The husband had recently returned from prison for beating his wife previously. Upon his return he discovered that his wife had become pregnant by another man in his absence. He became outraged by this infidelity and beat the woman so severely that she had to be hospitalized. Upon her release from the hospital he beat her once again, this time killing her.

Case 5: Murder.

A man killed his wife by forcing his fist into her vagina. The woman died in hospital as the result of a ruptured bladder, poisoned by her own urine. The husband believed his wife was being unfaithful to him and wished to punish the part of his wife's body which was "used" during this act of infidelity—hence the attack on the vagina.

The offender had been reported to have beaten his wife extensively in the past.

As we have previously noted, incidents such as these accounted for approximately 30 percent of the homicide and attempted murder files which have taken place in Newfoundland over the twenty-five year period.

Let us turn for a moment to the incidents in which women kill. As we have mentioned before, women rarely kill or try to kill. In eight of the fifteen incidents which we examined where women have killed, or attempted to kill, they killed or tried to kill their husbands. The other incidents were categorized as "infanticides" where women killed their newborn children. Because of the high frequency of women killing their husbands, we will pay particular attention to these types of incidents.

From the information which was collected, it is evident that women who kill or attempt to kill their husbands do so for rather different reasons than men who slay their wives. We examined eight such files and in all of these situations (according to witness accounts as well as statements made by these women offenders) women committed these acts in desperate self-defense. Here are some short descriptions which will illustrate the conditions under which women kill their husbands in Newfoundland and Labrador.

Case 1: Murder. Acquitted on the grounds of self defence.

A woman shot and killed her husband with a shotgun. At the time of the incident both the offender and the victim were drunk and arguing over the husband's allegations that the woman was unfaithful. Specifically, the man was upset because he felt that his wife was having an affair with his brother. According to relatives' statements contained in the police file, the woman had been beaten by her husband for years. According to a statement made by one of the investigating officers, "Mr. X had the weakness of his race," but he didn't think that he was an evil man. On the contrary, the officer believed that the offender was a good man who occasionally showed "moral weakness" and that his "worst fault" was that "he did not exercise enough influence over his wife." In other words, it was felt that the offender had let his wife 'go too far.'

Case 2: Murder.

A woman stabbed her husband in the middle of a drunken argument which concerned the husband's belief that his wife was being unfaithful. According to statements contained in the file, it was not the first time that the woman had stabbed her husband and the man had a history of beating his wife. The husband reportedly beat the wife when *he* was drunk, and according to the wife she had recently begun beating the husband while *she* was drunk. "It's just like paying him back for what he did to me" she said. "I didn't mean to kill him, but I just wanted to show him what it was like to be hurt, but I think I went too far this time."

Case 3: Murder. Dismissed.

A woman stabbed her husband in the chest with a kitchen knife. The couple had returned home from a local club where a fight between the two of them started and continued into the house. The husband was beating the woman when she pulled a knife out of the kitchen drawer and stabbed him to death.

When we examine the differences in homicide rates between the island of Newfoundland and Labrador, we see considerable differences. Labrador has a population of approximately 32,000 people (with natives accounting for about 5,000 of the total population for the region) which is less than 6 percent of the Newfoundland's total population. Yet Labrador accounted for 20 percent of the homicides and 10 percent of the attempted murders in the province between 1977 and 1984. When these differences are examined more closely, we discover that most of the homicides and incidents of attempted murder take place between native people living in that part of the province. In fact, between 1977 and 1984 nine homicides and three attempted murders took place in Labrador and out of this total, natives were involved in seven of the homicides and one of the attempted murders. In other words, natives in Labrador who comprise approximately 15 percent of the population accounted for 78 percent of the homicides and 33 percent of the attempted murders which were reported to police during this period (adequate data was only available for this eight-year period). Looking at these figures in a different way, we see that homicide and attempted murder which occurred between native people accounted for 10 percent of the province of Newfoundland's homicide and attempted murders for this period—a remarkable statistic if we consider that the native population in Labrador accounts for less than 1 percent of the total population of Newfoundland. In this way, the homicide rate among natives in Labrador is 20/100,000 population while the rate for the province in general since 1933 has never exceeded 1.6/100,000 population.

These data which were obtained from police files have provided us with a general picture of the *character* of homicide and attempted murder in Newfoundland. Although not all incidents which have taken place in the province were available for the analysis, nonetheless it has provided us with a general level of understanding about the "crime of crimes." Even though we feel we have a reasonable grasp on the *unchanging* level of this phenomenon and the general character of it, we remain at this stage still uncertain as to whether or not this typically *mundane* character is changing. For instance, at this point we have not mentioned a sex murder which took place in Corner Brook in 1983, (which was not contained in the set of police files which we examined) where two young men raped and killed a young woman. Crimes such as this were referred to in the first section of the analysis, and were felt by some to be a "new" form of violence in Newfoundland, which was presumed to be on the increase.

However, the information does not indicate that such 'mainland' style acts of violence are on the increase in Newfoundland. Rather, we have demonstrated that the quality of 'mundaneness' had changed very little over this period. Men continue to be involved as offenders considerably more often than women and both men's and woman's chances of becoming a victim of this violent crime have not changed over time. In this way then, the "sex murder" which took place in Corner Brook does not represent a *pattern*, as these forms of violence are not on the increase in Newfoundland; they merely occasionally occur. The vast majority of murders in Newfoundland continue to take place between family members, other relatives or between acquaintances. If there is any evidence of an increasing *trend* in a certain type of murder in Newfoundland, perhaps it is to be found with increasing numbers of young men under the age of twenty who have been involved as homicide or attempted murder offenders. According to our data, numbers of young men and boys killing family members and other intimates may be increasing in Newfoundland. However, we must be careful not to make the same sort of mistake with general assumptions which others have made based upon limited information. Hence, caution, will be used in any attempt to interpret this statistical trend.

Between 1978–1984, ten homicides or attempted murder incidents occurred in Newfoundland where young people were involved either as offenders or suspects. These incidents accounted for roughly 25 percent of the total number of people who were involved in a homicide or an attempted murder. Prior to 1978, it was a rarity to come across a case of this nature, as only three files in our data involved cases where people under the age of twenty were charged with a homicide or attempted murder. We will provide a brief synopsis of these incidents so as to better understand the essential characteristics of this statistical "trend."

Case 1: *Manslaughter.*

Three boys were drinking in a cabin when one of them was shot and killed by a .22. The boy who was shot was lying on the bed at the time, sick from too much alcohol. The offender (eighteen) had aimed the gun at the victim and it accidentally fired. The offender had also been drinking and throughout the day while the boys were in the woods he was constantly scaring the victim and another youngster who was also there by aiming the gun close to them and firing into the dirt. The offender had a criminal record for assaulting his mother and had been convicted for liquor violations. According to the psychiatrist who examined the boy, "he has been aggressive to members of his family in the past while under the influence of alcohol and he is an epileptic who doesn't take his medication and becomes violent especially while under the influence of alcohol."

Case 2: Second degree reduced to manslaughter.

A seventeen-year-old boy stabbed his father to death shortly after he returned home from a dance. According to the boy's friends he had a considerable amount to drink that evening, and his behaviour was described as "bizarre" as he was threatening to kill himself. Apparently the boy and his father had fought earlier that evening and the fight continued after the boy had returned home from the dance. According to the offender, "I never done anything to hurt him. He kept getting on my nerves and making me mad. I never meant to hurt him but when spite gets into me I get a quick temper."

Case 3: Murder.

A fifteen-year-old boy stabbed his father to death with a knife. When the police arrived at the scene of the crime the offender was leaning over the dead body in what police described as a "dream-like trance." The boy was reported to have been suffering from epilepsy and was described in the file as being a "trouble maker" in school. Both of the boy's parents were alcoholics. Shortly after the boy was paroled from prison and returned to his community, he died from a drug overdose.

Case 4: Attempted murder.

A fifteen-year-old boy dragged a thirteen-year-old girl off a dirt path going through a wooded area into some bushes and cut her throat with a pocket knife. The police suspected that the boy had originally intended to sexually assault the girl, but when she began to scream and resist, he tried to "silence" her by putting a jack-knife to her throat. The boy was reported by teachers, parents, and those who knew him as "normal."

Case 5: Manslaughter.

A twenty-year-old man got into a fight with another man (twenty-four) over a film projector. The offender believed that the victim was "ripping" off the local people by charging them admission to the films he was showing with the projector (as it was community property). The victim died as the result of the offender hitting him over the head with a leg of a table.

Case 6: Attempted murder.

An eighteen-year-old stabbed two of his friends on the way home from a dance (one seriously). Apparently one of the victims was responsible for the offender's girlfriend leaving him. The offender had drunk twelve beers that night and in his statement to police he said, "He had it coming to him." He was charged with two counts of attempted murder.

Case 7: Murder/suicide.

A sixteen-year-old boy shot a sixteen-year-old girl in his community—he then put the gun to himself. According to various statements contained in the police report, the boy was "infatuated" with the girl as he was constantly trying to make dates with her. The girl apparently had no romantic interest in the boy and only considered him as a "friend" and sometimes a "pest." The boy had the girl's initials engraved on many pieces of property which he owned such as his ski-doo helmet. The incident took place because the boy discovered that the girl had a new boyfriend and the girl's mother told him to "lay off." The boy had an "unremarkable history" as he was a good student and was no trouble in his community or to his family.

Case 8: Manslaughter.

An eighteen-year-old male shot and killed his mother and father, then himself. The boy had just returned to his community from a series of foster homes. Both of the boy's parents were alcoholics, and the police were very "familiar" with the family.

Case 9: Attempted murder.

A twenty-year-old man fled to a friend's house to seek refuge after he had committed a break and entry in the community. Once he made his way into the house he checked to see if anyone was home and while checking in the master bedroom he found a couple asleep in bed. He then went over to the bed and stabbed a man in the throat as he apparently was "shocked" to see the bed occupied by someone he was not familiar with. The offender had been drinking heavily the previous day and had a long history of being in trouble with the law in addition to having spent a considerable amount of his life in the "Boys' Home."

Case 10: Infanticide.

A fifteen-year-old girl gave birth in the washroom of her home and smothered the child after it was born. The girl apparently did not know that she was pregnant until shortly before she gave birth. According to the opinions of various professionals involved in the case, she was totally ignorant of sex. There was also evidence that the father of the child may have raped her.

In general terms, these incidents *do not* conform to the stereo-typical image of youthful homicide. That is, the people involved in these tragedies do not confirm the typical mass media image which has developed in North America (as well as in Newfoundland) which essentially portrays the youthful murderer as someone who is psychologically disturbed, sex crazed and intrinsically violent. Rather, these thumb-nail sketches essentially depict incidents and contexts which are for the most part *unsensational* yet tragic. In this way, youth interpersonal violence is in many respects similar to the types of incidents in which adults (those who are over the age of twenty) are involved. Despite the generation gap, fatal, or near fatal, incidents of interpersonal violence, whether they involve young people or adults, may be located within the context of normal and everyday situations surrounding family or friendship relations. However, it is also important to recognize that alcohol seemed to play a significant role in these sorts of incidents.

Although a small number of what could be described as 'mainland' murders involving the young have taken place, they have not been responsible for the increasing numbers of young people who have killed or attempted to kill in Newfoundland in recent years. Indeed there is little evidence to suggest that this 'trend' (more youth becoming involved in homicide incidents) can be explained in terms of the changing *character* of youthful homicidal violence.

While we have only briefly examined homicide and attempted murder, our investigation has nonetheless revealed some important aspects which are for the most part contrary to the popular image of homicide in Newfoundland. Contrary to popular perception, homicide has not recently been increasing in Newfoundland and in fact the level (rate) of this type of sudden, non-natural violent death has not increased since the 1930s. The unchanging incidence of homicide in Newfoundland differs from the situation in Canada generally, as, according to official statistics, the Canadian rate of homicide (although remaining quite low compared with the USA) has been increasing over the past fifty years.

The popular perception that the *character* of homicide may have recently changed in Newfoundland was also seen to lack empirical support. Although some sensational homicides have occurred in Newfoundland in recent years, they continue to represent a small proportion of the total number of these types of violent crime.

This brief analysis of homicide in Newfoundland has also demon-strated that the vast majority of offenders who kill (or attempt to do so) are men. This has not changed over time as men continue to over-represent women as offenders, while women and men are practically equally distributed as victims. In terms of women who kill (or attempt to do so) we have shown that they commit such acts for the purposes of self defence — particularly from violent husbands.

When we examined the incidence of homicide across the province, we discovered that Labrador (with a population of less than 6 percent of the total population of the province) accounted for about 20 percent of the homicide and 10 percent of the attempted murders. In particular, we found that the native population in Labrador contributed significantly to the number of homicides which take place in the province.

Finally, almost half of the homicides which have taken place in Newfoundland from 1953–1984 have been between people who have had an intimate or otherwise close relationship or friendship. We also have shown that the victim-offender relationship does not really differ between generations, as both young and old kill or attempt to kill those they are close to — although younger people (those under the age of twenty) are now committing these acts more frequently in recent years than in previous years. However, since the frequency and the circumstances of these incidents are relatively recent (1978–1984) we are not in a position to speculate why this may be the case.

Robbery in Newfoundland: Retail Hold-ups or Parking Lot Punch-ups?

The crime of robbery has provoked considerable public concern in Newfoundland in recent years — particularly in the city of St. John's. According to the study of "retail crime" conducted by the St. John's Board of Trade in 1985, the total number of robberies rose by 26 percent between 1978 and 1983. However, when these statistics are critically examined, a rather different picture emerges. That is, if the study had used other years, say 1978 and 1982, or 1979 and 1983, as comparison points, there would have been a *decline* in robberies. Along with this dubious use of statistics, the figures used in the report were not standardized by population rates. This was a serious omission because in 1981 the jurisdiction of the Royal Newfoundland Constabulary (whose annual reports were used in their analysis) was expanded by approximately 60,000 people, and now included the town of Mount Pearl. If the report had compared rates, rather than incidents reported to police, different results would have been obtained.

Figure 7 shows the statistical trends for rates of robbery in St. John's from 1962–1985. The information in the figure demonstrates that the incidence of robbery in St. John's has *not* been increasing at an alarming rate. In fact, on a per capita basis, the rate of robbery in St. John's seems to have reached its peak in 1979, and to have lowered since that time—although there have been fluctuations.

The study conducted by the St. John's Board of Trade was also inaccurate in its use of the statistical category of "robbery" to measure the incidence of robbery at retail locations. That is, the report used an aggregate total which included the sub-categories of robberies with other offensive weapons, and other robberies. Therefore, no attempt was made to differentiate between robberies which take place at retail locations (the types of robbery which the report was most interested in examining), particularly involving the use of a firearm, and other types of robberies. If the Board of Trade had made these distinctions, they would have discovered that the majority of what are commonly referred to as "armed robberies" essentially comprise only a fraction of the total number of robberies which are reported to the police. For instance, between 1981 and 1985, approximately 50 percent of robberies which were reported to police did not take place at retail locations, although the way in which they were included in the Board of Trade's figures would suggest that they had. Furthermore, roughly one-half of all robberies which took place in St. John's between 1981 and 1985 did not involve the use of a weapon, and they were incidents which would be popularly described as "muggings." Therefore, the data used in the Board of Trade's study are misleading, as they *do not* reflect the incidence of armed robberies which took place at retail locations in the St. John's area.

Looking at the "problem" on a provincial level, the incidence of robbery (all types) is relatively low in Newfoundland when it is compared with the Canadian average. In fact, between 1974 and 1984 the average incidence of all categories of robbery in Newfoundland which were reported to police was 11/100,000 population, compared with the Canadian average over the same period which was 93/100,000 population. Newfoundland has a robbery rate almost nine times lower than the Canadian average. And when the different categories of robbery are compared between Newfoundland and Canada in general, "robbery with a firearm"—what is most often referred to as "armed robbery"—takes place in approximately 20 percent of the robberies in Newfoundland, compared with 33 percent of those which take place on the mainland. The combined categories of "other offensive weapons" and "other"

Figure 7: Robbery Incident Rates in St. John's, 1962–1985

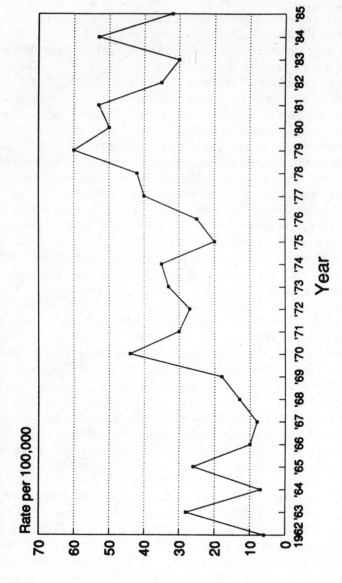

Source: Compiled from Annual Statistical Reports, Royal Newfoundland Constabulary, St. John's.

robberies—where no weapon is used and which may be referred to as the "mugging" variety—comprise 80 percent of the robbery total in Newfoundland while the same figure is 67 percent for Canada generally.

The preceding discussion has demonstrated that the level of robbery in Newfoundland, particularly in St. John's, has *not been increasing at an alarming rate*. In fact, the majority of robberies which are reported to the police do not conform to the dominant and stereotypical images of this type of crime as seen in the media where, for instance, armed robbers are depicted as violent heroin or cocaine addicts. We will, therefore, proceed by examining the specific characteristics surrounding the crime of robbery in Newfoundland so that we can compare these with the more popular images.

Let us begin by examining in more detail the qualitative differences between the sub-categories of robbery. As we have already pointed out, the majority of robberies which are reported to the police are located in the "other" robbery category, and these are essentially "muggings." This sub-category of robbery accounts for approximately half of robberies committed in Newfoundland over the past ten years—a ratio which has not changed to any marked degree. After examining the information about this type of crime, we were struck by the fact that this is the category of robbery where most people were injured! According to our sample, (based on a 10 percent random sample of robbery incidents which were reported to the police between 1979–1983) in 30 percent of these incidents the victim was injured. Of this 30 percent we discovered that the majority (70 percent) of these acts of violence could be described as muggings, rather than robberies which took place at retail locations. That is to say, robberies that involve attacking people in a parking lot of a bar or on the roadside and taking their money or valuables, are the most likely to involve victim injury. In fact, only one death has taken place at a retail location in Newfoundland where a person working in a convenience store was robbed and then stabbed with a knife. Table 9 gives a better illustration of the types of robberies which have taken place in Newfoundland where a victim was injured.

In terms of the 30 percent of people who were hurt in robberies (of which the majority were in the "other" category), 7 or 37 percent were acquaintances at the time of the incident while 3 or 16 percent were friends. Actually, less than half of all robberies involving injury take place between strangers.

Table 9

Robbery Incidents where Victim was Injured or Uninjured (by Location of Offense) 1979–1983

Location	Injured No.	% of Total	Uninjured No.	% of Total
Victim's Home	5	7.5	8	12
Convenience Store Attached to Private Dwelling	0	0	3	4.5
Convenience Store	2	3	8	12
Gas Station	3	4.5	8	12
Fast Food	0	0	3	4.5
Club/Bar	5	7.5	3	4.5
Street	1	1.5	6	9
Bank	0	0	2	3
Car	3	4.5	6	9
Total	19	29%	47	71%

Source: Compiled from a random sample of 66 robbery incidents (on file) in the Royal Canadian Mounted Police record department, "B" Division, St. John's, Newfoundland.

The following vignettes illustrate the kinds of incidents in which people have been injured:

Case 1.

A fifty-three-year-old man reported to the police that he had been beaten and robbed of his wallet. The victim was drunk and could not recall very many of the details surrounding the crime. The crime took place while the man was walking home from a club.

Case 2.

A foreign sailor who was in port reported to the police that he had been beaten and robbed of his watch and his wallet. The incident took place in the parking lot of a bar.

Case 3.

A woman reported that two masked youths broke into her house and stole her husband's money. The victim of the crime was sixty years of age and while trying to resist being robbed he received a few bruises.

In the first section of this analysis, we looked at the popular perception (voiced by a judge in a robbery trial) that the number of robberies which involve the use of a firearm has dramatically increased in Newfoundland in recent years. However, according to the information in Table 10, the use of firearms in the commission of robberies in Newfoundland between 1974 and 1985 has *not increased at an alarming rate*. Although there is some evidence in this table to suggest that use of firearms has increased to some degree over this period, it has not increased dramatically and has been subject to considerable fluctuation. In other words, there is no sign of an upward *trend* in the use of firearms in robberies. Moreover, the incident rates of robberies which take place in Newfoundland where firearms are used are substantially lower than rates registered for Canada as whole.

It is most important to note that these figures do not necessarily represent the 'real' incidence of robberies which involve the use of firearms in Newfoundland. There is evidence to suggest that the number of firearms said to have been used in the commission of robberies may in fact be higher than the number which were actually used. In 1985, for instance, a young man was charged and convicted of five robberies — one with a firearm. Although *at least* one of these "armed robberies" was categorized in the official statistics as a "robbery with a firearm," since the young man's court trial, evidence has been uncovered (by Schacter in a piece of investigative journalism) which challenges this. Schacter has revealed that the defendant may have actually used a pellet gun with a broken trigger to commit these offenses. However, during "due process," both the crown and the defence suggested that the defendant plead guilty to the charges. They in turn would recommend to the judge a six year sentence as he was told that the evidence was "overwhelmingly against him," and that pleading not guilty and contesting the charges before a jury would be "straining the patience and mercy of the court thereby increasing the likelihood of a stiff sentence" (Schacter 1986:4). Besides the fact that the judge issued the young man an eleven year sentence rather than the six years which both lawyers had recommended, this turn of events was no doubt reflected in the official statistics which classified these offenses as taking place with a firearm, rather than with an "other offensive weapon" (see Table 10).

Robbery in Newfoundland, particularly in the St. John's area against retail merchants, is *not increasing at an alarming rate*, and instances of these types of crimes are not approaching 'mainland standards' as many people have believed. Furthermore, approximately (74 percent) of all robberies which involved injury to the victim were due to muggings. And despite the fact that a person was killed during the commission of an armed robbery at a retail location in Newfoundland, this incident, although tragic, was highly atypical. Moreover, in 1984, the year when Newfoundland recorded its highest robbery rate in recent history, this figure was still the *lowest recorded for any province or territory in Canada.*

Table 10

Incident Rates/100,000 Population of the Use of Firearms in the Commission of Robberies in Newfoundland, 1974–1985

1974	1.7
1975	.7
1976	1.4
1977	1.7
1978	4
1979	2.2
1980	1.8
1981	1.7
1982	1.4
1983	3
1984	5
1985	2.5

Source: Compiled from Statistics Canada, Canadian Crime and Traffic Statistics 1974–1985.

Child Abuse and Child Sexual Assault

Recently there has been considerable concern that child abuse — particularly child sexual assault — is statistically on the increase in Newfoundland. Concern has also been expressed over the belief that the official statistics underestimate the "real" incidence of this phenomenon, since many of these crimes are not reported to the officials.

Despite the fact that we share the 'expert' assumption that the incidence of child sexual abuse and child sexual assault is underestimated in government statistics, we do not share the belief that this particular crime is necessarily *increasing* in the province. It is difficult to determine where this mistaken impression comes from, since many people and groups who have expressed concern on this issue are well aware that official statistics do not accurately measure the 'real' incidence of this crime. For instance, the *Blueprint for Action* (Community Services Council 1986), claimed that the official statistics represented less than 1 percent of what they felt to be the 'real,' or most accurate, measure of child sexual assault in Newfoundland.

We would agree with the *Blueprint for Action*, that the incidence of child sexual assault is greatly under-reported in the province and that social services statistics represent only a fraction of all incidents. However, we will argue that the recent increases which have taken place in the number of reported cases of child sexual assault in Newfoundland do not necessarily mean that more of these events are now taking place than was the case in the past. Rather, these increases are more of a reflection of recent social developments in the province which have *improved* and *encouraged* the reporting of these events to authorities.

In Newfoundland, it was not until 1974 that the Department of Social Services first began to collect statistics on the incidence of child sexual assault. This awareness also parallels a more general social awareness of the problem which occurred at roughly the same time. That is, it has only been over the past fifteen years or so that a significant level of social concern has emerged over child sexual abuse and this has been expressed by women's groups, public health professionals (including the medical profession), teachers, day care workers and social workers—particularly those employed by the Division of Child Welfare. The concern of these groups has developed into a broader level of social concern and awareness of this once "hidden problem," and this has encouraged more people to report such incidents to the authorities.

More substantial evidence suggests that increases in the 'official' incidence of child sexual assault may in fact be due to increases in *detection personnel*. For instance, the majority of cases of child sexual assault which have come to the attention of the authorities have come from the St. John's metropolitan area, rather than from rural areas of the province. This is the part of the province which has been more developed in terms of providing services for victims and offenders, and it is also the area where child "streetproofing" programs have been most common. It is interesting to note the fact that shortly after the implementation of a child education and prevention program in May 1984, primarily in the St. John's area (such programs, according to the *Blueprint for Action* are urgently needed in other areas of the province), there occurred a dramatic increase in the numbers of incidents of child sexual assault which were reported to the authorities. In fact, in 1983–1984 approximately thirty-five cases of child sexual assault were reported to the authorities, whereas in 1984–1985 the number had doubled to seventy-three cases—most of which originated from the St. John's metropolitan area.

It would be absurd to suggest that, based on the use of official statistics, the incidence of child sexual assault has dramatically increased in the province in recent years, particularly in the St. John's region. Undoubtedly, if more services and programs were to be established in other areas in Newfoundland, there would also be increases in the number of these crimes reported. Therefore, there is very weak empirical evidence suggesting that the rising statistical incidence of child sexual assault in Newfoundland is due to any breakdown in 'normal' family relations, nor does the evidence support the popular theories of "greater permissiveness" or "alarming levels of unemployment" bringing about this purported increase.

Violence Against Women: Sexual Assault and Battering

The perception that sexual violence against women has recently increased in Newfoundland is widespread. However, when the evidence is critically examined, problems arise regarding the ability of official statistics to measure accurately the 'real' incidence of these crimes.

We will show that the increases which have taken place in the incidence of these types of crimes are more a reflection of changes which have taken place in terms of recording practices and reporting than actual increases in sexual violence against women.

Figure 8 shows that in Newfoundland the incidence of sexual crimes (the majority of which are sexual assaults against women or rape/sexual assault) increased drastically between 1960–1961. In fact, the rate per 100,000 population increased by over 500 percent. This increase, however, coincides with the establishment of the Uniform Crime Reporting System in Newfoundland. Prior to this period the record keeping practices of the Royal Newfoundland Constabulary were not conducted in any systematic fashion, and many of the crimes which may have been reported to the police were not recorded and not contained in the annual reports of Statistics Canada. The point is simply that administrative changes in record keeping, not actual increases, were responsible for the drastic increase in these types of offenses which may have otherwise been interpreted as 'real' changes in these forms of criminal behaviour.

Other factors also indicate that changes in official statistics of sexual offenses are not simply a reflection of actual changes in violent behaviour. In an analysis of 116 reported cases of rape in Toronto, Clark and Lewis (1977) found that the progress of a rape case case through the criminal justice system reflected a "highly selective process of elimination." According to these authors:

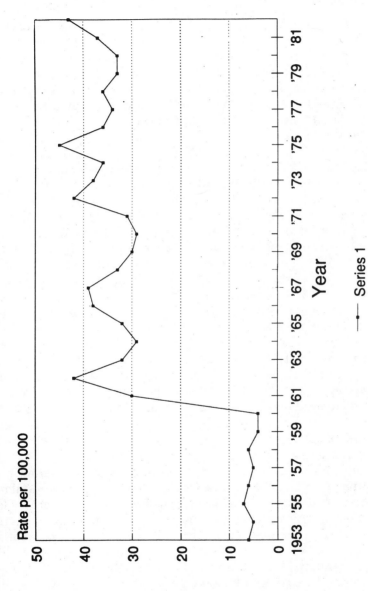

Figure 8: Sexual Crime Incident Rates in Newfoundland, 1953–1982

Rate per 100,000

Year

— Series 1

Source: Compiled from Statistics Canada, Canadian Crime Statistics, 1953–1982.

Only a fraction of all rapes are reported; only a fraction of reported rapes are classified as founded; only a fraction of founded cases lead to an arrest; and only a fraction of suspects are convicted (1977:57).

The first two steps of this "filtering process" are especially important to our analysis regarding the accuracy of the rape/sexual assault rate as a reflection of the real incidence of this type of violent behaviour. In terms of the numbers of rapes which are in fact reported to police in Newfoundland, it would appear that only a fraction of these are indeed reported. For example, in 1981 results from the Canadian Urban Victimization Survey found that 60 percent of sexual assaults in St. John's were unreported—the national average was 61.5 percent. Regarding the second step of the process identified by Clark and Lewis, a number of the incidents reported to police are not necessarily classified in such a fashion that they are represented in the "rape rate." For instance, a large proportion of these types of crime are categorized by the police as "unfounded"— and the rape rate is calculated using crimes which are in the 'founded' category, or in Statistics Canada's terms, "Actual Offenses." In 1983, 5 out of the 7 reported cases of aggravated sexual assault, 3 out of the 17 reported cases of sexual assault with a weapon, and 56 of the 238 reported cases of sexual assault were classified by police as "unfounded." In other words, roughly 1/4 of all cases of sexual assault reported to the police in that year were classified as "unfounded." These figures only become important when they are compared with other types of violent crimes which are reported or detected by police. The category of sexual assault/ rape has approximately three times the number of "unfounded" reports compared to other crimes of violence. Furthermore, according to information from the St. John's Rape Crisis Centre, less than 5 percent of all reports actually result in convictions where the offender receives a prison sentence (Duggan 1986:20).

Taking all of this into account, it would be foolish to assume that the statistical incidence of rape/sexual assault in Newfoundland accurately measures the 'real' level of these crimes which are taking place in the province. More specifically, we can demonstrate that the increase which took place in the level of rape/100,000 population for St. John's between 1976 and 1977 (it increased from 4–15/ 100,000 population) was likely due to the fact that in that same year Newfoundland's first rape crisis centre came into operation, and women were then encouraged to report these offenses to the police. Moreover, this was the period when what has been referred to as an "anti-rape" movement was gaining support and momentum in North America generally—and Newfoundland was no exception.

Considering what has been said, it would be very difficult indeed to *prove* the popular assumption that the 'real' incidence of sexual crimes—particularly against women—has actually increased in Newfoundland in recent years. Consequently, beliefs which have attempted to explain these *increases* in terms of changing behaviour patterns resulting from the proliferation of 'pornographic' cultural material must be re-evaluated. In other words, to say that the increasing levels of pornography in Newfoundland during recent years have been responsible for increases in sexually violent behaviour is very difficult to support empirically. We are not arguing that there is no relationship between pornography and violence towards women in society, but we are suggesting that taken as a bi-variate relationship, it is questionable whether exposure to pornography actually incites individuals to violence and aggressive behaviour. Until researchers begin to understand what triggers sexual excitement; how it is "produced by everyone"—not just in deviant groups; what "maintains and protects it;" and what makes it "recur or subside in time into boredom;" we will not understand the multi-variate relationship between sexual arousal and aggressive behaviour (see Wilson 1983:135–168).

Until fairly recently, the issue of physical and psychological violence against women was not a public one. However, during the past decade or so, many have developed the impression that this form of violence is increasing in Newfoundland. These increases have been seen as connected with what is believed to be the growing number of families which are breaking down under the pressure of economic hard times—commonly measured by rising levels of unemployment or else by declining moral standards.

How strong is the evidence that more women are being battered today than was the case in the past? Is it reasonable to assume that the rising number of calls to battered women's centres in recent years are evidence of more women requiring shelter than in the past? Are rising levels of unemployment, for instance, the reason why this disquieting situation has occurred?

During our earlier description of the 'facts' of this problem, we pointed out that the development of services for battered women in Newfoundland could be seen as a response to an increase in the level of this type of violence. That is, according to popular sentiment, government funding was provided in order to establish the first battered women's shelter as it had been recognized that the problem was increasing (statistically) and these women had to be protected.

However, this perception of the reasons for government assistance is erroneous as it fails to understand the process which led to the establishment of services for battered women.

In 1972, the Newfoundland Status of Women's Council (NSWC) was formed in St. John's and during these early and formidable years of "feminism" in Newfoundland, women who were associated with the movement were involved in a considerable amount of activity which was designed to: "raise the consciousness of women, to improve their status, and to promote the recommendations of the Status of Women report" (NSWC 1982:3). To help accomplish these goals, in 1975 the NSWC first approached government with a proposal for a Transition House for battered women in St. John's. These women (particularly those involved in the 'anti-rape movement') recognized that many women in Newfoundland were being battered and were therefore in need of refuge from such violence. The proposal, however, was turned down by government. Though this was a grave disappointment, work and pressure for a Transition House continued for six years until finally, in 1981, funds were provided by the Canadian Employment and Immigration Commission and the Newfoundland Government. A Transition House was officially opened in St. John's by Premier Peckford in June of that year.

Although persistent pressure was exerted on various levels of government, the successful struggle for the establishment and funding of a Transition House—and the other homes located elsewhere in the province which followed—has to been seen in a broader context. By 1981, many other provincial governments in Canada (and in the United States and in some European countries) had already provided funds for battered women's shelters. The successful establishment of a shelter in Newfoundland may have been in part the result of the political pressure which these other shelters may have exerted on the Peckford administration. Newfoundland lagged behind most other Canadian provinces in this regard, and the issue began to be publicly and politically recognized as a 'legitimate' problem and 'deserving' of government funding.

It is difficult to argue that the 'shelter movement' grew in response to the sudden surge in the numbers of women and children seeking refuge or the increasing number of Newfoundland families 'breaking down' because of rising levels of unemployment and other social problems.

Unemployment, for example, may not necessarily cause the battering of women. Most of the calls received by police in St. John's come from regions in the city where there is a high concentration of unemployed people or those living on social assistance. However, according to police, these are not necessarily the calls which are viewed with greatest concern. Rather the calls which are defined by police as being most serious are those which come from those living in the more "affluent" sections of the city. According to one member of the Royal Newfoundland Constabulary:

> And the high-class people very seldom call. Area 4, if you get a call from a drunk and disorderly, it's heavy. You've got to watch it, knives, guns, could be anything (McGahan 1984:86).

This certainly implies that not all domestic violence takes place in the homes of the unemployed, the poor, or the working class. Although police do in fact receive more calls from these sections of the city, it may not necessarily mean that this is where the majority of domestic battering takes place. Consequently, there must be social and cultural reasons why middle-class women report being battered to the police only in situations where they feel their life is in immediate danger. There must also be factors influencing working-class and poor women to report less serious incidents to the police more often than their middle-class counterparts.

With respect to middle-class women, they may report only the most serious and perhaps life threatening incidents because they may have more options open to them. They may have the opportunity to leave the home in situations which might be labelled as 'less serious.' Or perhaps, the 'minor' batterings may not be reported to police by middle-class women because their understanding of the roles of wife and mother calls for dependence on men; thus making them more reluctant to report 'lovers' spats.' Furthermore, some middle-class women who do not have paying jobs or access to their 'own' money and rely solely on their spouses' incomes, may fear losing their 'security' if they report being battered to police (Schechter 1982).

Working-class women or those who do not have much money may not have the opportunity to leave the battering situation, and hence have to deal with the violence in other ways, such as reporting the incidents to the police. According to Schechter (1982:236), working-class women, out of their struggle to survive, may have developed more resourcefulness and less fear of being alone than their middle-class counterparts. Poor women frequently use the courts and welfare, and are more prepared to struggle against institutional abuse.

For these reasons, therefore, it would be very difficult to assume that because more battering is reported to police by poor women, this necessarily indicates that domestic violence is isolated to families of unemployment and poverty.

Battering in the home is not a new phenomenon in Newfoundland, but it has been brought out of the closet in recent years by the feminist movement. The movement has helped to create an atmosphere in which women can begin to understand and talk about battering, and it has influenced the evolution of the 'shelter movement' in the province.

Vandalism

During the second half of the 1970s, the crime of vandalism, and other crimes generally associated with youth were seen to have reached a crisis. Although the problem of vandalism had not disappeared from the public eye, in the 1980s it certainly was not being treated in the same fashion as it was during the middle of the 1970s. When we examine the official statistics and the patterns and trends which they reveal for the crime of vandalism (official statistics define vandalism as wilful damage to public and private property) some interesting points emerge. Let us begin by examining official rates of vandalism for both the province and the city of St. John's.

According to data in Figure 9, the rates of vandalism for the city of St. John's do not seem to be alarmingly high. This particular crime has generally been increasing on a year to year basis (although not necessarily uniformly) before and after the 'panic' of the mid 1970s. The lowest rate of vandalism recorded during the entire period occurred in 1975, the same year in which the idea of a curfew was considered as a measure to control the "crime wave" of malicious property damage! In fact, the rates in 1985 were more than twice the 1975 level. Despite these differences, and although the problem of property destruction has been a recurring one in the 1980s, in no way has the *response* to vandalism been as strong as it was during this earlier period.

The statistics in Figure 9 certainly suggest that rates of vandalism do not necessarily respond to the degree of social censure waged against them. In this way then, the social response to the crime of vandalism does not correspond to its statistical level. If there were a relationship, then there would be considerably more concern and anxiety about vandalism in the 1980s than was the case in the 1970s.

Why, then, was vandalism such a strong issue in the 1970s in Newfoundland? Although we did not have the opportunity to thoroughly investigate this issue, we recommend that to do so, it

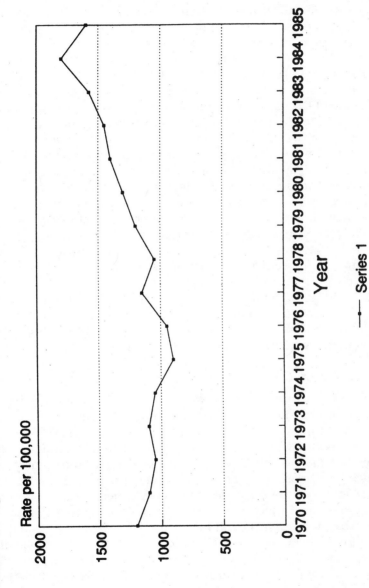

Figure 9: Malicious Damage Incident Rates in St. John's, 1970–1985

Rate per 100,000

2000

1500

1000

500

0

1970 1971 1972 1973 1974 1975 1976 1977 1978 1979 1980 1981 1982 1983 1984 1985

Year

—■— Series 1

Source: Compiled from Annual Statistical Reports, Royal Newfoundland Constabulary, St. John's.

must be specifically situated in its social, political and economic context (see Hall *et al.* 1978). We may begin to account for these differences in response by taking note of the fact that in St. John's during the mid-1970s a first attempt was made to "develop" and "revitalize" the downtown core of the city. This project was essentially the work of city government but was encouraged and supported by many downtown merchants who wanted the area "fixed up" so as to regain customers now attracted to new shopping malls located in the outskirts of the city. Vandalism may have been seen as one of the clean up measures which were required in order that the downtown area be properly re-developed. The activities of "vandals" or more generally working-class youths who were living in the downtown area, may have been used as a scapegoat or perhaps as an ideological symbol to mask the more serious problems which were involved in successfully re-developing the downtown area — particularly problems which were of an economic nature.

Moreover, it was during the time when the downtown area in St. John's was becoming gentrified and taken over by the new middle class: the neighbourhood improvement movement associated with the community movement was formed as concern grew with respect to property values and 'atmosphere.'

While these comments do not fully *answer* the question of why the reaction toward vandalism was much more pronounced during the mid-1970s than in the 1980s, they may serve as first steps towards more systematic research in the area.

Crime and the Oil Boom

In terms of the future, should Newfoundlanders expect a crime wave to take place once offshore oil production begins? Concern has been expressed in this regard, but how strong is the evidence? Although many have linked what they fear will happen in Newfoundland with the social turmoil which they *impressionistically* assume took place in Calgary when oil development boomed in Alberta during the mid-1970s, very little scientific evidence has been used to support such statements. In fact, when we examine the scientific evidence reviewed by the Newfoundland Petroleum Directorate, we find little support for the notion that increasing levels of crime will accompany oil development. The evidence is at best inconclusive. For example, in the Newfoundland Petroleum Directorate report the "existing" scientific information on social problems which accompany energy development, and offshore development in particular, was said to be "incomplete." It was concluded that "social science has only scratched the surface in terms of understanding the types of social problems which may be associated with energy development" (Cake 1986:3). Summarizing the "state of knowledge" on social problems in the boomtowns of the western United States, the report included these words by two American researchers:

> We don't really know *what* happens to the individuals and the community as they undergo rapid change, much less why it happens; *who* it happens to or *when* the effects may be observed (Lantz and McKoewn 1979:48, cited in Cake 1986).

With regard to the literature which particularly examined changes in reported crime in energy development areas, the report found that these studies were "somewhat inconclusive [and] scanty" and generally questioned the results of this research because the field of study was thought to be in "an embryonic state of development" (Cake 1986:5). Thus, after reviewing all of this material the author could have easily inferred that the available literature suggested that crime rates *may not* increase disproportionately in energy-impacted communities, rather than concluding that "crime rates *may* indeed increase" (Cake 1986:8).

RETHINKING POPULAR IMAGES OF VIOLENCE

We have demonstrated in this analysis that although Newfoundlanders are not exempt from interpersonal violence, and although some of the crimes do resemble the types of violence most commonly associated with the mainland, *there is very weak empirical evidence that the level or character of interpersonal violence has recently undergone significant change in Newfoundland.* We have shown that the majority of interpersonal violence which takes place in Newfoundland is *mundane*, as it takes place between people who have established social relationships—particularly between family members where men are most often the offenders. This being the case, where does the feeling come from that crime and violence is increasing and changing character (becoming more violent) in Newfoundland in recent years? Can it be that it is a product of false impressions, anecdotal information and the questionable (to say the least) use of statistics by various interest groups? Or is it the disproportionate media attention to what is considered to be newsworthy? The frequency of Newfoundland crimes may have increased although the rates/population have remained relatively stable when we controlled for various changes in record keeping and reporting practices. To answer these questions a number of factors need to be examined. We will begin by taking a closer look at the role Statistics Canada has played in the production of official criminal statistics.

We have pointed out that on occasion Statistics Canada and/or the police have released crime statistics to the media without first stressing or even providing the necessary cautions which should have accompanied these figures. In turn, the media have presented the material to the public in a generally uncritical fashion and this may have fostered the impression that crime and violence are rapidly growing in Newfoundland. Many people's estimates of their personal safety may be rooted in a transference of criminal statistics to what McKie and Reed have called "a rational calculation of jeopardy." That is, a "ratchet effect" may be taking place whereby when people hear that crime and violence are increasing their estimate of personal risk may be revised upward; but where statistics indicate a decrease in the crime rate (as the press and other forms of media in Newfoundland have at times reported over the years) personal risk estimates are not revised downward (McKie and Reed 1979:5).

In addition, crime statistics may affect people in another way. People may become *concerned* or perhaps *anxious* about the integrity and stability of what they take to be the *social order* when they are constantly presented with 'facts' stating that crime and violence are reaching unprecedented levels. Furthermore, when increasing crime statistics are situated within a wider picture of how the social fabric may be crumbling in other ways (such as increasing levels of unemployment) the situation is disquieting; especially when crime is constantly discussed in popular discourse as an *empirical event* which may or may not be likely to happen to someone.

Together with the striking increase in the scope and magnitude of official statistics following confederation with Canada, there have been consequent increases in various social problems which have been subject to statistical quantification. In this way, then, these 'social facts' which are typically presented as being untainted by social values or ideology may indeed have had the effect of shaping public opinion, by intensifying a general sense of fear, anxiety and/or concern in some people's lives regarding the 'growing crime problem.'

However, it is not true to say that these 'effects' have occurred because Statistics Canada has failed to recognize some of the more obvious inadequacies of the information they produce, or has kept these 'deficiencies' from the public. In fact, if we examine the publications which Statistics Canada has produced over the years in which crime has been counted, we find that they have at times underlined what they have felt to be the "limitations" or inadequacies of their data. For example, as long ago as 1947, the Dominion Bureau of Statistics (DBS) stated in their annual report that, "crime statistics, no matter how complete, cannot tell us all that we need to know" (Annual Crime Statistics 1947:1). However, it was not until a decade later that the problems associated with crime statistics were explained in more detail.

In 1958, DBS raised the issue of the comparability of crime statistics between different jurisdictions. The reason for these difficulties was said to rest on the fact that certain regions of the country were more developed than others in terms of the numbers of police departments submitting their crime statistics to Ottawa. In other words, police in certain areas of the country had not yet been convinced of the importance of submitting statistical information to DBS. In fact, this problem had been first dealt with in 1947 when officials from DBS visited certain parts of the country "in an attempt to obtain greater accuracy and uniformity in reporting criminal offenses and to create interest in the gathering of required data by pointing out the invaluable aid the information that is collected, is in the prevention and control of crime," for: "as confidence in their [statistics] utility grows the objections to all that they involve by way of labour and inquiry will weaken" (Annual Crime Statistics 1947).

Moreover, the DBS also brought to public attention the fact that it is impossible to compare the information collected prior to 1949, with figures collected after that year because in 1949 the basic unit for compiling statistics of indictable offenses was changed from *convictions* to *persons*.

In 1960, readers of DBS's annual Canadian Crime Reports were advised that data which they had published in that year "left much to be desired in the way of completeness and uniformity." Although DBS had taken steps to ensure that the data they published were accurate, the bureau said that it could not "vouch for the validity of the information" as variations in crime rates between different reporting units were found to be the result of police departments' different interpretations of reporting instructions (Introduction, Annual Report 1960). The following are examples of a "few apparent inconsistencies" which were *discovered*:

(1) Offenses are reported as concluded where no offenses were reported or known. Some of these may be accounted for by old crimes being concluded in the current year.

(2) The proportion of concluded offenses compared with offenses known to police varies widely. Some departments report offenses as known but no information is reported on the conclusion of

these offenses; in others, all offenses known are shown as concluded.

(3) The number of prosecutions are reported instead of the number of persons prosecuted.

(4) In a few instances there has been difficulty in the interpretation of terms in the French language version of the monthly returns. In these cases, *vol* (theft) and *vol qualifie* (robbery) have apparently been confused as well as *vol* (theft) and *voil* (rape) (Introduction, Annual Report 1960).

In 1962, DBS began its Uniform Crime Reporting system, which they hoped would allow for the publication of more "complete and meaningful data" on the incidence of crime in Canadian society. Despite the improvements which were said to have come with the new system of reporting, a number of "factors" were still felt to be influencing the "coverage and quality" of the data to be used for comparative purposes between different parts of the country. DBS wrote:

> Users of data are cautioned against drawing conclusions from comparisons of reported data between areas without first considering the two factors of complete coverage and quality. . .which may cause variations between areas, whether provincial, metropolitan areas, communities, etc. such as: the density and size of population; population mobility, sometimes within areas; composition of the population, including age, sex and other social characteristics . . .strength, training and efficiency of local law enforcement agencies and facilities; variations in attitude regarding the reporting of offenses to the police, towards law enforcement, prosecution (Introduction, Annual Crime Statistics 1962).

In addition to these "factors" which may have an effect on the crime rate, DBS reminded users in their 1966 Annual Report that their data cover "reported crimes" and that any increase in the number of crimes may indicate an actual increase in "offenses committed," or merely "an extension in record keeping practice." It is also interesting to note that from 1947 to 1984, in most publications of crime statistics, Statistics Canada advised readers that every effort had been made to improve the quality of criminal statistics.

In 1983 Statistics Canada decided not to use decimal places in the computation of crime rates. There is evidence that this decision gave rise to the belief that their data were not as 'factual' as before. The policy was changed as the agency felt that the publication of rates with one decimal place gave the impression of far more

accuracy than was warranted. The change even applied for comput-
ing homicide rates. This is particularly interesting in that homicide
has always been regarded as the crime which can most easily and
accurately be measured in terms of a rate depicting the 'real'
incidence of the 'crime of crimes' in Canadian society. Perhaps
officials who made this decision had come to realize that the homicide rate may not be so 'exact' as it was once felt to be. Conceivably,
events such as missing persons, certain traffic deaths, occupational
accidents, some deaths by so called natural causes are recognized
as areas where people may have been 'murdered.' For various
reasons these deaths may have not been officially defined as
homicides and therefore have not been included in annual crime
statistics. In fact, in a recent book on policing in Canada, Sewell
writes:

> A generally agreed upon estimate is that for every murder known
> to authorities, another three or four are never reported. Some
> writers put the ratio at one to nine (1985:62).

As a response to the "sad state of affairs" of Canadian crime
statistics, the Ministry of Justice felt a need to have the "crime
statistics industry" in Canada reviewed so that some of these
problems could be resolved. In 1981, a report entitled, *The National
Project on Resource Coordination on Justice Statistics Information in
Canada* dealt with what was called the "present and extremely
problematic" state of affairs of justice statistics in Canada. According to the final report of this commissioned study group:

> In Canada, nationwide information about crime is so fragmented,
> unreliable, untimely and varied that it is impossible to state with
> any reasonable degree of confidence, conclusions about the state
> of crime or the criminal justice system of the Nation (*The National
> Project on Resource Coordination on Justice Statistics Information
> in Canada, Preface*).

The report's concluding comments strongly reflect the findings
of their research; that is, the abysmal condition of justice statistics
in Canada.

> . . .[they] are so lamentably far behind economic statistics that the
> sooner a start is made to improve the situation the better. It is truly
> astonishing how little we know, or how little we pool out knowledge,
> about what is happening "out there" and particularly in an area
> which affects all of us as citizens, *viz* the area of justice. Any
> business enterprise which is equally unaware of the state of its
> market, the efficiency of its operators, the number of its customers
> and how many times they have used the services of that enterprise

would quickly be bankrupt. It is illogical, if not inconceivable, that the present situation be allowed to continue (*Conclusion*).

Despite the fact that criminal statistics are usually regarded as authoritative and objective sources of information, Statistics Canada and other agencies of the Canadian state have not been solely responsible for the 'scientific' status which has been given to crime statistics. In addition to this "state" critique of the limitations of criminal statistics, many social scientists have also pointed out the problems in employing official statistics for research on crime, and these criticisms have permeated to some extent through the larger society. Thus, the use of statistics has not been exclusively responsible for the fact that so many people accept the notion that crime and violence are increasing in Newfoundland.

***

Another dimension of this recent anxiety about crime and violence in Newfoundland may have to do with the tremendous growth which has taken place in communications technology in recent years. This rapid growth in communications (television, radio, telephones, etc.) has occurred at a time when the *number* of homicides reported to the police has more or less doubled—between the 1950s and the 1980s. Therefore, because there have been more sources of communication available to disseminate tragic news, people may have been alerted to events (ranging from those within the community to those which may have taken place thousands of miles away from Newfoundland) which previously might have gone unnoticed. Here is an example of such an increase in communications in Newfoundland:

> Between 1973 and 1981, the number of telephones in rural areas increased by 47 percent. Although the urban increase was larger at 69 percent, this can be accounted for by the faster growing population in urban areas, as well as the growth in the service sector of the economy which is primarily located in urban centres (Newfoundland Department of Rural, Agricultural and Northern Development 1983:152).

Additionally, newspapers have become more widely available in the province, particularly in rural areas: in 1969, 68 percent of families purchased newspapers, and by 1978 this figure had risen to 83 percent. Television and radio have also become more widespread in Newfoundland in recent years. There were seven radio stations and relay transmitters in rural areas in 1970, 14 in 1975 and 17 in 1981. In urban areas, the number of stations and transmitters was 19 in 1970, 24 in 1975 and 25 in 1981 (Newfoundland Department of Rural, Agricultural and Northern Development 1983: 155, 157).

Television—perhaps the medium which informs most people— has also witnessed a "tremendous growth:"

> In 1970 there were 10 television stations and rebroadcasting stations in rural areas, in 1975 there were 28, and in 1981 there were 100. This amazing growth has made television broadcasting available to all rural areas, although the most remote communities only receive the broadcasts of the Canadian Broadcasting Corporation (Newfoundland Department of Rural, Agricultural and Northern Development 1983:158).

On a general level, it may be suggested that this growth in communications—especially with regard to television and more particularly "cable" television (where it is now possible to receive such major American networks as CBS, NBC and ABC) has had its "effects" in terms of producing a more 'mainland,' or more specifically *American*, image of crime and violence. Discussing the images in the American-produced police shows and their effect on the way in which crime and violence is "commonsensically" perceived, Taylor states:

> Day in and day out, these programs portray an image of urban life in North America as a dangerous human jungle, where the prospect of criminal assault and homicide is almost random and immediate. Human life is seen to be threatened, in particular, by the presence (especially in the street but also in everyday business and personal relations) of psychopathic individuals, intent on murder and general mayhem (1983:82).

Commenting upon the influence which these types of portrayals may have on viewers, Taylor adds:

> It would be obviously absurd to suggest that media portrayals of homicide and violence are without "effects" in the specific sense of helping to manufacture a widespread, popular ideological understanding of the character of social order, the changing sources of danger to personal well-being and security, etc. Countless research studies have produced evidence of widespread, and apparently increasing, fear of crime in most industrial societies (1983:82).

Popular television drama cannot be seen as a medium which necessarily *incites* all individuals who view it toward violence (although some research does indicate that aggressive films do have an effect on viewers' levels of aggression, e.g., Goldstein *et al.* 1975) but it can be a strong source of information which plays a part in forming popular beliefs about the nature of crime and violence.

In addition to drama on television having this "effect," it has also been suggested that the *news* on television may be responsible for increasing anxiety about crime and violence (see Chibnall 1977). Since the time of the Vietnam war, television news has been responsible for bringing onto the screens of millions of television sets film clippings of various types of mayhem—ranging from reports of local murders to film coverage of the carnage inflicted in various war zones throughout the world.

If in fact these views are correct—and there is good evidence suggesting that they are—and television is the medium from which most people receive their news and entertainment, then this exposure may have elevated people's images of violence. It may even have helped to redefine what is considered to be violent since the "sensationalist" material which saturates both American news and drama do not parallel the empirical reality in terms of the quality of violence in Newfoundland. That is, these anxieties are not related *statistically* to the probability one has of being victimized—particularly by psychologically disturbed strangers in Newfoundland. There is also empirical evidence suggesting that a considerable amount of interpersonal violence which takes place in urban America is inaccurately portrayed in the "sensationalist" media, since a large proportion of murders which take place in American cities involve family members or individuals with previous social or business relationships (Taylor 1983:93).

As important as it is to consider the changing forms of media which have developed in Newfoundland and the types of programming which have developed along with it, this explanation is too simplistic on its own to account for the popular fear and anxiety about growing crime and violence. We do not think that increased levels of fear about crime and violence have been *caused* simply by "false images" constructed in large part by television and other forms of media.

Other researchers have argued that there is a relationship between crime frequency and criminal justice expenditures—particularly police expenditures, and that this spending may be linked to people's perceptions that crime and violence are increasing (MacDonald 1986 and MacLean 1986). Is there any evidence to suggest that something like this has taken place in Newfoundland? Table 11 indicates that there is a relationship between the violent crime rate and levels of policing.

As Table 11 shows, from 1962–1984 the rate of violent crime recorded by the RCMP and the RNC has been increasing (except for the slight dip in the rate of violent crimes recorded by the RCMP in

1972). If we examine these increases in more detail, we find that the rate of violent crime recorded by the RCMP has increased by 473 percent while data taken from the RNC indicates an increase of 188 percent. These differences become significant when we note that the numbers of RCMP per 1,000 population in Newfoundland have doubled from .9 in 1962 to 1.8 in 1984. On the other hand, the rates of RNC per 1,000 population have actually decreased (this was the result of the RNC expanding their jurisdiction in 1981 by 60,000 people to include the town of Mount Pearl). Can we therefore assume that the differences recorded in the rate of violent crime for the RCMP and the RNC have been the result of changes in police personnel, that is, increases in spending in the criminal justice system? To a degree, I think we can. Although there is certainly no evidence suggesting that more police in Newfoundland have *caused* more violent crime to happen, we do have evidence to suggest that the growing expenditure in this area has in fact increased police surveillance (more detachments and more police) in many areas of the

Table 11

Rates of Violent Crime Per 100,000 Population by Police Force in Newfoundland, 1962–1984

	Police/1,000 pop.	No. of Violent Crimes	Rate/100,000 pop.
1962			
RCMP	.9	479	123
RNC	2.7	158	226
1967			
RCMP	1.0	1172	287
RNC	2.4	198	232
1972			
RCMP	1.2	1178	270
RNC	2.4	338	383
1977			
RCMP	1.4	2255	486
RNC	2.6	374	429
1984			
RCMP	1.8	2893	705
RNC	2.2	1042	651

Note: Violent crime rates/100,000 population may appear to be high as we used incidents which were reported to the police rather than "actual offenses"—therefore, some incidents which were recorded as being "unfounded" by police have been used.

Source: Compiled from Statistics Canada, Canadian Crime and Statistics 1962–1984.

province, and that this has improved the ability to *detect* more crime. Furthermore, this increase in spending has also made police more available, which may have had the effect of increasing people's reporting behaviour for certain crimes. For example, consider the isolated communities in Newfoundland at the time when the RCMP presence was low. During that period, say in 1962, police response time to calls was no doubt slow, as roads were undeveloped and many families did not have telephones. It was therefore less rational or practical for people to report crimes to the police. In fact, in 1969 only 65 percent of rural families in Newfoundland rented telephones, and the percentage was no doubt lower than this in 1962. Thus, the growth in communications (telephones) and the development of roads, coupled with the extension of police detachments to more areas of the province have *increased the number of violent crimes which have been reported to the police.*[11]

***

The tendency to simplify the causes of crime and violence may be another reason why so many people believe that these problems are increasing. We have demonstrated that there is a widespread belief that crime and violence are a product of social breakdown or disruption of some kind. The prime features of this 'theory' have been rooted in the notions that both the unemployment crisis and the cultural upheaval (or the North Americanization) of Newfoundland which has been popularly perceived to have taken place, have inevitably produced a social breakdown. This in turn, is seen as leading to increasing social problems—and crime and violence are seen as the most serious indicators of this social breakdown.

In recent years there has been great concern about the demise of Newfoundland tradition, identity, and lifestyle. References to this loss liberally sprinkle newspaper columns, a variety of small magazines, and the speeches and slogans of all political parties and popular songs (Overton 1985). A simple and humanistic society once based upon hospitality, self-reliance, religion, a strong work ethic, personalism, and egalitarianism is perceived as being dismantled. This line of argument (which first surfaced after World War II, but became profoundly influential during the late 1960s), according to Overton (1985), laments the loss of a traditional way of life (centred on the outports and independent production) and blames this decline on the 'new realities' of mass culture, consumerism, the welfare state, industrialization, urbanization, corrupt politicians, and inappropriate development. This disjunction between old and new cultures has led to a breakdown of traditional forms of social control in the province. The "North Americanization" of Newfoundland, then, is changing society's techniques of conflict avoidance. Traditional social controls such as the family, the church and community are believed to be eroding—especially in the urbanized areas of the province. As a result of this disintegration, people (especially youth) are seen as having to survive in an environment of impersonality, social distance, and permissiveness. Thus, what used to operate in the past to keep crime rates down has been weakening over time.

This type of social change theory implies what Pearson has referred to as a "historical deterioration in public manners, stressing the novelty of crime and violence, while harbouring assumptions of harmony and tranquillity in the past" (1985:15). Pearson elaborates on this social theory in which change is automatically seen not only by "low opinion" but by a very prominent brand of social theory grounded in what he called the "Durkheimian legacy," as a cause of the break-up of tradition and authority. Pearson writes:

> Among the many questions which impinge upon the question of 'modernity,' the one most deeply rooted in popular convictions insists that the advance of civilization brings in its wake a deluge of crime and violence. We know only too well the string of accusations, often summed up as the advent of 'permissiveness,' which are brought against the present tense: the break-up of the family and traditional authority; the erosion of community in the place of 'rootless' urban anonymity; the demoralizing effects of 'affluence;' the incitements of television and cinema; the surge of irresponsible freedoms among the rising generation. . .things have 'gone too far' (1985:15).

Coupled with the notion of a 'cultural breakdown' in Newfoundland is the popular connection between *unemployment* and social breakdown—personal, family, and community. This breakdown can be manifested in a number of ways, and is similar to the negative effects believed to be produced by cultural breakdown in that: individual alienation and despair may lead to suicide and mental breakdown; vandalism may result as frustrations are turned outward; the family may disintegrate leading to problem children; or community tensions may increase and people may become involved in radical politics (O'Grady and Overton 1986:7).

It should be recognized, however, that this type of response in which impressions of increasing levels of crime are linked with unemployment in a rather simplistic fashion is by no means confined to a Newfoundland context. This has developed into a conventional wisdom which has been used by others as a theory to explain increases in crime and violence. The assumption derives to some extent from established academic wisdom. According to Box and Hale:

> Traditionally, criminologists tended to limit their theoretical reasoning to one banality, which consequently became enshrined as orthodoxy. Reduced to its bare essentials, this orthodoxy states that as unemployment increases, the rate of criminal behaviour increases, and this not only results in more persons being sent to prison, but also leads to an extension of the period for which they are imprisoned. (1985:215)

Box and Hale have also argued that:

> as unemployment increases, more individuals are tempted to break the law, and many of these have less reason to resist because —being unemployed or anticipating unavoidable future unemployment—they have fewer important economic or social bonds acting as brakes on their deviant motivations; consequently, the rate of crime reporting, arrest, and conviction, produces an automatic work load increase for the judiciary, and this results in more persons being sent to prison (1982:20).

If people do embrace this kind of theory, and there is considerable evidence that they do, then it is not surprising that they now feel anxious and can find evidence to confirm their worst fears. Thus it is hardly surprising that more people have been sent to jail in Newfoundland in recent years—and for longer terms —since some judges in Newfoundland work with this same set of assumptions about the 'causes' of crime, and the recent growing unemployment seems to be a strong influence on their sentencing behaviour. According to research by Box (1983), a similar process is occurring in Britain, where more people are being sent to prison. Between 1971 and 1981, the number of persons who received prison sentences rose from 60,429 to 88,110, an increase of 46 percent. The courts have also been sending offenders to prison for longer periods. The average length of prison sentences in England increased considerably during 1961–1977; it dipped slightly at the end of the decade, but rose again in the early 1980s. There is some evidence to suggest that this sentencing pattern is occurring in Newfoundland as well: despite the fact that violent crime has not been increasing in the province, judges are nevertheless sending more people to prison. Thus the conventional wisdom that increasing levels of violent crime lead to more people being sent to court and imprisoned does not hold up to rigorous empirical examination.

If the current situation gives cause for concern, unemployed youths—who are growing up in a culture which is being affected by increasing 'permissiveness' etc.—seem to be the focus of particular fears. Many of the early 1970 make-work schemes in the province were directed to this group; as the jobless rate among young people has climbed (to the current rate of 40 percent), so has concern about the effects of unemployment on the young. Youth is seen as a group which is particularly disaffected, estranged and demoralized. The fear is that they will become resentful and antagonistic and will resort to crime: excluded from society by being denied a useful role, they risk becoming hostile and dangerous. Discipline and careful control are considered necessary.

If there is so much anxiety about youth, it may be seen as a particular problem in a province with such massive unemployment as Newfoundland. It may not be surprising that the 'criminal' behaviour most often associated with unemployed youth (such as vandalism and armed robbery) is a symbol of danger and social malaise and the focus of so many anxieties.

However, the popular 'social breakdown' theory that more unemployment coupled with other problems of 'modernity' (such as permissiveness) leads to more crime and more people imprisoned is *false*. For instance, if there were indeed a simple relationship between unemployment and violence, Newfoundland would be on the verge of chaos as its unemployment rate is the greatest for any province in Canada! The increased use of imprisonment in Newfoundland is not a direct response to any *rise* in violent crime, but rather seems to be a response to the *perceived threat* of crime posed by growing numbers of unemployed persons—especially young males. As Box (1983) has argued for England, there is evidence that in Newfoundland members of the judiciary may be acting in this way:

> It is not that members of the judiciary conspire to instill more discipline into the unemployed as a means of defusing their potential threat to social order, but when it comes to sentencing, each judge and magistrate, as a matter of routine practice, takes into account a number of legal and EXTRA LEGAL factors. If, as is likely, many of the judiciary believe that unemployment leads to more crime—and chances are that during periods of rising unemployment the level of recorded serious crime and especially its amplification in the media (Chibnall 1977, Hall *et al.* 1978) will confirm this—then extending the use of severity of imprisonment, in an attempt to increase its deterrent and incapacitation effect, will appear as nothing less than a normal and rational response

any sensible person would take. In the aggregate, these individual decisions form a pattern (1983:214).

It is also well known that judges and other law enforcement officers associated with certification and punishment of crime (such as probation officers in Canada) have a considerable amount of freedom "to base their actions on personal theories of what causes crime, who is likely to reform spontaneously, and who is likely to respond to various punitive or rehabilitative strategies. . . .Evidence suggests that wherever discretion is available it is used in ways ultimately damaging to poor people" (Tepperman 1977:159).

For example, a study by Haldane, Elliott and Whitehead (1972) observed that Halifax working-class juveniles before the court were more likely to receive a harsher punishment than middle-class juveniles. According to Tepperman:

> This study shows prejudice against working-class children, but not prejudice against them alone. Judges have a more refined theory of criminal causation than one that simply assumes lower-class children are the most given to delinquency. One can infer another significant part of the "theory" from these data: a stable and 'normal' home life is thought to be a good guarantor of future lawfulness, reducing the need for the major disposition (1977).

Tepperman (1977) continues by suggesting that these "untested theories" become entrenched over time:

> They may begin as the causal reflections of scholars, teachers, or ministers and become implemented by their students, persons of piratical affairs: the judges, politicians, and other managers of our society. When sociologists later examine criminal records of offenses, arrests, or convictions, all of which result from discretionary judgments and the application of "practical reasoning": (Turner 1974:7-11 *et passim*) they find that working-class children and children from broken homes are indeed over-represented. As a result, recorded juvenile delinquency and crime more generally are found to be highly correlated with poverty and family instability (e.g., Chimbos 1973).

It is important to recognize, however, that this differential treatment in courts is not the result of overt attempts by judges to penalize the unemployed and the poor. Rather, this discrimination may be partly the result of the way in which these officials "theorize" on the causes of crime and violence and on the social characteristics which are said to predispose certain types of individuals to violent behaviour. Judges may be working under the assumption that members of the lower class (which often include those who are unemployed) are prone to violent behaviour, and, consequently, believe that these individuals are disposed to higher levels of criminality. Swigert and Farrell, in a study of American homicide have provided a "clinical description" of this criminal imagery which they refer to as the "normal primitive":

> the primitive is comfortable and without mental illness. He has little, if any, education and is of dull intelligence. His goals are sensual and immediate—satisfying his physical and sexual needs without inhibition, postponement or planning. There is little regard for the future—extending hardly beyond the filling of his stomach and the next pay day or relief check. His loyalties and identifications are with a group that has little purpose in life, except surviving with a minimum of sweat and a maximum of pleasure. He has the ten-year old boy's preoccupation with muscular prowess and 'being a man.' Unfortunately, he lacks the boy's external restraint and supervision so that he is more or less an intermittent community problem and responsibility (1976:5).

Swigert and Farrell also note that the image of the "normal primitive" is reflective of a social scientific approach to the problem of causality, where a similar imagery is seen to exist more generally in society, and more importantly, "within those institutions officially charged with the control of criminal behaviour (1976:96). Swigert and Farrell further declare:

> to theorize that blacks and members of the lower classes are prone to violent behaviour, is to state a specific aspect of a more popular belief that these individuals are prone to higher levels of criminality. While symbols may vary over time from the "dangerous class" to the "criminal element," the imagery remains the same. A conception exists in our society that members of lower-class groups, through mass media accounts and conventional wisdom, come to be defined as criminally motivated. The scientific 'discovery' of a violent subculture is testimony to the success with which this stereotype has been applied (1976:96).

Such ill-informed sociological 'theories' of crime and punishment are firmly entrenched among those who work in the criminal justice system in Newfoundland. One example concerns the case referred to earlier which involved an eighteen-year-old man, charged with a number of armed robberies in St. John's (in total he stole slightly over $1,000), who had no adult criminal record. The man (who apparently had a drug problem) came from a large working-class family, had a poor employment history, did not complete high school, and was unemployed at the time of his arrest. Although he was charged with robbery with the use of a firearm (he later claimed that he had used a pellet rifle—with a broken trigger) in all of the hold-ups, the police had failed to recover the weapon for evidence.

Essentially the case rested on the evidence of several clerks working in the stores that he had robbed, who claimed that the weapon they were confronted with resembled a "shotgun." The defendant was encouraged by his lawyer to plead guilty. The Crown and the defence plea-bargained and the Crown advised the judge that he would be pleased with a sentence of six years. The judge deliberated for a week and returned to the court with a verdict of guilty and sentenced the young man to eleven years in prison. In his comments during sentencing the judge said that the defendant was involved with drugs and with "seedy and unsavoury characters," and although he did not have an adult criminal record, this was because he was "barely old enough to commit adult offenses." To put a halt to armed robbery as "there is a lot of public concern about the incidence of this crime," the judge issued an eleven year sentence to act as a deterrent to others of "like mind" (*Evening Telegram* 6 December 1985).

No doubt the judge in this case felt that this eighteen-year-old was beyond rehabilitation: he *had* to be, as he was unemployed, had a drug problem, grew up in a large working-class family, and had quit school at an early age. In other words, this man had to be severely punished as his social profile indicated that if he was 'set loose,' or given a light sentence, he would be a dangerous threat to society: this offender fitted the image of a "normal primitive."

Although we are not attempting to generalize with these examples, here is an another case where a different set of social circumstances undeniably influenced the judge's decision. A twenty-year-old man was apprehended by police as he was attempting to sell a quantity of LSD and marijuana. The drugs were valued at over $1,000; someone found guilty of such a crime would usually stand a good chance of being sent to jail. However, it appeared that this young man had considerably more going for him than the armed robber who was sent to prison for eleven years. He was "working with his brother as an apprentice plumber," and according to his defence lawyer, the young man "from a solid family background," was described as a "clean liver," and the event, according to the crown prosecutor, seemed to be an "isolated incident." Although the judge described the incident as a "wild and irresponsible act" he felt that "*With a fair education and good family background, it was strange for you to decide on this course of conduct.*" The judge noted, "All the support of family and teachers you had up to eighteen years (his age at the time of the incident) was thrown out the window," and that he was lucky that he was "nipped in the bud" before he had a chance to get more involved in the drug scene. The judge said that while the public was entitled to be protected, the offender appeared to be a man who was entitled to rehabilitate himself and "get back on the track by earning money honestly." The defendant was fined and placed on probation. (*Evening Telegram* 20 February 1986). Additional research in this area would be very useful for demonstrating just how representative these examples may be in terms of determining the extent to which the decision-making process in courts is being influenced by these stereotypical images of criminals.

Although there are no statistics available on the numbers of inmates who were unemployed at the time of their arrest, the figure must be high. In 1984, for instance, almost 90 percent of those admitted to Newfoundland correctional facilities were between the ages of 17 and 29 and over 80 percent of inmates had less than a grade 10 education. Therefore, a large proportion of these inmates must have been unemployed, as very few Newfoundlanders who have low education levels and are under the age of 30 find employment.

Thus, the popular conception which sees a relationship between incarceration rates and unemployment, suggests that rising prison populations are caused by unemployment. However, this relationship appears to be the result of increasing sentencing in a period when violent crime *is not increasing*. This raises some serious questions about the impact of the social breakdown theory which links increasing levels of crime with unemployment. In the words of Overton:

> To what extent have unionists and academic radicals agitating government to reduce unemployment contributed to reinforcing existing stereotypes of the unemployed and making them a breed apart, to be pitied and helped but also to be feared because of their violent, dishonest, suicidal, subversive tendencies? (1986:28–29)

Moreover, have those well-intentioned people, who have studied increasing levels of crime and violence in Newfoundland (child sexual assault, women battering, etc.) unintentionally fuelled the kind of panic which has been the basis for unemployed people being punished more severely than previously for breaking the law? (Overton 1986:28)

The popular notion which so many people have used to explain *increasing* levels of crime and violence in Newfoundland has been undermined. This is not to say, however, that unemployment is *unrelated* to criminal behaviour, but rather that it is not related in any simplistic fashion. For example, a drop in standard of living might lead the unemployed to attempt illegal ways of obtaining money and so on (Carr-Hill 1985:343). However, there are arguments which suggest that unemployment may in fact *reduce* crime. According to Carr-Hill:

> Where there is more unemployment it is possible that communities are poorer and this may make individuals less prepared to take risks. . . .The unemployed may perceive themselves to be subject to heavy punishment and this would also work to reduce offenses. Finally, the employed may be less likely to commit offenses if they fear unemployment more (1985:342–343).

There are arguments for and against the idea of unemployment leading to increases in criminal behaviour and "we cannot pretend that the effect of unemployment on behaviour is clear, *a priori*" (Carr-Hill 1985:343).

We believe that this research has raised some very serious questions regarding the ways in which violence is commonly thought about, not only within a Newfoundland context, but in Canadian society generally. In much of the talk about violence, whether it be statements from academics, social workers, judges or others, violence has been treated as though it were an empirical fact, worthy of quantification, and thus capable of measuring changes in the real levels of human behaviour. Furthermore, these statistical changes in rates of violence are usually explained in terms of other changes which have occurred in the social structure, such as increasing levels of unemployment.

In order to demonstrate some of the drawbacks which are inherent in this type of approach, we will conclude this section of the analysis by examining the work of two Canadian academics who have used "official statistics" (as well as other not-so official statistics) as evidence that certain types of violence have been increasing in Canadian society.

Armstrong (1984) has used social statistics in a relatively uncritical fashion to argue that in Canada, "unemployment is increasing depression, anxiety, and mental illness as well as child abuse, suicide, alcoholism and crime" (1984:106). Armstrong attributes this *increasing* violence, against women and children in particular, to the "social and psychological" effects of "hard times" which many Canadian families have gone through. Particularly worrying are "personality changes in husbands:"

> Social interaction patterns can be upset since the loss of a job and income may diminish the unemployed person's status and authority. Shifts in roles within the family, coupled with changes in the unemployed person's personality, can provoke considerable stress and in extreme cases can lead to family breakdown (cited in

the Social Planning Council of Metropolitan Toronto 1980:24; Armstrong 1984:107).

To Armstrong, this "increasing tension" among families of the unemployed "not infrequently leads to violence and the violence is directed primarily against women and children;" and this violence is seen to be "widespread" as "their numbers are increasing" (1984:107). Armstrong uses some "devastating statistics" by Roberts (1983:14) to prove her point:

> In Ontario in 1981 over 10,000 women and their children fled to women's shelters due to wife battering, and many others went to other places of refuge. The 19 transition houses in Quebec sheltered nearly 5,000 women and their children that year (1984:107–108).

To further support her claim that unemployment leads to "family breakdown" which in turn leads to violence, Armstrong cites the results of a Toronto study which found that "Eighty percent of wife-batterers reported to Metro Toronto Police were unemployed" (cited in Mackay 1983:33). To make matters worse:

> While the violence increases, the opportunities for escape are reduced. Rising unemployment and falling wages for women mean they have fewer alternatives to accepting the battering at home (1984:108).

In terms of increasing levels of child abuse, Armstrong cites a study conducted by the Children's Aid Society of Metropolitan Toronto which was reported in the *Montreal Gazette* 15 October 1983. "The number of cases opened in the first six months of 1983 increased by 15.6 percent over the same time period last year"—the CAS director cited the economy as a major factor for this increase (1984:108).

In another piece of work, Taylor (1985) cites information collected by the National Clearing House for Family Violence in which, "research done in transition houses for battered women strongly suggests that wife battering is massively on the increase and that the forms of violence within the family are becoming more and more prevalent" (1985:33). In attempting to explain why these levels of interpersonal violence within the family are increasing in Canadian society, Taylor suggests that *increasing levels of unemployment* coupled with the decline of the patriarchal family have prompted a *real* dislocation in accustomed social relations in many parts of Canada—particularly those most "severely affected" by the recession (1985:338). In another source, Taylor uses evidence based on two

Macleans magazine articles where journalists linked "hard times" caused by unemployment to increases in social problems:

> Journalistic reports from the most severely affected areas of the country spoke of sudden, steep increases in social work caseloads, suicide calls to crisis centres, reports of wife battering and child sexual abuse and admissions to mental hospitals (1984:13).

Armstrong and Taylor both feel that unemployment kills—or at least has the potential to do so. The unemployed are viewed as 'dangerous,' and more prone than people with jobs to become violent. But how strong is Armstrong and Taylor's evidence linking unemployment with crime and social problems—especially violence? How accurate are their sources of information? If rising unemployment is simply related to levels of crime, then one would expect that Newfoundland, the Canadian province with the highest unemployment rate, would be experiencing unprecedented levels of violence. However, this clearly is not the case.

It appears then that these researchers, like many others, have based their assumptions on a quite uncritical acceptance of the evidence suggesting that unemployment is associated with violence. If both Taylor and Armstrong were to have critically examined their sources, as we have done in this analysis, they would not have concluded that the types of violence which they were examining were actually increasing—although there is no denying that such violence is in fact occurring in many Canadian homes and is a serious problem.

A LOOK BEYOND THE VIOLENT CRIME RATE

We have demonstrated that recent anxieties about the changing level and character of crime and violence in Newfoundland have been socially constructed by events and processes. This is not to say that all concern about violence in Newfoundland may be examined in this way. In our attempt to debunk these popular and transparent social constructions and images of crime and violence in Newfoundland, we do not wish to deny the undesirable occurrences and conditions which a considerable number of people really do experience and obviously see as worrying—especially for particular groups such as women, children, and natives. We will now show that a great deal of trouble, conflict, and difficulty which occurs in Newfoundland fails to be recorded in the "violent crime rate" and yet may contribute to the general level of fear and concern about crime and violence in the province. Results from the Canadian Urban Victimization Survey (1981) indicate that 67 percent of assaults, 56 percent of robberies (the majority of which are not convenience store and gas bar hold-ups), and 60 percent of sexual assaults fail to come to the attention of the police in St. John's (Solicitor General 1984:20).

There is also evidence to suggest that some "violent" crimes which are reported to the police are not conventionally regarded as "violent crimes" and are consequently not being recorded as such by Statistics Canada. Here we are speaking of offenses statistically categorized as "other provincial statutes" and "other offensive weapons," or in more common terms "drunk and disorderly in the home" and crimes such as: dangerous use of a firearm, pointing a firearm, careless use of a firearm, or carrying a weapon dangerous to the public peace.

We will begin by examining incidents which are labelled "drunk and disorderly in the home." Like the term "armed robbery," there is no statistical category which is called "drunk and disorderly in the home." In fact, it is extremely difficult to extract from Statistics Canada's annual reports the offenses which would be described in this way, as the offense is subsumed under the category "other provincial statutes"—which includes a variety of offenses other than "drunk and disorderly in the home." What does this term mean? According to the police, a "drunk and disorderly in the home" could be typified as a situation in which a person (usually a woman) calls the police requesting that an officer(s) come to remove someone who is drunk and causing a disturbance in the home (in most cases a man who lives with the complainant—usually the husband). Many "drunk and disorderlies" can be situations which resemble assault—and in recent years a large number are in fact being defined as such. According to official statistics, however, many such incidents continue to be classified as "other provincial statutes" and thus remain "non-violent." A "drunk and disorderly" may only become classified as an assault if the complainant reports to police that she (in most cases a woman) was assaulted. A "drunk and disorderly" on the other hand, is a situation in which the complainant wishes only that the person complained about be removed from the premises. In many cases, the complainant has indeed been assaulted or threatened with bodily harm, but since the victim's primary wish at the time is for safety, usually the complainant is concerned only with having the police remove the violent person from the home. Thus an assault, unless serious (e.g., requiring hospitalization), becomes a secondary issue. Here is an example of a situation which the police would define as a "drunk and disorderly in the home":

Well, a woman calls up. She'd called before. You can recall the
name, but you don't know what she's called for. Or someone calls
up:

"What's the trouble tonight?"

"He's drunk again."

"Okay, are you going to Court?"

"Oh, yes I'm going to court. Okay, I want you to take him out."

So we go off and arrest him, she's going to appear in Court. . . .But
if she's not going to Court, we still send someone there more or less
for protection. There could be children involved there, and we have
to see the condition of the fella. . . (McGahan:1984:85).

These are also the types of calls police view with greatest apprehension:

You got to approach it, you go to analyze the situation and approach
it that way—who's who, if there are any guns or knives. You got to
be cautious because one slip and that could be it. That's where
most police officers have been killed—[on] drunk and disorderly
calls. . . .You knock on the door, and stand back from it because
you don't know what's going to come. We've had a number of calls,
doors blown off by shot guns. We've been lucky (McGahan 1984).

Clearly, "drunk and disorderlies" may sometimes be *overtly*
violent situations. Also, in many cases these types of calls are pleas
from women who are in fear of their lives—even though they may
not have been directly physically assaulted by the "drunk"—and
even if they were, their prime intention is not to pursue a charge of
assault, but to get the trouble-maker out of the immediate environment as soon as possible.

How many of these types of calls do police respond to? As we
have pointed out, annual official statistics published by Statistics
Canada do not allow for this figure to be easily computed. However,
the 1984 and 1985 annual reports of the RNC have in fact reported
the number of calls to the police which were labelled as "drunk and
disorderly." In 1984, police received 417 calls in this regard; the
following year the RNC received and responded to 461 of these calls.
In this way, we can discern that in 1984, 57 percent of "other
provincial statutes" were offenses which were "drunk and disorderlies in the home," while in the following year, the percentage rose
slightly to 60 percent as there were 461 "drunk and disorderlies"
and 769 offenses in total. Although this information is not available
on a provincial basis, we may roughly estimate this occurrence using
data from the RNC as a baseline. If we assume that half of "other
provincial statutes" across the province as a whole involve instances

of "drunk and disorderly in the home," we may estimate that in 1983, for example, there were approximately 1,800. In this way, we may estimate that the provincial rate for "drunk and disorderlies in the home" was approximately 250/100,000 population—in fact, *this is a rate which is almost half of the total assault rate for the province in that year!*

Hence, a considerable amount of "violence" takes place in the province which is commonly referred to as "drunk and disorderly in the home" but which is not included in Newfoundland's violent crime rate—the same of course applies to data for the country as a whole, since other police forces in Canada record these offenses in a similar fashion. This may be changing to a degree in certain parts of the country, as police are being encouraged to lay assault charges in many instances which would otherwise be simply labelled as "drunk and disorderly in the home."

The second category we will examine is again not classified as a "violent crime" as it falls under the general statistical category of "offensive weapon violations;" more particularly under the sub-category "other offensive weapons." This includes such offenses as: careless or dangerous use of firearm, pointing a firearm or carrying a weapon dangerous to public peace. We randomly examined 78 RCMP files involving these types of offenses between the years 1979 and 1984. Of these 78 files, or police investigations, 28 percent (22) involved complaints where a man was threatening his wife (including common-law) with a gun, knife, or other offensive weapon—in most cases a firearm. Another 3.8 percent (3) involved complaints where women were threatening their husbands (including common-law) with a weapon—again usually a firearm; 7.6 percent (6) were incidents where children threatened parents; 5.1 percent (4) were incidents which took place between other family members; 39 percent (29) took place between neighbours or other close acquaintances; 11.5 percent between strangers and the remaining 6.4 percent (5) involved the police and civilians. In 44 percent of these incidents a shotgun was used: 23 percent were rifles; 26 percent were knives; whereas, the remainder involved "replicas" of offensive weapons. In only 7 percent of these cases was there an indication from the police file that somebody was injured and had to be hospitalized (not because they were injured by a weapon but rather by an assault). However, in 43 percent of the cases somebody was reported to have been assaulted, but did not seek medical attention.

Although it was very difficult to obtain information about the circumstances behind these incidents, (as in 58 percent of these files no information was gathered in this regard) we were able to ascertain

that in 10 percent of these cases, the established motive involved
sexual jealousy (in most cases this involved situations where husbands were threatening wives); 5 percent involved a "break-up"
between married or unmarried lovers; 6 percent concerned financial
problems which a couple was reported to have been experiencing;
and 17 percent were defined by police as incidents which resulted
from a person (in most cases a man) getting "blind drunk" as the
result of being depressed.

Here are some examples of the types of incidents which were
statistically categorized under "offensive weapons"—a non-violent
crime. Within a domestic context:

> A thirty-five-year-old woman telephoned the police and reported
> that she was afraid to enter her home as her husband was in the
> dwelling, drunk and armed with a .303. Police arrived on the scene
> and confiscated the weapon.

> A women was reported to have threatened her husband with a gun
> in order to "scare" him. In her statement the woman reported that
> she was "fed up" with the problems her husband had recently been
> giving her and decided to "take some action to put a stop to it." She
> was convicted on the charge of pointing a firearm and placed on
> probation for two years.

> A forty-five-year-old man threatened to shoot his wife and
> daughter with a 12 gauge shotgun. Police arrived at the scene and
> confiscated the weapon. The man was charged and was prohibited
> from using a firearm for five years.

> A woman called the police from a hotel near her home and reported
> that her husband had chased her from the home with a shotgun.
> Police came to the scene and confiscated the weapon from the
> man—no charges were laid.

Here are some instances which involved confrontation between
neighbours or friends:

> A woman called the police and reported that while her husband
> and neighbour were fighting in her kitchen, the neighbour pointed
> a gun at her husband. The case was brought to court and dis-
> missed.

> A group of men went to a bar after they had finished hunting. After
> the men were in the bar and drinking for a considerable period of
> time (according to the bartender) one of the men pulled a knife on
> another and put it up to his throat as he was annoyed at the other's
> "bragging" about his "moose skinning" skills. No charges were laid.

> A group of men were drinking in a house and one of the men was
> "thrown out" for behaving "bizarrely." Shortly after, the man
> returned to the house and threatened the other men with a shot-
> gun. Probation for one year.

Two men were in a local "club" drinking and an argument broke out between them after one had driven the other home and then demanded money for his services. The passenger refused to pay, ran inside his home and came out with a shotgun and pointed it at the driver of the car. No charges laid.

Three boys were in a neighbour's backyard stealing apples. The neighbour caught the boys doing this and pointed a gun at them threatening to shoot them and fired a shot into the air. The case was dismissed in court as the judge felt the defendant was "guarding his apples against intruders."

Here are some vignettes involving incidents with strangers:

A group of boys were wandering in the woods and stumbled across a man whom they described as a "hermit." The hermit threatened the boys with a gun as he wanted them to get off his property. The hermit received two years probation.

A travelling salesman was threatened by a man with a "machete" in a public washroom. The suspect was not apprehended by police.

A man claiming he required a "boost" for his car forced his way into a woman's apartment. The stranger then proceeded to grab the woman and put a knife to her throat. When the woman asked the stranger what he wanted he replied, "What do all fellows want?" He attempted to sexually assault the woman but she managed to escape unharmed. The man was first charged with "dangerous use of a weapon" but later this changed to "assault with a weapon" and he was sentenced to three years in prison.

In terms of the frequency of these "non-violent" crimes, their statistical occurrence is greater than crimes which are popularly defined as "armed robberies." In fact, the incident rate offenses involving "offensive weapon violations" in 1983, for instance, was more than *double* the robbery rate for that year—13/100,000 versus 31/100,000.

Examining the "non-violent" crimes of "drunk and disorderly in the home" and "weapons violations" has clearly demonstrated that many violent acts are in fact taking place in Newfoundland, but because of differences in definition, they are not recognized as violent crimes, despite the fact that a considerable degree of danger is present in both these sets of instances.

Our data suggest that the way in which police in Newfoundland handle "drunk and disorderlies" and "weapon violation" offenses is consistent with the way in which police react to these sorts of incidents in Britain. Research conducted by McCabe and Sutcliffe (1978) in Salford, England indicates that many police investigations of "domestic" incidents involving aggressive attacks on women resulted in either no charge at all, or else a charge of drunken and disorderly behaviour was issued. In fact, in Salford, only 11 percent of reports of domestic violence ever ended up as a recorded crime. What McCabe and Sutcliffe's research suggests then is that the responses of uniformed police officers to reports of violent family disputes made by women are formalized around the stereotypical conception police as a group hold about "domestics." McCabe and Sutcliffe (1978:82) suggest that police initiative seemed to have its source in stereotypes of individuals as the events and circumstances giving rise to police action in such cases seemed to be less important than the outward appearance or suspected proclivities of the individuals observed. In some respects, it would appear that police label these sorts of incidents as "victimless crimes."

Considering the evidence we provided earlier on police perceptions of "drunk and disorderlies" in Newfoundland, our data suggests that such stereotypes held by police may not in fact be isolated to Salford, England.

In these sorts of incidents, then, crime reports are either not being recorded by police, that is they are *no-crimed*, or else are being recorded as something which is less serious than it really is, or *down-crimed* (see Jones *et al.* 1986:78). In other words, standard definitions of crime are constructed so as to exclude many similar, and in important ways, identical acts that are committed frequently.

In summary, our data on "drunk and disorderlies" and weapon violations covered in this analysis of police record files illustrates that the frequency and distribution of *violence* is quite different from what common conceptions or police statistics taken at face value would suggest. It is quite clear that when domestic violence is taken into consideration as a form of criminal assault, it is mainly women who are exposed to much of the violence occurring in Newfoundland society. Considering the levels of homicide which we discussed for native people in the province, natives are clearly another group in Newfoundland society whose victimization is not being seriously recognized.

Unfortunately it is beyond the scope of this essay to adequately answer the question of why these types of crimes are not considered violent, and other researchers may wish to examine this in the future. Nonetheless, the data in this analysis would suggest that many crimes are taking place in Newfoundland with little critical comment and with relative impunity.

CONCLUSION

This research has raised some very serious questions about popular perceptions of crime and violence in Newfoundland. We have shown that although a considerable amount of violent behaviour does occur, there is no valid evidence to suggest that violence is rising. Many of the assumptions made by individuals and groups regarding the *causes* of violence are to say the least *questionable.* As we have demonstrated, official statistics do not accurately reflect changes in levels of interpersonal violence and, therefore, it would be very difficult to say with any degree of certainty that Newfoundland is a more violent place today than it was in the past. Consequently many of the assumptions about the *causes* of these perceived increases in violence are questionable. Our work has also raised some serious questions about the conventional wisdom that crime rates are *directly* linked to unemployment or other factors which have caused a breakdown in the social fabric of Newfoundland society. This research has gone some way in demonstrating that stereotypes about crime are in many respects merely claims about *simple* correlations. To understand the meaning of violence, let alone issues of causality, the use of simple correlations must be abandoned. By no means is violence a "social fact"; social life is a configuration of many complex phenomena and must be understood as such.

Our effort in exposing the public stereotypes of crime or fears of crime should not be taken to suggest, however, that official statistics and police record keeping practices are meaningless in terms of providing information on the human consequences of violent behaviour. While we have provided some strong evidence illustrating how problematic it is to use official statistics to determine whether or not levels of violence are changing, in our argument we have provided data which suggest that these statistics may be quite useful if they are treated with caution and used in a critical fashion.

By conceptualizing violence *sociologically*, and by not basing assumptions on conventional wisdom, this essay confirms what other researchers working with victimization surveys have found, namely that "the more vulnerable a group of people are to crime, the less likely are the official figures (whether police statistics or victim reports) to reflect the real situation that they face." Furthermore, and of significant import, is that the "greater degree of vulnerability, the greater the underestimation" (Kinsey *et al.* 1986:65). In fact, based on data from national and local victimization surveys conducted in urban areas in Britain in recent years,[12] "Serious crime is underestimated, but not randomly" (Kinsey *et al.* 1986:65).

Groups who are poor and powerless in society are victims of violence much more often than official sources taken at face value would suggest. For this reason, then, the fear and anxiety about crime which is tapped by victimization surveys may in fact be related to people's material experiences. The evidence we have presented here would indicate that this may be the case. Also while popular conceptions of crime and violence (e.g., armed robbery and stranger homicides) may not be related to general levels of public anxiety, concern about mundane and much 'unofficial' violence does have a rational basis. Consequently a great deal of the fear being expressed in victimization surveys is probably much in line with people's own experiences of violence (e.g., domestic violence).

We hope our analysis will encourage people to think more carefully in the future when they attempt to explain crime and violence as simply the result of 'social breakdown;' personal, family or community. For future research, it may be wise to do more than ritually denounce crime statistics, or any other information which tries to quantify crime and violence, before any attempt is made to explain crime causation.

We must go beyond these simple, and *dangerous* (in terms of the effects which they may be having on sentencing behaviours of judges) notions of what causes crime, to arrive at explanations which go beyond "wayward or unemployed youth" or "family breakdown" as being responsible for the conflicts, troubles and difficulties which many people do experience.

Research and serious investigation must replace conventional wisdoms and stereotypes.

Notes

1. According to Bottomley and Coleman (1981:9), "although the advocate of anomie theory, Robert Merton, argued that there were successive layers of error which intervene between the actual event and the recorded event, between actual rates of deviant behaviour and the records of deviant behaviour, official statistics were nonetheless put to practical use in research and theorizing."

2. There has been a good deal of material which has been published in the area of "left realism" in recent years. For a good review of this position see Young (1987) and Matthews and Young (eds.) (1986).

3. This figure was generated by Leyton in his content analysis of the St. John's *Evening Telegram*, Newfoundland's largest daily newspaper which is described in the following chapter.

4. See Leyton's essay in this volume for a formal recantation of these notions.

5. This information was obtained from the files of Leyton's content analysis of the *Evening Telegram*.

6. Recent events surrounding child physical and sexual abuse in Newfoundland involving priests and brothers associated with the Catholic church will not be included in this analysis. Our research in this area took place before these events reached the public eye.

7. On 3 January 1983, Bill C-127 became law. This change in legislation, according to Statistics Canada, has "redefined the former categories of sexual assault and assaults (not indecent) and created a major discontinuity in the historical record of sexual assault offenses," making it no longer possible to "clearly compare different categories from each of the classifications" so the "historical record for sexual assault cases stops in 1982" (Statistics Canada, 1985, Canadian Crime Statistics). Thus, to keep in line with these changes, our time series data for rape will only apply to the period prior to 1983.

8. On numerous occasions the St. John's Coalition Against Pornography have publicly voiced their concerns against the proliferation of pornographic material in St. John's and surrounding area.

9. Although we are arguing that some feminists in their attempt to deal with the issue of pornography have in fact come dangerously close to aligning themselves with the 'fundamentalist right,' we are by no means arguing that pornography is not linked to violence towards women. Furthermore, we do not believe that all feminists approach the issue in this way. The point that we are trying to make here simply concerns the logic of analysis that some feminists have used to argue that pornography causes violent sexual crimes. For example, Maude Barlow, then special advisor to Prime Minister Trudeau on pornography policy, stated that "it's no accident that 48 percent of rapists and 14 pe cent of child molesters are pornography fans." However, to show that pornography causes these sorts of crimes she would have had to prove that the percentage of pornography fans who commit sexual crimes is higher than the percentage of non-fans who do (see Thomas Hurka, *Globe and Mail* 6 March 1990)

10. A certain proportion of this increase could perhaps be explained by the fact that a number of new correctional facilities have been built in the province in recent years, such as: Clarenville Correctional Centre, 1982; Bishop's Falls Correctional Centre, 1983; The Newfoundland and Labrador Correctional Centre For Women, 1981; and the Labrador Correctional Centre, 1984. These new institutions are now holding some offenders who have in the past served their terms in "lock-ups" in local police detachments. These statistics were not included as provincial admission statistics, and therefore were not included in the total admission statistics for the province's correctional institutions. However, it is also the case that the increasing admissions to Newfoundland and Labrador correctional facilities took place *prior* to the establishment of the above mentioned facilities. The increases which

have taken place then cannot be entirely 'explained away' by this change in record keeping.

11. The importance of the telephone as a means of communication between the police and the public has been discussed elsewhere by McCabe and Sutcliffe (1978). These researchers suggest that because of the anonymity associated with telephone use it is easier to complain to an unseen police officer about other people's behaviour than to risk embarrassment or discomfort at the station counter. Furthermore, McCabe and Sutcliffe's research indicates that the police seemed to give a more active response to telephone reports and complaints than to personal visits by aggravated and anxious citizens (1978:39–40).

12. Commencing with the British Crime Survey of 1982, a number of local crime surveys have been carried out in Britain in recent years. In 1984, Kinsey *et al.* were involved in the Meryside Crime Survey, which surveyed households in the Liverpool area. This was followed by the Islington Crime Survey in 1985. In 1986, two surveys were conducted in Tottenham, a focused survey of the North London area in 1987, and a survey in 1988 of Hammersmith and Fulham (Lea, Matthews and Young 1988).

Part II

The Theatre of Public Crisis

Elliott Leyton

> The worse the crime problem be-
> comes, the more professional growth
> can be justified (Cohen 1985:177).

Western democracies with high levels of state spending and state employment provide relatively free access to the mass media for private individuals, interest groups, and government agencies. This is especially the case in a country such as Canada, where the media tend to be less ideological, less systematically conservative in their politics, than in Britain or the United States (a "neutrality" rein-forced by national CBC Radio's concern for broad social issues). In such a milieu, there is a clear perception among politicians, proponents of various ideologies, and special interest groups, that if they wish to justify their behaviour, make their case to the public, or capture increased levels of government funding, then they must use the mass media to gain public recognition of their cause. To do so, they participate in a kind of media theatre, in which the stage is managed as much by the interest groups as by the media.

Thus rival ideologies and groups must compete with one another to secure media attention, for only then, they believe, will sufficient public pressure be generated to stir the government to support their cause. One of the primary stratagems for capturing media attention has been to discover, or manufacture, a "crisis"—a real or sometimes imagined, accurately described or sometimes radically embellished, hitherto neglected or unknown phenomenon. The press, and then the public, must be convinced, partially through the medium of emotionally charged and anxiety-arousing news, that the crisis is a legitimate one—and, moreover, that the discoverers of the crisis will have the most capable professional expertise to solve the problem, once funding is enhanced by a newly sympathetic public and government.

This manufacture of moral panics is well understood in the literature; but the manner of their orchestration has been explained primarily in terms of machinations by the media, usually on behalf of the ruling elites, police, and government. It is my intention in this essay to examine one ethnographic milieu in microscopic detail to show how these panics are generated by a much wider range of self-serving groups, and on an infinitely broader variety of issues. Such issues in recent years have included among many others, the AIDS Panic, the Herpes Scare, the Drugs Crisis, the Abuse Crisis, and the Greenhouse Effect. Regardless of their actual legitimacy, their stage management is strikingly similar. Provocative claims are made to first capture media attention on behalf of the new or established "industry"; the new industry exercises a tight political censorship (usually discussed as professional "ethics") on their broadcasts to the public, carefully controlling what their "objective" professionals and scientists may and may not say.[1] Moreover, there is an apparent tendency for the *rate* of claim inflation to increase as competing (or even cooperating) members within the new industry respond to one another, accept each other's claims, and are further validated by media attention. In any case, the claims generally function as useful stratagems for the establishment and reinforcement of social and scientific industries; and they do, in fact, often perform accordingly, eliciting media attention, sympathy from the public, and enhanced funding.

The Violence Crisis of the 1970s and 1980s appears to have had its origins in a similar dynamic. Unconsciously or otherwise, the increase in the national homicide rate that occurred in the late 1960s and early 1970s was retailed to the public by many Violence Industry spokespersons throughout the 1970s and 1980s (when rates were actually declining) in such a manner as to create a national climate of fear of crime. This in turn justified the massive expansion of the Justice Industry, as well as the enhanced subsidization and prestige for the professionals and ideologues associated with the enterprise. Thus the promulgation of a scare by one interest group, such as politicians or scientists, may create a *bandwagon* effect offering ideological justification and resource expansion for many others—for care-givers, researchers, bureaucrats, ideologues, and radical activists. Sometimes, of course, a single crisis may provide support for quite contradictory positions—as when the AIDS Crisis was used by religious fundamentalists as proof of their interpretations of Biblical injunctions against homosexuality and promiscuity; by a wide variety of scientists, medical officers, social workers, anti-drug agencies, and media personnel pursuing quite different funding goals; and by the homosexual community itself to elicit popular support and sympathy for their own social agenda.

The data presented below make it clear that it was by no means simply the media and the ruling elites that created the fear of violence in Newfoundland in particular, and in Canada in general. In fact, a loose and disorganized, often conflicting and contradictory, "coalition" of groups, professionals, government agencies, politicians, and ideologues seized upon the issue in order to strengthen their own positions. Thus the media were exploited almost as much as they themselves exploited the situation. Moreover, the various interest groups appeared to use the media as their testing ground to gauge public response to their claims. If a positive response was forthcoming, they continued to play the issue; while those professional groups, such as guidance counsellors or nurses, which did not invoke the appropriate social response, dropped out of the game to make room for newer claimants.

THE LITERATURE

What does the academic literature suggest about the prime sources of this widespread fear? What are their speculations on the origins of the cultural messages circulating through the public domain proclaiming a continuous increase in violence? How can 40 percent of the surveyed population of the sleepy capital of Newfoundland (and 60 percent of its elderly inhabitants!) be afraid to venture out of their homes at night for fear of being assaulted?

A substantial literature in sociology and criminology addresses this general question, and concludes that the mass media—and particularly the press—are largely responsible for the creation of public fears of crime waves. This explanatory tradition began with Stanley Cohen's analysis (Cohen 1972) of the 1964 Mods and Rockers panic in Britain. Here, bored working-class Londoners holidaying at a seaside resort found their personal fist fights transformed by the national press into socially meaningful and frightening, "gang wars." Cohen argued succinctly that the media's labelling of the "groups" created a moral panic which obliged the police to intensify their surveillance of the Mods and Rockers, resulting in yet more arrests. Moreover, this press attention to the differences in style between the groups, and their mutual antagonism, "encouraged adolescents to think of themselves in these terms" (Murdock 1982:79), thereby further increasing the tension between the two groups.

Following this insight, a more radical literature developed which explained the dissemination of fear of crime as a class stratagem used by the ruling elites to reinforce their dominant position. Thus, Murdock (1982:82) summarizes, "This accentuated sense of risk and insecurity. . .increases people's dependence upon established authority, legitimizes the increased use of force by control agencies, and mobilizes opinion behind demands for tougher law and order policies." In a similar vein, Stuart Hall and his colleagues studied the mugging panic of the early 1970s, and demonstrated how the media transformed an apparent increase in ghetto street crime into the explosion of an essentially new violent crime, "mugging." As with the British Mods and Rockers panic, the manufacture of public fear was the primary stratagem by "which a 'silent majority' is won over to the support of increasingly coercive measures on the part of the state, and lends it legitimacy to a 'more than usual' exercise of control" (Hall *et al.* 1978:221).

Throughout these analyses, the media are most often explicitly presented as the primary culprits, disseminating fear and false consciousness on behalf of the ruling elites. In his paper, "Crime Waves as Ideology," Fishman (1978:26) observes that "one cannot be mugged by a crime wave, but one can be scared. And one can put more police on the streets and enact new laws on the basis of fear. Crime waves may be 'things of the mind,' but they have real consequences." Similarly, Ian Taylor's essay (1981:43) "Crime Waves in Post-war Britain," notes that "reading the newspapers and listening to television news in 1980, we could be forgiven for believing that 'crime' and disorder are now an inescapable and overwhelmingly serious reality in our cities, a significant factor in everyday experience and, what is more, that they are problems of relatively recent origin." Taylor concludes that the law and order ideology of the 1970s was "an attempt to reformulate the posture of the police towards youth on the streets in general, towards black youth in particular, and the relation of the State to civil society as a whole" (1981:58–59).

Whether or not the scholars feel that the dissemination of fear of violence is a conspiracy between the ruling elites and the mass media, the vast majority seem to agree that the media are more than mere transmitters, that they are, in fact, *the primary creators* of this disinformation. Thus Sanford Sherizen (1978:203–204) notes that "from the limited research available, it is clear that the mass media play a major role in the creation and dissemination of beliefs about crime." He concludes that "Crime news is a constructed reality, selected from a series of events which occur and, from which, crime-newsworthy events are written as crime news" (Sherizen 1978:222). However, Stuart Hall and his colleagues, among the more astute commentators on these matters, have severely qualified this position, reducing the centrality of the media's role and assigning primary importance to others:

> The media, then, do not simply 'create' the news; nor do they simply transmit the ideology of the 'ruling class' in a conspiratorial fashion. Indeed, we have suggested that, in a critical sense, the media are frequently not the 'primary definers' of news events at all; but their structured relationship to power has the effect of making them play a crucial but secondary role in reproducing the definitions of those who have privileged access, as of right, to the media as 'accredited sources.' From this point of view, in the moment of news production, the media stand in a position of structural subordination to the primary definers (Hall *et al.* 1981:342–343).

Indeed. But precisely who are the "primary definers" of these perceptions, and are they exclusively from the power elites? If the analyst focuses narrowly on crime news, which contains a description of the crime along with reactions from the judiciary, the victims, the police and the government, as have so many of these studies (cf., Voumvakis and Ericson 1984; Dussuyer 1979), then the inevitable impression is that media institutions alone are responsible for the widespread fear of crime.

We felt, however, that an exclusive focus on crime news gave an entirely false picture of the actual number of public announcements of increasing violence. Our research project thus cast its net much more broadly than crime news, examining instead *all references to an increase in violence* which appeared in the press, regardless of whether it appeared in crime news, in editorials, in letters to the editor, or in interviews with prominent individuals and institutions. The data that resulted from this quite different emphasis were taken from a detailed examination of the microfilms of the *Evening Telegram*, the province's only journal of record and only major newspaper, for the period from 1 January 1975 to 31 December 1985. We focused exclusively on this newspaper partly because it was the only major paper to survive through the period of our study,

partly because it was neither a tabloid nor sensationalist in approach, and partly because it was the only media source which
consistently covered violence in journalistic depth (a radio or
television station might, for a brief period, devote itself to a particular
crime or series of crimes, but over an extended period there was no
consistent coverage of the subject by radio and television). The
province's only other major newspaper, the *Daily News,* which had
a much smaller circulation (the *Evening Telegram's* circulation
reached 53,000 copies for its Saturday edition) both within the city
and throughout the province, went bankrupt during the period of
study, and never at any time had the impact on public consciousness of the surviving newspaper.

The eleven-year period covered by the research was a time of
*rapid expansion of the Canadian and Newfoundland justice
bureaucracy,*[2] *and increased sensitivity to hitherto unacknowledged
"crimes."* The period also saw the *proliferation of professional and
special interest groups* to deal with these new systemic requirements. The reality uncovered by the research was that during the
eleven-year period, 55 types of institutions and/or individuals made
341 announcements that crime was increasing and/or changing in
character for the worse: an average of 31 announcements each year,
or almost 3 every month. The press made less than half (157 of a
total of 341) of these announcements, doing so in crime stories,
editorials, and coverage of "threatened" collective violence by labour
unions or proletarian youth. Governments and government
bureaucracies were responsible for 102 of the 341 announcements.
Members of an extraordinary array of social agencies, professional
organisations, and social action groups, as well as members of the
public, were responsible for 82 of the announcements. Although we
have no data to substantiate this speculation, it might be argued
that the announcements made by the social action groups were
taken more seriously by the general public, since it would be
assumed that they had a more professional (i.e., more objective)
motivation for their statements: thus their greater perceived social
legitimacy may have made their announcements even more
authoritative and plausible than those stemming from politicians
and the press.

The data suggest that Cohen's comments might be most acute,
especially what he calls "the general theory of professional growth,
aggrandizement and self-interest," in which he refers to the social
fact that "it is in the best interests of professions to enlarge the
system and attract more clients," which is to say that "to keep your
job, to justify your existence, to attract grants and subsidies, you

must keep on expanding" (Cohen 1985:167). If, as Cohen concludes, "much system expansion can be explained in terms of relentless professional self-interest," then many of the announcements of crime waves that appear in these pages may also be attributed to similar characteristics of the system. Table 1 shows the actual list of announcers and the frequency of their announcements.

The data force us to conclude with an infinitely less conspiratorial theory than is usually retailed, for there are 184 non-press announcements to the press's 157, and members of the major public and private social agencies and social action groups are major contributors. The remarkable openness of the Canadian press gives many groups the opportunity to participate in the press's function of isolating, developing, and labelling what is to become "news"—what Ericson and his colleagues (1987:142ff.) have described as the processes of simplification, personalization, dramatization, and continuity—and thus capture media attention. The appropriately tailored crime wave announcement could come from an isolated individual arguing some obscure ideological point, from an independent social agency legitimizing its funding, from an industry justifying the sale of its products, or from government bureaucracies anxious to expand their domains.

We do not wish to suggest that they cynically, or even consciously, manipulated violence statistics and anecdotes for their own political and economic agenda. Nor was there any monolithic conspiracy through an alliance of these interest groups. We make no suggestion that data were fabricated; merely that they were sometimes embellished; and that such embroidery was often found to be useful and effective. We simply observe that the thoughtless use of data, the succumbing to the desire to find evidence for what they felt (for political and ideological reasons) to be correct, were characteristic of a very wide segment of society. If many such individuals and groups stood to gain from the public's growing belief in a crime wave, we make no claim that they did so from any malevolent intent. Whatever their motivations may have been, and we can only speculate on these, the impact of their strategies was to heighten the public awareness of the violence "problem" as a means of enhancing their own position. As such, they managed the stage, and wrote the script for the Theatre of Violence Crisis.

One phenomenon that is worthy of note is what a colleague has referred to as "*baton-passing*"—that is, the fact that while some contributors appeared in the press throughout our time period, others surfaced for a short time and then disappeared, passing the violence "baton" to their successors.[3] We can only speculate on the

Table 1

Announcements of Crime Waves 1975–1985

GENERATORS	FREQUENCY	
The Press		
Crime stories	79	
Editorials	56	
Sensationalized union violence story	15	
Sensationalized youth violence story	4	
Sensationalized proletarian violence story	2	
Columnist	1	
Subtotal		157
The Justice System		
Judges or Magistrates in court	19	
Royal Newfoundland Constabulary Management	14	
Royal Newfoundland Constabulary Brotherhood	7	
Crown Prosecutors in court	7	
Royal Canadian Mounted Police	4	
Canadian Centre for Justice Statistics	4	
Solicitor General of Canada	3	
Canadian Police Association	3	
Police Chiefs of Canada	2	
Atlantic Police Chiefs Association	2	
Toronto Police Chief	1	
Retiring Probation Officer	1	
Federal Department of Justice	1	
Assistant Director of Public Prosecutions	1	
Subtotal		69
Members of the Public		
Letters to the Editor	32	
Victims of crime	5	
Unions	4	
City merchants	3	
Divorce lawyer	2	
Newfoundland Convenience Store Association	2	
Professor of Anthropology	1	
Subtotal		49
Social Agencies & Social Action Groups		
Status of Women Council	12	
Association of Registered Nurses	4	
Canadian Guidance and Counselling Association	3	
Coalition against Pornography	2	
St. John's Committee on Child Protection	2	
Pentecostal Assemblies	1	
Roman Catholic Priest	1	
Kiwanis Club	1	
Ex-convict's proposed Halfway House	1	

Table 1 (continued)

GENERATORS	FREQUENCY	
Academic Conference	1	
Children's Hospital	1	
Neighbourhood Watch	1	
Family Life Bureau	1	
Newfoundland and Labrador Human Rights Association	1	
Advocacy Centre for the Aged	1	
Subtotal		33
Politicians		
The Minister of Social Services	6	
Member of Federal Parliament	6	
Member of Provincial House of Assembly	3	
Mayor of St. John's	2	
Premier of Newfoundland	1	
Federal House Committee	1	
Ontario Cabinet Minister	1	
Subtotal		20
Government Bureaucracies (Non-Justice)		
Alcohol and Drug Addiction Foundation	4	
Statistics Canada	3	
Department of Social Services	3	
Avalon School Board	1	
Family Court Social Worker	1	
Family and Community Services	1	
Subtotal		13
TOTAL		341

motives behind a disappearance, but obvious possibilities include the achievement of their goal, or the discovery of an alternate means of garnering public approval. Thus in the mid-seventies, the primary contributors were the press, the public, and the politicians; but the justice system moved to the forefront in the late seventies, and in the early eighties was joined by various professional and social action groups making their own claims for special status. By the mid-eighties, professional and social action groups had retreated while the justice system, the press, and assorted politicians regained their ascendancy. Throughout this period, of course, the role of the press was constant, and it was especially virulent in the production of anti-union and anti-youth stories.

A second form of "baton-passing" was the implicit exchange of "information" between the groups. Here, an announcement from one sector, such as justice, functioned as both encouragement and reinforcement for the perception by the other sectors that there was indeed an upsurge of violence. This enabled them to retail their own positions with increased confidence and even stridency. Moreover, the effectiveness of the violence card in attracting public attention and funding cannot have been entirely lost upon the audience, composed as it was of many other potential beneficiaries.

Are these conclusions peculiar to Newfoundland? We think not. It is true that industries purveying anti-crime products and services, such as security systems, did not play a major part in this period, but that is a reflection of the province's underdeveloped economy. If the Royal Canadian Mounted Police played their typically un-provocative role, the Royal Newfoundland Constabulary were not so blameless. Still, their role was relatively minor compared to the pugnacious and unsubstantiated statements that are much more common in central Canadian regional police forces. Indeed, for the most part, management of the RNC and the RCMP appeared in the press to calm the public and dismiss rumours of an explosion of violence (for which they were sometimes savagely attacked by the press and various social action groups). We can make no solid claims in the absence of proper comparative data, but we do not feel that the data are distinctive in any other way, for politicians everywhere have used the fear of violence for their own ends, and the majority of the special interest groups we describe here are either local chapters of national and international agencies with broadly defined policies and strategies, or representatives of international social movement, be they anti-abortion, pro-capital punishment, or feminist in content.

This is not to say that exploitation of fears of violence on the cheapest imaginable level was entirely absent from the province. From time to time small-circulation weeklies and irresponsible media would grossly distort events and probabilities to play upon the public's fears. But this form of exploitation was relatively rare. Indeed, most of the individuals and agencies announcing the in-crease of violent crime were drawn from the middle classes (although the unions also learned how to use the fear of violence as an essential bargaining chip), the "educated" and "responsible" members of groups which presumably, merely wished the public to understand the enormity of the problem they were presenting. Yet in doing so, they appear to have left the public with the overwhelmingly powerful message that the rates of these crimes, and the significance of them in everyday life, were increasingly out of control, suggesting an imploding social order.

In what follows, I shall first offer a detailed discussion of a single case, and then proceed chronologically through the period 1975– 1985, examining all the references to violence in the *Evening Telegram*. I shall demonstrate how the repetition of such references rapidly developed to the point where violence became the symbol of everything that was wrong with society (cf. Pearson 1985, for a fascinating essay on the nostalgia of the non-violent past); the *proof* of any assertion (be it social, political, or religious); and the *ammunition* which permitted any individual or group to expand its domain (whether that be consolidating a public image, increasing political power, or arguing for increased funding). If these conclusions are surprising and disturbing, the solution is simple: progressive social movements and professionals, as much as self-interested and self-serving politicians, have a responsibility to address the public in a non-inflammatory language of discourse.

First, though, let me offer a *caveat*. The majority of the social groups and agencies responsible for the manufacture of public anxiety were "progressive" in ideology and altruistic in intent, with no conscious plan to promulgate fear among the populace. In releasing unanalyzed data without sufficient warnings of their un-reliability, or in yielding to the temptation to assume that an increasing awareness of a problem meant that the problem itself was increasing, or in selling ideas or merchandise, they were simply exercising insufficient caution, rather than cynically manipulating the public. Contrary examples were rare: our attempt to interview several individuals who had served as editors of the *Evening Telegram* yielded no useful data at all. Near the end of this project, one member of our research team *was* explicitly approached by the head of a powerful social agency and asked to supply her with data on violence that would justify a demand they wished to make of government: he was also asked for suggestions on how best to tailor the violence data to suit their case. Public fear was perhaps the latent consequence of other realizable political, ideological, and financial goals.

THE ANNOUNCEMENT OF A CRIME WAVE: AN ILLUSTRATIVE CASE

We have no data on the precise sentiments and motives, inclinations and prejudices, which lead individuals and institutions to announce the coming of a crime wave. Indeed, obtaining such data would be virtually impossible, since few are willing to expose for public consumption the manner in which they articulate their careerist self-interest.

The manipulation of public anxiety regarding violence need not be conscious or pre-formulated for it to be a significant force. The many players in the game we describe below may well have been motivated by the purest altruism, or the narrowest self-interest; but to attempt to determine this would be fruitless, for individuals and institutions with no vested interest in arriving at the truth can hardly be expected to undergo merciless examination or self-criticism. All we can assume here is what Dahrendorf tells us (1959:178), that membership in a group invests the individual with "role interests," and that these interests provide "undercurrents in his behaviour which are predetermined for him for the duration of his incumbency of a role." When these become conscious goals, the undercurrents direct the "emotion, will, and desire of a person," and operate to suppress, deny, or ignore alternatives.

Conveniently for this enterprise, one of the offenders in this matter proved to be myself. In an article written for popular consumption in 1982 (Leyton 1986), in an extended interview with the *Evening Telegram* in 1983, and in an interview on CBC radio in 1984, I repeated the errors for which this essay castigates a wide range of individuals, agencies, and institutions. This by no means comforting discovery provides at least a unique opportunity for a glimpse of motive in some depth, since my compelling desire to elicit useful material largely overwhelms my all-too-human desire to whitewash my own motives. Of course we cannot state with certainty that the motives underlying these particular announcements are in any way representative of those which informed the other announcements we witnessed in our eleven-year survey; but neither would we think they were entirely inappropriate. In any case, we present them below.

> Even the most self-serving of professional groups—academics are a good example—cannot expand indefinitely without appropriate financial and political support (Cohen 1985:168).

In a popular essay written in 1983 (but not published until 1986 due to various delays) I first made the same unwarranted claims that characterize the 340 other announcements. Having at that time only the most superficial understanding of the deficiencies inherent in official crime statistics, and both believing and being influenced by the unwarranted claims of increasing violence that the Department of Justice and other interest groups were pressing, I uncritically accepted the various claims and concluded that violent crime was 'radically' increasing in Newfoundland and would continue to do so in the future.

In reviewing recent decades, I wrote that the 1970s "brought radical and obvious change," and that "the society steadily increased its rate of serious crimes" when in fact the results of our research project have now made it clear that this is not the case. Moreover, without any evidence other than official government statistics, I managed to retail the prevailing myths of a "crime-free past" and a "crime-ridden present" which O'Grady and Overton so effectively demolish in their essays in this volume. Moreover, I discussed "disturbing rumours of violent assaults," assuming that because I was now personally hearing about these downtown assaults it must mean that they were increasing (in fact, I was hearing about them simply because for that brief period I was involved in the downtown bar life. In previous, or ensuing, years I had no personal contacts in the city's nightlife and simply had never heard of any isolated incidents). Similarly, based on a few isolated incidents, the gossip around the city, and the comments of the press and the various self-serving agencies, I managed to conclude that "by the 1980s, this escalation [of violent crime] was well advanced indeed, with casual knifings and assaults by strangers upon one another, with frequent rape, sex murder, and even matricide and patricide." In fact, there had been one incident of sex murder, and one young man had murdered his mother and father; yet the reader, and the writer, were left with the distinct impression that these acts were, or were about to be, widespread. Like many of the ideologues O'Grady discusses, I claimed that this was a consequence of a "rent in the social fabric," although I had no evidence whatsoever that this had occurred; and I managed to suggest that it was no longer possible "to walk the streets of old St. John's in complete safety."

In an extensive *Evening Telegram* interview published in 1983 (which O'Grady discusses in this volume), more complex and emotional cross-currents emerge. Ostensibly, the interview was a chat with a young journalist (a former student of mine) about the book I was writing at the time (ultimately published in 1986 as *Hunting Humans*), but I rapidly converted the interview into a political document for my own careerist ends, retailing mounds of unsubstantiated speculation to advance my case. Entitled *Memorial professor expects murder rate to climb here*, and appearing under a large photograph of myself, the article paraphrased me as claiming "the system we now have is 'utterly different' now than it was 40 years ago, and is based on hierarchy and inequality with the minimum wage worker and the long-term unemployed at the bottom." With no evidence of any kind other than a speculative report prepared by a senior RCMP officer, I claimed that the "oil boom will accelerate the destruction of the traditional system because it will mean big money for a few, modest amounts for a few more, but nothing for most people." I thus converted a vague left-of-centre political position into a scientific judgement on violence patterns, as in "Leyton sees an increasing number of mainland-type murders because of the gradual chipping away of traditional social and structural phenomena which have in the past operated to keep the rate down."

This unjustified speculation was soon transformed into a political document of quite another kind. In 1982 and early 1983 I had been especially active in attempts to develop practical social profiles of serial killers for the use of police. The assumption guiding my work was that serial killers would have similar social backgrounds (cf. Leyton 1983); that these profiles could be superimposed on the police suspect list in any individual case; and that the police use of these profiles might radically accelerate the time involved in apprehending the killers. These assumptions may or may not be correct. However, the work had suffered a series of rebuffs during its early stages, when I was intoxicated with excitement at my supposed discovery. The editor of an American police journal had seen an early, and unpublishable, draft of the essay and had insisted upon publishing it, only to reverse his decision several months later, claiming (with some justification) that the work was unfinished. At the same time, while I had received encouragement from the U.S. Federal Bureau of Investigation and the Royal Canadian Mounted Police for this work, neither of these agencies was able to supply me with the detailed social data on killers that I required if I were to make the social profiles statistically acceptable.

Further, my attempts to obtain such social data from the Solicitor-General's office in Ottawa were ignored. Feeling disaffected and unjustly denied, I took advantage of the request for an interview on my purely academic research to *make a political case* in an apparently purely objective manner, hoping naively that the authorities would then put pressure on Ottawa to release the data. Moreover, I argued that the social profiles were being unjustly suppressed, and cruelly reminded the police of the difficulty they have in capturing serial killers, while implying (without any evidence) that my work could certainly help them. I thus allowed myself to be presented in the following manner:

> About a year ago, Leyton was really excited because he began to develop techniques for compiling social profiles on mass murderers. The FBI and the RCMP were patting him on the shoulder,

but when he asked for access to data in police files, the police backed off. Leyton attributes this to RCMP distrust of outsiders. Without the data, he had to put the practical work on the back burner (*Evening Telegram* December 1985).

This clearly implies, as I meant it to imply, that actual murder cases might have been concluded more quickly, and lives perhaps saved, had I been given the information I requested.[4] Thus half-conscious desires and ambitions distort the interviewee's perceptions and encourage him or her to overstate the case, converting objective discussions into political documents for personal political ends — furthering the person's career, or expanding the interests of the group to which he or she is affiliated.

Finally, in a *CBC Radio* interview given at the time that I was first formulating this research project, I discussed the forthcoming work on violence in Newfoundland in terms of two utter misapprehensions. The first was a cluster of homicides in the province which gave me the "impression" that the murder rate was exploding; and the second was an official report from one government department which announced a 20 to 40 percent increase in violent crime in Newfoundland. I uncritically accepted the veracity of this government report, and assumed that the group of homicides was not a random cluster but an ominous trend for the future, perhaps primarily because it supported my own position — which was the need for a large research project. With equal lack of careful thought I assumed that remarks passed on to me from officials in the Department of Justice, which denied that there had been any real increase in the rate of violent crime, must be politically motivated. That is, I assumed that these officials were wrong, but had been ordered by their superiors to play down the increase in violence. My interests pressed me to consider that any contradiction of my 'insights' must be sinister in origin; since they offered no hard evidence to dispute my claims and, as important, their position defied my own anecdotal evidence while making my proposed research seem somehow less exciting and important. All these half-conscious distortions, sentiments, and motives had the effect of enhancing the importance of my research project and conveying to the public the feeling that I was to strip bare a social matter of significance.

In the examination of the eleven years between January 1975 and December 1985, and the 341 announcements of crime waves that appeared in a single newspaper, we shall see that such squalid sentiments, motives, and stratagems might not be entirely foreign to other individuals and institutions – some legitimate and noble in their ultimate aims, others less so. Regardless of their legitimacy, we all came to believe what we wanted to believe, allowing unconscious or half-conscious interests to influence our perceptions, announcing explosions of violent crime in order to validate the expansion and enhancement of our ideological, political, and economic domains. Figure 1 shows how these announcements varied over time, while Figure 2 charts the relationship between press and non-press announcements. Figure 1 makes it clear that the rate of announcements is not related to actual changes in violent crime rate (see figures in O'Grady, this volume), and Figure 2 demonstrates that non-press generated announcements were more frequent in six of the eleven years, and tied with the press in one: the press made more announcements than the non-press institutions in only four of the eleven years surveyed, and their announcements seemed primarily related to "crimes" which caught their attention, such as vandalism or armed robbery, rather than attention to any actual rates.

"SHOCKING REVELATIONS" – THE PRESS, LETTERS TO THE EDITOR, AND THE PUBLIC

Table 2 shows how the year 1975 was characterized by a kind of balance of announcements between the various institutions, and that social agencies and social action groups had not yet learned to use violence in the same manner.

1. *The Police Brotherhood.* The first reference to violence came neither from the press nor from any official source, but from the lobby group representing the rank and file of the local constabulary. The Royal Newfoundland Constabulary is the only unarmed police force in the Americas. For a variety of reasons, none of which have ever been publicly described, or admitted, the majority of the rank and file would prefer the force to be armed. No serving member of the force has ever been killed by a gun, and the absence of hostile gunfire from the public makes it difficult for the brotherhood to argue their case. This problem is resolved through the stratagem of drawing attention to killings of police officers which have taken place elsewhere, and implying that such killings are inevitable and imminent in Newfoundland. Under the January 6 headline *Police Brotherhood seeking sidearms for night patrols*, the story ran: "The Brotherhood President said that if crime continues to increase at the rate it has been for the past few years [there had been no such increase], 'then next year we will have to talk about having the

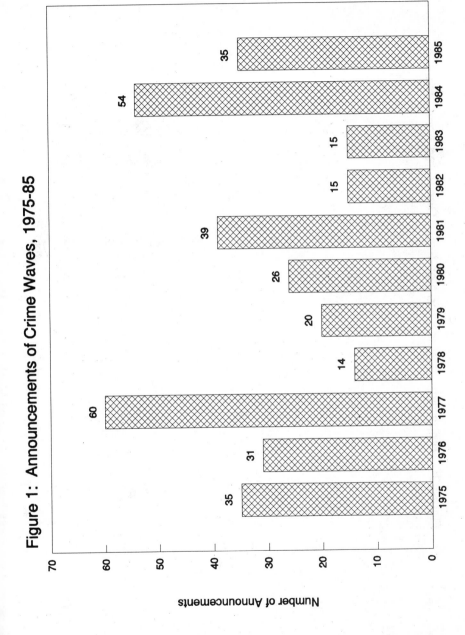

Figure 1: Announcements of Crime Waves, 1975-85

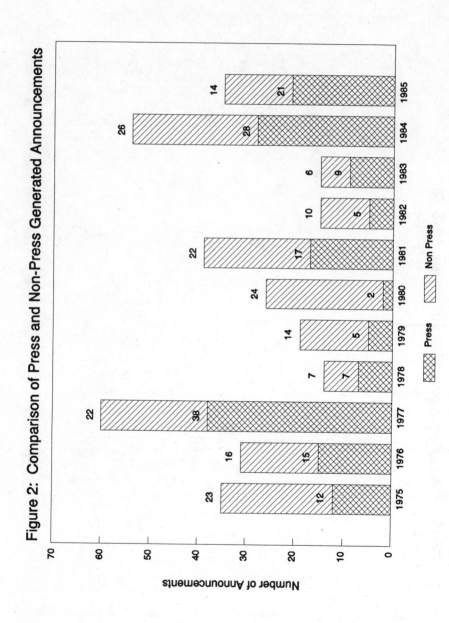

Figure 2: Comparison of Press and Non-Press Generated Announcements

Table 2

Announcements of Crime Waves in 1975

GENERATORS	FREQUENCY	
The Press		
Editorials	6	
Crime stories	5	
Union violence story	1	
Subtotal		12
Members of the Public		
Letters to the Editor	9	
City merchant	1	
Subtotal		10
Justice System		
Royal Newfoundland Constabulary Brotherhood	2	
Toronto Police Chief	1	
Probation Officer	1	
Police Chiefs of Canada	1	
Subtotal		5
Politicians		
Minister of Social Services	1	
Mayor of St. John's	2	
Provincial Premier	1	
Provincial Opposition Whip	1	
Subtotal		5
Government Bureaucraciies (Non-Justice)		
Statistics Canada	1	
Avalon School Board	1	
Subtotal		2
Social Agencies & Social Action Groups		
Pentecostal Assemblies	1	
Subtotal		1
TOTAL		35

evening patrols armed and then if it continues to get worse we'll consider arming the whole force.'" The newspaper did not question his assumption of escalating crime, and allowed him to continue with the following unnecessary caution: "Detective X said they will also be looking for a number of bulletproof vests as well as having a couple of men trained as firearms instructors." The president consolidated his argument by appealing to the sentiments of the readers, saying "they are also looking into the possibility of having a special insurance policy for brotherhood members whereby if a police officer is killed in the line of duty his family will receive an adequate income." He confirmed the imminence of such a tragedy by directly linking the force to other killings: "Three members of the organization [the Newfoundland brotherhood] will be in Toronto to attend a conference on punishment for the killing of police officers." If the argument proved unsuccessful, it rehearsed and established many of the themes that would be deployed by other interest groups in the ensuing years. These include the introduction of data from other parts of the country, or even from other countries, with the implication that they are directly relevant; the manipulation of data to leave the reader with the impression of an explosion of violence; and the use of emotive images such as bulletproof vests and grieving widows and orphans to enhance the argument.

On January 14, individual members of the brotherhood, who refused to identify themselves, issued a press release continuing their campaign to be armed by drawing dubious conclusions from rumours about the theft of guns from private homes in the city. Under the headline, *Police concerned criminals may start using stolen guns*, the reporter wrote:

> Criminals have stolen close to half a dozen hand guns from private homes in St. John's during the past couple of months, and a police officer says 'it's only a matter of time before they start using them against us.' The officer, who did not want to be identified, said the guns were taken during break-ins at private homes and not one of them have been recovered. While not giving the actual number of hand guns stolen, the officer said 'it is close to half a dozen. . . .We know that these guns are in the hands of "criminals" and how many more do they have that we don't know about?'

Implying that not knowing how many guns were in the hands of criminals was a new situation, the officer then went on to emotionalize his argument: "The officer said that during the past couple of years violence against policemen has increased in the city and there are indications that grudges are being built up against individual members of the constabulary." Thus the unidentified officer retailed rumours of thefts and "grudges," thereby converting them into a kind of reality. He emotionalized the issue by pointing out that the stolen guns were now in the hands of "criminals" who, he speculated, might be plotting revenge against individual officers. This speculation was apparently confirmed by the mention of the unsubstantiated claims of an increase of assaults upon officers. While utterly groundless, this press release might have been more effective if the chief of police had not immediately quashed the story, informing the newspaper that "he has information on only one hand gun that was stolen from a private home," and adding that "it is their [the police's] belief that the person who stole it threw the gun away."

On February 5, an anonymous letter to the editor was printed which gave even more emotional and unsubstantiated support to the police officers' demand for weapons. The writer argued that "members of the Newfoundland Constabulary are entitled to protect themselves," although he did not say what the threat was, given the complete absence of serious violence against the police. He or she then moved into an emotive illustration, conjecturing that, "If a policeman was shot to death in the line of duty, what do you tell his wife and children? How do you explain that he was not properly equipped to meet the demands of a job which expects him to place his life, in some situations [none of which had occurred in Newfoundland], on the line?"

2. *Politicians*, furthering their less apparent political interests, made five announcements during 1975. On January 29 the Minister of Social Services attempted to expand his bureaucratic domain by claiming an increase in social problems. He announced an increase in child abuse in the province, despite the fact that he had no evidence of this other than a rise in reports of child abuse to his agency. With such a small number of cases, any "increase" was statistically meaningless, or more likely to represent an increased willingness to report cases, as his advisors must have known, but it proved to be an effective stratagem for increasing his department's visibility to the public and arguing within the civil service for greater funding for his department. Under the headline *Child abuse on increase. 20 cases last year*, the *Evening Telegram* recorded that "Social Services Minister *X* feels that continual efforts are needed to create public awareness of the existence and seriousness of child abuse in Newfoundland and of the general public's responsibility to report all suspected cases to the proper authorities. Mr. *X* noted an increasing concern over child abuse throughout Canada and confirmed that the number of cases being reported is increasing."

On April 12, the Mayor of St. John's, responding to a few acts of vandalism that had occurred at the city hall, said she was "ashamed to be mayor of this city." The newspaper reported "People working at city hall should be paid 'danger pay' added the mayor, because a person is certainly taking his or her life in their hands by working there now." On closer examination, these "life-threatening" acts turned out to be the breaking of a few windows and a number of empty bottles of cheap "pinky" wine dropped in the city hall's parking lot. Similarly, on April 17, the Opposition Whip in the provincial legislature used a bogus increase in vandalism to score his own political points. Under the headline *Opposition Whip fails to get debate on vandalism*, the paper noted "Opposition Whip *B* failed Tuesday to have the legislature adjourn its regular business and debate what he termed 'the failure of this government to take appropriate action and implement moves to deal with the increase in vandalism that has occurred in the province over the past three years.'" Implying that the very fabric of society was coming apart under the sustained pressure of this bogus vandalism wave, "Mr. *B* claimed the Minister of Justice is 'no longer capable' of dealing with the situation and accordingly the House is forced to 'come to grips with the problem.'" His stratagem failed, but it was taken up in another vein by the Premier of the province on May 2, who discussed a non-existent wave of violence, without substantiation of any kind. Under the headline *Premier urges action to curb violence here*, the story read:

> Premier *C* says stern measures have to be taken to cut down on the violence which has hit the province recently. He said Thursday there are two things which have to be done — police surveillance has to be stepped up and courts in the province have to begin handing out sentences which are in line with the seriousness of the crime. 'This crime is no longer just vandalism. It's becoming very serious.' Premier *C* says for a long while there was very little crime in the province and Newfoundlanders were 'easy-going,' but, if the present crime wave is to be halted, the courts and the police will have to act.

As if to confirm the Premier's ideological call for stiffer punishment, and thus aggrandizement of the judicial and police domain, the newspaper added that "Meanwhile, ten persons and possibly more, will be charged with unlawful assembly in connection with an incident at the RCMP detachment headquarters. About 30 people gathered in the area and some entered the detachment before police ejected them." This reporting implied imminent insurrection, but was a common and long-standing Newfoundland pattern of a crowd objecting to the arrest of one of their members by protesting directly to police.

3. *Letters to the Editor* are widely read, appear on the editorial page, and provide an opportunity for members of the public to air their fears and ideologies. In 1975, there were nine letters in the *Evening Telegram* announcing a crime wave. On February 13, headlined by the editor as *Stealing has become a plague*, one citizen wrote that "Everyday facts concerning break-ins and shoplifting confirm that stealing is fast approaching a serious challenge to law and order." He continued, "Even the federal government has had reason to note that in St. John's thieves interfered with mail, e.g.,

Christmas parcels. . ." thus using rumours of a type of pilferage that occurs everywhere to signify a remarkable change in Newfoundland. On April 17, an editor showed an uncharacteristic flash of humour when he headlined a letter, *Stop vandalism: Bring troops home, mobilize militia.* The concerned citizen proclaimed: "Today in this island we are witnessing a developing state of anarchy well documented in your issues. . .I could add some personal evidence regarding property in Harbour Grace where lawless louts are busy dissecting it piecemeal." The writer continued by asking "How can people protect themselves from this uncivil outrage of person and property? For the nonce I would prescribe a flick of the 'cat' or the crack of a .410 but that puts you in an adversary position and pre-empts the law." Similarly, a letter on April 19 supported harsh punishment for such miscreants. Headlined *Strict punishment would stop destruction,* the letter read: "They are young brats of boys who have never felt the sting of leather to curb their unruly activities. Don't tell me I'm wrong. I've seen it and I know what I'm talking about." Again, on April 24, another citizen wrote: "People in St. John's are increasingly becoming fed-up with the growing vandalism and wanton destruction of public and private property. The trend in this sort of behaviour seems to be downward. Things are getting worse rather than better. One hears rumours of a demoralized police force. . . .It is difficult to know how one can try to persuade courts to be tougher on criminals. . . ." On October 11, a very long poem entitled *Violence Grows* specifically linked violence to the increase of wealth in the province, and an accompanying letter from the poet noted: "I believe our Newfoundland is fast becoming tainted with the detrimental effects of good times and the high standard of living which Confederation with Canada has brought us. . . .I believe the horizontal spread of progress is never satisfying to build a good society unless it can be balanced and enriched with Divine guidance."

Throughout the period studied, capital punishment was one of the issues producing the most letters to the editor. On May 6, in *Capital punishment is deterrent,* Pro Bono Publico wrote:

The man who deliberately takes the life of another human being forfeits his own right to life, as the Bible makes quite clear. . . .Does the anti-capital punishment politician really ask us to believe that the prospect of capital punishment has not 'deterred' many a potential murderer in the past, and would not do so again if restored? How does he explain the rising murder rate in Canada, from 180 in 1960, when capital punishment was suspended, to 440 in 1970? Of course capital punishment is a deterrent.

On October 30, another letter to the editor noted that "over the last nineteen years or so, the Canadian murder rate has nearly trebled," and that "over the same period, 1963–1974, capital punishment was increasingly liberalized in Canadian law, and not implemented at all in practice, [and] murders and attempted murders in Canada, and other crimes of violence have been skyrocketing."

4. *Newspaper Editorials* frequently asserted the existence of crime waves, doing so six times in 1975, and consistently using the fear of violence to support a variety of ideological positions. On January 25, agitating for a new federal prison for the province which would provide many jobs in both the construction and maintenance of the facility, the *Evening Telegram* drew attention to an article about a Newfoundlander serving his sentence at a federal penitentiary in New Brunswick. The article "was a shocking revelation about the kind of crime that goes on within such institutions and the conditions that provoke it," implying both that such conditions were too rough for relatively clean-living Newfoundland criminals, and that a Newfoundland penitentiary would not be so violent. Then, writing from an uncharacteristic "liberal" perspective, enabling them to argue for a prison in terms of the latest progressive notions of rehabilitation, thus converting an self-serving economic issue into an altruistic ideological one, the editorial noted: "Last December *Time* magazine published a searching story on Canadian prisons, and referred to Dorchester as being full of smouldering, dangerous tension." While pointing out that "Dorchester is so old and hopelessly decrepit that it is virtually impossible to introduce reform measures," the editorial did not specify the necessary link between the condition of a building and the rehabilitation of prisoners. However, it did connect these two issues when reporting on the local situation, adding that the Newfoundland prison is "almost twenty years older than Dorchester, is hopelessly out of date, and lacks both facilities and staff to provide 'meaningful rehabilitation.'" On other occasions, though, in editorials on other subjects, serving different interests, the newspaper consistently argued for harsher punishments and *less* rehabilitation. This editorial was accompanied, however, by a long and socially progressive article on the antiquated Newfoundland prison, entitled *Pen unable to provide good rehabilitation program.*

In a more typically reactionary stance, the newspaper ignored the provincial Minister of Justice's announcement that the vandalism rate had *not* increased, and pointed instead, in an emotionalized piece, to one act of vandalism—the destruction of the interior of a home. In a June 5 editorial, written with heavy sarcasm:

> We feel that Mr. and Mrs. R. . .would be delighted to have Justice Minister *D* tell them personally that vandalism is on the decrease. They might even believe that the near destruction of the interior of their home did not really take place and the mess they see is pure imagination. We suspect that if the minister's house were subject to the same treatment he would insist that the damage was done by mice and not by vandals. For some time now the Justice Minister has been telling the public that vandalism is not as bad as people think it is. He has the cooperation of the chief of police in making such statements [implying that the two are involved in some kind of conspiracy to keep the truth from the public] but the general reaction of the public is that neither the minister nor the police know what he is [sic] talking about. Their sheet anchor is statistics of recorded crimes and they refuse to swerve from that to anything near an admission that the level of vandalism is something to worry about.

Thus the paper used government statistics when they matched their ideological preconceptions, but denied them when such statistics were inappropriate to their argument.

5. *Crime stories* themselves, the customary primary focus of most criminologists, constituted only five of the year's thirty-five announcements of crime waves. Sometimes painted in lurid tones, their primary effect appeared to be an increase in fear. Thus when an elderly woman was held up for the first time, the story was presented in a manner that gave the impression that such holdups were increasing. Headlined *83-year-old woman sends robber fleeing. Threatened with a knife*, the story quoted her as saying: "'I gave him a good clout right down over the head. . . .It's an awful thing to be held up.' . . . Mrs. *G* said she has been running her store since 1957 and never had that kind of experience before." Equally typically, fears of the misbehaviour of youth, especially unemployed youth, were generated and fanned in sensationalized stories of trivial incidents, such as the series which began on June 19: *Frustrated city residents may form vigilante group. 'Living in fear' of punks* recorded that residents of the downtown core of the capital city were "'living in fear' because of increasing acts of vandalism and terrorizing behaviour of a gang of 'punks' roaming the streets at all hours of the day and night." One resident in a letter to the editor of the *Evening Telegram* said that in the past year, "residents have been victimized by assault, theft, destruction of property and intimidation by a group of 'young punks' who hang out constantly in the area

. . .the group hurls insults and filthy language at young girls and women when they are walking down the street." On June 20, the *Evening Telegram* reporter did a follow-up story, interviewing the 'punks': *'Punks' deny terrorizing district, police 'stupid bunch of baymen'* ("baymen" means country bumpkins) piously recorded that

> a gang of self-professed 'punks' and 'welfare bums,' washing their hands angelically of any responsibility for the waves of vandalism and thefts in the central area of the city, boasted yesterday of their run-ins with the local police, making no attempt to hide their contempt for the 'stupid bunch of baymen.' . . .The chief spokes-man for this gang, a nineteen-year-old with 'a record as long as this street,' laughed off charges by residents of the area that he and his group are terrorizing the district. . . .Pointing to the escapee from the juvenile home, a sixteen-year-old who has been on the loose for three days, the youth said the police 'won't get him. They're afraid of us.'

Heating the atmosphere still further, the reporter noted that "A number of other residents were reluctant to talk to the *Telegram* reporter because of the 'deep fear' they have of the group," although they did not specify the type of retribution they feared.

In a similar vein, the newspaper buried on page four an an-nouncement from Statistics Canada that Newfoundland had experienced the lowest murder rate in Canada and the smallest increase in criminal code violations for the previous year. On June 3, however, the paper ran *Violent crimes on increase here* without mentioning or explaining the distinction between increased reports of crimes and increased rates. The story selected crimes whose reports had increased, without giving similar attention to decreases in other crimes: "Rapes in Newfoundland last year increased 44 percent over 1973, Statistics Canada reported today. . . .Robberies increased by over 50 percent." The paper commented that "although violent crimes increased by only 5.1 percent in 1974 in this province, the lowest rate in Canada, the figures are still high [without saying what they were high compared to]," and concluded: "This brings to 2,354 crimes of violence in Newfoundland during last year compared to a total of 2,227 for 1973.

"TERRORISTS IN THE MAKING"—THE PRESS, THE JUSTICE SYSTEM, MERCHANTS AND UNIONS

Table 3 demonstrates that while the predominance of the press and the justice system in announcing crime waves continued through-out 1976, the generators of such announcements now tended to come from a more broadly-based spectrum of society, with labour unions and various social agencies such as the Status of Women Council and the Alcohol and Drug Foundation using violent crime to advance their own causes. The year's first reference to a crime wave came not from the press or the justice system, but from a social action group—the Status of Women Council—beginning their entirely legitimate agitation for a Transition House for battered women, but doing so by confusing increases in reports with increases in rates.

Table 3

Announcements of Crime Waves in 1976

GENERATORS	FREQUENCY	
The Press		
Crime stories	5	
Editorials	5	
Youth violence stories	2	
Union violence stories	3	
Subtotal		15
Justice System		
Royal Newfoundland Constabulary Brotherhood	2	
Canadian Police Association	2	
RCMP Chief Superintendent	1	
Magistrate in court	1	
Federal Department of Justice	1	
Subtotal		7
Members of the Public		
Board of Trade merchants	1	
Hospital Worker Unions	1	
Letters to the Editor	1	
Subtotal		3
Social Agencies and Social Action Groups		
Status of Women Council	2	
Roman Catholic Priest	1	
Subtotal		3
Politicians		
Federal Member of Parliament	1	
Provincial Member of Assembly	1	
Subtotal		2
Government Bureaucracies (Non-Justice)		
Alcohol and Drug Addiction Foundation	1	
Subtotal		1
TOTAL		31

1. *Social Agencies and Social Action Groups* opened on 10 January 1976 with the *Evening Telegram* devoting an unusually large amount of space (36 column inches) to *Wife-beating always a*

problem. Few charges pressed but more women seek counselling.
Suggesting an increase in the actual rates of wife abuse, despite the
responsible headline, the article read:

> The number of women seeking counselling to deal with the problem
> of wife-beating is on the increase, says Women's Centre employee
> D. "There is an awful lot of wife-beating," said Mrs. D. . . .Many
> women continue to take the abuse until they cannot take it any
> longer, she said. . . . "There has to be more counselling services."
> The volunteer group at the Women's Centre, including volunteer
> professionals who work after hours to counsel women who come
> there, does what it can, she said, but the staff is too small to take
> on long case loads.

Offering professional legitimization of their activities, while stak-
ing out their territory, the article continued: "Psychiatrists in the
city are already too busy to spend lengthy sessions with those who
need that amount of time and some have referred their clients to the
Women's Centre, [Mrs. D] said." Eight months later a similar article
appeared, *Wife beating a real problem*, in which the social action
group expanded its case and used an intensification of emotional
images to leave the reader with a visceral impression that there had
been an explosion of wife-beating in the city:

> The problem of the battered wife is very real in St. John's even if it
> is ignored, says *F*, a volunteer with the Women's Centre in St.
> John's which has assisted in "hundreds" of such cases over the
> past two years. "The problem was worst last Christmas time. . .our
> phone was rung off the wall," she says. The women call in despera-
> tion. In almost all cases the husband is in a drunken rage and she
> is afraid to stay under the same roof. The wife, and often children
> as well, need a safe place to stay at least until dad cools down. There
> is no agency to deal with the problem. The police are next to useless
> in coping with it, so the women turn to the Women's Centre. . . .
> What's drastically needed in St. John's is a 'transition house,'
> common in other Canadian cities, that would be a sanctuary for
> the afraid, embattled wife, *F* says.

Then, arguing its particular economic case:

> Such a large boarding house would have 24-hour staff including
> counsellors, who would help reconcile the couple once the anger
> subsides, or offer guidance if the wife doesn't want to go back.

Making the council's specifically political move, the article concluded, under the sub-heading NO GRANTS:

> The Newfoundland Status of Women Council, which runs the
> Women's Centre, applied to government for money for a down
> payment on such a house two years ago but was turned down flat.
> "The government still thinks a retired men's club is more impor-

tant," commented *G*, during discussion at Saturday's "Women and the Law" seminar at City Hall.

Similarly, various private and public individuals used the issue of violence as support for their ideological and/or political positions. On September 1, a Roman Catholic priest claimed that teenage prostitution and dope dealing were rampant behind a large shopping mall—although the police denied this. The priest called the perpetrators "terrorists in the making," so frightening that "people are afraid of the consequences if they report them." He offered no substantiation for these comments, other than a lack of sympathy with the morality of the younger generation. On January 22, in a clever letter to the editor, "Concerned Youth, Conception Bay South" used a recent incident of gang rape in his area as justification for the construction of expensive recreation centres for youth:

> Lately the youths of Conception Bay South have been getting a lot of vicious publicity about the incidents of sexual assault. It is not just the offenders, but we, the innocent bystanders of the area who are suffering. You hear parents and other people say that if they had any beneficial place to get the teenagers involved, these things would not happen. But that is just it, we don't; Conception Bay South is a sizeable community, and there is lots of space, and great need for recreational facilities. . . .What does it take to make our parents realize we need places to go?

Again, a prominent member of the federal parliament used the "crime wave" to argue against his personal obsession, television violence. In *P takes another swipe at TV violence*, the story ran: "Member of Parliament *P* has again lashed out at the 'growing incidence of violence' being aired on national television networks," and thus linked it directly to a supposed explosion of actual crime. "'Violence in the streets, an upsurge in the rate of violent crimes, vandalism on the increase and juvenile alcoholism are just a few of the results of watching such television programs,' Mr. *P* told a meeting of members of the St. John's United Church Women's Club last night." *P* then used the typical emotional image from anecdotal evidence as confirmation of his position: "Last year in Calgary, he said, a mother found her thirteen-year-old son in a bedroom closet hanging by a belt. Schoolmates testified the boy had been to a party where he and other youngsters emulated a mock hanging they had seen being performed on television by the American rock star Alice Cooper." "Experts," said Mr. *P*, calling upon professional legitimization for his position, "attributed the boy's action to watching this television program."

Finally, on July 26, a prominent social activist posited an "increase" in child battering in order to make his otherwise worthwhile point. *More public enlightenment on child battering*, argued that "Child battering is on the increase in Canada. There is no reason to suggest that the torture is any worse in Newfoundland than any other province. There are battering parents everywhere." He concluded with a dubious statement and a wild conjecture: "There appears to be very little public concern over the fact that hundreds of children in the country are battered to death by their parents every year. The exact numbers are not known but some estimates put the number over a thousand [which would put his estimates on child killing well over the nation's entire homicide figure for the year]."

2. *Labour Unions* began to use — consciously or otherwise — the fear of violence (directed against themselves or against society) as an effective bargaining chip in their political strategy. On April 9, 1976, unions used management's alleged violence against the strikers as a way of showing management's moral bankruptcy. *Cars try to break picket line but 'scabs' fail to get through. Another confrontation at shoe factory* recorded:

> The picket lines at *PR Shoe* were the scene of yet another confrontation yesterday morning between striking employees and workers described as "scabs" by the strikers. *T*, one of the 31 employees on strike for the past two months said last night that he was struck by a car driven by one of the scabs who attempted to plow through a lineup of pickets and approximately 25 other residents. . . ."I was hit and so were two other fellas" he said. . . .Mr. T said the man "gave me a kick and knocked me down" and then "the two of us got in a little fist fight."

On July 1, striking mental hospital workers used violence from patients as justification for advancing their wage claims. *Waterford workers attacked by patients. Broom, mop handles used as weapons*, implied chaos in the hospital, and imminent threats to the lives of the hospital workers:

> Four hospital patients attacked three male nursing assistants with broom and mop handles Sunday night in an attempt to escape from that institution. The patients, who are on the "maximum security ward," are in the hospital for various criminal offenses, said a spokesman for the institution. . . .He said the patients were "well armed" with handles of toilet plungers; and the patients demanded that the attendants hand over their pass keys to the ward and when they refused the attack took place. . . ."These guys figure they were fighting for their lives," he said, adding that the other two nursing assistants received bruises in the attack.

Then, explicitly playing their economic card:

> The local president said the incident demonstrates the danger that
> workers on the ward face, noting they have been attempting to get
> the same salary and pension benefits as the wardens at the
> penitentiary in St. John's. "It's like beating your head against a
> brick wall," said Mr. Q, noting that when their contract expires they
> will be going into negotiations for parity with the wardens.

Thus what must be a common event in any mental hospital, and
always a trial for the chronically underpaid staff, was now made
public at contract negotiation time to score a specific political point.
This stratagem was repeated on November 18, when the union
expanded on the frequency of such assaults and intensified their
impact by upgrading their label to "hostage-takings." *Staff facing
great risk in carrying out their jobs. Hostage-taking at Mental*
recorded:

> A hostage-taking incident at the mental hospital last Wednesday
> is the latest in a series of "continuous" occurrences at the institu-
> tion which has the hospital staff "facing great risk" and has dropped
> their morale to an "all-time-low." "The staff is being attacked every
> other week," the union spokesman said yesterday. "Someone is
> always getting smacked in the mouth or their nose broken."

Then, using emotionalized material, the report continued:

> Sources say the incident last Thursday began when a male patient
> in the Justice Ward, armed with an iron leg from a table, grabbed
> a female nurse in an apparent attempt to escape. "All we want is a
> half-decent wage and a 25-year pension" the union spokesman
> concluded.

3. *The Justice System* continued its activities, with police organizations of the rank and file using highly charged comments on
violence to back up their various positions. On June 23, in *Policemen
fear bill will lead to more violence, crime*, police used their position
to back pro-capital punishment debates:

> Policemen were the most vocal and angry group in Canada Tuesday
> as Parliament approved in principle a bill to abolish capital punish-
> ment. . . .Police Association officials throughout Canada said they
> were disappointed with the decision and expressed fear that the
> bill will only lead to more violence and crime in Canada.

Indeed, one Nova Scotian police official made an especially
irresponsible remark:

> In Halifax, the President of the Police Association of Nova Scotia
> said he feared policemen will now be forced to rely more on their
> weapons. "I don't think you're going to see too many policemen
> killed in the future," he said. "They're going to be watching this kind

of thing and if anyone goes for his cigarette package, look out. . . . The laws are so liberal that everybody is getting away with everything."

This position was echoed by the Newfoundland police local. *There will be fear in Canada. Death penalty decision brings strong reaction* noted:

"It's a tragic mistake," said the Police Brotherhood president. "Even though the law was not enforced before, it was still a deterrent, but now that deterrent is gone," he said, adding that the work of a police officer is going to be much more dangerous because of the government decision [to end capital punishment].

At the same time, on June 24, Canadian prison guards called for walkouts and other pressure tactics because, the story ran, "guards believe that abolition of hanging will remove a powerful deterrent to prisoners who contemplate killing as part of planned escape attempts."

4. *Non-Justice Government Bureaucracies* played a role, with the Alcohol and Drug Addiction Foundation, consistently one of the most extreme sensationalizers (and with the most transparently expansionist goals), announcing in a large article on September 10: *Marijuana smoking, drinking prevalent among Grade 6.*

Marijuana smoking and alcohol consumption among youngest teenagers—even those at the Grade 6 level—is a problem in the city, according to the Director of the Alcohol and Drug Addiction Foundation. The Director said yesterday during an interview that the foundation has 'definite knowledge' of frequent and widespread use of marijuana, as well as the increasing use of alcohol among Grade 6 to 9 students.

No hard data were offered for these' suppositions but they charged: "Police and school authorities seem unaware of the extent of the problem for varying reasons." Adding spurious professional expertise to his foundation's justifications, "The teenage counselling services provided by the foundation. . .bring certain cases to the attention of the foundation which usually would be unavailable to police or school boards because of the atmosphere of trust and strict 'confidentiality,' said the Director." Referring to a Foundation-sponsored 1975 "study" which concluded that 92 percent of 400 students with an average age of fourteen and a half years admitted to consuming alcohol and 24 percent admitted to driving a motor vehicle while drinking, the Director claimed his story was more reliable than most because of the pledge of confidentiality, and then came to what was transparently the point of his interview with the press: "There will be no study of the drinking habits of the teenager this year because of the lack of funds, said the Director. The 'shoestring budget' of the foundation just won't allow it. . . .Before the interview ended, the Foundation Director said the trend in increased teenage drinking is nationwide."

5. *The Press* announced crime waves in editorials, in crime stories, and in its coverage of union violence, yet these constituted less than half of the announcements in 1976. Inflammatory inter-views with the victims of crime featured prominently, as did the use of a number of incidents to indicate an increase in the rate of crime. On February 11, after a cluster of incidents of vandalism, the paper headlined *Vandalism on increase again* and interviewed one man at the scene of several hundred dollars worth of damage: "'They should be put in a gas chamber,' said an elderly customer [of the vandalized business]. . . .'This was just plain badness,' said Mr. *S*, adding 'the worst thing they ever did was to do away with the whip.' Another customer felt that the courts were too lenient on offenders," the story recorded, registering the newspaper's continuing ideological posi-tion on harsh punishment. Again, on April 21, in *Vandals on rampage, businessman wants gun*:

> A businessman says he sees no way to stop vandalism at his premises "unless I'm allowed to use a gun." Mr. *L*, who is "over 70," said he is expected to "go out and take a chance of jeopardizing his life to stop them because I'm not allowed to use any protection." He feels the "whole law is wrong," and those type of people are "no good to society." He feels the law is too mild and if vandals are caught and sent to jail, after six months "they're fat enough for the Last Supper." He advocates feeding them bread and water.

As commonly, the newspaper used purported increases in violence to justify its ideological stance, most especially on the issue of capital punishment. In a February 26 editorial, *Peace and Security*, referring to a current federal plan to eliminate the death penalty, the paper claimed:

> In recent years and months crimes of violence have been on the increase [in fact, they had not]. Between 1965 and 1974 there was a 200 percent increase in rape and a 140 percent increase in woundings and attempted murder. Murders committed with fire-arms rose from 178 in 1970 to 272 in 1974 and most of them were committed with rifles and shotguns, hence the need to control such weapons.

In making this reference to another of their ideological hobby horses, gun control, the editorial at no point referred to the fact that the figures were national (the Newfoundland statistics had not changed). Again, on June 24, the editorial ignored government figures when they did not meet the paper's preconceptions, and utilized the data when they coincided with the *Telegram* opinions. Here, an anti-abolitionist editorial on the death penalty quoted a self-serving Department of Justice pamphlet announcing the crime wave. "There is a growing public concern about the rising number of firearms incidents in Canada. Every year sees more murders, armed robberies, suicides and accidents than the year before," the pamphlet noted, as part of its own specious campaign to expand the bureaucracy coordinating gun control legislation.

"PUBLIC DISTURBANCES"—THE PRESS, THE JUSTICE SYSTEM, AND SOCIAL ACTION GROUPS

For 1977, the number of announcements of crime waves doubled compared to 1975 and 1976, as the viability of the violence symbol became increasingly apparent.

1. *The Justice System* appeared first during the year. On January 7, the new chief of the Newfoundland Constabulary called a press conference, ostensibly to improve relations with the press, but clearly to politick for a new police building—using fears of an increase of crime to buttress his case. As reported in *Lack of suitable building dividing city's police force. New Chief says divisions being created, efficiency hampered*, the "main purpose of the [press] conference was to exchange ideas with news media personnel and establish a better system of communications between the constabulary and the press. . . .The majority of the force's executive officers and its Criminal Investigation Division are housed in cramped quarters at a former barrack. . .while its patrol operates out of the courthouse." Stressing the need to stop this "waste of manpower" and resulting inefficiency, the new media-conscious chief turned naturally to what crime he could find to justify his case: "The chief also intends to take further steps to curb vandalism in the city. He feels vandalism has become 'almost a way of life with young people' and many of them feel there is nothing wrong with it as long as they don't get caught." Thus the behaviour of the younger generation was sensationalized and appealed to as a justification for the bureaucracy's desire for a new building.

On April 29, the new chief made his case once more, here turning to an increase in drugs. In *Crime rate is rising and chief blames the illegal use of drugs*, the chief left the impression that all crime was rising, not just drug offenses, in order to validate his argument: "The number of arrests for possession of marijuana for the purpose of trafficking has almost tripled over the past five years, and generally, the illegal use of drugs continues to spawn 'sharp increases' in the city's crime rate, says Police Chief," creating images of heroin addicts supporting large habits with which readers would be familiar from newspapers and television. Thus the increased use of soft drugs and increasing arrests for this use are converted, via the phrase "spawns sharp increases in crime," into an image of drug-crazed youth forced into crime. The chief made this explicit when "He associated the high level of theft to evidence which indicates that drug users, in order to foster the habit, have to resort to stealing," although he did not specify what his "evidence" was. The chief noted that break and enter offenses had actually experienced a major decrease, but he managed to convert this also into a political document by the expedient of attributing this decrease to his force's remarkable efficiency: "Chief

Table 4

Announcements of Crime Waves in 1977

GENERATORS	FREQUENCY	
The Press		
Editorials	15	
Crime stories	14	
Anti-union stories	8	
Columnist	1	
Subtotal		38
The Justice System		
Royal Newfoundland Constabulary	4	
Solicitor-General (Ottawa)	2	
Royal Canadian Mounted Police	2	
Crown Prosecutor	2	
Subtotal		10
Social Agencies and Social Action Groups		
Status of Women Council	2	
Kiwanis Club	1	
Ex-convict's Proposed Halfway House	1	
Subtotal		4
Members of the Public		
Letters to the Editor	4	
Subtotal		4
Government Bureaucracies (Non-Justice)		
Alcohol and Drug Addiction Foundation	2	
Subtotal		2
Politicians		
Federal Member of Parliament	2	
Subtotal		2
TOTAL		60

Z attributed the decrease to the department's booster shift program,"
which placed more police on the streets at critical periods.

On June 27, the chief went public on various incidents involving
working-class youths in a public housing project. *Attacks on police
rise. Chief promises action* recorded: "The Constabulary Chief claims
that attacks on police officers are increasing in St. John's, and
promises he is going to do everything in his power to see they are
stopped." This announcement left the reader with a sense of impending insurrection, and the chief developed it further, with imaginative
and dubious statements about increases. "'In the last 18 months
there has been growing evidence more of our people are being
attacked,' he explained. 'Groups of young people are employing
Detroit or Chicago-like tactics and their tendency is to gang up on
officers.'" Transmitting this sense of proletarian rebellion still further, an August 12 story, *Police are keeping area under close
supervision. Public Housing incidents*, reported:

> In the last few weeks there have been reports of slashed tires, public
> disturbances, and a policeman assaulted in the public housing
> area, long considered a "trouble spot" by the police. The most recent
> incident at the project occurred Wednesday night when a police car
> had its tires slashed and a young nineteen-year old was arrested
> for dangerous driving. These incidents in themselves aren't par-
> ticularly alarming. But what is surprising, and of particular
> concern to police, is that incident sparked a spontaneous street
> demonstration as crowds quickly formed and the level of emotions
> turned red hot. . . .There hasn't been anything in the area yet that
> compares to the Graves Street 'mini-riot' of a few weeks ago, but
> the Chief of Police feels the project "is getting to be a real Bogside."

Thus in order to respond to a perceived threat to their authority,
the police created an air of insurrection justifying an escalated
response.

In a similar vein, the paper carried the politicking of Ottawa's
Solicitor-General, apparently anxious to increase the funding of his
own department. Defining an increase in his budget as a "reform"
of the system, the Solicitor-General used the threat of violence to
justify his position: *Escalating violence, chaos predicted if report on
prisons is not acted upon* contained the warning from the Solicitor-
General "that failing to act upon it [the so-called reforms] will mean
continued chaos and resumed violence in federal prisons," as strong
a bargaining point as any bureaucracy could wish. He did not
explain how an increase in the funding and number of justice
bureaucrats would quell violence. The Solicitor-General continued
his campaign on August 31, justifying his ever-increasing budget in

terms of a bogus increase in crime. *Crime fighting costs increasing says Solicitor-General*: "The cost of fighting crime is increasing and may reach $7.8 billion a year by 1985, the Solicitor-General told the Canadian Bar Association. 'There is at least one striking feature to the picture over the past several decades — most things are going up,' he said." The wire story emphasized that "crime rates kept rising," although it did add, unfortunately without explanation or elaboration, the fact that violent crimes had actually decreased in the previous year.

2. *Social Agencies and Social Action Groups* produced only 4 of the year's 60 announcements, yet their special status as legitimate and politically "neutral" institutions may have increased the impact of their statements. On December 15, 1977 the usually responsible rape crisis coordinator at the Status of Women's Council announced an increase in sexual assault: "*R* believes that rape is increasing and that most cases do not get reported to the police. She bases her conclusion on the experience of the rape crisis counselling centre run by the Status of Women Council and on police statistics." Similarly, campaigning for their Transition House for battered women, the estimates were raised on the significance of the problem: *Government rejects proposal to fund transition house for battered women* contained revised estimates to buttress the legitimacy of their case. A general meeting was told that:

> wife-beating is more prevalent than any other violent crime committed against women. And the speaker estimated, that if the truth were known, 30 to 40 percent of all marriages in Newfoundland contain the battered wife — wife beater syndrome. "They're everywhere, from the bottom of the social scale to the very top."

Similarly, a Kiwanis Club meeting wildly exaggerated the case to develop its own program. A January 11 interview, *Kiwanis Club plans program to fight crime* noted:

> Because ever-increasing crime is an unfortunate reality of modern living [although not, of course, in Newfoundland, but that was not mentioned] the Kiwanis Club of St. John's is organizing a program to help ordinary citizens avoid being victims of crime. . . .The program will attack crimes against the home, children, and senior citizens. It will also deal with organizing a civilian surveillance program which the spokesperson said "is not a vigilante group" but just a means of alerting police to any unusual behaviour in the neighbourhood.

3. *Government Bureaucracies (Non Justice)* were relatively inactive during 1977, producing only two announcements by the Alcohol and Drug Addiction Foundation. Under the headline *Marijuana use*

zooming, statistics are startling, the Foundation "released" alarming data:

> Use of marijuana in the city is "continuing to zoom," there is a "slightly upward trend" in the use of chemicals, and a "small pocket" of people still use hard drugs such as morphine and heroin, says the provincial coordinator of the Alcohol and Drug Addiction Foundation. The coordinator said in an interview yesterday the most alarming fact about the use of drugs in St. John's is that younger people, "well down in the junior high school grades," are smoking marijuana.

On September 23, the Foundation continued its typically inflammatory practices, with the ADF's Director stressing that "there is a strong relationship between alcohol and crime." In providing statistics, he said that "65–70 percent of sexual attacks on children are alcohol related and between 30 and 40 percent of sexual attacks on women are alcohol related." The Director also noted that "present facilities to treat alcoholics are overburdened," and he "called for more care centres," thereby increasing the ADF's importance and its future budget.

4. *Politicians* announcing crime waves were represented in 1977 by the lone MP obsessed with sex and violence on television, apparently responding to his limited success by increasing the emotionalism of his announcements. On June 1, under the headline *Church accused of taking back seat. Fight against TV violence,* the MP pointed to:

> the harmful effects television had already had on the province's youth [although he had no evidence for this] . . .including increased vandalism and teenage alcoholism, and predicted that the "full catastrophe will come in a few months time" when cable television begins broadcasting in Newfoundland. The MP said that studies have proven that children have become walking "time bombs" programmed by what they view on television [a decade after this statement, nothing had changed in violent crime rates]. . . .He referred to the Police Chief's statement that St. John's has "gone berserk with vandalism" and to a survey which indicated that 95 percent of all high school students have had at least one experience with alcohol.

The MP thus ably demonstrated how the bogus figures of each self-serving institution support the next.

On July 9, in *MP loses out in bid to curb TV sex, violence,* the MP argued that "every day of delay in setting guides for violence and sex on television means young minds are harmed a little more. . . .He said a recent poll conducted by the American Medical Association showed that many doctors feel television violence is not only dangerous but can cause physical illness." This was not the first or the last time the MP would cite meaningless research.

5. *The Press* were, however, by far the largest contributors (38 out of 60 announcements) to the 1977 figures. They made their contributions in many editorials, in calls for stiffer sentences for criminals, in crime stories and in sensationalized accounts of union violence. A February 17 story, for example, quoted provocative descriptions from a lawyer with a vested interest in the case: *Lawyer says employees threatened with death. Burning result of 'drunken stupor'* followed an injunction taken against striking workers after a company security station had been burned, and RCMP flown into the area. "The lawyer described the people involved in the demonstrations as being in 'a drunken stupor' and resorting to such tactics as throwing beer bottles. He said there have been incidents of people telephoning the homes of other people and telling their children they will kill their fathers and burn their homes." This nonsense was retailed without any check.

The dissemination of anti-union ideology was continued in an editorial on March 12, in which the paper remarked: "In recent strikes there has been an increase in unruly and threatening behaviour and it was reported that in one strike supervisory personnel were bombarded with pieces of ice and beer bottles." Similarly, an article on March 16, *Mental hospital worker facing charges. Hockey game ends in scuffle* gave prominence to a minor incident in which striking hospital workers harassed police officers who were doing the jobs of the strikers during the dispute. Their source was the hockey arena's assistant manager, who "said that after the game finished and the teams were leaving the ice, a number of female spectators, whom he identified as striking non-professional workers at the hospital [how he could be so remarkably astute is not explained], began spitting at members of the Constabulary team." Thus a trivial incident was transformed into a threat of worker insurrection.

On June 11, the press continued their efforts to discredit the unions by retailing rumours of violence. *There could be trouble if picket line crossed. Mental hospital strikers feeling the pinch of strike* noted: "The rumour continues to float around the picket lines [that some strikers might break ranks with the union and go back to work], however, and some of the strikers predicted Friday that there would be 'holy war' if any of their colleagues attempted to give up the strike, cross the picket lines, and return to work." A June 21 story returned to the bogus incident at the hockey game: *Tension ran high so riot squad was called. Mental hospital worker in court over incident at hockey game* noted that:

> A veteran police officer told provincial court yesterday that a confrontation March 15 at the Prince of Wales arena between police and striking non-professional workers at the mental hospital was a "very serious" situation and it was necessary to bring about 30 members of the Newfoundland Constabulary riot squad in to control it. . . .Tension ran high from the opening whistle, he explained, because there were a number of Waterford Hospital employees at the game. . . .He admitted the hospital workers probably had a right to be upset because constabulary members were working at the hospital.

Thus, although the courts dismissed the charges against the workers, the distorted coverage of the event left the public with images of disturbing violence.

"SOCIETY GHOULS"—PRESS EDITORIALS, THE COURTS, AND SHOPKEEPERS

The years 1978 through 1980, inclusive, featured a sudden and dramatic decline in the number of crime wave announcements, although the press continued to contribute roughly half the announcements.

1. In 1978, *The Press* made its first announcement on March 15 in an editorial protesting the closure of the city's only Family Crisis Centre. The editorial stated the Centre's legitimate case in sensational terms, positing an increase in rates to bolster its position. "The need to have a refuge to which battered wives and children can flee in times of stress has been established. . . .The abuse and misuse of wives and children seems to be on the increase everywhere and some social workers regard it as one of the major social problems of today." A May 13 editorial appeared in support of the constabulary, who were at the time receiving criticism from certain quarters. The editorial used the bogus increase in crime rates to demonstrate how important the police were:

> The police of St. John's are busier now than ever before, according to the Police Chief. Almost every kind of crime is on the increase and the services of the police force are in greater demand than ever . . .Statistically, it looks as if the police are still winning, but to go on doing so requires constant vigilance and an alert and well trained and well equipped police force. From all the reports we hear, we gather that the Chief is producing that kind of force.

This theme, the expansion of the police, was argued for again on May 26, when the press distorted police statistics to buttress their argument. The editorial claimed that while the RCMP had clearly stated earlier that:

The slight increase in the crime rate last year can be mostly attributed to vandalism. . . .Now the annual report on crime in St. John's for 1977 has been published and the increase in the crime rate for that year over 1976 is only too obvious. In every area of crime there was an increase [this was incorrect]. . . .And if early observations are any indication of what will happen, 1978 will be another record year for that crime. . . .All these crimes place a heavy burden on the police force. . . .As crime increases so does the work of the police, so that it too must increase in size and range of activities to meet the extra challenge. The criminals must certainly not be allowed to gain the edge over the police.

Table 5

Announcements of Crime Waves in 1978

GENERATORS	FREQUENCY	
The Press		
Editorial	6	
Crime stories	1	
Subtotal		7
The Justice System		
Newfoundland Constabulary	2	
Judges in Court	2	
Newfoundland prosecutor in court	1	
Crown prosecutor in court	1	
Subtotal		6
Members of the Public		
Newfoundland Convenience Store Association	2	
Subtotal		2
Social Agencies and Social Action Groups		
Academic Conference	1	
Subtotal		1
Politicians		0
Government Bureaucracies (Non-Justice)		0
TOTAL		16

On September 28, a cluster of several armed robberies with no injuries to anyone provoked *Stop the robbers*:

Armed robbery seems to be the number one crime in St. John's these days. Hardly a night passes without a report of a holdup involving a weapon [a profound distortion of the actual frequencies]. The risk to the victim is even greater. What is at stake for him is his life. All the robber has to do is to squeeze the trigger or slash with his knife and the victim is going to die or at least suffer a serious wound [there had been no injuries, and air pistols—which are not life-threatening—were among the most common form of weapons used in the robberies]. That's why a solution has to be found to the armed robber.

An October 4 editorial, *Organized crime*, left the reader with the impression that the province had been taken over by the Mafia:

> The peddlers of drugs, be it on the small or grand scale, have been termed 'the ghouls of modern society.' The growth of this nefarious trade has rapidly increased within the past decade. . . .So it should not come as a surprise to learn that it is no longer a haphazard, individual operation, but a well-organized business. It is a setup worthy of the Mafia or other comparable organization and would suggest that, somewhere in the background some such sinister influence lurks.

Not content with lurking sinister influences, a November 13 editorial, *Concern over crime*, used emotive material and spurious statistics, despite the tiny increase even in official crime figures, to push its ideological position. It also justified why the editorial writers felt they could ignore statistics if the numbers did not suit their position on an issue:

> Every crime places a burden on some innocent victim and that is why it is wrong to think of crime in terms of percentages and numbers. A few years ago the Justice Minister pooh-poohed the public concern with vandalism because he as Minister had not seen any sign of an increase in the statistics. Yet those who suffered from the vandals could have easily put the Justice Minister on the right track if he had been prepared to listen. Now there is an obvious increase in the number of armed robberies and the rapes that are being committed are of a more sinister nature [they did not explain the nature of a non-sinister rape]. But the Police Chief would have the public believe that things are not as bad as they seem. He would prefer to have less publicity for these crimes.

Finally, the press began what would become its custom of recounting each armed robbery and providing the year's running total, making meaningless (because of the small size of the sample and the tiny number of robbers involved) "statistical" statements, as in *One arrested in armed robbery. Elizabeth Avenue bank hit*:

> In a daring daylight armed robbery. . .The last armed robbery involving a bank in the vicinity of St. John's occurred in Kelligrews five years ago. . . .yesterday's holdup brings to 25 the number of armed robberies this year. The net total last year came to 9, an increase of nearly 300 percent.

2. *The Justice System* was the second major producer of crime scares. On May 12, a very long story appeared under a photograph of the media-conscious police chief, captioned *Crime on the increase*. The interview appeared to be a political stratagem by the police chief in what was a purely internal political matter—the protest by rank and file officers over the disciplining of a fellow officer arrested for drunken driving. In an address to the city's Rotary Club, the chief said that "the operational efficiency of a police force is in direct proportion to the amount of discipline instilled in that force. Pointing out that crime is on the increase, he stressed that never was there a greater need for top notch discipline in the force than there is now." Thus the chief manipulated the fear of increasing violence in order to discipline his own rank and file officers. "He said drinking by young people has never been so widespread, bootlegging is on the increase, the use of marijuana is unabated and vandalism is increasing," appealing, presumably, for support from both public and police. Reaching for any evidence of an increase in crime, he stated:

> Never. . .were there so many so-called delinquent children of couldn't-care-less parents. As an example, he told the story of parents who gave their child a trail bike: a police officer was requested to apprehend the child while he was riding the bike on a public thoroughfare, in violation of the law. When approached by the officer, he said, the parents' reactions are usually unbelievable. They either tell the officer it is no wonder children have no respect for the police because they are being harassed by them, or they ask the officer if all he has to do is apprehend children riding trail bikes.

Warming to his task, the chief concluded, "These are topsy, turvy times and there is no doubt police must strive to set an example in their public and private lives." (In other words, the rank and file must stop their protest at the chief's discipline.)

Unfortunately, the chief's use of bogus statistics regarding an increase in crime seems to have caused disquiet among the public. On November 11, responding to sensationalized claims appearing in the tabloid *Daily News* about a huge increase in crime (suggested, of course, by the chief himself), the chief blamed the media for spreading the fears, and "assured city residents Friday that as far as crime is concerned, St. John's is comparatively quiet when compared to many Canadian cities." The chief stressed that "armed robbery and rape are the types of crimes the force is alerted to and 'everything is geared to it.' He said this type of crime is fostered by the misuse of alcohol and illegal drugs and the social climate." He added that the force's soon-to-be-constructed new building would "enable us to plan future operations with a greater degree of efficiency," thus reassuring the public, a measure necessary because he had previously disturbed them in order to make a political point.

3. *Members of the Public* made a small but significant contribution to crime wave announcements when the merchants in the Newfoundland Convenience Store Association used a small cluster of armed robberies to suggest that there was a major increase in such crimes, requiring drastic action. In *Store owners plan action on robberies*, the reporter observed:

> Concerned about the alarming increase in the number of armed robberies at their establishments, the membership of the Newfoundland Convenience Store Association will meet next Tuesday to discuss possible ways to protect their employees, themselves, and their businesses [no one had yet been hurt in these robberies] . . .'We're really concerned with what's been going on,' said the president of the association. 'One of these days somebody will get hurt.'

The association treasurer added that "in his opinion armed robbers are being let off too easily by magistrates," and called for a penalty of ten years imprisonment for an armed robbery. On October 4, the association announced a rewards scheme in *Storeowners hope award system will prevent armed robberies*: "Concerned about the alarming increase in the number of armed robberies in the St. John's region," the association had moved to "establish an award system for information leading to the arrest and conviction of robbers." Yet the name and aim of the system obviously had little to do with armed robbery, fears of which were used to justify "Operation Shoplift," aimed at a purely property crime of little concern to the public.

"THE REPRESSION OF CRIME"—THE POLICE, THE COURTS, AND THE PRESS

1979 continued the late-70s pattern of a small number of alarms, which the justice system and the press primarily generated.

1. *The Justice System* was the largest single offender. Their campaign opened on January 24 with a large photograph of the constabulary chief over the headline *Police Chief raps parents for ignoring their children*. Blaming an increase in armed robberies on poor parenting, the chief told the Rotary Club:

> Collective and coordinated action is needed by citizens at large if police officers are to operate effectively and crime is to be repressed . . .If an ideal society is one comprised of strong family units, then our society is far from ideal, said the chief. Day after day, he said, police officers encounter young children roaming the streets either

because there is no one at home to look after them or their parents are too drunk to care. He felt it is a sad reflection on society when parents choose to ignore the fact their children are using illegal drugs or alcohol.

Without an explanation of the meaninglessness of the figures, the chief "noted that the number of armed robberies increased by 311 percent," and "taking into consideration the use of illegal drugs and alcohol, the chief said it is difficult to predict whether or not the number of armed robberies will continue to increase this year." He announced that "in most categories. . .there were a higher number of crimes in 1978 compared to 1977." Lest the police be perceived as slack, however, "he stressed that the force's apprehension and arrest record was much higher in 1978."

Table 6

Announcements of Crime Waves in 1979

GENERATORS	FREQUENCY	
The Justice System		
Newfoundland Constabulary	4	
Judges in court	4	
Subtotal		8
The Press		
Editorials	3	
Crime stories	1	
Anti-union story	1	
Subtotal		5
Social Agencies and Social Action Groups		
Children's Hospital	1	
Status of Women Council	1	
Subtotal		2
Government Bureaucracies (Non-Justice)		
Department of Social Services	1	
Family Court social worker	1	
Subtotal		2
Politicians		
Federal Member of Parliament	1	
Subtotal		1
Members of the Public		
Letter to the Editor	1	
Subtotal		1
TOTAL		19

A few months later, in June, the tabloid newspaper, the *Daily News*, sensationalized rumours that a rapist had been operating in the city over a four year period. The chief responded to the furore in an ambiguous interview which appeared in the relatively staid *Evening Telegram*. The interview could have sent nothing but mixed messages to the public. First he admitted that there might be something to the rumours of a rapist, and then he insisted the public should pay no attention to such rumours: "Not all rape cases are reported, the chief said, referring to rumours in the city of numerous attacks on women, and it is possible there could be something to the rumours. However, the chief counselled the public not to panic at unsubstantiated reports." He then referred to a recent crime where a woman was forced into a car at a shopping mall and raped: the chief said only "We will catch him."

One week later, undoubtedly having been told of the ineffectiveness of his mixed messages, a long story appeared in the *Evening Telegram*. In *Chief denies rape rumours*, the chief "has dispelled rumours that St. John's has become the target for a wave of rapes and child molestations. The chief told a news conference Tuesday that certain news reports and rumours circulating in the city last week were not founded on fact and only served to terrify people." Under the sub-heading, CITIZENS UPSET, "He was unable to say how the rumours began, but, he stressed that he is upset with 'news garbage that upsets the population. . . .Rape is a major crime.'" The chief then confused the issue by adding, "I think we're extremely lucky more women are not being raped," referring to "the large number of women who hitch-hike by themselves." In order to quell the public rumours, he gave an illustration which suggested that many rumours of rapes are false, as when "the child confessed he had lied to his parents because he was late arriving home from school." Some of the force of this denial of an increase in violent crime must have been diluted by the release a few weeks later of alarming, and unexplained, statistics. *Armed robberies increase in St. John's 300 percent. Police report* announced that "There was a 300 percent increase in armed robbery during 1978, the annual report of the Royal Newfoundland Constabulary shows. There were 28 armed robberies reported during the year compared with nine in 1977. A fifteen-year-old youth was later charged in connection with nine of last year's robberies, one of which involved the shotgun theft of about $3,500 from a Bank of Montreal branch."

It was in this year that *judges in court* began to use dubious increases in crime rates to justify their increasingly heavy sentences. On February 1, under the headline *Man jailed for assaulting policeman*, the judge remarked that while "an assault of this nature on any person can never be justified or tolerated, it is even more reprehensible as it was an attack on two officers who were engaged in the execution of their duty. . . .The Judge continued that 'it was absolutely essential' that the general public have the 'utmost confidence' in the police force. 'That confidence will not exist if the courts treat lightly such assaults.'" Finally justifying his position in terms of an increase in crime, under the sub-head MORE VIOLENCE, "The Judge pointed to the importance of this by noting there is an ever increasing tendency to violence in St. John's, 'much of it directed towards the police,'" despite the fact that he had no solid evidence for such an assertion, and concluded that it was therefore essential that police "'be protected from the criminal element in society.'" Similarly, on March 31, under the headline *Bank robber gets prison sentence*, a judge said the sentence was "designed to deter others likely to commit the same offense and to hopefully check the increase in local armed robberies. 'If this rash of armed robberies continues, sooner or later someone is going to be killed,' the judge declared."

2. On January 12, *The Press* opened its year with a sensationalized series on a strike. Written from its usual anti-union perspective, *Abattoir hit by vandals* left the public with the impression of violent workers on the edge of insurrection. "During the first day of a strike by its employees, vandalism struck the Newfoundland Farm Products Corporation's abattoir. . . .The windshields of five parked trucks were smashed and the vehicles' tires deflated, 30 hog carcasses stored in cold storage facilities were thrown around the plant and 28 pigs kept in a barn were let loose to roam around corporation property." This less than bloody "violence" was picked up again three days later on the editorial page: *A deplorable act* commented that "the vandalism carried out by persons unknown against the abattoir on the first night of the strike of members of the Newfoundland Association of Public Employees was bound to damage relations," and "it was a nasty and vicious bit of work."

More commonly, however, the paper used spurious increases in various forms of violence for its own, not always obvious, ideological ends. On March 8, *Too many pubs* noted: "If some authority doesn't exert some control, Duckworth Street and Water Street will eventually become a solid wall of pubs, taverns, cocktail lounges and bars. . . .They are more than just a nuisance, they are a menace. In any city where there is a heavy concentration of drinking places there is usually a higher than normal incidence of violence [an utterly unsupported statement, at best], street brawling and general rowdyism." This allowed the press to increase public anxiety in general by commenting that "There are many people who are nervous of walking on the downtown streets after dark." The writer claimed that "they are afraid of being attacked and beaten by drunken rowdies," although such events were in fact extremely rare.

In the absence of crime news (and crime events) during the autumn, the paper invented a new crime, "verbal vandalism." An editorial commented:

> Vandalism takes many forms, but there can be verbal vandalism as well. On a recent warm Autumn evening, four young lads were strolling along following their evening meal; and the conversation was so brutal as to be frightening. Not a sentence without an obscenity. Not one. One wonders about the language used in the home, in school, at social gatherings.

In mid-November, a cluster of armed robberies permitted a more conventional alarm: On *Law and Order* claimed that

> Citizens are disturbed, alarmed, and rightly so, over the terrific increase in the number of armed robberies that are occurring almost nightly in the city and environs. In 1978, according to the report of the Royal Newfoundland Constabulary, there were three of these incidents. This year they are happening with frightening regularity. . . .The Police Chief was reported as saying [that] because of the current epidemic of armed robbery he fears that someone is going to get hurt, even killed if they're not stopped.

3. *Social Agencies and Social Action groups* played a relatively modest role during 1979. Their contribution began on August 18 when the Status of Women's Council, in quite correctly responding to "jokes" made in the provincial legislature about wife-beating, nevertheless did so by creating spurious statistics. "'Some of these people might think it's a joking matter,' a spokesperson retorted, 'but I can tell you it most certainly is not.'" Meanwhile, the Women's Council survey showed a 400 percent increase in charges related to wife-battering. (Clearly implying that the police chief's purported 300 percent increase in armed robbery, and the newspaper's "disturbed" and "alarmed" citizens, were insignificant compared to the 400 percent increase in wife assault.) To make their case, the Women's Council was reported as saying that "Two researchers were employed to compile the statistics in a report that is now being prepared," and that "A social worker with the family court said as many as 40 percent of the married men in Newfoundland physically abuse their wives," a statement without an iota of evidence. "And the crimes are on the increase," said the Council representative. "In 1974, there were 133 cases reported, in 1978 there were 312 cases dealt with. Also during 1974, there were 19 physical assault cases whereas last year there were 73. So you can see the increase is very

obvious and very serious." Thus a legitimate need to impress the public and the authorities with the importance of their case is translated into the retailing of meaningless and spurious "data" and the manipulation of rates to suggest an extravagant increase in actual rates of offenses, all leaving the public with the clear impression of a terrible growth of violence.

4. *Politicians* no longer played a major role in the manufacture of public anxiety, although on October 29, the federal member of parliament obsessed with television made a curious admission. Under the headline *Sexual perversion threatening very existence of family life. Conference told*, the politician blamed the media, "especially television advertising and soap operas" for the increasing degeneracy of society. Speaking as a "concerned parent," the MP "said he was appalled that the daily rosary, once part of family life, 'has been replaced by *Another World*,'" and without any apparent self-consciousness, admitted "And I have to go through the weekend papers to see if there is anything there that will embarrass my teenage daughter. We've gone the limit," he claimed, complaining that the emphasis on violence in the 1960s has now "come full tilt" to sexual perversion "that is threatening the very existence of the family."

"STRIKING WORKERS ATTACKED"–THE PUBLIC, THE COURTS, AND SOCIAL ACTION GROUPS

The year 1980 demonstrated most aptly how little consistency there need be over the years in the origins of announcements of crime waves, for in this year the press, politicians, and non-justice government bureaucracies virtually resigned from the task, passing the baton to members of the public, the justice system, and various social agencies and social action groups.

1. *Members of the public* were especially active during the year. On January 18, members of the Newfoundland Association of Public Employees Union who worked at the Boys' Training School—for some of the lowest salaries in the province—used the issue of violence, dubious at best, as their bargaining chip in demanding a wage increase. The report read:

> A union spokesman says there have been at least three instances in the past week that justify contact pay for employees of the Boys Home [implying a surge of violence against their staff]. The President of local 6203 of NAPE which represents the striking workers said yesterday there have been three instances where a staff member was 'physically attacked' by inmates. "As a matter of fact,

we have one man off since last Friday as a result of a kick in the stomach," he said. "I don't know how much contact we have to have to justify contact pay."

Conversely, on October 7, the press used violence as part of an anti-union story. Under the entirely misleading headline *Riot police called to picket lines*, the story revealed only deep in the article that there had been no violence of any kind:

> The riot squad of the Royal Newfoundland Constabulary was called to the Sir Humphrey Gilbert Building on Duckworth Street in St. John's this morning to escort non-striking members of the Public Service Alliance of Canada and management across the picket lines established by striking clerks and regulatory workers. Approximately 25 officers arrived around 10:15 attired in helmets and carrying night sticks. The strikers moved away from the main entrance and the police formed two perpendicular lines to the door . . .There were no arrests and no violence.

Table 7

Announcements of Crime Waves in 1980

GENERATORS	FREQUENCY	
Members of the Public		
Newfoundland Association of Public Employees Union	1	
Divorce lawyer	2	
Victim of armed robbery	1	
Letters to Editor	3	
City merchant	1	
Subtotal		8
The Justice System		
Judges in court	3	
Crown Prosecutors in court	3	
The Solicitor-General	1	
Royal Newfoundland Constabulary	1	
Subtotal		8
Social Agencies and Social Action Groups		
Association of Registered Nurses	3	
Status of Women Council	2	
Neighbourhood Watch	1	
Subtotal		6
Politicians		
The Minister of Social Services	2	
Subtotal		2
The Press		
Crime story	1	
Anti-union story	1	
Subtotal		2
Government Bureaucracies (Non-Justice)		0
TOTAL		26

Thus the government's manipulation of the police to suppress the strikers is further manipulated by the press as part of its anti-union ideology through the simple expedient of headlining the use of the riot squad and playing down the absence of violence.

A respected divorce lawyer announced an explosion of wife-battering on January 26:

> One third of divorces in Newfoundland in 1977 were based on "mental and/or physical cruelty," the St. John's lawyer told members of the Corner Brook branch of the Status of Women Council.
> . . .And the brutality is on the increase with national statistics showing that 104 people had been killed by their spouses in 1973—fully 100 percent more than those recorded in previous years. "Eighty-five of the victims were wives," said the lawyer [continuing his blatant misuse of statistics]. . . ."In recent years in Canada, domestic murder is carried out by firearms as the first choice, fists as the second choice, with knives a close third as a tool of homicide."

Admitting the reasons for their crime wave announcement, the meeting "was called to gauge support for a refuge for victims of violence."

On February 23, the lawyer wrote an article for the newspaper which received the entire top of a page: it was a sensationalized "discussion" of family violence, and wildly overstated its case as part of a campaign for a refuge. Under the headline *Family violence: the need for social and legal responses*, the story read:

> Domestic violence knows few perimeters. . . .Clenched fists and household appliances are employed by husbands and wives to injure each other. Parents abuse their children with unwarranted beatings. Some siblings rise up in battery against mothers and fathers. . . .Many victims of this abuse suffer physical and emotional injuries. A number of them die. . . .What is the extent of family violence? The total of domestic homicides in 1973 in Canada represented a 100 percent increase in such killings since 1966. Wrote Barbara Amiel in *Chatelaine* magazine, "By any yardstick, murdering your mate is definitely a growth industry."

Warming to his theme, the lawyer continued: "Students of, and graduates in social work, with whom I have had contact during the past decade [many of whom, of course, have a vested interest in perceptions about the growth of violence] talk increasingly of encountering violent marriages in the course of their work." At no time did the lawyer mention that this increase in encounters of family violence might be because social workers' training now sensitizes them to the issue, rather than suggesting an explosion in the frequency of this crime. Similarly, on December 15, in order to encourage an upgrading of police surveillance of the downtown area, a city merchant whose store had been broken into several times announced that "the time has come for a serious review of law enforcement in downtown St. John's. We are being victimized by an unprecedented crime wave, and the police appear unable to do anything about it."

2. *The Justice System* was equally active during the year. On May 6, a city man received a three-year sentence on a conviction for armed robbery. The judge remarked that the public "has to be protected 'from young men like you'"; and the crown prosecutor used the notion of a crime wave to press for a harsh sentence when he "emphasized that the number of armed robberies in the St. John's area within the past year has grown considerably. He said the news media now reports one just about every week," implying that this cluster meant a clear trend of increased violence. "In asking for a lengthy period of imprisonment, he stressed the deterrence to others who may be tempted to commit a similar offense." Similarly, on May 7, a judge in court used the bogus crime wave to justify his refusal to reduce a harsh sentence. Describing armed robbery as "one of the most serious offenses," the judge remarked that "this type of offense is being committed in the St. John's area with alarming frequency, and it is the duty of the courts to make every effort to curtail it. The prime consideration must be protection of the public." Again, on June 6, a purse snatcher was sentenced with the inflammatory words from the crown prosecutor: "I'm concerned that elderly people, children and others should be allowed to walk safely in the streets without being attacked by hooligans or thugs," implying that the theft of the purse was much more than a rare and isolated incident. And on August 23, before the sentencing of an armed robber, the crown prosecutor remarked that "robberies of gas stations have become almost a common occurrence in St. John's," and the judge "agreed that in view of the epidemic of service station robberies the court must take a more serious view of these offenses" [when in fact it had always done so, regardless of the rate of occurrence]. On October 9, a judge repeated that "the number of armed robberies in this city is becoming alarming."

The federal solicitor-general used the bogus increase in violent crime to justify his department's expansionist strategies. A front page June 19 story headed *Fight against crime will top $1 billion this year* ran: "The cost of the federal fight against crime will top $1 billion this year but only one offender in 600 is ever jailed," the solicitor-general said enigmatically, "emphasizing the serious need for a much larger budget" by panicking the population with bogus statistics. "Property crime has doubled in the last 12 years while violent crime is up 50 percent since 1968."

During the course of this year, the media-conscious Royal Newfoundland Constabulary police chief retired, and his successors (housed in their expensive new building) were infinitely more restrained in their comments to the press and public.

3. *Social Agencies and Social Action Groups* increased their output of crime announcements to six this year, tripling the press's production. The newly formed Neighbourhood Watch used sensational terms on September 26 when the program's chairman, a lawyer, was reported as saying, "The Neighbourhood Watch program is designed to show people how to avoid being a victim. What the Neighbourhood Watch program hopes to do, he said, is to train people to take precautions," despite the fact that there was remarkably little to take precautions about. Moreover, giving substance to groundless rumours, he continued, "All sorts of bizarre things happen in the city everyday," and encouraging further speculation, he added "'the facts of life' dictate that precautions be taken. The trends of the 20th century have come to St. John's. . .you can't take things for granted any more." Here, the lawyer clearly stated that the peaceful "traditional" Newfoundland was gone, buried in a wave of American-style violence.

In November, the Association of Registered Nurses made a transparent appeal for incorporation into the fast-growing violence industry, providing an elaborate rationale for the notion that nurses, rather than other "professionals," would be best suited to deal with the problem of violence:

> Nurses have a vital role to play in re-orienting the health care system to more appropriate goals of family and community health, according to a Professor of Nursing. . . .She said the major health problem today is not cancer or cardiovascular disease but that of the unhealthy family which develops through destructive lifestyles. . . .Destructive lifestyles occur through disruption of a family through divorce, juvenile delinquency, job loss, battering, mental illness, crime and so on.

Having made the connection between family health and violence, the professor then linked both to nursing. She "stressed that health behaviours are learned initially in the family," and "she sees nursing as being a primary health resource for families and for the community." To demonstrate this primacy of the nurse, "A model of nursing was set up to complement services provided by other professional health care workers," and the model "gives a full role to nursing," as one might expect. The following day, under the headline *Nurses key figures in halting child abuse*, the nursing conference was given a major story, featuring preposterous claims by another professor that "nurses in hospital case rooms during the first four days of a child's life should be able to detect, with 85 percent accuracy, high risk patients who might batter or abuse their child. . . .Speaking at a family violence session during the Association of Registered Nurses of Newfoundland annual meeting, the associate professor of pediatrics said a nurse should study the parents' reaction to a new baby; how the mother looks; and what she says and does." Assigning preternatural insight to the nurses, the professor said "If the interaction between parents and child seem dubious the nurse should take steps," and these remarkable steps would somehow "hopefully prevent neglect or abuse of a child." The professor was rash enough to even detail the "negative behaviours" which would presumably alert the nurse: "Initial reactions of the potential child batterer include denial of the pregnancy and depression over it [a phenomenon more widespread than child abuse], no planning for the child's arrival [ditto], overconcern over the sex of the child [ditto], and concern over the child's performance and whether or not he is normal [ditto]." The professor quoted U.S. statistics which "indicate that one and one half million children have been abused in this decade," and without support of any kind, said "There are an estimated one million potentially abusive people in the U.S." The professor went on to give an emotionalized anecdote of how one child was cruelly abused, and then saved by a nurse. At the same panel, a nurse outlined some of the "necessary" services nurses could provide; thus specifically blueprinting the expansion of their professional domain. "She said a crisis nursery is needed for children under two so they can be protected and parents can be rehabilitated. There should be a foster parent training program [and] also a broader public health program so that nurses can visit more homes and probably prevent some cases of abuse." Exactly how visits from nurses would prevent such abuse was not explained. The talks ended with a standard technique for suggesting that great scientific thought and professional expertise had been injected in the matter, by categorizing and listing ten "types" of child abuse.

The Status of Women Council pressed its case on November 18, under the headline *Home for battered women may be established soon*. Announcing a crime wave in order to politick for the quite legitimate refuge, the article ran:

Showing a dramatic increase in the number of cases involving wife-battering, the Newfoundland Status of Women Council says a transition house for battered women in or around St. John's may soon be established. Final negotiations between the council and government agencies in the federal and provincial levels have begun to obtain funding for such a home. Statistics from the Royal Newfoundland Constabulary show, for the St. John's area alone, there are about five reported cases each day where women ask for police assistance in family disputes involving violence. These statistics also indicate a 130 percent increase over three years in the number of violent incidents involving women. In 1978, the reported cases numbered 834. Last year, the number of reported cases jumped to 1,275 and, already during the first six months of this year, police report 946 such cases.

Until the end of the year no mention whatever was made of the distinction between an increase in actual occurrences and a heightened sensitivity to the problem leading to more reports. Thus, in order to confirm the legitimacy of their case for a transition home, statistics were presented without explanation and were misinterpreted as a kind of avalanche of recent violence against women, for which there was no reliable evidence. The only negative comments on these announcements at the time came from a St. John's woman who remarked, in a letter to the editor, that "you have to hand it to the group of girls who operate under the trade name of Status of Women—Women's Centre-Planned Parenthood. . .for their ability to manufacture employment for themselves with your tax money and mine." This comment was ignored by the Minister of Social Services, eager to expand his own domain, who echoed the figures and the statistical distortions on December 20: "As the minister noted," ran the report, "the number of documented cases of wife beating has increased in recent years. In 1978 there were 834 cases reported to the police. In 1979 there were 1,275 cases and another 946 cases during the first six months of this year." Untypically, both the minister and a member of the Women's Council stressed that "the number of incidents reported does not necessarily mean family violence is on the increase. Rather, women have decided they won't accept this type of abuse any more and are taking appropriate action."

"BREAKDOWN OF FAMILY LIFE"—THE PRESS, SOCIAL AGENCIES, AND THE COURTS

Unlike actual violent crime, announcements of waves of violent crime increased by 50 percent in 1981 over the previous year. Less than half of these announcements were from the press, and politicians played a relatively minor role, while social agencies and the courts moved to the forefront.

1. *Members of the public* appeared only in letters to the editor, and their four contributions both announced, and explained, crime waves. A graduate of a correspondence course in criminology wrote on February 5 under the headline *Breakdown of family life contributes to crime waves*:

> Crime and violence are becoming a way of life in much of the world today. Shocking crimes which a decade or two ago would have made front page headlines are now so numerous that, in many cases, they are no longer news. Offenses of murder, armed robbery, aggravated assault, rape, burglary, arson, vandalism and the like continue on the upswing around the globe, despite ever-increasing expenditures of law enforcement. The crime wave is sweeping underdeveloped and developed countries, democratic and communist. Why is crime skyrocketing? It's back to the home—the basic building block of society—that's where most crimes can ultimately be traced. The breakdown of family life and the home is a major social trend in nation after nation. Consequently, the home which should stand as a strong bastion of resistance against permissive and lawless influences of society is no longer playing its proper role.

The same writer followed this up on March 3 with *Pornography corrodes the pillars of civilization*:

> Under the guise of constitutional rights and freedom of expression, the floodgates of filth and perversion have opened wide. The experience of many law enforcement personnel who have caught savage sex criminals with a room full of pornography tells a different story. The news media daily relate the wave of rape, crime and other despicable acts all over the world. Wherever it [pornography] is permitted to take root, it breeds criminal vice and violence.

While the police brotherhood had consistently used the crime wave to argue that the force should be armed, another citizen on March 13 demonstrated the flexibility of ideology by using the crime wave to justify his claim that police should *not* be armed. Under *Don't arm the policemen*, he wrote: "the ever increasing number of police officers killed or wounded [suggests] that if our police are permitted to carry firearms, then there is one thing for certain—the criminal will likewise have to carry firearms to give them the added protection."

2. *The Press* began its announcements on February 14, with an editorial on the subject of arming the police, which sent profoundly mixed messages to the public: it urged that the public should not

panic despite that "fact" that "Most citizens are alarmed at the
increasing increase [sic] in the number of 'stickups' and armed
robberies around the city, especially at service stations and other
establishments open during the nighttime." An editorial on May 11,
Thought for Police Week, mused on "the frequency of crimes of a kind
that once were few and far between. . . .Everyone recognizes that we
are facing a new dimension in crime, alongside of which the latest
rash of 'stickups' will look like a game of 'cops and robbers.' In this
Police Week, let's think about it—but everybody!" *Trouble in Saint
John* on May 28 drew attention to chaos that purportedly took place
in another province when police went on strike, but suggested that
such riotous conditions would also prevail in Newfoundland: "We
have seen how quickly a relatively peaceful Canadian city, like our
own, can be thrown into destructive turmoil and terror, as soon as
the men in uniform leave the scene [the "terror" was some drag-
racing and looting of shops]. That fact should make us all appreciate

Table 8

Announcements of Crime Waves in 1981

GENERATORS	FREQUENCY	
The Press		
Editorials	8	
Crime stories	8	
Anti-proletarian story	1	
Subtotal		17
Social Agencies and Social Action Groups		
Canadian Guidance and Counselling Association	3	
Status of Women Council	2	
Committee on Child Protection	2	
Subtotal		7
The Justice System		
Judges in Court	4	
Constabulary's Crime Prevention Unit	3	
Subtotal		7
Members of the Public		
Letters to the Editor	4	
Subtotal		4
Government Bureaucracies (Non-Justice)		
Department of Social Services	2	
Family and Community Services	1	
Subtotal		3
Politicians		
The Minister of Social Services	1	
Subtotal		1
TOTAL		39

what a good police force means to a modern community." On June 16, *Keeping the RCMP* observed: "The evidence is all around us that new kinds of crime are developing, e.g. the armed robberies and associated felonies, and most observers are predicting a real upsurge in criminal activities, of a truly nefarious nature, when the offshore oil development begins to move." Finally, on December 23, in reaction to the tragic sex murder of a young girl, the editorial noted: "That kind of death, that kind of crime is almost foreign to our midst. The fact that it has raised its ugly head among us is a signal to indicate the reefs that lie ahead, the evil of the modern, permissive society with its greed, passions, liquor, drugs and other forms of high and licentious living, that have penetrated deeply into our once pure and well-behaved towns and cities." No evidence was offered for either of these assertions—that the province had once been "pure and well-behaved," or that such murders were a new kind of crime—indeed, they were not.

Crime stories endlessly repeated these notions of an increase in crime, and a new sinister character to these crimes. By March 24, *Armed robberies have increased in city* appeared on page two: "The number of armed robberies or attempted armed robberies in St. John's is up this year from last with 11 reported so far, compared to 5 in the same period last year. A spokesman for the Royal Newfoundland Constabulary said that last year there was one armed robbery in January, another in February, and one attempted armed robbery in each of January, February and March." Making a meaningless comparison, the paper added that "So far in March there have been two attempted armed robberies and four armed robberies." This pattern of rehashing the year's robberies with each new robbery, and comparing them to the previous year's continued, as on October 15, *Armed robbery at grocery store* recorded that "a masked man, armed with a knife" had robbed the store. "It marked the second armed robbery in the city this week," the reporter noted, implying a new crime wave. "So far this year there have been 17 armed robberies and four attempted armed robberies reported in the city."

3. The *Justice System* produced seven of the year's 39 announcements. On February 13, a judge in court explained his decision not to release an alleged armed robber from custody: "He described the offense as a serious one and stated that there are 'too many armed robberies in this town.'" On February 28, another judge justified his sentence for a woman who had been bullied into participating in a bank robbery: "In passing sentence, the judge

pointed out that armed robberies in the province have become very frequent. 'They are becoming more serious with each offense committed,' he said," although he offered no evidence for this assertion.

On April 22, the Royal Newfoundland Constabulary's newly-formed Crime Prevention Unit held a seminar for business people on the correct manner in which to respond to an armed robbery—but this was, after all, their job, and they performed it without recourse to emotionalized metaphors or spurious statistics. Again, on October 9, under the headlines *Crime in city on the upswing*, the CPU spoke rationally and without sensationalizing the material, while pointing out that the increase in recorded crime in the city was primarily in break and enter, and armed robbery. It was left to the reporter to point out that "In the past year the frequency of armed robbery in the city has jumped 400 percent." The CPU constables reminded their audience that "most of the robberies in St. John's are 'penny-ante stuff,'" and correctly observed that the recent surge in crimes can be traced to "a growing population, expanding boundaries [meaning constabulary jurisdiction over more citizens], and the perennial high unemployment rate throughout Newfoundland." They urged "caution" rather than panic. At the end of the year, the CPU reminded the press that "fear of crime is not present in many neighbourhoods because they are not being subjected to a great deal of vandalism or theft." According to a December 10 story, *Constabulary hoping to reduce high number of armed robberies. Seminar held for store employees*, the CPU informed business people that "the number of armed robberies in St. John's has increased about 70 percent in the first ten months of this year." In an attempt to involve the public in their programs, the CPU also reminded business people that "You could become a victim any day at all."

4. *Social Agencies and Social Action Groups* were responsible for seven announcements during 1981. The Status of Women Council, politicking the municipal council for permission to renovate its Transition House, was interviewed on March 24 and given extensive coverage on page two. "The Newfoundland Status of Women Council wants the centre to be a haven to which battered women can retreat and take stock of their situation without harassment. . . .The Transition House will have an administrator, a secretary and four counsellors trained in social work and family counselling, the council's official said, and added the centre will also have federally-funded child-care workers." Having sketched the size of their unit, they justified it in the usual manner:

According to statistics released by the Social Services Minister, when announcing the provincial funding last December, 946 calls for intervention in family violence were made to police during the first half of 1980, compared with 1,275 cases reported in 1979. For every call made, four more go unreported but show up later in hospital and police reports, according to the council official, [allowing the figures to swell impressively] who adds that family violence is increasing in the province.

On October 7, having established the Transition House, the officials launched a campaign for additional funding. In order to justify these additional demands, communications with the press implied that levels of wife assault in the province were now unprecedented. *Local Transition House operating near capacity* explicitly noted that violence was increasing at such a rate that their original accommodations were now insufficient:

> Women and children have been filling the Transition House for battered wives in St. John's to near capacity since the facility opened. The House Administrator said yesterday things were so hectic. . .a waiting list had to be drawn up by the house staff which could have filled two more transition houses of the same size. . . .
> Now, when there are more demands on the project than can be dealt with, the administrator said, like four weeks ago, members of the Women's Council have been called upon to house battered women. . . ."That's a very difficult thing to do and we do it just for safety when we're blocked and faced with a woman in an absolute emergency."

Only at the end of the story did the official announce that "operating costs for the house" had turned out to be "higher than anticipated," and she noted that "the Status of Women Council and other concerned groups and individuals are gearing up now for a fundraising effort before Christmas," thus explaining, perhaps, why the interview had been given.

Speakers at the three-day conference of the Atlantic Chapter of the Canadian Guidance and Counselling Association stressed the "increase" in crime, and the unique ability of guidance counsellors to deal with this social problem. On October 9, *Violence on upswing among Canada's youth* presented "statistics" showing that one-third of the fifty-six youths serving heavy terms in federal penitentiaries in Canada came from the Atlantic region—a fact that has many potential explanations, but which was here used to suggest quite unreasonably that (a) the Atlantic region was in a most precarious state, and (b) that guidance counsellors could somehow remedy this. "Whatever the reasons, Mr. *X* of Family Court services in Prince Edward Island says violence has increased dramatically among

Canada's youth since about 1974." He said, "The group which instigates real violence is easier to pin down. 'People from poor families, lower classes, physically or mentally abused and deprived people, the undereducated and drop-outs,' are the people to whom crimes like murder, manslaughter and armed robbery are attributed." He distinguished between the model youth on the one hand, and the delinquent youth on the other, observing that there was a third group which "needed" guidance counselling and, presumably, many more guidance counsellors to deal with them. "This is the group of alienated, non-cooperative youth—standing outside the realm of crime, but needing attention."

Similarly, a group formed against child abuse agitated for funding on October 27, in an article that stretched across the entire page with a large photograph of four officials over the caption "Child abuse conference ends today." Headlined *More public awareness, better services needed. 70 children abused monthly*, the chairman of the Committee on Child Protection said "There are as many as 70 cases of child abuse and neglect reported in the city each month [and] the incidence of sexual abuse and incest are also increasing, but he [the chairman] had no figures available on the actual increase." The following day, the same conference produced *Services currently unavailable for new child abuse program*, which baldly stated that "incestuous behaviour which is now the most prevalent form of child abuse in the province is a relatively new problem [although it offered no evidence for this statement] which is demanding services that are just not available." Here, two social workers with the child welfare division of the provincial Department of Social Services made the case for the expansion of their domain, suggesting they might be able to provide these services, arguing that "100 referrals of child abuse have been received at the St. John's office [implying a major increase] and that more than half of these are incestuous behaviour reports." They then emotionalized their case by reporting that "the average victim of incest is the oldest daughter, nine years old, sometimes younger," but admitted that "Reports of incestuous behaviour have increased in the past two years because more daughters are reporting it and due to increased public awareness of the problem." They pointed to the special expertise of social workers in dealing with the problem, "because social workers are more experienced [than whom?] in noticing the signs of it in the family. He explained that incest is often hard to diagnose in the family and is often discovered in the diagnosing of other problems in the family." Unfortunately, although "efforts to improve the services offered have been expedited in the last year with the introduction of a regional child protection team. . .there are only a few private agencies providing help available for families" and, they hastened to add, "there is a great need for more services."

5. *Politicians* used the remarkably assertive Alcohol and Drug Dependency Foundation to argue for an expansion of both their domains. Under the headline *Province planning major battle against alcohol and drug abuse,* the story noted that "debate began in the House of Assembly Tuesday on legislation to set up an Alcohol and Drug Dependency Commission, which the Social Services Minister says will provide an 'opportunity to bring all existing forces together in a cooperative effort, with the necessary funding, to provide at last a real chance to those suffering from such dependency.'" The minister manipulated data to imply there was an unusual alcoholism problem in the province, when in fact alcohol consumption was *below* the national average: "In stressing the critical importance of the legislation, the minister pointed out that the per capita consumption of alcohol in the province increased from 1.3 gallons in 1970 to 2.4 gallons in 1978, and researchers predict that within two years, it will exceed the national average consumption of 2.6 gallons." Moreover, to provide additional impact to the "researchers'" results, "Additional statistics quoted by the minister indicated that teenage drinking in the province increased by 90 percent between 1970 and 1980," although how they could possibly obtain such a figure was never explained. Similarly unexplained was their assertion that the "estimated 20,000 alcoholics in Newfoundland increased by seven percent per year." To clinch his argument, the Minister took the appropriate action—linking the problem to violence: "The Minister noted, for example, that based on national figures [which is to say they had no idea what the provincial figures were] approximately 1,000 Newfoundland children were victims of alcohol-related child abuse in 1978, and that upward of 50 percent of violent crimes are alcohol related." This connected suspicions of increases in alcohol consumption with clear hints that tragic violence would similarly increase, and justified the expansion of the revised Alcohol and Drug bureaucracy. In the days that followed, the paper ran reaction stories from other groups with a vested interest in such programs, such as the Salvation Army's Harbour Light Commission: "Social agencies in the city of St. John's have—without exception—reacted positively to announced plans by the provincial Department of Social Services to establish an alcohol and drug addiction commission."

"INCREASINGLY LAWLESS SOCIETY"—THE PRESS, LETTERS TO THE
EDITOR, AND SOCIAL AGENCIES

There was a major slump in crime wave production in 1982. The
numbers dropped from 39 in 1981 to 15 in 1982. The largest
generators were the press and members of the public, with no
participation from non-justice government bureaucracies.

1. *The Press* opened on March 16 with an editorial entitled
Extending police force, commenting that "As every reader knows, we
are living in an increasingly lawless and violent society, when
protection by police and other security forces is more important than
ever." Expressing "concern" over recent reshufflings in the geo-
graphical jurisdictions of the Royal Newfoundland Constabulary
and the Royal Canadian Mounted Police, it called for a "royal
commission or some other form of special inquiry" to look into "the
entire field of law and order," describing it as "the only major and
vital area of provincial life that has not been subjected to an in-depth
scrutiny," and insisting that such a venture was vital in this time of
accelerated violence. *Murder in the courtroom* on March 22 referred
to killings between rival factions in the Toronto Sikh community
thousands of miles away, but left the reader with the impression
that it might also occur in Newfoundland. "The courtroom is the
place where murderers are tried for their crimes; it's hardly the place
where murder is committed, gory and grisly murder, right in front
of the eyes of so many horrified witnesses. . . .It's very disturbing to
think that one is not safe from violence even in a courtroom."

A September 30 editorial used a concocted increase in violence
to justify the newspaper's consistent semi-abolitionist ideological
position on gun control. In *The climate of fear*, the writer observed
that "Over the years, Canadians have become very smug about the
safety and security that exists in their country." Suggesting the
readers should feel neither safe nor secure in order to make his
ideological point, he wrote: "But it's beginning to be apparent that
Canada is no longer a place where one can escape from grisly
killings, savage assaults, multiple slayings that can match almost
anything that has occurred below the border [a grotesque abuse of
statistical reality]." Referring to a family annihilation in British
Columbia, he wrote: "Their killers have not been found, and no
motive, other than bestiality, insanity, or greed, has so far been
determined. . . .One of the worst side-effects of this new 'climate of
fear,'" he argued without a shred of evidence, "is the growing
inclination and tendency among ordinary travellers to carry guns
along with them, for their own protection." This was a bad thing, he

wrote, because "one of the basic causes of the frightful crime rate in the U.S. is the availability of guns."

Table 9

Announcements of Crime Waves in 1982

GENERATORS	FREQUENCY	
The Press		
Editorial	4	
Anti-proletarian story	1	
Subtotal		5
Social Agencies and Social Action Groups		
Family Life Bureau	1	
Association of Registered Nurses	1	
Subtotal		2
Members of the Public		
Letters to the Editor	3	
Newfoundland Association of Public Employees	1	
Subtotal		4
The Justice System		
Canadian Centre for Justice Statistics	1	
Canadian Police Association	1	
Subtotal		2
Politicians		
Member of Federal Parliament	1	
Federal House Committee	1	
Subtotal		2
TOTAL		15

Similarly, a story about a neighbourhood dispute in a working-class downtown area was reported as a virtual workers' revolution. *Police launch investigation into incidents on city street* appeared on March 11 under a 30 square inch photograph of a burned house, and claimed "Residents are being intimidated by a group of young people and it appears police are afraid of them. . . .What started out as an argument between two families over a parking spot has led to a man having his home burned down." In a letter to the *Evening Telegram*, a writer had alleged that someone "tossed a firebomb into an upstairs window," and that "the same man and his family were verbally abused by the group for several days with the group repeatedly gathering outside his house and challenging him and his wife, who was eight months pregnant at the time, to come out."

2. *Members of the public* were relatively active as generators, primarily in the form of letters to the editor. On January 29, the day after the Canadian Centre for Justice Statistics announced a

decrease in the homicide rate in a wire copy story printed in the *Telegram*, a letter to the editor entitled *Human nature hasn't changed in a thousand years* commented: "Instability is the hallmark of our times [which are characterized] by violent outbursts of rampant human passion." Commenting on a recent tragic murder, the letter continued:

A child has been brutally murdered in our own quiet city and it probably won't be the last. . . .It is human nature plain and simple. . . .Our cities have become hotbeds of violent and brutal crime. Families nag, scream, shout and curse at one another. Diplomats hurl invectives.

On March 19, a spokesman for a Calgary-based group, used a purported increase in violent crime to justify their pro-capital punishment ideology. "Have the values of Canadians changed to the point where outrageous acts of violence have become an accepted part of everyday life?" the writer asked. He did not specify the manner in which this change of values might have taken place, and referred only to the alleged "cold-blooded murdering of people which occurs across this country with unsettling regularity." The writer claimed that "Violent crime is visibly and statistically on the increase," justifying his position by pointing not to the fact that it has been stable for years, but at the sudden and world-wide increase in the 1960s which enabled him to say that the "average" rate of increase had been 4 percent, clearly implying a consistent escalation of violence every year.

The Newfoundland Association of Public Employees, a union of government workers, used the alleged danger of violent assault on their workers once again as their bargaining ploy for increasing wages and arguing against staff cutbacks. Under a large photograph captioned "Our lives at stake," although none of their lives had ever been lost, the May 1 story referred to an "illegal strike" the union had staged:

Protesting what they termed a lack of employee safety on certain wards of the mental hospital. . . .NAPE President is concerned staff reductions at Waterford Hospital are seriously threatening the health and safety of employees and will lead to serious labour relations problems. The most acute situation exists on Ward West 1B where, in spite of the fact there are 67 documented instances of patients physically attacking staff members during the past 3 months [implying an increase without stating it], the hospital administration insists on staff cutbacks.

The union then offered an emotional and personalized "case" of violence, in which an "attendant was attacked from behind by the patient and sustained superficial cuts to his mouth, ear and neck."

3. *The Justice System* contributed only two announcements in 1982. On August 24, a front page wire service story was run with the inflammatory headline *Crime in Canada every 18 seconds*: "A property crime such as theft, robbery or arson is committed every 18 seconds in Canada and a violent crime every four minutes, the Canadian Centre for Justice Statistics reported," leaving the reader with the impression of an extraordinary rate of crime. The report stated that "Violent crimes, such as murder, kidnapping and sexual assault, increased 17 percent in the five year period," but did not mention that the increase could have been largely a result of increased *reports* of sexual assault. On August 26, a federal member of parliament responded to these releases: "He declared that the statistics actually understate the amount of crime" because so much crime goes unreported, a massive abuse of interpretation which left the reader with the feeling that the actual rate of increase was even higher than the figures admitted.

4. *Social Agencies and Social Action Groups* made a small contribution, as when, on October 7, the nurses staked their claim for special expertise in violence directed against the self. In an article entitled *Suicide rate is soaring to epidemic proportions. Nurse's conference is told,* the conference of the Association of Registered Nurses in St. John's was informed "that suicide is the third largest cause of death between the ages of 15 and 30 and is a growing epidemic." The conference speaker said "when a suicide occurs, there is always evidence the warning signs were there but not seen by family or friends." (Thereby suggesting that the persons best equipped to see these signs are registered nurses, who would be professionally sensitized to them.) "The good news," the article continued, "is that between 50 and 75 percent of potential suicides can be prevented," although it gave no indication of what evidence it had for these figures. "The remainder cannot be prevented even with several interventions," the speaker admitted. "She said for the professional that can be the most frustrating part of the work, but they should never feel they have failed."

"VIOLENT CRIME UP"—THE PRESS, THE PUBLIC, AND THE POLICE

Announcements remained relatively low again in 1983, with the press being the major single contributor. The year was opened on February 12 with my own announcement—which I have already investigated in some detail.

1. *The Press* gave considerable coverage to crime stories, although it should be noted that even the most sensational murder

received no more coverage per day in the press than other issues —for example, an article on the discovery of a new enzyme in seal stomachs with considerable practical and economic potential. The press began counting armed robberies once more, giving front page attention to *Captain Quik robbed*, noting that "a man wearing a ski mask and brandishing a sawed-off shotgun" was the second robber to hit a store in that "general area" during the week. "It's getting to be a habit around here," they quoted one store employee as saying, suggesting that armed robberies were now so common that towns-people were blasé) about them. By June 28, *Another armed robbery at confectionery store* observed that a masked man, "believed to have been armed with a gun," created "the fifth [armed robbery] in the city and the third at a Captain Quik store in just over six weeks." Similarly, a July 13 front page story on a sensational murder took the opportunity to count and re-hash all the murders of the year, implying a radical change in the homicide rate. Thus the murder of a golf club watchman "marked the fourth murder in St. John's since December 14, 1981 when fourteen-year-old Miss *X*" was killed. This was in fact the usual low Newfoundland homicide rate, but present-ing the figures in this manner left the reader with the contrary impression. The list ran:

> A St. John's man was found guilty by reason of insanity earlier this year for murdering his father and mother March 3, 1982. Another city man is waiting trial for the murder of a Water Street bartender September 29, 1983. There have been three murders in other parts of the province since Miss *X* was killed. Earlier this year a Holyrood woman was convicted of stabbing her ten-year-old son to death May 3, 1982. Two Corner Brook men are waiting trial for the January 14, 1983 murder of a twenty-year-old woman in that west coast city. A St. John's man has been charged with the murder of another man June 26, 1982 in a motel at Victoria, Carbonear.

On October 14, this procedure was repeated with *Seven facing charges of murder in province*, leaving the impression that these seven murders constituted an increase. This was compounded on October 15 with a misinterpretation of the Royal Newfoundland Constabulary annual report, which was summarized in the news-paper in such a way as to look as if there had been a major crime wave. *Constabulary reports increase in crime* claimed that "The number of major crimes in the area policed by the RNC increased more than 12 percent from 1981 to 1982." Although the story did note that "the reader should bear in mind that the jurisdiction of the RNC was continuously expanded during 1981 and 1982," the article invalidated that observation by stating that "The major crimes that showed an increase during 1982 were murder, attempted murder, assault, break and entry, theft, possession of stolen goods and impaired driving." Although it did observe that "the number of reported rapes decreased, as did armed and other robberies," the casual reader was nevertheless left with the impression that the expansion of police jurisdiction was some incomprehensible form of statistical quibbling, and that the rates of major crimes were in fact dramatically increasing.

Table 10

Announcements of Crime Waves in 1983

GENERATOR	FREQUENCY	
The Press		
Crime Stories	8	
Editorials	1	
Subtotal		9
Members of the Public		
Professor of Anthropology	1	
Letter to the Editor	1	
Subtotal		2
The Justice System		
Royal Canadian Mounted Police	1	
Maritime Association of Chiefs of Police	1	
Subtotal		2
Social Agencies & Social Action Groups		
Status of Women Council	1	
Subtotal		1
Government Bureaucracies (Non-Justice)		
Statistics Canada	1	
Subtotal		1
TOTAL		15

2. *The Justice System* was by now much more discreet, but police associations of various kinds continued to use spurious statistics for their own political and ideological goals. Thus the Maritime Association of Chiefs of Police, disapproving of parole for dangerous prisoners on what may well have been legitimate grounds, nevertheless justified their stance in terms of a bogus increase in crime in the Atlantic region. "The Maritime Association of Chiefs of Police has recommended that parole not be granted to inmates considered to be dangerous and violent offenders," the story ran. "The Chiefs of Police discussed the rise of violent crimes such as attempted murders, assaults, armed robberies, and sexual assaults on children and women in the Atlantic region. The Association said many

offenders who commit violent crimes are repeaters," and without explanation, added that "increasing numbers of offenders released are considered to be dangerous and a threat to society."

3. *Government bureaucracies (non-justice)* made their modest contribution via Statistics Canada. Their announcement presented what seems primarily to have been improvements in police record-keeping procedures as a genuine increase in violent crime (see O'Grady, this volume). On September 1, *Violent crime up in Newfoundland* contained a sensational story: "Crimes of violence took a 19 percent jump in Newfoundland during 1982, Statistics Canada has reported. The federal agency's annual report on uniform crime shows the rate of violent crime reached 579 per 100,000 population, the highest rate in the Atlantic region," leaving the reader with incontrovertible "proof" that Newfoundland society was in serious danger.

"CAUGHT IN FEAR"—CRIME STORIES, UNIONS, POLICE AND JUSTICE BUREAUCRATS

1984's announcements more than tripled the previous year's, and although the press continued as the largest single generator, non-press institutions and agencies played an equal role in this vastly expanded enterprise.

1. *Members of the public* generated announcements of crime waves in several forms. There was an increased tendency for victims of crime to be interviewed immediately after the event, and their naturally emotional responses were quoted in detail. Thus on January 12, under a 24 square inch photograph of the owner, captioned ". . .in less than three weeks two armed robberies have taken place. . .," a large page three story appeared entitled *Owner changes method of running gas station. Two robberies in three weeks.* The owner was quoted as saying that the second robbery had "upset everything at the business," and that "the effect has been hardest on the employees. . .the man who was on during the robbery quit because of it." The owner drew unwarranted conclusions from a coincidence by noting that while armed robberies were not new at his station, "the last two have involved handguns as opposed to knives or other weapons." He implied a new sinister and more deadly quality to the recent armed robberies. Similarly, a first robbery was converted to an increase on January 17 when, under the headline *Stiffer penalties urged for armed robbery, theft,* the manager of a chicken bar said:

that although her store has been the target for a rash of malicious damage, it was the first armed robbery there. She felt the news media should do more to make the public aware of the number of robberies and break ins that are occurring in the St. John's area. She also felt the media should call for longer prison sentences for those convicted. . . ."Most of these guys are in and out of jail. . . . It's a vacation for them."

Again the front page story on May 18, *Armed robbers get $250,* made a similar suggestion when the manager of the drug store said that while it was not the first time he had been robbed, "it was the first time a robbery had taken place with weapons. He admitted it was frightening and hoped that armed robberies were not becoming a trend."

In what appears to have been an orchestrated campaign, anti-pornography activists used the fear of violence to justify their ideological position in letters to the editor. On November 26, *Caught in fear* complained:

> I am not free to walk on a city street at night. . .others in my society feel free to disseminate hate literature against me. This is what I judge the banned Penthouse magazine to be. Could the Klu Klux Klan or any group distribute pictures of blacks in bondage or being injured? Why do girlie magazines feel free to do the same thing with women?

On November 28, "Disgusted" wrote to praise the media-conscious fieldworker for the Coalition Against Pornography:

> All honour to Mrs X, yes it is indeed a victory. Are we not of the Christian faith? Our poor old (once safe) Newfoundland, so long beleaguered with one wrong and another, beset with violence of thieves, drug users, those who are to usurp the laws of God, must now endure another creeping evil unless people like Mrs X are with us. Sweet purity thy spotless garments turn aside lest muddy evil stain.

On November 29, Mrs X herself stated her case, linking pornography with what she called a "time bomb of violence." "In Britain," she wrote, "a special parliamentary enquiry, set up to examine the effects of violence on videos and television, is asking the question, 'does the adulation of violence among children and teenagers that is revealed in this survey mean that we may be priming a time bomb of violence that could explode upon our city streets in some five or ten years time?'" In a surprising irrelevancy, she drew attention to the exploitation of children in other countries, suggesting that this in some way proved similar abuses were widespread in Canada: "Children are being kidnapped and used in the pornography in-

dustry in the United States, in the Philippines, in Central America
. . .In Canada a recent study has shown alarming statistics about
the widespread abuse of children." She complained that "In this
province magazines are being sold that condone children being used
as victims of incest and other forms of abuse." On December 15,
another letter emotionalized the problem with: "I was greatly sad-
dened, angered and disgusted while reading about a St. John's
woman raped as she jogged along Ridge Road. I feel his [the rapist's]
hatred for women in my gut. I, and all women are imprisoned by our
fears of the faceless men (or boys) who might do this to us if we walk

Table 11

Announcements of Crimes Waves in 1984

GENERATORS	FREQUENCY	
The Press		
Crime stories	18	
Editorials	6	
Anti-union stories	2	
Subtotal		26
Members of the Public		
Victims of crime	4	
Letters to the Editor	4	
Newfoundland Association of Public Employees	4	
Subtotal		12
Social Agencies and Social Action Groups		
Coalition for Equality	1	
Newfoundland & Labrador Human Rights Association	1	
Mental Health Association	1	
Status of Women Council	1	
Subtotal		4
The Justice System		
Canadian Centre for Justice Statistics	3	
Royal Newfoundland Constabulary Association	3	
Assistant Director of Public Prosecutions	1	
Lieutenant, Royal Newfoundland Constabulary	1	
Canadian Police Chiefs Association	1	
Subtotal		9
Politicians		
Minister of Social Services	2	
Liberal Opposition Leader	1	
Ontario Cabinet Ministers	1	
Subtotal		4
Government Bureaucracies (Non-Justice)		
Alcohol and Drug Dependency Commission	1	
Subtotal		1
TOTAL		56

alone (or jog)." Quoting an ideologue who claimed that "'men are increasingly unable to handle their excessive power over women,'" "Time for a Change" concluded that "We will not see a reduction in rape (or wife-battering) as long as the philosophy and false advertising promoting the hatred of women is available through the burgeoning business of pornography."

2. *Social Agencies and Social Action Groups* made a relatively smaller contribution in 1984 than in recent years, but a greater variety of such groups were now recognizing the political shock value of the subject. On February 24, the Newfoundland and Labrador Human Rights Association moved to expand its domain and influence with *Child sexual abuse a growing problem*. After submitting a number of recommendations to government for an expansion of government-funded services, the report claimed that "child sexual abuse is a growing problem in Newfoundland," despite the fact that it had no data on which to base such an announcement, and justified its claims on an assessment of the problem in another country. "There has been very little data collected in the province," they admitted, "but based on a U.S. survey that 10 percent of women and five percent of men have been sexually abused as children, the association says it can be assumed that about 7,500 Newfoundlanders age six to 10 have experienced some kind of sexual trauma." Having used data in this manner, they turned to a local source, once again confusing increases in reports of a problem with increases in the rate of their actual occurrence: "The association says in its report the Janeway Hospital has noticed a significant increase in treatment of young children who have been both threatened [here, the invention of a new category of offense, "threat," allows the figures to swell still further] and sexually abused." The Human Rights Association then went on to recommend a large-scale expansion of facilities for the monitoring of sexual abuse and treatment of victims and offenders.

In an October 11 story, the entire right quarter of the page was occupied by a long report with photographs, referring to a series of speeches in which the Coalition for Equality (a political coalition of union leaders, women's groups, and various social action groups) used the fear of violence for its own political ends in the workplace. Decrying "the actions of management personnel and governments," Rev. *P* said that instead of progressing to a more humane and more civilized society, it appears as if Newfoundland is slipping back into a more brutal society." The president of the Newfoundland Association of Public Employees, speaking at the same meeting, added that the "intellectual, bureaucratic arrogance demonstrated by governments and private sector companies with regard to labour negotiations may lead to bloodied confrontations—and we may end up behind bars for fighting that."

On October 18, the president of the Mental Health Association's national committee on unemployment appeared in a large 29 column-inch article linking violence to his political ideology. In *Stress on the rise due to jobless rate*, the president said that "psychological and emotional problems are increasing in Canada with the ever-increasing unemployment rate," and also claimed the studies "have shown a relationship between high unemployment rates and increasing crimes, sexual assaults, ill health including heart attacks and psychological and emotional stability," thus converting speculation into hard scientific "fact." He stated that "in one survey of 100 wife beaters, 80 percent were unemployed [and] unemployment also contributes to incidents of child abuse."

On December 1, as part of a new campaign for additional funds for Transition House, the fundraisers used their usual ploys—so unnecessary in such a legitimate case—to state that "since the mailout campaign began [for more funds], the number of distress calls has doubled," implying yet another rapid explosion of wife-battering in the province. "We're full, [a spokesperson said]. We need another house!"

3. *The Justice System* was especially vocal in 1984. The Royal Newfoundland Constabulary Police Association (formerly the "brotherhood" representing the police rank and file), still campaigning to be allowed to carry sidearms despite the fact that no member had ever been shot on duty, used its familiar tactic of referring to murders of officers in other parts of the country in an emotionalized manner, and implying that such tragic events were imminent in Newfoundland. On August 27, *Police association head says officers are targets* related an interview with the association: "Two police officers in the Toronto area have been murdered on the job over the past week, and the president of the RNC association says the same could happen here. 'We are doing the same duties as other police forces in Canada,'" he stated, while failing to note the rather profound differences in assault rates on police officers, or the degree of their severity. Then, without any justification whatever given the nature of the local situation, he continued: "It's a little discouraging thinking that we have people who want to take revenge." He did not mention how being armed would stop a revenge-seeker from shooting him, nor why such an act had *never* happened in the province.

On August 28, a front page story, *RNC men want to be armed*, exploited a different argument, this time referring to a new "fear" — that criminals in Newfoundland might be armed already: "'Members of the RNC should be armed for their own protection and the protection of the public,' says the president of the Constabulary Association." The president noted that in the past, one of the main arguments against arming the force had been that if the police were armed, then the criminals would arm themselves as protection, and he therefore proceeded to offer spurious evidence that criminals were now armed. "The President said that many criminals in St. John's carry firearms." As examples, he cited cases where criminals used firearms in armed robberies and break ins (although he did not mention that a large proportion of these "firearms" were in fact pellet guns: nor did he mention that no injuries had yet taken place). "We've been fortunate so far. Sometimes the public should be aware of some of the situations our members have to face," he said, reminding the readers that two officers in Toronto had been murdered during the previous week, and repeating his earlier comments about officers being targets for revenge-seekers. These themes were repeated in October by both the Canadian Police Chiefs Association and the RNC members association following the tragic murders of eight police officers in Ontario and Quebec. One Canadian police chief making inflammatory and irresponsible remarks told his men "they don't have to be shot at before they shoot." As before, the chief was arguing for the return of the death penalty, while the RNC association was demanding the right to be armed.

Yet the most provocative and misleading announcement of the year—and perhaps of the decade—came from the Director of the Canadian Centre for Justice Statistics, whose speech to the Rotary Club in St. John's was given extensive coverage under the headline *Statistics show violent crime on the increase in province*. With the unimpeachable authority of his position, he stated flatly that "Detailed data showed that violent crime rates are growing in Newfoundland. During 1982, there were 3,305 crimes of violence reported to police in the province. The following year, the number was 3,483." The newspaper reported that the director "had no explanation for the increased number of violent crimes in Newfoundland," but then went on to quote him as offering three different theories. "He said one theory was the violent crime was related to a population in 'turmoil,'" while another "could be that the crime rate was in close relationship to the rate of people between the ages of 17 and 25, and if Newfoundland had a growing number of young people, that might explain the higher number of violent crimes." His

third theory, however, suggested that in fact he might have understood that it was improvements in police record keeping procedures,
not changes in the true violence rate, that were responsible for the
increase. "A third explanation, the Director suggested, might be
found in the way police recorded spousal assaults. In Manitoba, that
had been the case. The crime rate had jumped considerably from
one year to the next and the reason was that incidents connected
with domestic disputes were recorded as violent crimes in the latter
year." Moreover, on November 16 a report was released in such a
way as to give the impression that the explosion of violence was even
greater than the increased statistics had suggested: *Many criminal
offenses not reported to police* noted that "More than half the
estimated criminal offenses committed in St. John's are never
brought to the attention of police, says a report from the Canadian
Centre for Justice Statistics." It did not mention that this was not a
new phenomenon, and merely added with bogus precision that "61
percent of the estimated crimes were not reported to police."

4. *Government Bureaucracies and Politicians* coordinated their
efforts for clear-cut political purposes on September 29, under the
headline *More money needed to combat effects of alcohol and drugs*.
The Alcohol and Drug Dependency Commission, a government
agency under the Minister of Social Services, "prepared" a report
which "puts the total economic cost to the province because of
alcohol abuse at more than $56 million annually," although how
they arrived at such a precise figure was barely explained. The ADDC
chairperson, demonstrating unprecedented confidence in the utility
of the ploy, said the commission "now has support for raising public
concern over the economic, as well as the social costs of alcohol
abuse in the province," and asked that the level of funding for the
ADDC be "multiplied six times" [sic] so that they might come to terms
properly with the social problem. In turn, the ADDC's political head,
the Minister of Social Services, described the empire-expanding
report as "critically important," and added: "'I don't think anyone
could reasonably question that alcohol abuse has far more consequences on the family unit and the social fabric of this province.' He
said alcohol is a major contributor to the abuse of children, the
abuse of women, and 'no doubt,' the abuse of men," thus linking the
argument for a vastly expanded budget to violence and the need for
its suppression. Similarly, demanding more police protection from
the wave of violence, the Opposition Leader on April 11 referred to
the "recent increase in violent crime" and asked "What has happened
to our once happy province?"

5. *The Press* was the largest single generator of announcements in 1984, contributing almost half of the total. Six editorials discussed violence, arguing their ideological cases. On June 7, *The abused child* noted: "There are no statistics readily available, but there are indications that reports of child sexual abuse is on the increase," although it did not say what these "indications" were, and it urged that public awareness of the problem be heightened through the funding of conferences. On August 27, responding to a government-sponsored report on child abuse, the editorial raised the estimates of sexual abuse of children "to one half of all women and one third of all men are victims," and urged tougher laws. By September 4, having decided that *Tough laws not working*, the editorial made another—and gigantic—leap, now suggesting that the "majority" of adults were involved in some way in child sexual abuse! "There are a great many people out there who either see nothing wrong with making sexual advances to children or who are unable to control the desires within them which force them to make sexual advances to children. It is difficult, in fact, to avoid the suspicion that a majority of adults fall into one or other of the categories," the editorial writer concluded, and called for yet-tougher laws and "education."

Eighteen of the press announcements took the form of crime reporting. Minor incidents of shoplifting were transformed into major crimes through sensationalizing and emotionalizing the events. For example, on August 30 a front page story, *Shoplifting gangs hit St. John's supermarkets. Staff threatened with violence* read: "The major supermarkets in the St. John's area are increasingly becoming the targets of gangs of shoplifters who often threaten violence when confronted by store staff." The violent images provoked by this statement certainly blurred the impact of the actual description of the event given later in the story: "In one incident two men entered the store, walked behind the counter, took a carton of cigarettes and started walking away. 'When a store employee confronted the two, they threatened to stab him with a knife,' said the store's Chief of Security. 'We really can't expect our employees to be risking their lives against these threats.'"

A cluster of armed robberies during the year was subjected to hyper-emotional reporting in which meaningless statistics and a sensitivity to "firsts" contributed to an atmosphere of mounting popular anxiety. Statements such as, "This is believed to be the 32nd armed robbery or attempt of an armed robbery in the city this year" were retailed without explanation of the significance of the number, or any comparison with other similar-sized cities in the country. On

November 5, *Two more armed robberies in St. John's* reached the front page, remarking that "this year has been St. John's worst for armed robberies." On November 9, another story was accompanied by a 24 square inch photograph of a police officer staring at a tableful of confiscated weapons, clearly implying that vicious and armed assaults were happening everywhere. This form of reporting culminated in a November 13 editorial, *Reassure the public*, in which the state of affairs was presented as being so chaotic that the public needed reassurance:

> A crime, practically unheard of in recent years, is fast becoming a common occurrence in St. John's. Armed robbers are prowling the streets at night, preying mostly on convenience stores and service stations. All types of weapons are being used—knives, pistols, rifles, shotguns, crowbars, etc. It is only a matter of time before the wrong move is made and someone is either maimed or killed. The general public, the convenience and service station owners and employees need reassurance. And who can blame them?

The editorial then called for stiffer sentences for offenders.

The use of "firsts" appeared frequently, as in *Liquor store robbery first for province*, in which the newspaper observed that a single robbery contained two "firsts": "The first armed robbery to take place in a liquor store in Newfoundland happened Wednesday night in Wabana, Bell Island. It was also the first armed robbery to take place on the island."

The paper reached a strident pitch on November 16, when *Store owner says someone bound to get hurt or killed. Fears increase in armed robberies* claimed that "Armed robberies have reached epidemic proportions" in the city. Finally, an editorial on December 15 summarized their position:

> St. John's witnessed more armed robberies this year than for any similar period in its history. Weapons of all descriptions were used; and the robbers seem to become more bold on every occasion. The latest incident was more brutal than most. Two men wearing ski masks and armed with a pistol, two wooden clubs and a can of dog repellent entered a St. John's Brewers Retail Store, hit the manager with the clubs and sprayed the repellent in his face. The question is: How long more before someone is seriously injured or killed?

"BOMB SCARES INCREASING"—CRIME STORIES, THE COURTS, AND SOCIAL ACTION GROUPS

The year 1985 was a remarkable one in which the authorities announced a 30 percent decrease in all criminal activity while the press, responsible now for well over half the announcements, continued to report, or suggest, increases.

1. *The Press* now consistently distorted statistical reality and ignored the insistence of the police and government that there had been a major drop in violent crime. This intensification of the newspaper's tendencies towards sensationalism may have been a response to the fact that the province's tabloid newspaper had gone out of business, and the *Evening Telegram* may have been attempting to claim the tabloid's readership. Whatever the cause, the manipulation and distortion of crime news became both more routine and more complex. Now, increases in crimes were headlined, emphasized, and put into percentages, while decreases were simply relegated to the bottom of the story and not put into percentages — as in "armed robberies up 100 percent," while a drop of total murders from three in one year to one in the next was simply passed over without comment. Falling into line with more ideological newspapers elsewhere in the English-speaking world, the newspaper now accentuated its tendency to put increases of crime on the front pages, while relegating decreases to the back pages. Moreover, it used the notion of a "rash" or a "wave" of offenses, not to refer to a random cluster of crimes in a short time period, but to give the impression that this "rash" constituted an actual annual and statistical increase. This enabled the press to talk about a crime wave when in fact there was a *decrease* in actual crime, as in the June editorial, *A crook's a crook*, which opened with the statement: "Should you be one of the unfortunate people who have been a victim of the recent break-in wave in St. John's. . . ."

Blatant manipulation of the public was apparent in the bomb "scare" of August and October. On August 16, under a large headline, *Bomb scares in St. John's are increasing in number*, the *Evening Telegram* managed to distort the reality that there had never been a bombing in the city. The paper reported that "Bomb scares in St. John's have been made against schools, department stores, and shopping malls," but it did not explain that the bulk of the scares traditionally came from students wishing to avoid examinations or aggrieved employees irritating their employers. This manipulation was repeated on October 18, with half of the front page given over to a supposed bomb story, with a large photograph of a police officer holding a "bomb," a large map of the downtown area with shading indicating streets and houses that had been evacuated, and a picture of a police officer wearing a flak jacket. The huge headline concealed an utterly meaningless story of a prank: *Bomb scare in St. John's* left the reader to discover that "a novelty item resembling a bomb caused a brief, but real, scare for occupants of homes and businesses on Duckworth and Henry Streets." The paper drew attention to the fact that the police response to a woman's discovery of her friend's imitation bomb included six constabulary vehicles, a dozen police officers, three fire department trucks, and members of the constabulary and RCMP bomb disposal squads. "The armed forces were not alerted," the newspaper concluded.

Table 12

Announcements of Crime Waves in 1985

GENERATORS	FREQUENCY	
The Press		
Crime stories	17	
Editorials	2	
Anti-youth story	2	
Subtotal		21
The Justice System		
Judges in Court	5	
Crown Prosecutor in Court	1	
Atlantic Police Chiefs Conference	1	
Subtotal		7
Social Agencies and Social Action Groups		
Status of Women Council	1	
Coalition of Citizens against Pornography	1	
Advocacy Centre for the Aged	1	
Subtotal		3
Members of the Public		
Letters to the Editor	2	
Subtotal		2
Government Bureaucracies (Non-Justice)		
Statistics Canada	1	
Subtotal		1
Politicians		
Member of Federal Parliament	1	
Subtotal		1
TOTAL		35

Most common of all, however, was the conversion into a crime wave of the fact that a handful of individuals were perpetuating a few armed robberies. *Robbers strike again* created what would be a state of mounting tension in a series of seventeen crime stories, commenting that "There appears to have been an increasing number of armed robberies in and around the city in recent weeks." With each successive armed robbery, the situation was re-hashed, as in *Armed robber holds up store*: "There was another armed robbery in St. John's last night. . . .So far this year there have been eight armed robberies and seven attempted armed robberies in the area policed by the Royal Newfoundland Constabulary." The paper suggested a crime wave by converting a cluster into a pattern with "Five of the armed robberies and two of the attempted armed robberies have taken place since September 1." While noting that "in 1984, there were 37 armed robberies and 10 attempted armed robberies in St. John's and area," the newspaper did not draw the reader's attention to the fact that armed robberies in the city had *decreased* during 1985.

In late October, the report of the tragic murder of a young woman store clerk during an armed robbery noted: "The incident marks the first time a murder was committed in the process of an armed robbery in Newfoundland," and the accounts were emotionalized with disturbing eyewitness interviews. This was followed up several days later with a province-wide review of storekeepers' reactions to the murder. Thus, *Stores, gas bar owners concerned with a rash of armed robberies* ignored the actual decrease in armed robberies to write: "In the wake of Saturday night's fatal stabbing of a twenty-two-year-old convenience store clerk in Gander and a rash of armed robberies in St. John's during the past two months, employees and owners of convenience stores and gas bars are worried. . . .In a survey of employees and owners of convenience stores and gas bars throughout the province, the consensus is that the courts are too soft on armed robbers."

2. *Social Agencies and Social Action Groups* played a relatively modest role during 1985, perhaps because many of their immediate political objectives had been achieved. Anti-pornography marchers received major attention on February 19, when the chairman of the Coalition of Citizens Against Pornography claimed that a "huge volume of psycho-social studies have shown a link between pornography and violent behaviour," and a prominent anti-pornography activist was quoted as saying "that many women who end up in transition houses for battered women are there because they were forced to act out the actions portrayed in sexually violent magazines." Manipulating violent images for ideological purposes and without corroboration of any kind, "She said 'We are seeing students drawing pictures that are pornographic and violent.'"

On June 14, a new constituency was staked out by social activists, using violence as the justification for their program: In *Abuse of elderly widespread problem*, the head of a Toronto advocacy centre for the aged was paraphrased as saying that "Abuse of the elderly is so widespread it should be taken as seriously as child abuse and wife beating. . . .'Elderly abuse as a family violence problem has received little attention compared to child abuse,' she said. 'This is because the elderly haven't had a voice,'" she claimed, offering to provide such a voice. She continued by quoting some spurious statistics and concluded with emotional passages designed presumably to strengthen her political case: "A recent U.S. government study found the frequency of abuse of the elderly to be only slightly less than that of child abuse. The study estimates that more than a million elderly people in the U.S. are victims of abuse [such as] tying old people in chairs with ropes and wires to keep them out of the way."

3. *The Justice System* ran a poor second to the press, but judges and prosecutors in court often used purported crime waves to justify their decisions. Thus on March 30, a few weeks before the police chief officially announced a major reduction in violent crime (particularly of armed robbery) in the St. John's area during the first three months of the year, a judge sentencing a man for an armed robbery warned "that someone is going to be shot during a holdup in the city. . . .Armed robberies are a problem in St. John's," insisted the judge who added that "the robberies, which involve guns in many cases, are becoming 'more daring,'" although he did not specify what this meant. Justifying his heavy four-year sentence, the judge said "The court has to impose a sentence on armed robbers that will discourage others from committing the offense." Similarly, on June 1, under *Convicted of sexual assault, man gets three-year term*, the judge said in handing down his sentence "that sexual assault on children is becoming too frequent, and children must be protected from those who 'prey upon them for sexual purposes,'" although he had no evidence for claiming such an increase. In the October 30 trial of a prominent citizen on a charge of sexually assaulting a seven-year-old girl, the crown prosecutor insisted that "'Child abuse is a growing problem' and the courts take the view that it won't be tolerated." The judge repeated this claim a few days later at the sentencing. The newspaper paraphrased him as saying that "Society's greatest responsibility is looking after the very young and the very old," and that "Child sexual abuse is a growing problem and cannot be tolerated."

On December 6, under *Man, eighteen, gets 11 years for five armed robberies*, the judge justified his punitive sentence with the comments that "armed robbery is 'one of the most heinous crimes that society is aware of.' . . .It is one of the most frightening things that can happen to an individual, he said. He said the incidence of armed robbery in the city and area as well as other areas of the province is increasing," although the police had publicly made it clear it was not increasing. "There is great public concern about the incidence of this type of crime," said the judge observing that "a person was recently killed during an armed robbery, and it is undoubtedly inevitable that others will be injured or killed if this crime continues."

SUMMARY AND CONCLUSIONS

We have tried to describe the sources of the fear of increasing violent crime in the province—a fear so profound that, as elsewhere in Canada, close to half the adult population are fearful of assault, despite the low incidence of actual violent crime. In order to determine the sources of this fear, we concentrated on one of the primary sources of news, the province's major daily newspaper. It is customary in much of the scholarly and popular literature to assume, or categorically assert, that the press is the primary source of fears of crime—retailing hysteria in order to sell more newspapers, attract a wider audience, or dispense conservative ideologies—and this assumption is given no little credence by an examination of the manner in which crime news is distorted and inflated by the international press. However, we found that by casting our net beyond simple crime news, by examining instead all local references to an increase in crime and violence, that the local press was merely one of the six primary disseminators of fear, and that the volume of their announcements of crime waves actually constituted less than half the total during the eleven-year study period.

Similarly, many scholars assume that the police, anxious to expand their personnel and powers, are the primary culprits—dispensing fear of crime and criminals for their own expansionist ends. However, while certain mainland Canadian urban and regional police officials frequently abused their powers in this way, RCMP officials *at no time* seized the opportunity to capitalize on such misperceptions (even when their presence was being reduced in the province, and it might have been to their political advantage to manipulate fear). On the contrary, RCMP officials appeared in the press only to claim and reassure the public, or to make rational and non-inflammatory statements about changes in crime rates. Even the RNC (with the exception of one media-conscious chief politicking for a new police building and frequent self-serving statements from the rank-and-file brotherhood) behaved with relative responsibility. Indeed, the RNC's most publicly visible department, the Crime Prevention Unit (which frequently addressed the public through the press and the media) consistently reminded the public of the "penny-ante" nature of most Newfoundland crime, and merely exercised its professional mandate of informing the public of techniques for defeating burglary and armed robbery.

What we found was that a wide range of politicians, government agencies, professional associations, and social action groups "discovered" violence in the mid-1970s, and learned to harness it to their own ends. Violence became the material which the "professional and managerial classes" used to "generate and then mould reforms to meet their own interests" (Cohen 1985:112). Fear of violence among the public became vital political and economic ammunition for not only right wing newspapers and left wing labour unions, but for the employment and "emergence of those distinctive bodies of people — specialists, experts, professionals of all sorts — each of which took its 'own' category of deviants and established a monopolistic claim over their lives. Only the experts know what to do (knowledge); only they should be allowed to do it (power)" (Cohen 1985:101). Violence became the symbol of everything that was wrong with society, and the *lingua franca* in which rival ideological groups expressed their cases for or against capital punishment, abortion, women's rights, divorce, war, the family, religion, and many other current "issues." Individually and severally, a wide range of persons and institutions had much to gain from a public perception of a crime wave, and relatively few exercised much restraint in the exploitation of this reality.

Notes

1. For example, AIDS industry spokespersons are typically not "permitted" to discuss the social and sexual behaviours that may underlie "homosexual" AIDS. Occasionally, spokespersons will even justify this censorship on the grounds of "ethical" concerns that research funding might evaporate if the disease were relegated to the netherworld of unprotected anal intercourse and drug abuse (CTV, "Shirley," March 1990). Similarly, refugee industry spokespersons dealt with perceived unease among the Canadian public at the "queue-jumping" of a large number of Bulgarian "economic refugees" by staging an emotionally charged interview with a federal official discussing the actual persecution, torture and murder of *political* refugees from Latin America (CBC Radio, St. John's, March 1990).

2. Cf. Brian MacLean's "State Expenditures on Canadian Criminal Justice," (MacLean 1986:116). "Expenditures outgrow crime rates by 4525 percent per year on the average" in the period 1950–66 alone.

3. Personal communication, anonymous SSHRCC reviewer.

4. In the years since then, the FBI Academy in the U.S.A. and the "Investigative Psychology" unit at the University of Surrey in England, have in fact successfully developed these crude ideas.

Part III

Riots, Raids and Relief, Police, Prisons and Parsimony

The Political Economy of Public Order in Newfoundland in the 1930s

James Overton

> The task of a critique of violence can be summarized as that of expounding its relation to law and justice (Benjamin 1978:277).

INTRODUCTION

This essay explores the economic and political context of collective violence and protest in Newfoundland during the Great Depression of the 1930s. We examine the relationship between this collective action and state policy regarding unemployment and public relief and the maintenance of law and order. One aim of this work is to question some current assumptions about the non-violent nature of Newfoundland's past. This is achieved by the detailed documentation of violence connected with unemployment and public relief issues in the 1930s. From this it is clear that under certain circumstances large numbers of Newfoundlanders have been prepared to break the law and engage in violent acts. The study also goes beyond documentation to examine the complex and shifting relationship between economic and political change, state policy, and collective action. As such, it provides a case study of how one particular type of violence can be understood.

An initial discussion outlines some of the issues and reviews some of the approaches which inform the subsequent account of the 1930s which proceeds, by and large, in chronological fashion.

The Past and the Present

I take it as axiomatic that our efforts at historical understanding are shaped by present concerns and patterns of thought and that, in E.H. Carr's words, the pursuit of history is an "unending dialogue between the present and the past" (1986:24). As circumstances change, as alternative perspectives develop and as particular issues become important we look to the past asking new questions and reformulating old ones in order to better understand the present.

It is the task of the social investigator to stand back from events, to attempt to see the larger picture, to look for patterns, to sift the essential from the unessential, and, if possible, to explain what happened and draw lessons from this for today. In this context objectivity is no more than a willingness to try and see all sides of a question, to be skeptical of all received and offered accounts, and, while not ignoring any piece of evidence, to construct the most reasonable account of events using the concepts at our disposal. This does not mean letting the facts speak for themselves (as if this were at all possible); it means creating an interpretive framework for events. Given this, it is clear that different people working at different times will pose rather different questions, will utilize different concepts and will uncover and select different evidence to emphasize in their narratives. But in historical research we cannot control our characters or influence events. As John Berger suggests, we can only follow and oversee (Berger 1984; see also Dyer 1984). The time and the story do not belong to us, "yet the meaning of the story, what makes it worthy of being told, is what we can see and what inspires us." We can bear witness to past events. But "those who read or listen to our stories see everything as through a lens" and it is this lens which is "ground anew" in every story.

What can a study of collective violence and public order in Newfoundland in the 1930s add to our efforts to understand the current concern with crime and violence in the province? As has been well documented by Elliott Leyton and Bill O'Grady, there has developed amongst academics, the police, writers in the media, a variety of interests groups, and perhaps the population generally the notion that crime and violence in Newfoundland are increasing. Already this belief is informing action. Groups are lobbying government for tougher measures to deal with crime and harsher sentences are being handed out to lawbreakers.

All statements of concern about present and future crime levels in Newfoundland are explicitly or implicitly comparative in nature. "Newfoundland is becoming more violent than it used to be," it is suggested. Or, "Crime levels here are fast approaching mainland levels." Such statements may be supported by the selective and uncritical use of statistics. Usually, however, they are offered as self evident truths, occasionally backed up by anecdotal information and personal observation. Thus, current commentaries about crime waves and increasing levels of violence juxtapose a chaotic, lawless, and threatening present and immediate future against a past when Newfoundland was relatively non-violent and peaceful, a past which, incidentally, is rarely given any more specific identification than "traditional Newfoundland society" or "pre-Confederation days."

The strength of the belief that in the past Newfoundland was a peaceable place, was brought home to me recently when I gave a talk about public relief policy in the 1930s in Newfoundland and noted that the period saw a number of riots and many raids on merchants' stores. After my talk, one man who had lived through the period asked me where I obtained my information about raids and riots. He wished to challenge the facts I had presented and was at pains to assure me that the country was not at all violent in the 1930s. To talk about riots and raids was to cast a shadow over the supposedly non-violent character of Newfoundlanders and to challenge the standard version of the past offered in the following statement:

> And all through these years of incredible hardship, no violent political protest ever seems to have occurred. While other western peoples were having revolutions, revolts, riots and strikes, Newfoundlanders endured with unbelievable patience, keeping their kindliness and good-humour and dignity (Cutler 1969).

In fact, the idea that Newfoundland has been a law abiding place has a long pedigree. Prowse's *Newfoundland in 1900* made much of the "moral qualities" of the population and emphasized that the inhabitants of the country were "orderly, law-respecting and sober" (Prowse 1900). This kind, charitable, and hospitable population lived "peacefully among themselves" while "outbreaks of bigotry or fanaticism" were said to be "almost unknown." P.T. McGrath expressed similar ideas in 1911 when he wrote that "the country is absolutely crimeless, law abiding, moral and temperate" and "the Colonial Penitentiary is often scarcely occupied" (1911). Such views were expressed by many writers in the early part of this century, and in assessing their reliability it should be remembered that people like McGrath were acting as publicists for Newfoundland, very often in the hope that they would attract investors and tourists to the country.

The work of social anthropologists in the 1960s and 1970s also conveyed the impression that Newfoundland society (especially rural areas) had been and still was characterised by friendliness, tolerance, conflict avoidance, and honesty.[1] Lack of crime and violence is thought to be typical of what has come to be called "Newfoundland's traditional way of life." However, in the last fifty years traditional Newfoundland society has begun to break down under the combined influences of Confederation and modernization (Leyton 1986; Overton 1987).

Newfoundland's past golden age of independence, virtue, and peace has in recent years performed yeoman service for those who have mounted a certain kind of critique of "modernization." The idealized past has been used as a stick to beat the present. It has been posited that the changes which have occurred in the province since Confederation have weakened traditional patterns of social control. Thus, urbanization and modernization are thought to have weakened the social fabric and to have led to more crime. Future developments such as oil exploitation will continue the rot. Ed Kavanagh, long-time probation worker, expressed his concern about the current "downward spiral" of vandalism and destructiveness in Newfoundland in 1975 by contrasting the present with the good old days when young people respected their parents, the police, the law, and the clergy (*Evening Telegram* 11 October 1975:4). Now these traditional social control mechanisms have been weakened by permissiveness and a pleasure-seeking youth is out of control.

Most present-day discussions of crime and violence rest on the assumption that the past was peaceful and non-violent. Many accounts implicitly or explicitly offer some kind of explanation why crime is on the increase. In these accounts increased crime tells a story. It has a meaning.

Rising unemployment and economic crises are often connected with a wide variety of social pathologies (including the deterioration of mental and physical health, increases in child abuse, vandalism and other forms of violence) and an increased likelihood that social unrest and even revolt will occur. In Newfoundland, as elsewhere in the western world, mass unemployment has been associated with a variety of images of danger and has become the focus of much social anxiety for commentators of both the left and the right (Overton 1986). The main assumption of this view is that the loss of control associated with being without work and poor leads to crime and violence. Two excerpts from submissions to the *Royal Commission on Employment and Unemployment in Newfoundland and Labrador*, contained in a background report (Clarke 1986), illustrate current thinking about unemployment and crime and violence:

I see the young people in our community getting very upset and possibly there could very well be a sudden rage from the people towards the Government, and maybe in our own community, towards whatever groups of people they see as being in authority, who are seemingly not doing anything to help. It's like a time bomb which is very soon, I would think, ready to explode (Placentia Public Hearings).

The correlation between crime and unemployment is a reality. Many individuals find themselves in a rut. As long as the present unemployment situation continues, the crime rate will continue to rise due to the poverty cycle and the social and psychological effect that this cycle has upon the individual (Rocky Harbour Public Hearings).

Again, a threatening and dangerous present and future are ranged against a more stable and peaceful past. This is true whether it is "good times" or "hard times" which are identified as the cause of increased criminal activity.

One of the striking features of the current preoccupation with lawlessness is that, to use Pearson's words, it is a "structure of feeling" which with "different degrees of refinement, emphasis and commitment" unites both "'high' theory" and "'low' opinion and sentiment" (1985). Popular sentiments are paralleled by criminological and social theory and together these constitute an overwhelming orthodoxy which indicts social change and loss of social control as the cause of increased crime and violence.

On the basis of this discussion, it is fair to say that to a large degree current statements of concern about crime and violence *depend* on the view that in the past things were less violent and more crime free in Newfoundland. But, how much stock can be placed in the idea that the province/country has until recently been law abiding? Certainly, if we are to draw the obvious conclusions from the work of Elliott Leyton and Bill O'Grady, not much. Crime waves have been identified hundreds of times over the last decade on very slim evidence, contrary evidence or no evidence at all. A variety of interests have (perhaps unwittingly) announced these waves to further their aims and, in the process, created a general impression that crime and violence are on the increase. If we accept that with all the sophisticated data and techniques currently in the hands of government officials, academics, and other researchers it is not possible to show a marked change in patterns of crime and violence in recent years, then surely we should be more than a little skeptical about statements which suggest Newfoundland was peaceful in the past.[2] In fact, there has been very little historical analysis of crime and violence in Newfoundland which could be used to support or

refute the widespread feeling that Newfoundlanders have traditionally been non-violent and unwilling to break the law. Given this, it
would seem unwise to make sweeping generalizations about the
past, and by extension the present, without some attempt to examine changing patterns of crime and violence and without being
specific about the kinds of activities, the places, and the periods for
which we are making our statements.

At one level this essay raises some serious questions about the
myth of the peaceful past in Newfoundland by documenting for the
1930s the nature and extent of violence in connection with unemployment and public relief. This was a period of severe
unemployment and acute poverty, of slow starvation and the loss of
political control associated with Commission of Government in
1934. It was a period in which several riots took place and many
raids on merchants' stores occurred. Spectres of "absolute revolt"
and "mob action" and the issue of law and order troubled the
authorities. Major changes in policing occurred and observers began
to express the idea that there had been a fundamental change in the
law-abiding character of Newfoundlanders.

However, the main aim of this essay is not to provide a simple
resolution to the question of whether or not Newfoundland in the
past was a peaceful or violent place (if this were possible in any
simple sense) in order to undermine or confirm current statements
about crime waves.[3] It is rather to help create an awareness of the
great complexity of the issue of the causes of violence by examining
what was perhaps the most characteristic and important type of
violence in the 1930s in its political, economic, and historical
context. The study is also concerned with uncovering the broad
social and political meaning of violence. What factors affected how
violence was seen and what determined the authorities' reaction to
violent acts.

Approaching Crime and Violence Historically

Although deviance in general, and crime and violence in particular,
have been much studied and there is now what Nye calls a "rich
array of methodological alternatives readily at hand" for those
interested in studying such phenomena, there is currently considerable debate and disagreement over the value of various
approaches (Nye 1984). Recently there has been a shift away from
what may be called traditional criminology with its emphasis on the
etiology of deviance and its pragmatic orientation towards the location, investigation, and treatment of deviance, but this traditional

orthodoxy is still powerfully entrenched. It may even be rather too optimistic to argue, as Gatrell, Lenman and Parker (1980) do, that "the days of the uncritical and anecdotal history of crime are past."

In research on the relationship between patterns of violence and crime and social change there is still a tendency to favour global theories which may be mechanical and one-dimensional (Nye 1984). Historical work is still too much influenced by "uncritical criminology" which treats crime as a "social fact" (Hay 1982), while the grave dangers of "vulgar Durkheimianism" have been made much of in recent historical work on suicide (MacDonald 1986; Anderson 1980). A similar argument is made by Geoffrey Pearson in his critical review of discussions of lawlessness and social change. He questions not only "the vast authority of the Durkheimian legacy" but also "the work of the Chicago School," various "marxist or neo-Marxist formulations" and some studies of "crime in the Third World" (Pearson 1985).

The powerful hold of criminological orthodoxy has also been noted by Box and Hale (1982). In examining the relationship between crime, unemployment and incarceration, Box and Hale have noted that both traditional criminological thinking and common-sense wisdom are limited "to one banality. . .that as unemployment increases, the rate of criminal behaviour increases" (1982). Box and his co-workers also go some way towards demonstrating that this criminological orthodoxy does have very real consequences (Box 1983; Box and Hale 1985). They argue, for example, that in Britain prison incarceration rates increase during periods of rising unemployment. However, this is mostly due to judges handing out tougher sentences to people in order to deter them from criminal activity. Judges, armed with the idea that unemployment leads to crime, translate this theory into practice by sending more people to jail for longer periods in order to prevent crime increasing. What Box's work suggests is that there is a connection between incarceration, crime, and unemployment, but that the connection is not the one normally supposed.

Box's argument is supported by the work of Swigert and Farrell on "the discretionary dispensation of justice" in the United States (1976). Swigert and Farrell suggest that "the criminal stereotype" of the "normal primitive" operates throughout the legal system to ensure that certain people get better access to legal assistance and get more lenient sentences. High status persons are consistently dealt with more favourably by the legal system and judges operating within the "calculus of loss and pain" consistently provide lower status persons with heavier sentences than those who appear to be of higher status. During a period of rising unemployment, therefore, more unemployed people (lower status) might tend to appear before judges and this might 'naturally' lead to a rise in the proportion of people being sent to prison even if crime rates remained constant.

In this way different theories of the causes of crime and violence, as well as the orthodox and popular assumptions about criminals and proper punishment, can play a key role in framing legal practice. What we think of as explanations for the observed facts of crime and violence can influence the very observations themselves. This further supports the idea that 'facts' and 'theory' are inseparable. We should exercise great caution in our theorizing not only because our explanations might be wrong, but also because theory guides practice.

One area in which vulgar theory is dominant is in the research which tries to use crime and violence statistics as indicators of what is termed the quality of life of a society. At least since the late seventeenth century people have tended to regard the extent of crime and violence in a country as an indication of its moral condition (Gatrell, Lenman, and Parker 1980:3–4). In 1670 Sir William Petty, the father of "political arithmetic" advocated the collection of "the number of corporal sufferings and persons imprisoned for crime" in order "to know the measure of vice and sin in the nation" (Petty 1967:197). In the eighteenth century Jeremy Bentham argued that data furnished by the courts on all cases tried could provide "a kind of political barometer" which would indicate to the legislator the "*moral* health of the country" (Gatrell *et al.* 1980:3–4). By the early nineteenth century, countries such as Britain and France were making crime rates available for this purpose. Since that time the problems associated with using these statistics and with the validity of any conclusions drawn from them have been much debated. Even so crime rates, divorce rates, suicide rates, and abortion rates are still used as indicators of the health of the society in a *simple* fashion. A recent example of this is provided by the Economic Council of Canada's study *Newfoundland: From Dependency to Self-Reliance* (1980). Crime rates, divorce rates, etc. are used as indicators of "social disruption" and the low rates in Newfoundland, compared with the Canadian average, are used to suggest that the "human condition" in the province "may be fairly good" despite high levels of unemployment and poverty.

Challenges to this kind of orthodoxy have come from research in a number of disciplines in recent years. If, in the past, the consideration of crime and violence has been subject to what Nye (1984) calls the "tyranny of numbers" and characterized by an obsession with measuring changes in crime rates and explaining these in terms of one or two simple "factors," now this approach is being seriously questioned.

First, there has been a recent growth in the willingness to look seriously at what numbers can tell us about crime and at the many problems associated with their use. Much of this work reveals very clearly the great difficulties of using official statistics and demonstrates that even thoughtful researchers have not always exercised sufficient caution. However, the critiques of official statistics, developed since the 1960s, have still not been given the recognition they deserve.[4] Today it is common to find most users of statistics and commentators on crime, perhaps after a word of caution about the shortcomings of the data, persisting in using crime statistics *as if* they unproblematically indicate the *real* level of crime in a particular area. Statistics on the incidence of murder or assault are used *as if* they indicate *how much* violence exists in a given place at a given time. Rates of crime and violence are then correlated with other social indicators (unemployment rates, alcohol consumption, income, the price of bread, etc.) in order to confirm or challenge existing theories about the causes of crime and violence.

The whole approach rests on the assumption that, by and large, existing statistics on crime can be used as a fairly accurate indicator of the amount of crime or violence in a society and that this indicator is valid through time. It also assumes that violence can be unproblematically defined and measured; that is, that incidents of violence can be added up to give a picture of the amount of violence at a particular time and place. This approach is reductionist in the full sense of the word. Discrete and sometimes very different events end up being classified in the same way as a "riot" or an assault and given the same weight. In the process all the difficulties of defining precisely what a "riot" is are forgotten. In fact, the process of classifying any act as violent involves a great many judgments which vary from place to place and time to time. Whether such acts get translated into official statistics as "incidents" depends on public attitudes, policing and judicial practices, record keeping procedures, and many other factors which work together in complex ways.

Much recent work on crime statistics should act as "a counsel of caution" in the words of Carr-Hill and Stern (1979). These researchers even show "that the process generating criminal statistics differs substantially from year to year" and that because of this "it is difficult to say whether actual offenses have decreased or increased" (1979:271). This does not mean that we should not, under certain circumstances, use official statistics, but that when we do we should be fully aware of the difficulties of "statistical inference" in the face of problems such as "simultaneous causation and unobserved variables" (1979:312). We should also be fully prepared to use statistics only after police practices in relation to criminal behaviour and the production of official data are "disentangled" (Farrington and Dowds 1985:70–71).

Once we begin to ask questions about the social production of statistics and begin, as Bill O'Grady has done, to interpret such statistics in the light of the process by which they are made, then we become acutely aware of the difficulties associated with drawing firm conclusions about changes in patterns of crime and violence over even relatively short periods of recent history within the same jurisdiction.

The immense difficulties associated with identifying historical trends in criminal activity are brought out by much of the work now being produced by social historians. Beattie notes that commentators in eighteenth-century England made much of the "rising tide of crime" and argued that "the social bonds were disintegrating" (Beattie 1974). He attempts to assess whether this perception was correct or not by means of a careful examination of data based on court records. What his study reveals is the great difficulty of explaining fluctuations in recorded crime and the virtual impossibility of deciding whether the observed fluctuations reflect actual changes in the incidence of crime. This point is also brought out in a recent debate in *Past and Present* about T.R. Gurr's work on historical trends in homicide rates (Gurr 1981; Stone 1983, 1985; Sharpe 1985). Even when there is some broad agreement about overall trends (allowing for substantial errors) there very often still exists considerable disagreement about the meaning of such trends. Many of these points are also supported by recent work on the relationship between suicide and industrialization. Anderson's research challenges orthodox thinking by showing no correlation between industrialization and high rates of suicide in Victorian England. She suggests that further investigation of the problem of suicide should focus on the history of ideas in order to try to understand where the notion that "modern industrial society is associated with deviant behaviour" came from and why it has "reverberated" through society since Victorian times (Anderson 1980:86, 171–173). MacDonald's more recent work on suicide in England in the period 1660–1800 also suggests that "prevailing models of social and cultural change are oversimplified" (1986:111, 95).

The studies reviewed above suggest that we need to be concerned with the social and historical context of deviant behaviour. Crime and violence and even crime statistics should be studied as one aspect of social, cultural, and political history. Increasingly researchers are focusing on these kinds of problems, directing their attentions towards revealing how deviance is constructed and how definitions of normality gain acceptance. They stress the importance of appreciating reactions to criminal, deviant, and violent behaviour as well as trying to understand such behaviour in its own right. As Pick suggests, it is now commonplace to say that "theories of crime are inevitably connected with the particular political world in which they emerge" and to note that "the designation of the criminal is bound up, in complex ways, with the opposing but reciprocal process of defining the good citizen, or the good subject, in specific societies, in particular periods" (1986:21, 61). Likewise, the work of Foucault and his collaborators has focused attention on the nature of "discourses" such as criminology and their relationship to techniques of power in history (Foucault 1975, 1977).

It is certainly true that, as Hall and his associates suggest, "the complex relationship between crime, political movements and economic transformation have not yet had the attention they seem to deserve" (1978:186). However, there is a growing body of valuable work which does focus on the historical problems of the relationship between crime, violence and deviance, power and politics and social and economic change. Many of these studies point out with great force the fact that crime and violence cannot be treated as independent of broader questions concerning the nature of power and authority and the workings of the legal system—the police, the courts and the prison system (Brewer and Styles 1980:11–12; Hay *et al.* 1975; Thompson 1975). This approach has also been characteristic of recent work on riots and "moral panics."[5] The urban riots in the United States in the late 1960s stimulated research in that country and the riots of the early 1980s in Britain have led to a great deal of concern (Friedland 1983; Unsworth 1982:(1)63–85). In Britain the work on moral panics has been particularly well developed by Hall and his co-workers in their study of the mugging controversy in the 1970s (Hall *et al.* 1978). The recent revival of interest in the sociology of law has also produced important studies which place the operation of the legal system in its political, economic and historical context. This work emphasises how laws are made, enforced and changed and it directly parallels the concerns of social historians such as E.P. Thompson. The 1984 miners' strike in Britain has also provided the stimulus for a tremendous upsurge of research on legal issues and policing and their economic and political dimensions.[6] The approach discussed here has also made some headway in the area of development studies (Sumner 1982; Snyder 1980:14(3)723–802; Fitzpatrick 1980:4, 77–95).

Without, for the most part, tending towards economic reductionism, this work nonetheless does give full weight to the economic factors operating in particular situations (Thompson 1971). The best studies reveal the great complexity of the issues of crime, violence and deviance. They lead out from particular acts or incidents to broad discussions of social and economic issues, class structure and even social theory. The measure of their success is that they have stimulated heated discussion and disagreement about a vast range of important issues. New questions are being asked, old ones reformulated and fresh avenues opened up for investigation. If the questions raised are unsettling, it is because pre-conceptions are being challenged as many of the general theories we work with prove to be inadequate when exposed to the "jungle of history."[7] More and more, simple ideas of the relationship between crime and social change are being questioned and the great difficulty of relating violence and crime to political and economic conditions revealed.[8] Even the widely held notion that consistent distinctions can be made between rural and urban areas when it comes to crime rates has proved to be incorrect (Sharpe 1985).

The aim of this study is to confront vulgar explanations of violence. It seeks to show how violent events were embedded in the social, political and economic life of the 1930s in Newfoundland and to demonstrate how violence in turn shaped the course of events. As such, the study addresses a series of questions which cannot be approached quantitatively and comparatively. Rather, attention is drawn to the social meaning of violence (Hobsbawn 1982:15; Williams 1976). Violence is not assumed to be a universal type of behaviour which is constant throughout history. It is regarded as a moral and political concept with socially and historically varying meaning. Clearly changing social attitudes influence what is considered to be violent behaviour. Thus, as Hobsbawn notes:

> So long as husbands are assumed to be entitled to beat wives, or fathers children, or schoolmasters pupils, nobody will regard an example of a schoolmaster beating a pupil or a husband a wife as an example of violence (Hobsbawn 1982:15).

Perhaps we are less tolerant of certain forms of violence today than in the past? It may be, for example, that an increase in recorded incidents of domestic violence does not, in fact, indicate real increase in such violence. Such increases may reflect a less tolerant attitude towards such violence as well as a shift in patterns of policing and institutional methods for dealing with that violence.

This makes any comparisons between past and present very difficult. The question of whether a society is violent or not does not seem to be one which can be answered in simple, quantitative terms. Recently, for example, considerable public anxiety has been focused on armed robberies in Newfoundland, this type of crime being presented as something rather new and threatening in a New-foundland context. But how do we compare this crime with the scores of raids on merchants' stores which occurred in the 1930s? Many of these raids involved large numbers of men who used violence or the threat of violence to obtain relief supplies. Some of the men were arrested for their actions, but the numbers arrested represented a small fraction of those involved in breaking the law. How do we compare the 'amount' of violence involved in such actions with today's handful of armed robberies? Would it be worthwhile to even try and do this? The 'amount' of violence involved even in two events classified as "riots" is hard to assess. Views of the severity of riots may vary greatly and reactions to any incident will depend on a great many factors, including the strength of the forces of law and order, and the political climate. The work of Victor Bailey shows that the impact of riots depends on where and when they occur and, in a broad sense, on the "meaning" they are given (1981:94–125). Under certain circumstances, even not very serious riots can send "shock-waves through the nervous system of the propertied" (Bailey 1981:96). In periods of heightened public sensitivity, "normal" crimes can sometimes take on a very threatening character as Davis demonstrates in her study of the "ticket-of-leave" scares and the London garotting panic of the early 1880s (Gatrell, Lenman and Parker (eds.) 1980:190–213).[9]

Such work points to the importance of trying to understand public and official perceptions of and reactions to violence and crime. Why are some events particularly threatening? Why is it that crime waves are announced when they are? What roles do popular theories, like that put forward by Alex Parsons, the superintendent of the Newfoundland penitentiary in 1927, play in creating a heightened anxiety about crime during periods of economic crisis?

> It is noticeable that "waves of crime" usually occur in seasons of extraordinary want and depression, and that the centre of the "wave" is also the centre of population, where social and individual factors of crime converge with greatest intensity upon the given point. The nerve-tension is always more extreme in the city than in the outport, and in the city, also, are the social vices most

numerous. Precipitate upon these conditions a condition of unusual depression and an epidemic of crimes against person and
property may be expected to follow.

The overwhelming majority of thefts in this community are committed by men of unsettled pursuits and no established
occupation; and it is evident that they who, from whatever cause,
cannot produce for themselves, will most naturally attempt to take
the produce of others. Conspicuous among crime-breeding conditions is that state of political apathy or civic stagnation wherein too
many of the better classes become neglectful of their civic obliga-
tions.[10]

We should also raise some questions about the perceived
relationship between outbreaks of collective violence and crime. This
is important because at least since the nineteenth century there has
been assumed a connection between collective disorder and crime.
As is evidenced in contemporary discussions of unemployment
these are both seen as stemming from the same cause (Overton
1986). And, since Cesare Lombroso's (1836–1909) day, a firm connection has been thought to exist between criminal behaviour and
radical politics (Pick 1986). The frequency with which criminals
placed themselves at the head of the masses was often noted and
political subversion has frequently been linked with various forms
of degeneracy.

In a similar fashion Durkheim linked the rise in crimes of
"irreflection. . .and of impulsiveness" to periods of war and political
crisis (Nye 1984:193). His argument was that in such periods
collective passions run high. He also suggested that the intensity
with which society reacts to such crimes varies with the level of
"passion" in the collective unconscious (Nye 1984:193–194). Clearly
people working with such ideas would expect a rash of crime and
violence during a period of crisis. Such expectations could have a
major role in shaping policy concerning policing and law and order.

We need to examine societal perceptions of violence and responses to this (What does the violence mean? What is it held to signify
about the state of society?). To do this it is necessary to examine
violence in its broadest context. This means looking closely at events
and reactions to them. It means looking at the way in which specific
incidents or behaviours become the focus of fear and anxiety since
"no one thinks about violence in the abstract" and "any. . .society
shapes conceptions of its objects of fear out of images presented by
everyday culture" (Nye 1984:194). Nye's work on France provides a
good model for this approach. He examines the period 1905–8 and
the widespread belief that "new and more dangerous forms of

deviance were taking shape" in the country and that "traditional institutions and processes of repression were unable to cope with them" (1984:172). He argues that in fact there was no real shift in patterns of deviance, but that "the extraordinary series of external and internal crises that occurred in this brief era combined to produce an unusually high level of public concern about security" and that in this atmosphere of anxiety "the threshold of public tolerance for deviance" was particularly low. A medical model of cultural crisis emerged in which crime, mental illness and alcoholism became signs of national debility and degeneration. This suggests that public and official anxiety about violence and crime can be heightened by events which in themselves are not violent.

Poverty and Relief

> . . .get yourselves together and make history. Don't let history make you. You make it. Start in to sweep poverty away. (Pierce Power)[11]

Even a brief glance at the history of Newfoundland shows that the main problem faced by small producers and the working class has been, as indeed it continues to be, the basic insecurity of existence resulting from low wages and fish prices, unemployment, illness, and accidents and old age.[12] For many, obtaining minimum subsistence, let alone an adequate income has been a constant problem, periodically becoming acute. The struggle over the living standard has been carried out on many fronts: in the workplace, over the price of fish and the prices charged by merchants for basic commodities; against taxation and the game laws which regulated access to food; and over the provision of health care, education, pensions and relief for the permanent, casual, and able-bodied poor.

The provision of relief for the unemployed has, since the last century, been a focus of political struggle (Gunn 1966). In the period between the two world wars the provision of relief became one of the key political issues in Newfoundland. The questions of the extent of the state's responsibility for the poor, the form that relief provision should take, the level of relief to be provided, who should be eligible, the political rights of paupers, the best way to administer the public relief system and how it should be financed were all given a great deal of attention. The central concern of those attempting to work out relief policy was the need to restrict its provision both to keep costs down and to prevent pauperization of the population by making relief more attractive than work. This latter imperative is captured well by Thomas Lodge, one of the Commissioners who governed Newfoundland in the 1930s:

> The tragedy of Newfoundland is not that the scale of able-bodied relief is so low. It is that the scale differs so little from the standard of living enjoyed by the workers who manage to retain their complete independence and keep off the "dole." To make relief more attractive, or less unattractive, in a community in which one-quarter is already forced to apply for it, is to risk the complete collapse of the social structure (Lodge 1939:233).

Clearly, state policy concerning public relief was one of the main factors influencing the terms and condition under which workers and small producers would labour for those who purchased their products. If many of those who could find work were faced with slow starvation on inadequate incomes, there were also vast numbers of people who could not earn a living. Either no work was available, or piece work rates were so low and expenses so high as to make working a way of getting into debt (in the logging industry, for example), or people were unable to fish because they had no equipment and could not get credit or find a buyer for their product. With dole the only alternative—and in the face of efforts to restrict its provision—many were led into conflict with the state. The struggle for subsistence and for the dole took individual forms as people attempted to 'abuse' the system by making false declarations, hiding food and money and creatively exploring a variety of other possibilities. But the struggle also took forms which were political in both a narrow and a broad sense. In particular, collective action by the unemployed attempted to wring concessions out of intransigent governments and on a number of occasions this led to violent confrontations with the state. It was such violent confrontations and the policy of restricting the dole which had the most important impact on policing policy in Newfoundland in the 1930s.

THE ECONOMIC AND POLITICAL CRISIS OF THE EARLY 1930s

> . . .in 1914 you responded, your fathers responded to call of arms; you fought for democracy, you fought for it, but you have not got it. Millions of lives were given for it, but we have instead. . .soup kitchens, starvation, and dole rations. We never had democracy. (Pierce Power)[13]

With the onset of the Great Depression conditions deteriorated very quickly in Newfoundland. While both layoffs and wage cuts were made in the mining and forest industries, it was in the fishing industry that the situation became most serious. This had a drastic effect on all other aspects of the economy. The export value per quintal for dry cod fish fell from over $9.00 in 1929 to $4.53 in 1932 and $4.00 in 1936 (*Evening Telegram* 15 February 1932:2). The total value of this export fell from over $16 million in 1929 to $7.3 in 1936. As prices for cod fell, so the debts of those engaged in fishing rose. In 1932 it was estimated that only half of the supplies given out to fishermen on credit in 1930 had been paid for at the end of the fishing season.[14] In 1931 only a third of the supplies were covered. As credit was curtailed and small merchants went out of business, and as fishermen lost their equipment to pay off bad debts, many were forced out of the industry. With the possibilities of finding work in the woods and mines limited and with immigration to Canada and the U.S.A. curtailed, there was no alternative but to apply for the dole. The winters of 1931, 1932 and 1933 were ones of unprecedented misery in Newfoundland as the number of people who were totally destitute and receiving public relief rose to a maximum of 90,000, approximately a third of the population. As the costs of public relief mounted to over one million dollars, government revenue, derived mostly from customs duties, fell sharply from a high of $11.6 million in 1929–30 to $8 million in 1932–33.[15] Budget deficits averaged $4 million in the period 1930–33 and interest payments on the debt accounted for over 60 percent of annual revenue. Financial disaster began to loom perilously close.

With revenues falling and the country finding it increasingly difficult to borrow funds, the government began to cut expenditures. Serious efforts to limit the fast growing relief bill were undertaken. This, however, led to a spate of break-ins at merchants' stores all over Newfoundland and the government was deluged by telegrams and letters reporting starving conditions.[16] In some areas organized action followed initial protest. And in the summer of 1931 Prime Minister Richard Squires was anxious enough about the situation to contact the governor, Sir John Middleton, about persons of "Red tendencies" organizing the unemployed in Conception Bay and St. John's.[17] Facing a serious situation, Squires resorted to the use of the British navy.

In 1931 the financial state of Newfoundland was so precarious that default was narrowly avoided by bank loans which were provided on the condition that tariffs be revised and a strict policy of retrenchment followed by the government. The Squires government also sought assistance from the British government in managing its financial affairs. In the fall of 1931 Sir Percy Thompson of the Board of Inland Revenue in London was given the job of financial advisor to the Government of Newfoundland. His task was to suggest ways in which the country's financial position might be improved. Thompson was assisted in his work by a British Treasury official, J.H. Penson, who took on the task of deputy minister of finance. In addition, a Montreal businessman, R.J. Magor, was hired to undertake a reorganization of the country's public utilities with a view to cutting expenditures in this area.

The Liberal government responded to the crisis of 1931 by initiating a savage program of retrenchment and by raising taxes.[18] This program was extended and intensified by the conservative United Newfoundland Party which came to office in June 1932 after the defeat of the Liberals. The civil service suffered severe cuts. Overall spending on salaries was cut from $1,682,977 in 1931 to $1,187,021 in 1934 and in the same period the number of civil servants was cut from 3,230 to 2,476. In this short period over 300 post offices were closed and the number of mail couriers was more than halved. Those government employees who managed to keep their job experienced deep cuts in salaries in this period. Many government departments had their already limited budgets slashed between 1931 and 1934 forcing them into extreme economy measures. The budget for the General Hospital was cut from $163,441 in 1931 to $114,574 in 1934 and most of the savings were made by trimming salaries and by cutting the costs of food for patients.[19] Medical aid to paupers was also cut at a time when poverty-related diseases such as beri-beri and tuberculosis were becoming epidemic.[20] The two departments which had budget increases in this period were Public Health and Welfare and Justice, the increase in the budget of the former being a result of relief costs and the latter the increased costs of policing the population.

Those who were most affected by retrenchment were not in a position to put up a struggle against the tide of cuts in wages, employment and services.[21] Only a very small proportion of the population was unionized (about 7,000 workers) and most of these were in the Longshoremen's Union and in the forest industries (Gillespie 1980, 1986:55–66). In any case, even the unionized workers were not particularly successful at defending themselves against wage cuts. Opposition was also made difficult in political terms by the fact that many of the attacks were coming from the party which had claimed to be representing the interests of the masses against the classes.[22]

The Magor Ration

In November 1931 Mr. Magor turned his attention away from the reorganization of the transport and communications systems and public works, where substantial cuts had been made, to the Public Charities Department. In the area of public relief, spending was escalating in an unplanned and uncontrolled fashion despite attempts to discourage people from applying for state assistance. In 1931–32 it reached well over one million dollars.[23] Moreover, the Charities Department was "seriously in arrears" with the payment of bills for relief supplies issued through the various business houses, and merchants were threatening not to issue dole supplies until the government paid its debts (*Evening Telegram* 14 November 1931:4). This in turn increased the likelihood of raids occurring in small settlements where single merchants had control of the supply of relief rations. There was also considerable evidence of corruption and laxity in the distribution of relief.[24] As the financial crisis developed the press increasingly campaigned against the dole and this fuelled the fear of mass pauperization which gripped the middle classes.[25] All this, and the expectation that the winter of 1931–32 would see widespread distress, made the need to re-organize the relief system an urgent one.

On November 19 Mr. Magor announced his plans for relief.[26] These changes were to coincide with a scheme of treasury control being inaugurated by Sir Percy Thompson and Mr. Penson. From December 1931 no government expenditure would be recognized unless it was duly authorized in advance by the appropriate department and the budget of that department had been approved by the Department of Finance. By this means it was hoped to eliminate all *ad hoc*, unauthorized and unplanned spending. The financial reorganization was also a condition of further bank loans to the country. With the bulk of state revenue (from customs duties) directly under the control of Sir Percy Thompson and Mr. Penson all spending could be strictly rationed.

Mr. Magor's scheme was intended to help ration relief. He divided the country into relief districts under the control of "keymen." These men were to be recruited from magistrates, policemen and other "responsible" officials with the aim of ensuring that "under no circumstances will the work be influenced by politicians or their representatives." Thus the view that relief provision must be divorced from politics if expenditures were to be controlled was central to the Magor system (*Evening Telegram* 19 November 1931:4). The keymen would be responsible for surveying conditions in their districts using the existing body of relieving officers, policemen, and other state officials. The surveys would provide a basis for estimating fairly accurately the relief needs of the district in advance. A budget for relief spending could then be drawn up and approved on a month-by-month basis. In addition, the keymen were instructed to encourage the formation of local relief committees where this seemed appropriate. These committees would organize self-help schemes and thus lighten the relief burden of the state. They would also be responsible for organizing the community work which was to be required from all able-bodied relief recipients as well as advising relief officials on which applicants for relief were deserving of assistance.

As part of the Magor scheme a statutory declaration was to be required from all relief applicants and a standard ration issued to those who were successful in their application for support. This ration consisted, initially, of 25 lbs. of flour, 1 qt. of molasses, 3 3/4 lbs. fat back pork, 2 lbs. beans, 1 lb. split peas, 2 lbs. corn meal and 3/4 lb. cocoa (*Evening Telegram* 6 January 1932:12). This was the maximum to be issued to an adult for one month. Relief officials could, if they saw fit, issue a lower ration. Children received lower rations. The total cost of the ration varied depending on the cost of commodities. However, the Magor system did attempt to control prices paid to merchants for relief supplies and on this basis it was estimated that the cost of the ration in the outports would be $1.80 per month and in St. John's $1.43 1/2 per month. When the Magor ration was introduced to St. John's, however, it was decided to include vegetables with the order and to provide an extra fifteen cents *per order* for such items as oil and soap. For each order issued a sum of five cents was also sent to the Child Welfare Association so that from time to time milk or fats could be issued to children.

The new relief arrangements were part of an effort to put the allocation of state assistance to the destitute on a businesslike basis. This meant limiting the possibilities for abuse by both those administering the system and those being supported by its rations. The introduction of Magor's scheme coincided with a propaganda campaign aimed at the poor. They were told of the acute difficulties facing the country and asked to do their patriotic duty by not becoming burdens on the state. At the same time the authorities adopted a tougher attitude towards relief frauds and those thought to be abusing the system. People who were dependent on the state were quite regularly represented as unpatriotic and of low moral standard. In one account those applying for relief who were *not* totally destitute were held to be "in the same category as one who steals from a church poor box" (*Evening Telegram* 12 January 1932:4). The following statement made in January 1932 suggests that Mr. Magor was quite willing to hold a whole area to ransom in the quest to cut out abuses of the relief system:

consideration is now being given to the possibility of discontinuing relief orders in that particular section in which these violations are taking place. Such discontinuance will be enforced until the people in these communities unearth and report fraudulent cases and show willingness to cooperate (*Evening Telegram* 12 January 1932:4).

The views expressed by Magor were widely supported in the press. They fitted well with an analysis of the relief problem which saw abuse of the system, either through ignorance or deliberate action, as the only possible explanation for there being a quarter of the country's population on the dole.

The introduction of the new scheme in late 1931 and early 1932 proved difficult. Lack of detailed information supplied by less than competent officials as well as rapidly deteriorating conditions made it difficult to accurately budget for relief. The ration issued was inadequate and in several areas the population experienced acute hardship as a result. Many protests and some raids on merchants' stores resulted. In a few cases raids were narrowly avoided by the issue of rations, as occurred at Spaniard's Bay on New Years Eve, 1931.[27]

It was soon evident that under the new system control of relief spending was not going to be easy. Those closest to the poverty of the people, the relieving officers and relief commissioners, were spending too much. The only way to limit this was "to keep the pressure on these keymen to the utmost limit," in the following way:

where the first two months of some keyman's expenditure was thought high they were warned that, unless a reduction in their lists was immediately made, they would be subject to a 25 percent cut in their expenditure.[28]

Further relief economies were achieved by putting the permanent poor and pensioners on the Magor ration if they proved to be destitute(*Evening Telegram* 19 January 1932:4).

Early in 1932 an attempt was made to introduce the new ration to St. John's. The capital city enjoyed higher relief rates than the outports in recognition of the fact that there were less opportunities for hunting, fishing, and growing vegetables than in rural areas. With unemployment rising and efforts underway by employers to cut wages, the issue of public relief was a very important one in the city. Workers in St. John's also had a recent history of organized involvement in the unemployment issue. Organizations of the unemployed had existed throughout the 1920s and some of their members now took up the task of resisting the imposition of the Magor ration. At the end of January a meeting was held in the Armoury at which dissatisfaction with the proposed food ration was expressed (*Evening Telegram* 2 February 1932:4). A committee was instructed to arrange a meeting with Mr. Magor in order to present the case of the unemployed. As a result about 300 people marched to the meeting, and a delegation headed by Stanley Rideout spent half an hour with the Montreal businessman. They got no satisfaction from the meeting and on February 2 the unemployed assembled again to discuss matters. They categorically rejected the rations and passed a resolution to that effect (*Evening Telegram* 3 February 1932:5). They also rejected the declaration under oath which had been introduced on the grounds that existing investigations were ample proof of need.

As opposition to Magor's scheme was mobilized, it was announced, on February 6, that the new dole ration would be introduced the following Monday. The new dietary regimen had, it was argued, been determined in consultation with Dr. Brehm the Medical Officer of Health for the Country. He had analysed the food and found that it provided a total of 59,781.71 calories per month, or 1,990.62 calories per day for an adult. This ration was "well balanced and. . .quite sufficient as a maintenance diet" (*Evening Telegram* 6 February 1932:4). In addition, it was pointed out that the ration was not intended to supply all the needs of the unemployed. They were expected to fend for themselves and to avail themselves of the support of friends, family, and community. Many of the destitute were, in fact, being aided by charity. The St. John's Civic Relief Committee had been established to raise funds by donation which would be used to supply the destitute with fuel.[29] However, the fund was slow in climbing. On February 8 the Unemployed Committee reported in the press that the five cent-a-day ration was "absolutely insufficient to live on" and the following day a meeting at the Majestic Theatre chaired by James McGrath produced a resolution which stated its opposition to the new ration in no uncertain terms (*Evening Telegram* 8, 10 February 1932:5). In the absence of any response from the authorities to their demands, the unemployed decided to press their case further. On February 11 hundreds of men, women, and children assembled in front of the Court House in the vicinity of the Relief Bureau at 10:30 in the morning (*Evening Telegram* 11 February 1932:5). From there they marched to the Prime Minister's office. After waiting for over an hour for Richard Squires to appear, they were informed that he was too busy to attend to them until the afternoon. The crowd dispersed and following a further meeting at the Armoury a decision was made to try to see Squires. In the afternoon there was an orderly parade to the Court House to present the following letter to the Prime Minister:

We hereby desire to give you formal notification that, we the unemployed committee, have practically exhausted all possible efforts to secure a peaceful settlement of the Dole Question. Unless, therefore, some immediate provision be made for handling the situation we cannot hold ourselves responsible for any act or acts by those men who, seeing the failure of our efforts on their behalf, may decide to take matters in their own hands.

As we have no desire to bring about anything in the nature of an unlawful disturbance we are sending you this notice so that you may be able to take any steps you may deem necessary (*Evening Telegram* 12 February 1932:4).[30]

Again, Squires refused to meet those assembled in front of the Court House. The huge crowd waited from 2:40 until 4:45 while several requests were made for him to receive the committee of the unemployed and address the crowd. In the end the crowd decided to go into the Court House and see the Prime Minister. They entered the building and invaded the Council Chambers. A tense situation ensued. Some windows were broken and Squires was assaulted. The situation was only calmed when the Prime Minister told the protesters to go to the Charity Organization Bureau where they would receive dole orders under the old conditions. That evening rations to the value of $1.75 per person were handed out to 560 applicants. The following day another 700 were relieved. In all, $7,000 of dole was distributed. Where petitions and meetings failed, face-to-face confrontation succeeded. The threat and use of force may have been the last resort for desperate people, but it was to be increasingly used in the next few months as the struggle over the dole continued.

The resort to violence (if indeed it can be seen as a tactic rather than something which just happened in the course of events) was not without its costs. It was used to generate hostility to the unemployed. The editor of the *Evening Telegram*, for example, thought that although the authorities were not without blame in the incident, the unemployed, in assaulting Richard Squires and damaging property, had crossed the important line separating order from chaos (*Evening Telegram* 12 February 1932:6). Under no circumstances could violence and lawlessness be justified and the breakdown of law and order was "something worse than any form of hardship." Further, violence was alien to the Newfoundland character. If the unemployed were suffering, then they should resort to "self-help" to see them through their difficulties—this was presumably viewed as a part of the Newfoundland character—and not take to the streets to wring concessions out of a bankrupt government by means of meetings and confrontation. Instead of organizing and protesting the unemployed should be hunting and fishing, cutting wood, and cultivating vegetables.

The actions of the unemployed were also criticized by the *Fishermen's Advocate* when it jumped to the defence of Richard Squires. The unemployed, in their petition, might have appealed for "British Justice," but now they were accused of "Un-British Conduct." The "nauseating scene" in St. John's was an "outrage" which raised serious political questions:

> Well-reasoned persons may well ask if in any degree the Tory papers and irresponsible Tory agitators in St. John's are responsible for such conduct (*Fishermen's Advocate* 19 February 1932:4).

The *Advocate* laid the blame for events at the door of "Tory soreheads who stood in the background whilst their willing dupes did their dirty work." Comparing the actions of "the mob" with those of the Longshoremen's Protective Union in their recent strike against the Employers' Association, the *Advocate* found further reason to condemn the unemployed.[31] The Longshoremen had taken a "firm stand for what they regarded as their rights" and conducted their affairs on "sound business principles" with "no rowdyism" and "no attempt to create disorder" (*Fishermen's Advocate* 19 February 1932:4). The model offered by the responsible labour movement contrasted sharply with the unemployed's "strike." The message was clear: in its quest to upset the government, Toryism would not stop short of using "mob force and physical violence." Using this argument the *Fishermen's Advocate* avoided even acknowledging the grievances of the St. John's unemployed.

Although the idea should not be dismissed out of hand, there is little evidence to suggest that the unemployed were being manipulated by powerful political interests at that time. However, some conservative observers thought that the unemployed might play a crucial role in bringing about the end of the Squires government. John Hepburn, one of the St. John's directors of Baine Johnston Company Ltd., described conditions in Newfoundland in early 1932 as "shocking." However, despite the February confrontation, Richard Squires was still in office, even if his position was increasingly difficult:

> At the present time things have not been finalized. They have still to make another scene before they leave him. To my mind all that is wanted here is a leader to get the unemployed a-going, and when they do things will be very nasty, almost as you have there in Spain, because Newfoundlanders when their blood is up are not very easily handled.[32]

The unemployed had "showed their teeth" and Squires had handled the situation very badly.[33] With the banks "now showing their teeth" by refusing further loans to the government, it was clear that the Prime Minister had "finished himself." It was just a question of time and of "who are we going to put in that is any better?" Certainly the merchants and middle classes of St. John's had mobilized opposition to Squires at least from mid-1931 when Hepburn wrote the following:

> One thing is certain, that the country and all those interested in it are now favourable to calling a show-down at the present moment, rather than let things go on from bad to worse, and I think that is the wisest policy to pursue.[34]

But whether this involved *using* the unemployed in any simple sense of the word, rather than using the unemployment and relief issues to further undermine an already struggling government is open to question.

Certainly the Squires administration in its own defence suggested that the Court House incident was part of an effort to unseat the government. In its despatch dealing with the event it described James McGrath, chairman of the unemployed and the leader of the "raid," as a "gangster" (*Evening Telegram* 18 February 1932:15). It emphasized the violence of the incident and suggested it was caused by Tory agitation. It even raised the spectre of sectarianism. This account, which tried to make Squires a "martyr and a hero" was absolutely rejected by the *Evening Telegram* as an attempt to give a simple case of "disorderly conduct" a great "political significance" (*Evening Telegram* 15 February 1932:6). The government's version of events also brought a strong protest from James McGrath and Weston Dick of the Unemployed Committee (*Evening Telegram* 18 February 1932:15). They countered the "vicious and slanderous" attack by emphasising the intransigence of the government over the relief issue and the fact that the Prime Minister ignored the huge crowd of people assembled to present its position regarding the dole:

> We marched in order to the Premier's office, and whilst the women and men waited in the street, the committee entered, but again they were refused an interview. For nearly an hour we waited in the hallway. Outside the crowd were getting restless and, remember, they were cold and hungry. Fearing that they would get out of hand we made effort after effort to get a few minutes of the Premier's time, but to no avail. And right here I would like to say that the only explanation I can see for the Premier's ignoring hundreds of cold and hungry men and women as he did that day is either profound

stupidity, ignorance of human nature, or a deliberate plan to goad the people to some desperate act.

I place the entire responsibility for the outbreak on the shoulders of the Prime Minister. He could have prevented it, instead he invited it—he drove the desperate hungry to a point where they had no other course open; but only, mind you, after they had gone to the very limit as peaceable and law abiding citizens (*Evening Telegram* 18 February 1932:15).

On February 18 it was announced that the Magor ration had been abandoned in St. John's and that Mr. Magor had gone back to his task of trimming postal, telegraph, transportation and other services (*Evening Telegram* 18 February 1932:4). Relief outside the capital city was put in the hands of Mr. Taylor and a committee consisting of senior politicians, while J.H. Penson of Finance, Superintendent P. O'Neill and Inspector General Hutchinson of the Constabulary were to be responsible for organizing relief in St. John's (*Evening Telegram* 20 February 1932:4). Those in need would be required to register with the government and all investigations were to be undertaken by the police (*Evening Telegram* 19 February 1932:4). The ration for those in St. John's was increased.[35] The new rates were arranged on a sliding scale which provided a single person with $1.50 per week, two adults with $2.50 per week and a family of thirteen with $5.00 per week. This very much improved support for smaller families and single persons, but the improvement for large families was marginal at best. Very large families were worse off under the new system than they had been under the arrangements which pre-dated the Magor ration. However, the weekly ration made it easier for those on relief to budget their food. It was also announced that the requirement that the able-bodied work for their dole was to be relaxed.

In the short term, the improvement in relief rations had calmed a troubled political situation in St. John's, but the long term prospects of the country were not good. The government had managed to squeak through one crisis, but the treasury was empty and financial disaster was fast overtaking the politicians' frantic efforts to prevent the ship of state from foundering. The *Evening Telegram* in reviewing the situation argued that "even the present expenditure on relief cannot be of long duration" (23 February 1932:6).[36] Clearly a "miracle" was needed if the following winter was going to be faced. Increasingly the *Evening Telegram* and many other middle class commentators on the desperate situation argued that the only possible way out of the crisis was to cut relief by encourag-

ing a back-to-the-land, self-help movement amongst the unemployed.[37]

But events were not standing still. Pressure for the government
to abandon the Magor ration began to mount outside St. John's
following the triumph of the city's unemployed. It was particularly
well-organized in the Carbonear Area of Conception Bay.[38] Deputa-
tions from Victoria, Perry's Cove, Salmon Cove and several other
communities assembled at the Court House in Carbonear in late
February. Informing the authorities that they were unable to live on
the Magor ration of the equivalent of about $1.80's worth of food per
month, they demanded this ration be given every three weeks. In
many cases these people were living in circumstances not very
different from the working classes of St. John's. Many were unemployed miners who had returned from Bell Island and Nova Scotia
and they were not fitted out for fishing or providing their own food.
They also had a history of militancy which the authorities found
unsettling.

The situation in St. John's remained tense. Wages were reduced
for those still in work and unemployment was increasing as trade
ground to a halt and the government's retrenchment program took
its toll. Any accumulated savings were quickly eaten up and the
respectable working-classes and even some of the lower middle-
class were being haunted by the possibility of destitution. By the
end of February the unemployed were again holding meetings, this
time to press the government for work (*Evening Telegram* 1 March
1932:4).

In early March the Squires administration announced a new
budget. Under continued pressure from the Canadian banks who
were providing the government with loans, efforts were being made
to implement economies recommended by the government's financial advisor Sir Percy Thompson.[39] Cuts in the pensions of war
veterans were proposed as well as tariff increases which it was
estimated would raise the cost of living by 30 percent (*Evening
Telegram* 2 March 1932:5).[40] The budget even reduced the vote for
agricultural encouragement from $15,000 to $10,000 despite its
obvious value in assisting people to grow their own food by providing
advice and seeds (*Evening Telegram* 9 March 1932:4). The proposed
cuts in war pensions, in particular, generated considerable opposition from the Great War Veterans' Association. According to one
observer this group was able to alter the government's proposal by
threatening violence.[41]

Amidst increasing evidence of corruption in high places, resentment mounted as austerity measures were extended. Opposition to

the government was widespread. Taxes had been introduced on a number of items which had previously been untaxed, including flour, beef and pork, and income tax, profits tax and sales tax had also been increased. Merchants complained bitterly that the increased taxes would make profitable business even more difficult than in the past. Mr. Collingwood, of Baine Johnston Ltd., thought the situation in Newfoundland was now very poor and that there would be trouble, but he also thought that a "good row would clear the atmosphere, and might be the means of getting rid of Squires and his gang."[42] In anticipation of this event most of the Water Street firms, including Collingwood's, had covered their premises and stock against riot and civil commotion at what they considered to be a very reasonable premium, that is, 1/8 of 1 percent.[43] In addition to the opposition to the Squires regime, more and more serious questions were being raised about the costs of democracy in Newfoundland:

> Surely no country has ever had to pay so high a price for democracy as the people of Newfoundland are now paying, (*Evening Telegram* 9 March 1932:4).

The Fall of the Squires Government (1932)

Amidst charges of wrongdoing at the highest levels and mounting opposition to further austerity measures the government's ranks began to crack. By mid-March, Dr. Mosdell, minister without portfolio, was openly critical of the new budget (*Evening Telegram* 16 March 1932:5, 13). The government was, he claimed, "grinding the faces of the poor" by trying to balance the budget. It was driving fishermen to abandon industry. Mosdell talked of betrayal and warned of the wrath of the people. When the House of Assembly opened briefly to pass the tariff proposals on March 23, Dr. Mosdell and two other members of the government resigned (Noel 1971:201).[44]

Amid calls from church leaders for more intensive cultivation of the soil, "rigid economy. . .to the point of sacrifice and self-denial" and a return to "the adventurous spirit of our forefathers," the unemployed in St. John's continued their efforts to improve the dole and get work (Archbishop E.P. Roche, *Evening Telegram* 14 March 1932:10). On March 30th it was reported that the House of Assembly opened and that it was protected by over thirty policemen, both mounted and on foot. It was also reported that all business and office premises in the city were vacated for the occasion. On March 31, 250 unemployed marched to the House of Assembly after a meeting

at the Armoury (*Evening Telegram* 1 April 1932:4). They carried a
Union Jack and presented a petition to the House.[45] The unemployed committee claimed to speak for the 2,300 unemployed
people of St. John's and their 6,000 dependants. Complaining of
"malnutrition and semi-starvation" which was seriously affecting
their capacity to work they argued for a 50 percent increase in the
dole ration. They also noted that the recent tax increases (especially
on flour) had reduced the value of the dole ration. The petitioners
further requested that something be done to prevent evictions for
non-payment of rent as well as to provide employment on public
works. Squires promised to give the matter his attention and the
parade ended without incident.

On April 4 a letter was forwarded to the representatives of the
unemployed informing them that a committee was to be established
to deal with any threatened "ejectment" and that meetings were
taking place "with a view to a substantial reorganization of the
present allowance" and establishing "a work program" (*Evening
Telegram* 5 April 1932:12).[46] It was suggested that the reorganized
system would come into effect "on Saturday next." Apparently, a
"small readjustment" of the ration which had been in effect since
February 20 had taken place on March 26.[47] This provided a slight
increase in the relief scale for families of from three to ten persons
(one dollar per month for most families). Inspector General Hutchings of the Constabulary in his capacity as relief controller for St.
John's was in charge of negotiations with the unemployed. On April
7 he reported that he had met with the unemployed committee and
then submitted a proposal for new relief rates to the government.[48]
This represented the minimum required by the unemployed. However, Hutchings had "no assurance from the Committee that it would
be acceptable to the unemployed." The unemployed committee was
scheduled to meet on April 8 to discuss the government's offer. In
the delicate political situation which had developed the unemployed
were clearly pressing their case as far as possible. Even so, in the
end there was room for compromise. Responding to the government's pleas "that our finances are strained well nigh to the breaking
point," they agreed to accept a 20 percent increase in rations rather
than the 50 percent originally demanded.[49] The new ration system
came into effect on April 9.[50] It provided $1.80 per week for an adult
and on a sliding scale allowed $3.90 for a family of five and $6.00
for a family of thirteen. The new rates greatly increased expenditure
on relief for the approximately 1,800 people supported in St. John's
at the time. While these negotiations had been taking place a

political crisis of major proportions had been brewing creating a set
of circumstances which worked in the favour of the unemployed.

Opponents of the government chose the opening of the House of
Assembly on April 5 as the occasion to confront the Squires administration over its alleged wrongdoings. On Monday, April 4 a
meeting had been held at the Majestic Theatre to plan the action
(*Evening Telegram* 5 April 1932:5). Many prominent St. John's
merchants were present including C.P. Ayre, Eric Bowering, Gordon
Winter, and W.S. Monroe. At the meeting it was decided that the
citizens of St. John's would march to the House of Assembly the
following day to demand an investigation into the charges against
Squires' ministers. At 2 p.m. on April 5 people met at the Majestic
Theatre to line up for the "monster parade" (*Evening Telegram* 6 April
1932:6). Those assembled were instructed to make sure that there
would be no breaches of the law. The *Evening Telegram* described
the parade thus:

> The Guards band headed the parade, Mr. H. Winter with the
> petition, Rev. Mr. Godfrey, chairman Howell and members of the
> committee were in the front ranks. Ex-servicemen, naval reservists
> and members of the Mercantile Marine fell in first and after these
> citizens in general who walked in ranks six to eight deep. . ..
> Prominent businessmen, doctors, legal men and a large number of
> women were in the parade. It was a demonstration of citizenship
> representing every section of the city, such as was never before
> witnessed in the history of St. John's. As the parade proceeded
> along hundreds joined in and it is estimated that between eight or
> ten thousand people were in the demonstration (6 April 1932:6).

The parade marched through the centre of town to the Colonial
Building. Many St. John's businesses had closed for the occasion
and their employees swelled the parade.

The House met at the usual time of 3:15 p.m. and when the
parade reached the Colonial Building a number of people were
queuing to gain admission to the proceedings.[51] A squad of about
thirty policemen, including four mounted officers, was stationed at
the foot of the steps leading to the building. Many women and
children had been walking in advance of the parade and they
crowded into the yard in front of the building. The mounted police
used their horses to clear a path through this crowd for the parade.
When the petitioners reached the steps of the building they raised
the Union Jack amidst the cheers of the crowd. Members of the
citizens' deputation led by Winter, Godfrey, and Chairman Howell
mounted the steps in order to present the petition, but were forced
to wait about thirty minutes before they were allowed into the

building. Meanwhile the Guards band stuck up the "Ode to New-foundland" and the vast crowd "stood with bared head until the piece was finished." Once the delegation had been admitted and presented its petition at the Bar there was a further delay as procedure was discussed in the Assembly. At this point the crowd became restless and those at the back began to press forward. With the aim of keeping the people back, the mounted police took up positions in front of the steps. Pressed from behind and from the front by the police, trouble erupted and the mounted men were attacked and forced aside. An attempt was then made to enter the Colonial Building. In an effort to diffuse the anger the party with the Union Jack attempted to move off, but the flag was prevented from being removed. Soon the deputation returned from the House and Mr. Winter asked the gathering to march back to the Majestic Theatre. His efforts to re-assemble the parade were only partially successful and many remained in front of the building. Further attempts to gain entry to the House were made, but the doors were bolted and supported from the inside by the twenty-five or so constables who were present. A battering ram was obtained and "one door panel was quickly reduced to matchwood," but the police used their batons to prevent entry to the building. The mounted policemen attempted to disperse the crowd outside while those inside held the fort. One last attempt was made to quieten the situation by Superintendent O'Neill addressing the crowd, but this had little effect and soon the flagpole flying the Union Jack was being used as a battering ram. Armed with fence palings and stones part of the crowd stormed the east side entrance of the building, but were again repulsed by police.

At this point the police made a baton charge from the front entrance of the building. In the course of this "scores fell under the rain of blows" and both "young and old were hit." In less than a minute the steps of the building were cleared of all except the fallen. With this attack, according to the *Evening Telegram*, "*anger over-came reasons*":

> Like a flame, a desire for revenge took possession of the crowd and the police had to run for shelter within the building. Stones, sticks and every kind of missile obtainable were hurled through practically every window in the place. There were no leaders, but the crowd appeared to divide into sections to prevent the exit of the police and executive heads of the Government (6 April 1932:4).

By 4:20 p.m. a crowd of youths had demolished the door on the western side of the building, while the "stoning of the building continued uninterrupted." The four mounted policemen in a frantic effort to control the large crowd which had laid siege to the House of Assembly charged around and "into some thousands of innocent people who were assembled in the grounds." Some were knocked to the ground and injured, but most escaped into Bannerman Park by tearing down a fence. Before long, however, the mounted policemen were put out of action by the crowd. One was hit on the head by a stone. He lost control of his horse and was dragged from the saddle and trampled on before being rescued and rushed to the General Hospital. Another mounted officer was also taken to hospital after being knocked out by a stone. The two remaining officers suffered spills and decided to retreat to the barracks at Fort Townsend. After this rout the basement of the Colonial Building was broken into, a piano was hauled into Bannerman Park and "completely destroyed" and some youths consumed four plundered bottles of White Horse whisky. Both the mace and the sword of the Sergeant-at-Arms were stolen, but quickly retrieved. During the melee some of the members of the House of Assembly managed to escape.

Efforts were made to try and restore order by some ex-servicemen and messages were sent to the clergy to come and help calm the crowd. Dr. Wylie Clark made "an impassioned appeal for peace," but this was rejected. Mr. Cashin, Mr. Garland, and Superintendent O'Neill tried to arrange the terms of a peace. Mr. Cashin went to Inspector General Hutchings and told him that if the police gave up their batons then he would undertake to see that the crowd withdrew. Mr. Garland gave the crowd an assurance from the head of the police force that batons would never again be used, but in response the crowd demanded the resignation of the Inspector General of Constabulary. Several clergymen made further efforts to calm the situation but without much effect. Still trapped in the building were Sir Richard Squires, Mr. Bradley, and the Inspector General. Rev. Godfrey took forty volunteers and escorted the Prime Minister out of the building. On the way to a waiting car he was recognized by some of the crowd. A nasty incident was avoided by the pleadings of Superintendent O'Neill of the Constabulary, but it took one hour for the group protecting Squires to reach the refuge of a house on Colonial Street. A huge crowd continued to wait outside the house for Squires.

Meanwhile the Prime Minister was spirited out of the back door of the house, over some fences to a house on Bannerman Street, and then into a taxi. By the time the crowd had searched the house on Colonial Street, Sir Richard Squires had made his escape. Even so it took well over an hour and a shower of rain to disperse the crowd in Colonial Street. It was after midnight when the large assembly outside the Colonial Building finally dispersed. The police made their exit from the building late in the evening in two groups, the last leaving about 11 p.m. after a squad of about twenty ex-servicemen under the control of Lt.-Col. Paterson and Commander Howley, R.N. had arrived to protect the property for the night. Other groups of ex-servicemen were on duty throughout the city that night. In particular, they were called upon to protect the Liquor Controller's premises. The East End Controller's premises had been partially looted during the latter part of the disturbance and later in the evening the West End premises had been practically cleaned out of all its stock. During the night the situation remained tense. Some stores were broken into and looted and the same happened with several Chinese restaurants (*Evening Telegram* 6 April 1932:4). The following morning, while liquor was being removed from the West End Controller's premises to the Central Department, a box of beer fell off the truck. This was grabbed by one of the crowd who had assembled to watch the proceedings and he managed to get away with the prize despite the efforts of a special policeman to capture him.

The day following the riot St. John's was relatively quiet. An attempt to raid the Central Liquor store was made using a battering ram obtained from the water front (*Evening Telegram* 7 April 1932:4). But this was prevented by a flying squad of ex-servicemen and Major Peter Cashin, who addressed the crowd and informed them that Sir Richard Squires had promised to resign. Thereafter the liquor stores were patrolled by armed volunteers while the street was "closed off with barbed wire entanglements" according to the *Fisherman's Advocate* (8 April 1932:1). The attacks on the Central Liquor Controller's premises on April 5, 6, and 7 were beaten off "with much difficulty" as was a raid on a steamer loaded with liquor which was in the harbour;[52] but even so it was reported on April 8 that "liquor was selling in the city yesterday for small prices by youngsters who had got hold of many bottles" (*Fishermen's Advocate* 8 April 1932:1). In all it was estimated that over $1,500 of liquor had been taken during the riot, probably much of it by the unemployed who had been forced to give up their liquor permits as a penalty for being on the dole.[53] The situation in St. John's remained tense but quiet for some days. On April 9 the head of the Constabulary reported to the governor that rumours were circulating of a plan to steal gunpowder and:

> Destroy the Power Plant so as to put the City in darkness and then begin a season of looting, commencing at Rennies' Mill and Circular Roads.[54]

In the light of this, pickets were placed at the oil premises, the powder magazine, the banks, and all public buildings. Picket duty was performed by a special force of ex-servicemen raised by the Great War Veterans' Association following the riot. The force soon consisted of 1,000 men who were divided into squads to police the city. A flying squad was also established and 250 citizens were sworn in to act as special police at a cost of $2.50 per man per day.[55] The authorities were in a state of considerable anxiety for days after the riot. It was reported by the Department of Justice that Bishop Field College had been broken into and that six carbines had been stolen and clearly more serious trouble was anticipated.[56] In the event it was decided to send for the British Navy and the H.M.S. *Dragon*, a B Type cruiser of 4,650 tons, armed with 6.6 inch guns and a complement of 400 men, arrived in St. John's to help keep the peace (*Evening Telegram* 12 April 1932:6). However, the situation remained calm and the ship soon left.

The riot of April 5 profoundly shook St. John's. The defeat of the police and the looting showed that there was but a slender hold on law and order. The St. John's merchants were particularly apprehensive. On April 7 a local agent for the Phoenix Insurance Company advertised that "we can cover you immediately against loss from Riot and Civil Commotion" (*Evening Telegram* 1 April 1932:1). According to the governor this anxiety was one of the main factors (along with requests from the G.W.V.A.) which led to his decision to call in the navy:

> I ascertained that there was evidence of serious anxiety on the part of the mercantile community in St. John's as to the ability of the Constabulary Force to repress disorder in a crisis and that insurance of property against riot was being affected which in a few weeks rose to nearly five million dollars.

More generally he commented on the situation:

> Mass movements of this description cannot fail at the best of times to be something of a menace and consequently it is not surprising that given the disregard already shown by a section of the population for law and order a real crisis should have arisen.[57]

In part Middleton was attempting to justify his actions in calling in the navy. The situation had been bad. The police force was inadequate. The Great War Veterans could only be relied on in the short-term since half of the force raised consisted of solid men of property who, although dependable, wanted to get back to business and the other half were mostly unemployed men who could not be depended upon in an emergency.[58] By this time Middleton was also justifying the government's decision to increase the police force by 100 men (*Evening Telegram* 14 April 1932:4).

However, it was the sending for the *Dragon* which was particularly problematic. In Britain the *Daily Express* and the *Manchester Guardian* had taken up this issue (*Evening Telegram* 14 April 1932:4). As quoted in the *Evening Telegram*, the British government was accused by the *Guardian* of interfering in the affairs of an independent Dominion:

> Is our Government actually claiming the right to interfere in the internal affairs of one of the sister nations of the British Commonwealth?

While the *Express* argued that:

> Newfoundland is a self-governing Dominion. The request for a warship was ridiculous. The sending of it was sheer melodrama.

The governor had acted in accordance with what he understood to be his duty as outlined in the British government's 1918 circular on measures to be taken in the event of civil disturbance in the colonies. The constitutional niceties of this action and its implications were outlined by Arthur Keith:

> The dispatch of a British war vessel to Newfoundland illustrates another side of the responsibilities of a Governor. It is clear that it is the elementary duty of a Dominion Government to maintain order locally by its own authority; when it has to seek the aid of Imperial forces the Ministry places itself in a position in which it cannot claim exemption from a measure of control by the Governor. If the Imperial Government has to intervene to prevent the possibility of overthrow of constituted authority by mob violence, it is bound, through the Governor, to seek such a reorganization of the Ministry as shall remove the risk of further manifestations of popular displeasure with a discredited Administration, and the sooner this is accomplished the better in the interests of Newfoundland (1935:285–6).

The legal situation might be reasonably clear, but many were unsure about whether Governor Middleton had acted hastily and misread the situation. The riot was serious but not too alarming according to Mr. Hepburn of Baine Johnston Ltd.:

> The rough-and-tumble sort of Newfoundlander is an aggressive fellow, who will always create trouble and is always looking for a fight, but the average Newfoundlander is more of a man than that, and besides he is a gentlemen, not a hooligan. You will see from this that we were in the hands of hooligans at the time the rioting took place. Fortunately we were sitting here, quite comfortably although a little bit alarmed. What made us feel so comfortable was

that we were fully insured against not only fire but against riot and civil commotion.[59]

By the time the cruiser arrived on April 12 the *Evening Telegram* could make light of the event (12 April 1932:6). The warship came as "a rainbow after a storm" and "a pleasant stay" was wished to the "Navy men." The city was back to "business as usual" now that "practically the whole body of the citizens of St. John's" had "effectively dealt with the suppression of the comparatively small element that participated in the occurrences of Tuesday last."

Immediately after the riot the *Telegram* had appealed for order in the city, reiterating its established position that lawlessness and disorder would achieve little and were totally unacceptable to the community at large (*Evening Telegram* 6 April 1932:6). The paper went to some lengths to absolve the organizers and leaders of the "immense parade" of any blame for what happened. The efforts of Superintendent O'Neill and the police were praised. For the *Telegram* the government's delay in receiving the petitioners was "tactless in the extreme" and held to be partly responsible for what had happened. However, "a very small fraction" of the crowd "either participated in or were in sympathy with the disorder" and most of the damage was the "work of youths rather than responsible men." The paper's interpretation of, and response to, the riot cannot be separated from its efforts to undermine and discredit the Squires government. For stability it appealed to a higher authority:

> There can be no minimizing the grave state of affairs that exists. With the Government in a condition of uncertainty, the country looks to His Excellency the Governor in the first place that the control of public affairs will be resumed without delay (*Evening Telegram* 6 April 1932:6)

But it was also made clear that responsibility for restoring "normalcy" was in the "words as well as deeds" of individual citizens. "Common sense" had to prevail.

In fact, in the wake of the riot all seemed anxious to distance themselves from responsibility for its occurrence. The leaders of the unemployed quickly appealed to their followers for full co-operation in maintaining law and order while their negotiations for an increase in relief continued (the new ration came into force on April 9) (*Evening Telegram* 7 April 1932:1). The *Evening Telegram* even preferred not to talk about a "riot" but described it variously as a "wild demonstration" and an "unfortunate occurrence" (6 April 1932:6). As with most riots, the blame finally seemed to be lodged with the body of young hooligans which, it was argued, was always ready to make the best of any opportunity to cause trouble.

Whether or not it had happened exactly as planned, the big parade had been intended as a final showdown with the Squires government. A campaign against the government had been mounted, a confrontation engineered and a pitched battle had resulted. It is dangerous to read too much symbolism into the actions of those involved in the riot, but for a government such a breakdown of law and order has very serious consequences. The calling in of the British Navy, even though the ship's fuel was paid for by Newfoundland, was a further indication that the government was losing its ability to govern. The police force might be increased and calm restored but the damage had already been done.

For some the situation might be resolved by a change of government, but for many people the riot and the events which had preceded it were further proof that, in Newfoundland, politics had ceased to be workable. In the wake of the riot the *Fishermen's Advocate* reiterated its call for Commission of Government (8 April 1932:4). This idea had been launched by Sir William Coaker as early as 1925 (*Daily Globe* (St. John's) 26 November 1925:1, 5). Now some called "for a bloodless revolution" to install a "dictator," others for a body of honest men to dedicate themselves to saving the country from ruin (*Evening Telegram* 12 April 1932:4).

Following the April riot, the governing party decided that a general election should be held as soon as possible. The election was set for June 11. It was clear, however, that the Liberal Party under Squires was doomed. Abandoned by most of its ministers, the Liberal Party had nothing to offer the voters. The alternative to the Liberals was the United Newfoundland Party, "a formidable collection of merchants" led by F.C. Alderdice (Noel 1971:203). This party had but one election pledge, to look into the "desirability and feasibility" of placing the country under a form of Government by Commission (*Evening Telegram* 23 May 1932). It was, however, made clear that this would not be done without the consent of the people. This was a popular position. The comments of Mr Collingwood of Baine Johnston Ltd. are typical:

the fact of it is that the intelligent people are sick of politics and what I would like to see personally would be a suspension of the Charter for a period of 8 or 10 years, and the Country governed by a Commission from the Old Country with the aid of a few local men. By that time all the professional politicians would have passed out. There is very strong feeling here against the Prime Minister, the Chief of Police, and also the old Government.[60]

In the meantime Squires would be kicked out and replaced by Alderdice, even though some thought him to be "a very weak disciple" without "sufficient strength to lead a party."[61]

One month after the St. John's riot, Sir William Coaker resigned from government.[62] In bidding farewell to those who had elected him, Coaker conveyed a deep sense of pessimism about the future. He warned of hardship to come and the possibility of civilization vanishing in a "stupendous upheaval." All he could do in the face of this possibility was to urge people to store vegetables and dried caplin for the winter. He noted that:

> A change of Government will not bring us prosperity. Do not expect any such happening, but it is absolutely necessary that out of the present political situation must come a National Administration composed of the best possible material (*Fishermen's Advocate* May 6, 1932:4).

Thus he urged Newfoundlanders to end the struggle between the "ins and the outs" and support Alderdice's program. Although he was withdrawing from "ordinary political activities" due to poor health, Coaker made it very clear that had he continued he would have worked for the establishment of Government by Commission. When the election came the United Newfoundland Party won all but two seats and Squires himself was defeated.

Throughout the period leading up to the election, conditions continued to be very serious in Newfoundland. The destitution in St. John's had been eased somewhat by improvements in relief rations, but outside the capital city many areas were still subject to the harshness of the Magor ration. A constant stream of reports provided the government with details of the crisis which existed throughout the country. Clergymen from Greenspond reported in late April that "people are now collapsing daily in the streets and in their homes."[63] Elsewhere, merchants were refusing to fill dole rations and outfit people for fishing due to the government's non-payment of relief accounts. The calling of the election also presented particular problems as far as public relief was concerned. According to a 1929 amendment to the act governing the election of members to the House of Assembly, it was unlawful for the Department of Charities to issue any able-bodied relief from the date of proclamation of an election until the date of the election.[64] Relief could be issued in cases of exceptional hardship but only if a certificate was issued by a magistrate or clergyman. In view of the obvious hardship in many areas it was decided by the government to relax the existing legislation and while complying with the law "as far as practicable" to issue relief where necessary.

Alderdice Takes Charge

The Alderdice government assumed power in June. Immediately it set about finding ways to further cut expenditures. In the firm belief that spending on relief had been too lax under the Liberal regime they turned their attention in that direction. The Magor system of keymen was quickly dismantled and a committee, headed by the Prime Minister, was set up to look at the relief issue.[65] At a meeting early in July, Mr. Penson, the Deputy Minister of Finance, produced a chilling review of the financial situation. Virtually nothing ($50,000) had been budgeted for public relief for the financial year 1932–33 by the Liberal government in the vain hope that this signal would help stem the demand for state assistance. But by mid-1932 well over a half million dollars was already due in relief arrears. And the winter was yet to come. Mr. Penson thought that they could not expect to spend much less than a million dollars on relief for the whole year and that this would have to come out of total expenditures (excluding debt servicing) of just over $5 million. Penson concluded that "to continue able-bodied relief on the most moderate scale" the government needed "to effect sweeping reductions in some of the. . .large social services." This would involve cutting war and civil pensions, education, and the police. Some small cuts might also be possible in the Post Office.

Elections are, in part, won on promises. But the politics of governing are very different from those of garnering support. By mid-summer 1932 and certainly by the fall it was clear that the Alderdice government intended to extend and intensify the retrenchment program initiated by the Liberals. The new government also adopted a much harsher attitude towards relief for the able-bodied. Penson's position was clear:

> It is absolutely imperative to break at once with the idea of any wholesale issue of relief and with the principle that the population has a right to receive the dole.[66]

In line with this he suggested that from the middle of July relief should only be given (1) "in individual cases personally approved at headquarters," and (2) "in certain bad spots where. . .there are specially difficult conditions as to the finding of employment." Unlimited relief had to cease at once. Strict rationing was to be imposed. He suggested that no relief should exceed $1.80 per head per month, including St. John's and Bell Island, but this might be issued weekly in the city and fortnightly in "the bad spots." This was to be the maximum figure allowable. In the bad districts relief was to be issued by making "a fixed grant for the month" paid in cash to local relief commissioners. They would be responsible for allocating the sum provided amongst the destitute of their area. Elsewhere all relief was to be issued through headquarters and handled by local relieving officers. This system, it was thought, would make possible "strict financial planning month by month" to fit in with the need to control spending. Changes in headquarters' organization were also suggested to go along with the new arrangements.

When it came to putting Penson's proposals into practice, difficulties were soon encountered. It is not clear how far the government went in trying to cut relief in St. John's. One source suggests a cut of 10 percent was ordered but then a compromise cut of 5 percent was accepted in July with a further cut of 5 percent to come into effect in September.[67] Certainly by the third week in July the unemployed in St. John's were protesting the rations being issued (the scale was said to amount to 72 cents per adult per week).[68] The Unemployed Committee was also pressing for relief work to be started. Their meeting with Penson was, however, not encouraging. He claimed that the government had no money to spend on labour and clearly tried to deflect the pressure placed on him by the unemployed:

> Mr. Penson then put this idea to us, to get the names of outport people residing in the city for the Government, and suggested a scheme whereby the Government would defray their expenses home by paying transportation (*Evening Telegram* 20 July 1932:4).

From this time there was increasing evidence of tension between the governments' financial advisors (Penson and Thompson) and Alderdice (*Evening Telegram* 11 July 1932:5). Those concerned primarily with financial affairs continued to press for strict control over spending and to let financial realities inform their recommendations. The politicians, however, were more sensitive to public pressure. Alderdice, in particular, was concerned that further economies might provoke "an absolute revolt" (Noel 1971:205–206).[69] While Mr. Penson was willing to hold the line against the unemployed, Alderdice was more flexible. When confronted, he agreed on July 21 to restore the dole to the rates existing before the last reduction and to provide work (this was to be done by means of a bank loan for $100,000) (*Evening Telegram*. 22 July 1932:7).

The work was slow to materialize. As tension mounted, the leaders of the unemployed appealed to their members to be calm and wait for the bank loan to come through. But the moderate leaders were challenged by a group of "hotheads" who argued that the government was trying to dupe the unemployed on the question of work (*Evening Telegram* 25 July 1932:5).[70] On the evening of July

25 an unemployed meeting under the chairmanship of Thomas Hickey took place at the Armoury (*Evening Telegram* 26 July 1932:4). A discussion of the loan of $100,000 for relief work led to a decision to call on the Acting Prime Minister H.A. Winter in order to clarify the situation. The parade of 200–300 people started down Harvey Road heading for the residence of Mr. Winter. As they passed the Nickel Theatre some of the crowd threw stones at two constables on duty there and further down the road, cars were held up by the parade and one or two of the vehicles were struck with stones. The parade soon attracted a body of spectators and by the time it reached Winter Place it was about 1,000 strong and some of the marchers had armed themselves with fence pickets. However, Mr. Winter, one of the leaders of the April 5 parade, was not at home. The crowd left without doing any damage and headed for the centre of St. John's, followed by the twenty constables and the patrol wagon which had turned out to protect Winter Place. Passing down Prescott Street the crowd smashed thirteen plate glass windows in the Royal Stores (reportedly owned by a friend and supporter of Squires). Before the store could be looted the crowd was dispersed by a squad of policemen. During the police charge a number of constables were hit with stones.

From this point accounts of what happened differ somewhat, but several stores on Water Street had their windows broken and there were attempts made to steal liquor. These raids were successfully driven off by squads of police which were quickly organized to defend the liquor stores, banks, and other stores. A flying squad was also set up. Through the night there were more attempts to steal liquor and during the riot several stores were looted and boots and shoes, fruit, dry goods and cakes, pies and pastries were stolen. The glass in the Board of Trade building was smashed as well as the windows of five Chinese businesses.

The main confrontation of the evening took place when a group of about 400 strong, armed with pickets, stones, and pieces of iron, marched down Barter's Hill to Adelaide Street. There a crowd of about 2,000 people (according to the *Fishermen's Advocate*) witnessed a clash between the police and a body of young men (27 July 1932:7). Press reports differ on what happened. According to the *Evening Telegram*, a group of about twenty policemen baton-charged the marchers and a fight broke out which led to injuries and a number of arrests. In the words of the *Fishermen's Advocate* correspondent, however, it was "a company of police, about 50 strong" who "were proceeding up Water Street" when they were halted at Adelaide Street and "charged there by about 500 men and boys"

(27 July 1932:7). In any event, five police officers were injured severely enough to be sent to the hospital for treatment and one was so badly hurt that he had to be relieved of duty for several days (*Evening Telegram* 26 July 1932:4). As in April, the Great War Volunteer Association came to the assistance of the authorities and patrolled the street during the night. The following day, 100 members of the association were enlisted as a special police force. Over thirty people were arrested as a result of the events of July 25 and 26, half of these being charged with riot and the rest with larceny and loose and disorderly conduct. One of those arrested was Henry Saunders. He had been identified as a ringleader during the battle of Adelaide Street by Superintendent O'Neill who was directing police operations (see *Evening Telegram* 31 October 1932:4). At his trial Saunders showed that he had got caught up in the riot while out buying some fish and chips after a visit to the hospital and a few drinks with a friend. He told the court that since his arrest he had been informed that he was to be fired from the railway because he had been mixed up in the riot. He was found not guilty. Others were not so lucky.

On the afternoon following the riot the unemployed met to discuss the possibility of rescuing those who had been arrested, but they failed to find a leader and abandoned the plan (*Evening Telegram* 27 July 1932:5). In the evening a huge crowd of thousands assembled on Water and New Gower Streets in the expectation that they would observe another incident. They stayed till after midnight. The regular police force and ex-servicemen patrolled the city and kept a careful eye on a group of several hundred "of the younger element" who assembled in the vicinity of Barter's Hill, but no trouble resulted. Another crowd assembled at the Court House where one woman demanded the release of her arrested husband. This request was refused by the police who were well prepared to repel an assault.

On Wednesday morning four members of the unemployed committee were arrested and charged with rioting (*Evening Telegram* 27 July 1932:5). They were remanded on bail of $2,000 each. Those arrested included Thomas Hickey, the chairman of the unemployed and John McGrath, an ex-constable. Two of the committee had police records. It was later reported that all the committee except Hickey had been released and that his trial had been set for October. When the trial did take place in late October, Hickey was found not guilty of incitement to riot and he left the court room to a standing ovation.

This further outbreak of violence was denounced in terms similar to those used in April. The *Fishermen's Advocate* saw the incident as "simply an outbreak of the hooliganism which had been lying dormant. . .ready to break out at any opportunity" (27 July 1932:4). For the *Evening Telegram* such "futile vandalism" just made a bad situation worse (27 July 1932:4). The message of these statements was clear. No hardship or difficulty could justify people resorting to force to try to influence the government. Moreover, the occurrence of violence threw into question the actions of the whole unemployed movement. Given the delicate political situation and the widespread popular resentment of government and police, any agitation was problematic because it was likely to trigger an outburst of violent anger.

The July riot showed very clearly that the unemployed were only a loosely co-ordinated body. Within the unemployed movement there were differences of opinion about the most effective tactics to be used against the authorities. In 1932 a series of battles were fought within the leadership of the unemployed. For some "soliciting alms" and apparently endless and ineffective negotiations with the government—where the government was willing to meet the unemployed—were not enough given their pressing needs and anger.[71]

There is also some evidence that the unemployed were not assisted or well supported by organized labour in St. John's. Many of the unemployed might have belonged to the L.S.P.U. but that organization consistently refused to allow its hall to be used for meetings. We can only speculate, but the position of such organizations as the L.S.P.U. and also the *Fishermen's Advocate* seems to have been that they were the voice of respectable labour and concerned to maintain as much distance as possible from the confrontational stand of the unemployed. Organized labour still hoped to operate within the established system of politics.

Individuals like J.R. Smallwood, the founder of the Newfoundland Federation of Labour and a Liberal supporter, were working behind the scenes to undermine the Alderdice government and build an opposition.[72] Smallwood was even willing to use the issue of unemployment and relief to build this opposition, but when violence erupted he was careful to absolve himself from any part in "inciting disorder":

> I appeal to your sense of justice for space in which to protect myself from the malignant and baseless rumours which have this week been bandied through the city about me. These rumours. . .lay upon me, at least in part, responsibility for what happened Monday night.

Mr. Editor, I am as guiltless as you or any other person in this matter. I do not believe in force, violence, lawlessness or disorder, any more than you do. I have never in my life advocated them. I have never excused them. The use of violence is absolutely foreign to my nature—repugnant to every idea or opinion I possess. Furthermore, in the present position of Newfoundland I most especially realize the utter futility of force or any sort of disorder as a way out.

To inspire or in any way be responsible for lawlessness or violence is criminal, and if I or any-one else is guilty of such a crime, swift trial and severe punishment is the only just course (*Evening Telegram* 27 July 1932:14).

Many people condemned violence or the threat of violence by the unemployed. However, it is clear that this was one of the few effective ways of influencing governments bent on reducing state expenditures on relief to the absolute minimum. Petitions and pleadings could be ignored indefinitely, but parades and shows of force could not. Particularly so, since the government was anxious that the forces under its control were insufficient to control a really serious outbreak of violence. It was no accident that within a few days of the July riot relief work was started in St. John's. There was also a renewed interest shown by the St. John's middle-class in self-help schemes for the unemployed. Allotments in the city might take the edge off the hunger and anger of some of the unemployed (and reduce the costs of relief and the tax burden), but much more drastic action was needed. Increasingly, land settlement was promoted as "an investment worth considering" (*Evening Telegram* 29 July 1932:14). The July riot was taken as further proof that settlement on the land was the only long-term solution to the problem of the unemployed in St. John's. The members of the Land Development Association argued that "if [they] were dictators" they would cut out unproductive expenditures on doles and make work and "draw from the town its unemployable. . .definitely and for good." The "wilfully idle and troublesome," those who "lack initiative and need a lead in the right direction" and those who "given a chance on the land. . .could care for themselves" could all be removed from town to farming colonies where eventually they would become self-sufficient. The scheme might also be used to solve the problem of "juvenile delinquents" and to lessen the possibility of more violence in the capital:

For $200,000 the whole of the unemployable surplus could be removed from the town. For combined with this plan we are talking of, we could in cooperation with the government, set up a special Borstal colony for dealing with the troublesome youthful element from which most of the mischief is springing. One of the most dangerous features of the unemployment question is the large number of idle youths growing into manhood under the worst possible circumstances. Unless these young people are helped to self-respect, our prisons will show the effects of the education they are receiving, for many years to come.

Viewed "in the cold light of finance" (*Evening Telegram* 29 July 1932:14) the value of a land settlement scheme could not be denied.

Trouble Round the Bay

Oh, out near Conception,
Oh, out round the "Bay,"
We had no molasses to put in our "Tay."
We got all excited; cut dole off in our ears.
But now I won't worry for twenty-one years (Kirwin 1982).

While attention was focused on events in St. John's in the summer of 1932, conditions were deteriorating in other parts of the country and opposition to the government's new relief policy was developing. Early in August "a feeling of unrest" was reported to be "strongly evident" throughout the Corner Brook district with "severe comments. . .being freely expressed" in the industrial centre (*Bay Roberts Guardian* 12 August 1932). The cause of this was layoffs by the International Pulp and Paper Co. and a wage cut of 10 percent which had been forced on their employees (*Evening Telegram* 12 July 1932:4). Reports of more serious trouble came from other areas. By mid-July the government was attempting to implement its new relief policy. Sergeant Russell was in the Carbonear area conferring with the local relief committee which had been set up under the Magor scheme (*Bay Roberts Guardian* 22 July 1932). What he said caused them some alarm and an urgent telegram was sent to the Secretary of State, Mr. Puddester:

Our executive had conference with Russell here last night and are puzzled and anxious because of the whole situation. In order that you might understand us and yet be assured of our sympathy may we say our committee is political and during recent campaign declared under your authority dole would be continued for the needy under Alderdice Government until work could be substituted. This being so we will be held responsible for any cuts effected in quality and otherwise and will leave property and lives of our personnel open to wrath of any uprising that may develop. Again our committee functioned for the town of Carbonear only and if protection is afforded us against all outside raids we would gladly cooperate with clergymen and citizens of the town to help meet the situation here as best we can. We are of the opinion that the personal dole allowance of six cents per day cannot be safely lessened for the small family but can be adjusted somewhat in the case of large family recipients and after careful and thorough investigation a weeding out process can effect elimination of those not in real need. If extreme measures must be taken we must seek your protection to property and personals and respectfully suggest cutting all high pensioned salary allowances as well as scaling all salaries beginning at top first.[73]

These words of warning proved prophetic.

Not only were new relief rates brought into force in mid-July but the government also issued instructions that all relief was to be paid for in work. Relieving officers were told to inform their relief recipients that if they refused to work for the dole then there would be "unnecessary trouble" when they came to get their next ration.[74] The response to the new relief regulation was strong and immediate. From Britannia the government received a threatening message and the relieving officer was also threatened.[75] This situation was calmed by the issue of half a ration. The relieving officer at Trinity reported threats of a raid by men from the communities of Port Rexton, Champneys, Trinity East, Dunfield, Trouty, Ivanhoe and Little Harbour.[76] Again a half ration was issued to prevent violence. At the end of July three men were brought into St. John's from Maryside, near Harbour Main, charged with rioting (*Evening Telegram* 30 July 1932:4).

Reports of starvation and trouble soon came in from other areas. Once the government had been confronted and had given in to pressure in one area the word of this quickly spread elsewhere and others organized to make similar gains. The communities on the northern side of Conception Bay were relatively well-organized and able to mount effective pressure on the authorities. The destitute of Britannia, having been successful once, in August again tried to squeeze a relief increase out of the government. Again they threatened to raid local stores if not relieved and then to proceed to Clarenville to tear up the railway tracks.[77] Apparently, like St. John's, some areas of Conception Bay had managed in 1932 to resist the imposition of the Magor ration. Fearing widespread violence the government had stepped back and as late as August 1932 large sections of the Bay were receiving dole at the rate of $1.80 every three weeks. The government's plan to cut this to $1.80 per month was flatly rejected throughout most of Conception Bay.

In August the unemployed committee representing Bay Roberts, Coleys Point, and Country Road informed Mr. Puddester that they had decided not to accept the dole cut because, while it had been hard enough to live on $1.80 every three weeks, it would be impossible to live under the new regulations.[78] Most opposition was thus to be found in what had been identified as "the Bad Spots." Elsewhere those on relief existed in relatively small numbers and they could have their rations cut without being able to do much about it except protest. In many areas, therefore, the relief ration was cut well below the $1.80 maximum in the fall of 1932. In Lady Cove, Trinity Bay it was down to $1.15 per person.[79] In Channel $1.13 rations were issued, and in Harbour Breton the maximum issued was $1.60. The latter maximum was also being issued at Twillingate, while at Catalina relief was exactly half this amount in October when a public meeting was held to protest the matter and threats to raid the local stores were made.[80]

Under the new relief system instructions had been issued for relieving officers to cut expenditures as far as possible. In some cases they were issued with a lump sum which had to cover all relief for one month in their area. This led to vastly different relief rates all over Newfoundland. Many relieving officers took to the new system with great enthusiasm, doling out the government's money with as much parsimony as if they were spending their own dollars. One such officer, Mr. Moss administered what he liked to call "Moss's purge" and he carried on his lonely crusade even in the face of mounting local hostility and several physical assaults.[81] Other local relief officials complained that they could not manage on their allocations. One magistrate spent $541.40 of his $800 allocation within three days of receiving it, much to the consternation of those in St. John's who were administering the system.[82] In response the Charities Department was all for sending a constable to investigate. The Secretary of State acknowledged that it was now standard practice to undertake such investigations but did not think it proper that a constable should investigate a magistrate.[83]

Where investigations were undertaken a wide variation in the practice of relieving officials was uncovered.[84] In one case the official had cut all rations to those under the age of six. In another case, all rations were issued at $1.20 but a family of six was only provided with four rations. Where families had some vegetables they might receive less relief than those who had none.

The standard response of the government to evidence of distress was to ignore it. Requests for more relieving officers were rejected because "the rule is the more relieving officers we appoint the more expense is entailed."[85] The fact that many people had to travel vast distances (ten to twenty miles was not uncommon) to apply for relief and that they might have to repeat the journey several times was seen as a means of preventing those who were not really desperate from becoming a burden on the state. However, the strategy of ignoring acute distress carried with it many dangers. The distress might give rise to anger and trigger a raid on a local store or even a riot. This led to considerable pressure on the government from local merchants to provide protection. However, the Secretary of State's position was that:

> If people break in stores and take the food they can only do so once and then get themselves in hands of law.[86]

Desperate relief officials were informed that no more money was available and that threats would not move the government.[87] Cases of theft should be reported to the Department of Justice. But here the government faced the problem that it could not effectively police the outports. In some cases those involved in raids might be arrested and made an example of, but there was really no way of preventing raids from occurring without yielding to pressure. That so many raids did occur is testimony to the desperate conditions in many areas, conditions which drove groups of men to break into stores and take only that to which they felt themselves entitled.

Faced with this mounting unrest, the government extended the use of the police force. Constables were used to investigate both applicants and relief officials. A new system of statutory declarations gave officials wider powers to investigate relief applicants, including their bank accounts and insurance policies.[88] Magistrates were also instructed to issue "proper and suitable punishments" to those found guilty of relief fraud.[89]

Coercion was one side of the war against relief, the other side was the use of propaganda to educate the poor about their responsibility in the crisis. As Norbert Elias shows, efforts to foster prudent habits amongst the poorer classes have a long history (1983:229–258). Self-discipline and restraint, thrift and acceptance have all been regarded as essential virtues for the lower orders by their rulers. With the onset of the Great Depression, a veritable flood of this kind of material was unleashed on the suffering population of Newfoundland. By means of fables, speeches, and poems, moral and patriotic lessons were pressed home by state officials and politicians, writers in the press, religious leaders, and teachers. In the fall of 1932 police constables were being sent round to outports to lecture the population on the part that they could play in saving the country from ruin. They were to "try and earn their own living and keep off the dole."[90] The Prime Minister transmitted the same message to the country. Further borrowing was difficult and unwise and relief spending would have to be restricted. The appeal to the destitute was direct:

> every time you take a dollar or a pound of food you could do without, you are taking it from others who cannot do without it. We have enough only for those who are really destitute, and who cannot work.

> Do not ask for relief until you are honestly destitute. Do not ask to be helped by your neighbour while you have a dollar left or can support yourself in any way. Keep your independence while you can; there was a time when people considered it a disgrace to take relief. Do not defraud your fellow citizens. Remember that if you take a dollar or a pound of food you could do without, you are depriving us of the means to help those who are really helpless.[91]

Efforts to limit the dole were justified and even made acceptable by arguments which set out to persuade the population at large, including those who might be in need of support, that not only was dependence on the state too costly for the country to bear but that it was a moral evil as well. These arguments were supported by statements that abuse of the relief system had reached epidemic proportions. In many cases the attack on the relief system was extended into a general attack on a state which had in the period during and after World War I, gone too far in providing a helping hand to many sectors of society. A process had been initiated in which people had become aware of their needs and wants and translated them into an open-ended set of demands on the state. People had begun to see state support as a right. This had, on the one hand, encouraged dependency and undermined initiative and the work ethic, and, on the other hand, it had led to increased taxation and the growth of the national debt. In a situation where people were increasingly feeling the burden of taxation it is perhaps not surprising that there should be support for a program to limit spending on relief (one of the largest items in the country's budget).

However, in spite of the propaganda campaign, in mid-July, 1932, efforts to modify the relief arrangements in the Conception Bay area immediately ran into stiff opposition. By late July, men from Bay Roberts met with Sergeant Russell and informed him that they would not perform work for the dole and they would not accept a cut in rations from $1.80 every three weeks to $1.03 for the same period (*Bay Roberts Guardian* 22 July 1932; 19 August 1932). A similar confrontation occurred at Carbonear in mid-August when 500 men assembled to inform the local relieving officer that they would accept no cuts in rations.[92] This was a serious confrontation in which the Court House was damaged and the son of District

Inspector March was assaulted. The incident on August 18 led the relieving officer to instruct the government that any attempt to cut the ration would lead to serious problems. The outbreak was particularly troubling because it had occurred while the men were still on the old ration, an indiscreet release of information by the relieving officer galvanizing those on relief into action.[93] After this incident, relieving officers were instructed to maintain strict secrecy.

The riots which had occurred in St. John's under the Squires government had resulted in no arrests by the police. In accordance with its new, and harsher, attitude towards relief, the aim of the Alderdice government was to punish any violations of the law in connection with relief. Accordingly, an attempt was made to arrest the Perry's Cove man who had committed the assault at Carbonear on August 18 (*Fishermen's Advocate* 14 September 1932:5). However, the unemployed of the Perry's Cove area informed the Department of Justice that they would not allow the man to be tried. To support this stance some 600 men from Victoria, Salmon Cove, and Perry's Cove assembled at the Carbonear Court House. The Department of Justice reacted quickly. A special train with 115 infantry police and five mounted men was despatched from St. John's. The mounted men got off the train at Harbour Grace and "made an impressive cavalry ride upon Carbonear town" where they met the armed infantry for the march to the Court House. There they found "that the alleged unruly visitors had all gone home to bed" (*Fishermen's Advocate* 14 September 1932:5). The arrival of the police led to the arrest of the Perry's Cove man. He was tried and convicted, but (wisely) given a suspended sentence. A squad of twenty policemen was left behind in Carbonear and the rest returned to St. John's.

This was not the end of trouble in the area. Towards the end of September, Sergeant Russell who was responsible for supervising the dole in the area was "held up and not permitted to return to St. John's until he got an assurance that the rate of ration. . .was not to be altered" (*Fishermen's Advocate* 28 September 1932:4). However, the government continued with its plan to cut the dole in Conception Bay even in the face of stiffening opposition. The trouble was not long in coming. Early in October a body of men from the North Shore of Conception Bay marched on Carbonear to demand that the former rate of relief be restored (*Fishermen's Advocate* 12 October 1932:1). A very serious incident resulted. Somewhere between 300 and 500 men from Bristol's Hope to Perry's Cove assembled in the Court House fire break on October 6. The committees from the various communities called on Sergeant Bussey to inform him of their mission, the restoration of the ration of $1.80 every three weeks. The unemployed demanded to see the group of worthies who had been given local responsibility for relief matters (it was this group that had warned of trouble in July and had said they would be held responsible for any problems with relief). The committee men refused to meet the unemployed. The unemployed then used a local clergymen to present their demands to the government over the telephone. The reply was that $1.60 was the new ration and that no more would be given. The assembled crowd then decided to stop the train in order to go to St. John's and confront the government. Poles were placed across the track and the engineer removed from the train. Motor cars were also commandeered by "the mob" and "the owners forced to drive a delegation to Spaniard's Bay and vicinity to get the people who were getting dole to form up and allow nothing through from St. John's." The people of Tilton were also instructed to hold up any trains and cars from St. John's, especially if they had police on board.

The relief committee was also forceably brought to the Court House and, in the process, one man who tried to resist was "badly handled."[94] In fact, he was dragged there by his ears and his ribs were fractured by blows. His son was also injured by a rock. The committee reported "one by one" and were forced to contact the government to see what could be done. Again, a negative reply was received. The situation then became "very serious." Several "respectable citizens" were assaulted. The house and shop of the reluctant committee man were attacked and food was stolen. It was the actions of another committee member, Mr. John Rorke, in issuing the equivalent of one month's ration, which finally eased the situation. The train was then released and the situation became calm. Sergeant Bussey summed up the incident thus:

> I beg to say the object of the assembly was to obtain from the Government more food and to get back to the Magor ration of $1.80 per three weeks. No doubt the whole Town of Carbonear would have been wiped out but for Mr. John Rorke as there was no chance of getting assistance from St. John's.[95]

A day later violence erupted again. Men from Spaniard's Bay and area demanded dole of $1.40 every two weeks from the government and when refused they tore up the railway tracks, looted two bread vans, blocked the roads and expelled the three local policemen from the area (*Fishermen's Advocate* 21 December 1932:7). The following day a squad of police was sent from St. John's while a group of 500 to 600 men assembled in Spaniard's Bay "with the evident intent of resisting the police should they enter the settlement" (*Fishermen's*

Advocate 12 October 1932:1). A serious incident was, however, avoided when the Superintendent of Constabulary negotiated a settlement with the leaders of the unemployed on October 8.[96] In this the men agreed that in future there would be "no interference with the Railway" and that the rails would be replaced and traffic permitted to pass. They also agreed to accept the ration of $1.60 per month after a two week period, with the understanding that repre- sentations would be made to increase the ration by 20 cents per month. There was, however, an immediate settlement of $1.00.

The eruptions around Conception Bay came as no surprise to the government. On October 3 a constable had been sent to the town to keep an eye on the unemployed. Working under cover he had watched the movements of the assembling protesters. When the men "marched up through Carbonear in perfect order" he telephoned his superintendent in St. John's. Again at 4:00 p.m. he phoned his superior to report that the situation had become very tense:

> A young man, who I understand is a Doctor, and was intending to join the S.S. *"Kyle"* with his father, for the Grenfell Mission, was at the station with a camera, intending to take some snaps of the crowd when some of the mob eyed him. His camera was taken and he was badly beaten and his clothes torn. Later the camera was given back to his father. I was told that the man, or one of the men who assaulted this young man, is believed to be Albert Pilgrim of Carbonear. The man assaulted took a car back to St. John's and said he never wanted to see Newfoundland again.

> George Soper, clerk with John Rorke and Sons, left the store and went to the station to look at the mob. Some of them eyed him also and he was kicked and beaten back to the store. I could not take any more chances on 'phoning the Inspector General as the mob would know who I was.[97]

During the afternoon the three local constables were trapped in the Court House office. Constable Dwyer was upstairs with the light out spying on the "blood thirsty rather than hungry" crowd. Discretion proved the better part of valour for the local constables. However, they were able to forward the names of the men on the unemployed committees to St John's as well as those involved in damaging property and an assault on one member of the relief committee (Mr. James Moore). Constable Dwyer also warned:

> that the potato crop is mostly a failure in the vicinity of Victoria and a spirit of mob law prevails, and the same thing is going to happen again unless the ring-leaders are arrested and dealt with. It would be nearly murder to send Police to quell a disturbance of this sort unarmed.

Early in November the men named by the constables were arrested at Carbonear and Spaniards Bay and they were brought to trial in December (*Fishermen's Advocate* 6, 9 November 1932:6; 16 November 1932:5). While it was acknowledged that the people in the area were hungry, it was also thought to be important to try and break any resistance to government policy. Arresting the ringleaders was considered to be necessary since, according to one observer, "a socialist doctrine was being continuously preached over in the district" and "the crowd has the idea that everything should be divided up."[98]

Further Retrenchment: Towards Bankruptcy

Mr. Penson, the Deputy Minister of Finance, had informed Alderdice in June that cuts in spending would be needed if the country was to remain solvent. He had also argued that the extent of the cuts would depend on levels of relief spending. By the fall of 1932 it was quite clear that efforts to cut relief to the bone had been far from successful. Not only this, but revenues continued to fall, and with the country staggering from one debt payment to another the only short-term option available to the government was to retrench or to default. In September, Penson began to put considerable pressure on Alderdice to make cuts in war and other pensions, in civil service salaries, and in education, health and postal services. Penson even argued that such cuts would have a "beneficial" effect in a country which, according to his thinking, had become too dependent on the government (Neary 1985:42). But although further retrenchment might make sense financially, the politicians found it very difficult to put into practice. In fact, in terms of practical politics, Alderdice felt that the limit to which they could impose cuts had already been reached (Noel 1971:207). Virtually all the social services of the country had been eliminated. The Charity Organization Bureau, a by no means liberal group, was advising that relief rates could not be cut any further without serious consequences.[99] Generally, the country was fast-losing the last vestiges of civilization which it possessed. Not only were health problems such as beri-beri and tuberculosis reaching major proportions, but Alderdice feared that further cuts might be extremely dangerous in that they might provoke "absolute revolt (Noel 1971:206)."[100] In addition there may have been some anxiety about the continued reliability of ex-servicemen in policing any crisis because they had been particularly hard hit by retrenchment.

It was perfectly clear that disaster was but a short step away. Before he left in the fall of 1932, Sir Percy Thompson made a final assessment of Newfoundland's situation (Noel 1971:206). He noted that the government could not go further without the complete withdrawal of all services. He thought that any attempt to follow this course would produce a very dangerous situation which would not easily be controlled. To Thompson, default seemed unavoidable. It was just a matter of time. The relief issue was at the centre of the trouble and outbreaks of violence had already taken place with more likely to erupt.

One particular problem which needed immediate attention was that of relief arrears. Merchants were threatening *en masse* to refuse to supply the dole unless they were paid for supplies already issued (some of the bills were over a year old). In desperation the government pleaded with the banks for further loans to pay off some of the accumulated debts (*Fishermen's Advocate* 5 October 1932:5).[101] There were, it was argued, "grave threats of insurrection" and "mob rule" if the request was refused.[102] Under pressure, the banks yielded and some of the outstanding debts were paid. But events were moving inexorably towards a resolution of the crisis. New loans were only secured with strings attached. Stringent controls were imposed on the government's financial affairs and they were forced to agree to the establishment of a commission of enquiry into the state of the country and its future.

The gradual loss of control over the affairs of the country foreshadowed the end of democratic politics in Newfoundland. By late 1932, Sir Percy Thompson was arguing that no government could continue to govern successfully in Newfoundland (Noel 1971:206). Economy measures could not be imposed without a complete descent into barbarism and open revolt. Yet, the debts could not be met. Elected government was, Thompson argued, too close to the people and too subject to popular pressure to make the kinds of decisions necessary to save the country from financial ruin.

In fact, by the winter of 1932–33 Alderdice was already making plans to default and the British government had begun to look seriously for a solution to the Newfoundland problem.

The retrenchment program of late 1932 was another desperate attempt to keep the waterlogged ship of state afloat. Amidst cries that civilization was being wiped out in Newfoundland the government set about further unloading its responsibility for its citizens by trimming approximately one million dollars from its spending (*Fishermen's Advocate* 26 October 1932:2). Those dependent on the state were now to be left to their fate as pensions and health services were cut and the apparatus of government systematically dismantled.[103] Mail services were cut, more post offices were closed and the education system suffered drastically. If many felt that the lights were gradually going out in the country, they were not wrong. In December half the street lights in the capital city were turned off in order to save $34,000 (*Fishermen's Advocate* 7 December 1932:1).

Nevertheless, without the cuts the United Newfoundland Party could not continue to govern a solvent (at least nominally) country. Alderdice had no choice but to follow Penson's suggestions. These suggestions were only partially implemented, however, because "such determined and bitter opposition" was encountered. In all, state expenditure was trimmed to a minimum of $400,000 per month, excluding spending on able-bodied public relief. It was, however, the latter area which represented the most "disquieting factor" in the situation because the government was deeply in arrears to the merchants and because effort to limit spending in this area had been only partly successful.[104] In fact, able-bodied public relief was being financed by *special warrants*, there being no budget for this item.

Policing the Crisis

We tore up the railroad, we tore up the track;
We kicked up a rumpus, and then put it back.
They sent out the policemen, with horses that rears;
And, now, I'm in prison, for twenty-one years (Kirwin 1982).

Even if in most countries the law and its enforcement are for the most part formally independent of politics in a narrow partisan sense, and even if the ideals of impartiality and universalism (the laws apply equally to all) are held to be the central defining characteristics of these countries, it is clear that the legal system and its application are highly political in the broad sense of the word. The popular view that politics and policing don't mix may conform to the official and self-proclaimed role of the judiciary and the police that they are simply enforcing the laws of the land, but it is a view which will not stand any close scrutiny (Reiner 1985). If politics is defined broadly as about power in society, then it is obvious that both the law and its enforcement are key elements in power relationships in a class divided society (Reiner 1985:2). An examination of laws and their enforcement in Newfoundland during the 1930s reveals that these were an integral part of political and economic life. What may be called policing policy was inextricably linked with other policy areas and with politics. In some instances it is quite easy to see the class nature of the legal system and of law enforcement.

Throughout the crisis of the 1930s all major decisions about law and order were political. This was true of decisions to increase effective policing, to prosecute rioters, to conduct undercover surveillance of the unemployed, and to limit the circulation of what was considered to be subversive literature. The story of policing in Newfoundland in the 1930s is, then, but one side of the story of economic crisis, political disintegration, savage retrenchment, unemployment, starvation, and civil disturbance. To discuss any aspect of law and order or policing in this period without a full discussion of the political economy of the period would be to fail completely to understand these phenomena. Similarly, to try to discuss the politics and economics of the period without any reference to law and order would be to fail to capture the essence of events.

The unemployment crisis of the early 1920s brought the question of law and order to the fore in Newfoundland. At the end of World War I the police force stood at about 100 men, with most of these stationed in St. John's. Faced with the possibility of serious social unrest the government had resorted to the use of the British navy and naval reservists. It had also made the decision, in February 1922, to expand the police force and establish a seven-man mounted section armed with revolvers. A mounted force had existed in the nineteenth century. It had consisted of seven men in 1873 and ten men in 1893, but it had been disbanded in 1895.[105] Used originally to disperse strikes and control unlawful assemblies, it was reintroduced with the argument that "a mounted policeman handling his horse well is worth several men in a crowd."

Despite the increase in the police force in the early 1920s there was a growing awareness of the inadequacies of the force in the period leading up to the crisis of 1931–32. A report to the Minister of Justice in 1925 discussed the difficulties of policing the country. "Modern conditions and developments," it was argued, "demanded greater police supervision and attention" and were putting a great strain on the force of 138.[106] In fact, for the country there was only a ratio of one officer for every 2,000 people, a figure which was very low compared with, for example, the State of New York with its one policeman for every 500 people. The consequence of the small force was presented thus:

> Much of our territory has. . .to be ignored, and many crimes and offences undoubtedly go unpunished; in consequence the moral tone of the small community is often undesirable and becomes worse by contact with modern ideas disseminated through various agencies.

St. John's, it was argued, needed eighty men for normal work, but only had fifty. Already the police were burdened with the problem of dealing with unemployment:

We have unemployed troubles, which, during the winter, require the constant attention of four men for the purpose of investigations, and two men at the employment office.

Outside the capital the need for more policemen was even more urgent. This was particularly true of industrial areas:

The Humber territory had become by reason of the foreign element and the gravitation thereto of criminal classes, dangerous to law abiding citizens.

A request for an extra twelve officers was made, six being for St. John's. Later requests also identified the urgent needs of industrial areas such as Corner Brook, Buchans, Conception Bay, Wesleyville, and White Bay.[107] But, by late 1931 the total police force of the country was still only 152 including the inspector general and the superintendent.[108] Of this total, eighty-four were located in St. John's, but of these twenty-nine were employed by the fire department. They might be used in an emergency, but the effective force in the capital was a mere fifty-five men. The remaining sixty-six members of the total force were scattered outside St. John's, most of them in areas such as Grand Falls, Corner Brook, Bell Island, where there existed "works and plants of great value."

It was the introduction of the serious retrenchment program in the fall of 1931 which revealed the inadequacy of the police force. Government moves to reorganize relief and to cut rations to one standard level were resisted, opposition to the Magor ration being most fierce in St. John's, where the serious incident at the Court House involving Richard Squires occurred in February 1932. However, it was the riot of April 1932 which led to the urgent expansion of the police force. Governor Middleton was very disturbed:

Mass movements of this description cannot fail at the best of times to be something of a menace and consequently it is not surprising that given the disregard already shown by a section of the population for law and order a real crisis should have arisen.[109]

The government though, was already acutely aware of the inadequacies of the forces at its disposal to deal with unrest:

On the 22nd of July, 1931, when I was at Grand Falls. . .on my way back from Labrador I received a telegram from the Prime Minister in which it was stated that persons of "red" tendencies were attempting unemployment organization in St. John's and Conception Bay which if not checked would probably lead to serious breaches of the peace; that it would be particularly helpful if one of His Majesty's ships if not both of those in Newfoundland waters would visit St. John's before going to Canada; that the Inspector General of the Constabulary had reported that his entire available force on the Peninsula of Avalon. . .was "insufficient to cope with one major disturbance at one time in one place."[110]

However, little had been done to improve the force before the incident of February 11 forced the government to seriously consider improving the effectiveness of the police. This incident led to moves to arm the force with tear gas (*Evening Telegram* 25 February 1932:15). But it seems likely that it was not until later that this was obtained because at the end of March the sales manager of the Chemical Protection Co. of Toronto was still communicating with the Department of Justice about the capabilities of their wares. (It is also possible that the government had been considering tear gas before the February 11 incident):

> Further to our letter of February 12th in regard to Federal Tear Gas Police equipment, may I draw your attention to the Unemployed Demonstration at the Ford Factory at Dearborn Michigan, and the disastrous results there from.

> The Dearborn Police used Federal Tear Gas, but did not have a sufficient quantity to cover the large area occupied by the disturbers, and this, was responsible for the death and injury suffered by those present.

> Mr. Edsel Ford was present during this disturbance and was so delighted with the effect of our product, that he immediately telephoned long distance and placed a nice order for this equipment.

> We are enclosing a newspaper clipping, taken from the Toronto *Daily Star*, which is self explanatory and we wondered if your order had gone astray.[111]

The confrontation of February 11 led to increased pressure on the police. The government might have been forced to increase relief rations as a result of face-to-face confrontation by the unemployed, but it could minimize the cost of the increases by limiting the number of persons who would be eligible for relief. The systematic use of the police force to investigate relief applicants in St. John's was an attempt to limit relief spending without the risk of a serious confrontation with all those on relief. Individuals might from time to time be refused the dole or cut off from support, but they would not be in a position to bring organized pressure to bear on the authorities.

However, it was the serious riot in April that led to the decision to expand the police force by 100 men. The incident made it very clear that the police force could not hope to control a serious outbreak of violence. They had, in effect, been defeated by the crowd that laid siege to the Colonial Building. The use of the British navy was also problematic after the uproar about its use in British press. And while a militia raised from the ranks of the Great War Veterans' Association could be used in an emergency, it was thought to be not fully reliable. All considered, it was decided that the expense of expanding the force was not only justified but absolutely necessary. This put the authorities in a much better position to deal with lawbreaking than they had been in February and April.

Part of the art of successful government is to manage the society and the conflicts which are an integral part of our economic system without resorting to the use of overt force. It is the craft of persuading people that certain actions and compromises are the correct and only possible ones. However, coercion and force are also routinely used to enforce political will. Because of this, policing is "at the heart of the state's functioning" (Reiner 1985:2) and the art of successful policing is to minimize the use of legitimate force while bringing about the desired effect. The arts and crafts of government in Newfoundland were surely taxed to the limits in 1932. Caught between the incompatible imperatives of avoiding bankruptcy, maintaining the unemployed and keeping the peace (and all this while maintaining the existing power structure) the government staggered from crisis to crisis. Many Newfoundlanders accepted the fate handed out to them with quiet desperation. Others broke the law and these violent outbursts played a role in the breakdown of the political system. The lawbreakers were quickly identified as a minority and their actions condemned as an outrage. Even starvation was no excuse for breaking the law, hungry people were informed by the well-fed. In this context, we need to meditate seriously on the kind of social order which made such arguments not only possible *but* reasonable.

One of the difficulties of any discussion of violence is that the term covers a wide range of social activities, from rioting to assault. Yet, most studies of violence assume that such activities can be quantified and that by counting them up a measure of the degree of violence in a particular time and place can be arrived at. Was Newfoundland violent during the crisis of early 1930s? It depends very much on what measures are being used. Was Newfoundland then more violent than it is now? Again, it depends on what is being measured. Is a raid on a merchant's store by a crowd of 100 men armed with axes, who break down the door and take flour and molasses, the equivalent of 100 armed robberies today? Was violence in connection with unemployment more severe in Newfoundland in this period than it was in Britain? After all in Britain between August 1931 and December 1932 there were over 100 police baton charges against demonstrators, while in Newfoundland with perhaps 1/200th of the population of Britain there were at least two such charges (Manwaring-White 1983:3).

Of course one of the problems with this type of comparative and quantitative approach is that it by and large ignores the political, social, and economic context of particular events, such as riots. Clearly the meaning of a riot will vary greatly depending on the political climate at the time, the strength of the police force, and many other factors. There is also a very real sense in which the occurrence of a violent incident fundamentally alters perceptions of law and order. Thus exceptional circumstances must be given great weight in trying to appreciate something like policing policy. The point is that once a violent confrontation has taken place, once the power of the crowd has shown itself, then this haunts all those anxious about law and order. Once concessions have been gained from a reluctant government by force, then, in the future, threat of force may produce the same results. To call the bluff of those opposing the authorities, the government has to have enough power at its disposal to risk a violent outburst. Because of this, the shadow of 1932, with its three major violent incidents in St. John's and other disturbances in Conception Bay, hung over those responsible for law and order in Newfoundland throughout the 1930s.

Despite the increase in the police force which had taken place in April, the inadequacies of the force continued to worry the government. However, it was the eruption of trouble in Conception Bay and the fear that violence might break out in St. John's at the same time, that led the government to set about raising a force of 150 special policemen in the fall of 1932.[112] The recruiting drive only managed to turn up 100 men who met the specifications drawn up by the Head of the Constabulary. The men of the special police force were paid $5 per month and were under the full control of the police. They could also be used singly or as a unit in an emergency.

The fall of 1932 saw further efforts to equip the police for the task of riot control. In October, the Newfoundland High Commissioner in London was requested to provide quotations for the cost of trench helmets. The High Commissioner replied thus:

> On receipt of your first cable asking for quotations for trench helmets I got in touch immediately with the War Office. After being

referred to 'umpteen' departments I finally got into communication with an official who really knew something about trench helmets and their availability. I thought at first that there should be no difficulty in buying thousands of them right off but I was given to understand that the Jews had already been operating in this market and had brought them in enormous quantities for the use of the Chinese. That reminded me of our famous murder case 'Wo Fen Game' and of the many merry meetings of Counsel at my office during the adjournments.[113]

The High Commissioner had expressed the urgency of the Newfoundland government's request to the authorities and they had agreed to let them have up to 500 partly used helmets at seven shillings and fourpence each. The helmets were reported to be "in very good condition and. . .identically the same as those now being issued to the troops in this country." It was decided to buy 200. In passing the High Commissioner reported on the riots in London, adding a comment on the trench helmets: "I sincerely hope that it will not be necessary to use them but I think you are right in being prepared for any emergencies."

The success of the United Newfoundland Party's attempt to introduce a new and tougher relief policy rested on the coercive power of the state, that is, on its ability to overcome opposition to what was regarded by many as an unjust and blatant attempt to starve people. That this was only partly successful was due to the state's military weakness in the face of what was, in some areas, well-organized opposition.

The strategy of prosecuting rioters, or at least the ringleaders, proved to be more difficult than anticipated. The circumstances surrounding the St. John's riots meant that many identified troublemakers had gone unpunished, according to the Head of the Constabulary. The police simply did not have the forces to make mass arrests.

> It was not possible to take immediate punitive measures against those concerned in St. John's riots for the double reason that in case these should precipitate further trouble the Police Force was quite inadequate to deal with possible contingencies, and that there was at the time absolutely no prison accommodation available for the numerous persons who might be arrested (Amulree Report 1933).

When prosecutions did result from arrests, they were not always successful. The alleged leader of the unemployed in the July riots was acquitted of the charge of incitement to riot amidst a massive ovation from his supporters (*Fishermen's Advocate* November 2, 1932:1). Also the court system was put under an incredible strain by the number of serious offences which were being brought before the bench. Not only were there cases of riot to be tried, but the government was also conducting a campaign against dole fraud by both merchants and dole recipients. The prosecution of many of these cases was costly because witnesses had to be transported to St. John's and kept at government expense during the trials. In December 1932 the Supreme Court handled the greatest number of criminal cases in its 139 year history (*Evening Telegram* 19 December 1932:6).

The men arrested in the Conception Bay riots were tried in St. John's in December 1932 and convicted to terms in prison with hard labour. In passing sentence the judge made explicit the role of law in relation to relief policy:

> We are passing through difficult times at present and many or-
> dinarily independent people like most of you are compelled,
> through no fault of your own, to depend upon public assistance to
> support themselves and their families. But the resources of the
> authorities are limited and it is unlawful and criminal to try to
> compel them by force and violence to do what in their judgment
> they consider they would not be justified in doing. Riots and
> disorders will accomplish nothing. They merely lead to more suf-
> fering and privations. They destroy the means and the confidence
> necessary to restore the prosperity that will enable the people to
> live in comfort and happiness, and nothing could be more harmful
> at the present time. The enforcement of law and order is essential
> to the well being of the community and must be effected at all costs.
> Those of you who take the law into your own hands and by force of
> intimidation seek to impose your will upon the community must
> be arrested and adequately punished.[114]

The judge's statement belied the fact that it was precisely in those areas where there was extensive and coherent organization by the unemployed that concessions had been gained from the authorities. In both Conception Bay and St. John's mass protest, the threat of violence or actual violence had been used to prevent reductions in the dole rations.

However, in most small fishing communities, there was very little serious violence connected with public relief. Raids on merchants' stores did occur when those receiving relief were either denied assistance by the authorities or when the merchants refused to fill dole notes issued by relieving officers because they either did not have the necessary supplies or because the government was behind in its payment of bills. In such incidents the action of the people involved in the raid was for the most part very controlled. There was no looting, little violence against the persons operating the store, and the raiders only took the relief rations to which they felt themselves to be entitled.

In St. John's and Conception Bay, however, the violence was somewhat different. It was better organized, on a larger scale, and it had distinct political overtones. Many of the men involved in the unemployed movements in these areas were unemployed wage workers many of whom had worked abroad and been influenced by unionist ideas. Not only did these people have a limited opportunity to provide for themselves, but they were more prepared to organize in order to gain that to which they felt they were entitled. Given their importance in terms of protest and the activities of the unemployed, it is not surprising that the government was anxious to assess the influence of unionist and radical ideas in the major population centres.

The Prison Crisis

> Mr. Alderdice promised us progress, prosperity and profitable employment. Employment not prison ships. The crowd that have the profitable employment now is the crowd that has the jobs on the *"Meigle"* [a prison ship]. So Mr. Alderdice has carried out his promise to a few job hunters—at least. God help the poor of Newfoundland (*Fishermen's Advocate* 30 November 1932:6).

Early in 1932 a crisis began to develop in the Newfoundland prison system as more people were sent to jail for dole fraud, game law violations, riot, and other crimes. From the evidence it is not clear whether the rising rate of incarceration was a result of more serious crimes being committed or of a combination of factors. Certainly the police and others *thought* that the deterioration in the economic situation was responsible for an increase in crime. For example, the annual report of the constabulary issued in 1933 noted:

> Burglaries and larcenies have been very considerable during the period which has been termed "the period of depression," and the past year has had its share. Quite a number of cases can be traced directly to the condition of the perpetrators, many of whom would hesitate to commit their offence if it were not for their impoverished condition.[115]

It is probable, however, that this statement was based more on general impressions than on a careful analysis of trends in existing statistics (very crude at the time). It is possible that the crimes identified were on the increase in the early 1930s, but it is also possible that the much increased police force was detecting more crimes (the regular force stood at 280 by 1933 and had a much improved detective section) or that heavier sentences were being handed out to offenders who might previously have been dealt with more leniently. The above statement also must be appreciated as part of an argument that there were increasing pressures on the police force from a number of directions in spite of its greater manpower (implicit in the argument is a plea for a further increase in the force). One of these pressures was the result of the use of the constabulary in relief work (sixteen men in 1933), responsibilities which were not viewed with any enthusiasm by the police.

Without doubt the rising prison population was related to the deteriorating economic situation. From 1931 the government pursued with great vigour dole frauds perpetrated by both those receiving assistance and those handling supplies and administering relief. As this campaign intensified in 1932 many people were sent to jail. In September 1932 the Minister of Justice wrote to the Secretary of State about one such effort. New statutory declarations had just been introduced for dole applicants and this was providing the basis for more people to be charged with false pretences (nine people within the last few days). The situation was problematic from a number of points of view:

> I think we have to face the situation that within the next few weeks there will be many more arrests on similar charges. Each prosecution in the Supreme Court will cost us a minimum from fifty to two hundred dollars, depending upon whether the plea is "guilty" or "not guilty"; a great deal of this being out of pockets for witnesses. Furthermore convictions will be almost certain and an already over-crowded penitentiary will be unable to house them. In fact I am at present time considering suggestions for obtaining further accommodation at Harbour Grace. . .[116]

Previously, magistrates had been in the practice of fining people found guilty of false pretences the amount of the dole received plus twenty dollars. Now, however, the Minister of Justice was arguing that this penalty was "quite inadequate." He backed up his decision by noting that the existing penalty "holds no fear for parties who have bank accounts running into hundreds of dollars." But heavier sentences would make more prison accommodation necessary. Those unable to pay fines would have to go to jail and evidence suggests that, in spite of the minister's beliefs, many had already proved too poor to pay even the previous fines, in default, being forced to 'opt' for a prison sentence.

More people were also being sent to jail in connection with disturbances arising out of attempts to get public relief or improve rations. By March 1932 it was reported in the *Evening Telegram* that the "Hotel by the Lakeside" was full (15 March 1932:6). A constabulary officer had arrived from Grand Falls with three prisoners to find no room at the inn and the prisoners had been forced to double up until some vacancies occurred. By June the prison contained 150 people, a very high figure compared with the 55–80 average in the 1920s (Amulree Report 1933). Nor was there much possibility of accommodating prisoners in outport jails, most of which were just not suitable for anything but very short term incarceration. Jails which could handle longer term prisoners (for example, Harbour Grace) were also coming under increased pressure.

Under the circumstances the authorities undertook to jettison some of the less serious cases from the prison system.[117] First, it was necessary to make sure that the prison system was only used for the purpose intended and not as a kind of supplementary poor house:

> This is a course which, out of charity, Magistrates have been known to take from time to time in the past. We cannot, however, fall in with the arrangement, however desirable it may be in itself. The penitentiary is not a shelter for the poor; and if, as appears to be the case, Nixon [the case which had raised the problem being discussed] must be looked after by some department of the Government, this department is not the appropriate department.[118]

One of the problems was that with poverty so widespread and public relief rations so limited (accommodation was not included nor was clothing) prison might not have seemed such a bad option for those in desperate straits. This is borne out by an examination of prison diets in the 1930s. Almost one dollar a day was allowed for food while in prison and this provided a far superior diet than was obtainable on the dole, or, for the majority of people, by work.

The pressure on the prison system, and the penitentiary in particular, could be eased by early release of prisoners. This might also save the government money by cutting the costs of public relief. An example of this is provided by the case of a Paradise man who was serving four years in jail for incest.[119] His family of nine children had been assisted by the Public Charities "at very considerable expense." They were, however, "very improvident and lazy" and the opinion was that it was "impossible to do anything with them." Given this and the urgent need felt in 1931 to cut relief and the likely hardship of the coming winter, it was suggested by the Minister of Justice that "having regard to the interests of the children" the prisoner be given six months commutation of sentence and released to look after his affairs and provide for his family. Nor was this an isolated example. As a result of the Conception Bay riots of late 1932 some sixteen men had been sent to jail. In February 1933 over 2,300 residents of the area petitioned for the release of the men. In response to the public pressure and given the evidence of hardship being suffered by their families ("Its not the fuel that bothers me most its food that I'm short of"), the government undertook to seriously consider the release of the men. Powerful arguments in favour of release were put forward in the review of the situation. It was argued that the men were "not criminals in the real sense of the word" and that "in view of the fact that the spring is upon us and it is necessary for them to prepare their grounds and to get ready for the fishery" setting them free should be seriously considered.[120]

A pardon for the sixteen men made sense economically and might even have some political merit. But despite pressure, the Minister of Justice chose this time to be very clear about the conditions under which "the Royal Prerogative of Mercy" should be exercised. Sentences could only be modified if it was thought that the judge had erred on the side of harshness, or if circumstances changed which would shed new light on the trial, or, in the case of a juvenile, if it was thought that leniency would result in reform. None of these conditions applied in the case of the Conception Bay rioters. Under the circumstances, it was thought to be not advisable to set the men free:

> It must be realized that the friends of prisoners are naturally anxious for their release and will move heaven and earth for that purpose. Members of the House of Assembly are subjected to continuous pressure by their constituents to pull strings for the release of their friends. If a firm stand is not taken in connection with these one might as well open the Gaol. One release without justification leads to another.[121]

Not only would release set a dangerous precedent *at a crucial time* in the government's war against the dole, but it would put sentencing in the hands of politicians rather than the court. Thus release was rejected in this case.

The pressure on the penitentiary in St. John's was relieved in 1932 by sending prisoners to the Harbour Grace jail. But with the riots of the fall a very serious problem developed which was solved by the government renting the S.S. *Meigle* from the Reid Company to act as a floating prison ship. Moored in St. John's Harbour, and run by a person who had been one of the instigators of the April riot which had led to the unseating of the Squires government, it served as a prison hulk for the victims of destitution (*Fishermen's Advocate* 28 October 1932:4). The prison ship immediately became a potent symbol of Newfoundland's desperate situation and the government's frantic efforts to maintain law and order as the ship of state foundered and the crew mutinied (*Fishermen's Advocate* 26 October 1932:4).

Modifications to the penitentiary allowed greater numbers of people to be incarcerated after 1932 and the *Meigle* was retired. But when the Commission of the Government took over in early 1934 the prison was "overcrowded" with two or three men occupying each cell. Of the 375 prisoners, thirty-four were between the ages of ten and sixteen. Most of the overcrowding was due to people being jailed for longer periods:

> A serious feature of the situation is the fact that up to 3 1/2 years ago, the majority of commitments were for misdemeanours and for short terms, but during the last few years the situation has changed. Felonies now predominate with many sentences ranging from 1 1/2 to 3 years.

The problem of juveniles both within and without the prison was considered to be a serious one:

> The Grand Jury considers that the problem of juvenile delinquency is serious and must be faced at the earliest possible date.
>
> Undoubtedly the problem is to a very large extent due to the economic situation, causing lack of opportunities for employment; idleness, hunger, lack of clothing, drives many an honest person to commit crime, social conditions, bad housing, etc., is [sic] also a contributing factor. During 1933 about 200 boys and young men were committed to the penitentiary, no doubt many of whom leave at the termination of their sentences, little if any better either mentally or morally, than when they entered.[122]

This was part of a call for improved facilities at a time when it was to be expected that more government money would be likely available in Newfoundland.

But events were soon to put an even greater strain on the prisons. Trouble connected with those engaged on woods work in the summer of 1934 led to mass arrests which resulted in prisoners being accommodated in the broom cupboard at the penitentiary and to many prisoners being camped out in tents on the prison grounds (*Fishermen's Advocate* 20 July 1934:4). Later in the year a temporary reformatory for juvenile offenders was established at Harbour Grace (up to seventeen years). A prison camp was also set up on the railway to relieve overcrowding and provide employment for prisoners.[123]

Insufficient prison accommodation continued to be a problem throughout the 1930s. The lack of outport jails caused special difficulties, as one magistrate noted in his request for a prison in St. Anthony:

> It is singularly impossible to enforce the law in matters of minor importance, because the term of imprisonment is not sufficiently long to justify taking the offender to Twillingate or St. John's. The new result is to defeat the ends of justice while giving the offender a gratuity in the shape of a pleasant holiday to and from his home. The sentence is served in a boarding house and on a ship which carries him along.[124]

Again financial constraints set the limits to which law and order could be enforced and justice seen to be done.

The Struggle for Stabilization

The Alderdice government faced the winter of 1932–33 with a much strengthened police force. There is no doubt that this enabled them to take a much tougher line than previously on the question of relief provision. But still the situation was a delicate one from the point of view of maintaining law and order. In particular, "agitators" who incited the population to demand more relief were the bane of the government.[125] Under the circumstances it was thought desirable to provide some form of work for the unemployed during the winter months. Public works were not viewed very favourably. They had been considered in the fall of 1931, but rejected as too costly (it was estimated that they cost the government four times the amount needed to support people on direct relief). There was also the added problem that once government schemes were started in one area they tended to unleash a flood of requests for similar works from all over the country. To avoid this problem and to limit costs it was decided to provide work through private contractors during the winter of 1932–33.[126] Subsequently arrangements were made for some 90,000 tons of pit props to be cut for export by various contractors who agreed to employ people on relief to do the cutting. Competition for employment on these schemes did generate some conflict but overall they seem to have played a role in stabilizing conditions somewhat at a difficult time for the government.

Throughout early 1933 reports of starvation reached the government in large numbers from all over Newfoundland. In some areas threats were made against relieving officers, while in Wesleyville men refused to work for the dole.[127] There were threats of raids, for example, at Terrenceville, Conche, Burnt Islands and Seal Cove. Some of the worst hardship occurred in the middle of the year when the government made efforts to cut the dole during the productive season. In fact, what was taking place was a battle between the government and the merchants who would normally have outfitted men for the fishery. In the uncertain economic climate of the early 1930s merchants were increasingly loathe to risk outfitting fishermen. The government was convinced that they were trying to shift the responsibility for supply onto the state. If so, providing relief during the fishing season would encourage merchants to further cut supplies. Once relief was issued in an area or to some individuals it was thought that this would convey the message to the merchants that in the final analysis the state would step in and support people. The merchants would, therefore, feel free to unload their responsibilities for "their" fishermen.

The losers in this battle for responsibility were the pawns in the brutal game. By mid-1933 reports of starvation began to flood into St. John's from Chance Cove, Trinity South, Shoal Harbour, Queen's Cove, Hillview, Champneys East, Lethbridge, Newtown, Musgrave Harbour, Victoria Cove (Gander Bay), Loon Bay, Newstead, Exploits, Twillingate, New Bay, Westport, Bonne Bay, Rencontre East, Burin, Lamaline, Sound Island, St. Kyrans, Branch, St. Brides, Trepassey, Fogo, and Ferryland. In some of these places there were also threats made that stores would be raided. Force was used to obtain relief at a number of places, including Marystown, Westport, Hampden, West Clayton, Flower's cove, Come by Chance, and Victoria. A breach of the peace in connection with relief at Wesleyville in May led to two men being jailed, and riots occurred at Little Catalina and Salvage in June.[128] Serious incidents also took place at Greenspond and Bonavista. Fifty armed policemen were sent to the latter place and in both cases arrests were made.

Faced with such widespread unrest, the government was forced to issue relief and almost $100,000 was eventually paid out to 67,006 individuals in June 1933.[129] Throughout the summer and fall of 1933 relief continued to be issued in situations where this could not be avoided. Even so the occasional raid occurred, as at Flower's Cove in July.

In mid-1933 a new ration system was introduced in many areas. The following message, posted in Deer Lake, illustrates how the system worked:

> When June ration is given it will be the last under present system. Country cannot stand strain under present conditions and any dole given in future will take the form of Pauper relief consisting of flour molasses tea at so much per head and names of recipients posted in public places over the signatures of the relieving officers and relief controller.[130]

The new sliding scale provided a single individual with 42 lbs. of flour, 1/2 gallon of molasses and 1/4 lb. of tea per month. A family of five was allowed 112 lbs. of flour, 1 1/2 gallons of molasses and 1 1/2 lbs. of tea. The cost of the new ration was estimated at $2.06 per single individual, $1.57 per head for a couple, and about $1.00 per person per month for families over two people. There were, however, exceptions to the new system. One section of Conception Bay, that from Western Bay to Brigus, was still on the $1.80 per head per month ration and another section, that from Perry's Cove to Bay Roberts, was on a ration of $1.80 every three weeks.

In order to save money and reduce the inequalities in the system (which threatened to continue to be a source of political problems) a new scale was suggested for the dole season in late 1933. This would cut relief rates in Conception Bay and allow relief to be given at a higher level in the rest of the country, while saving an estimated $3,876.06 per month. The average cost of this new ration was estimated to be about $1.40 per person per month.

The dole reorganization of late 1933 was an attempt to re-introduce a degree of system into what had become a rather chaotic set of arrangements for supplying relief. There had been many complaints about the harshness of the ration from areas outside Conception Bay and the government acknowledged that these complaints had "a reasonable basis," especially for larger families. But the central issue which had been addressed was that of inequality in the system. The government admitted that "knowledge of this discrepancy in treatment" had "become general" by mid-1933. Agitation was showing signs of "soon becoming general" and it was thought advisable to "adjust matters on an equitable basis promptly and voluntarily" rather than waiting and then being forced to make changes to the system "under duress." Accordingly, it was decided to introduce the new relief ration first in those areas where conflict had already occurred and then deal with other areas.[131]

In late 1933 conditions continued to be quite desperate in Newfoundland. In much of the country people were being provided relief at well below the level which the government considered adequate for survival. Not surprisingly, the winter of 1933–34 produced widespread reports of starvation, although perhaps these were not as widespread as in 1932–33. Threats that stores would be raided also reached the authorities and several raids did occur, for example at Hebron in Labrador,[132] and at Port Saunders, La Scie and Marystown.

The introduction of the new relief system in 1933 generated opposition in those areas where rations were reduced. There was resistance to the new policy in several parts of Conception Bay, but although there were several confrontations no serious incidents like those of the fall of 1932 occurred. One incident did lead to a public outcry against the government, however. This arose out of some dole disturbances at Bay Roberts. Following the disturbances five policemen were sent to arrest two men. They entered the house of one of the men during the night and exploded one of the constabulary's new tear gas bombs at the head of the stairs. Meanwhile the man they had come to arrest escaped out of the bedroom window, leaving his family to the fumes. The police action led to a public meeting at Bay Roberts in which their excessive use of force (this was probably the first time tear gas, which had been obtained for riot control, was used in Newfoundland) was soundly condemned (*Fishermen's Advocate* 3 November 1933:5).[133]

It is hard to explain why serious confrontations did not occur after late 1932 (until mid-1935). Certainly, the government had become more adept at managing the relief issue, and the policy of arresting the leaders of the opposition no doubt weakened the organizations of the unemployed. Also, the political climate was changing from early 1933 when the Amulree Commission was collecting evidence in Newfoundland, and events seemed to be moving towards a resolution in the form of Government by Commission. In a very real sense the confrontations of 1932 had led to the government abandoning its plans for the wholesale elimination of relief. With a strengthened police force it seems that the two sets of opposing forces were now relatively well balanced and a standoff had been achieved.

Towards the End of Democracy

Ralph Milliband (1982), examines the "permanent and fundamental contradiction or tension" which exists in capitalist society "between the promise of popular power, enshrined in universal suffrage, and the curbing or denial of that promise in practice."[134] Democratic institutions and practices have provided "means of expression and representation to the working class, organized labour, political parties, and groups, and other such forms of pressure and challenge from below," but "the context provided by capitalism" has always required that these pressures from below be as far as possible contained and weakened. It is also clear that in certain places and at certain times (during crises, for example) efforts to weaken these pressures have greatly intensified, even to the extent of demolishing democratic institutions and limiting democratic practices.

One of the most dramatic features of political life in the West during the period after World War I was the growth of anti-democratic thought (Carr 1944:15–38; Spitz 1949; Griffiths 1983). This occurred at the same time that many countries were achieving something close to universal adult suffrage. However, it took the Great Depression to cause these smouldering sentiments to ignite into a series of flaming attacks on democratic institutions. In Newfoundland a certain disillusionment with party politics and an unease with democracy had been in evidence in the 1920s (Mc-Donald 1980:171–172; Elliott 1980:181–204; Overton 1990). It took the crisis of the early 1930s, the failure of the Liberal government in 1931 and the impending bankruptcy of the country to make people seriously consider replacing democracy with some form of exceptional state. It was around the issue of the dole that much anti-democratic feeling focused.

Sir William Coaker, the founder of the Fishermen's Protective Union, had made a strong appeal for Commission Government in 1925 (*Daily Globe* 26 November 1925:1, 5; *Fishermen's Advocate* 4 December 1926). The task of this Commission would be to "clean up" the government and put the country's "household in order." These tried and tested men would be responsible for producing reforms, establishing industries, placing the fishing industry on a businesslike basis, cutting out graft, and implementing a retrench-ment program. Coaker's suggestion for an end to democracy reflected his growing disillusion with party politics.

With the development of the financial crisis in mid-1931 the movement for some form of national administration gathered mo-mentum. There was widespread feeling that party politics was obsolete, or at least a major obstacle to swift and firm government action to deal with the crisis. This mirrored the growth of similar feeling in other countries, particularly in Britain. Party politics was not only seen as an obstacle to effective action, it was also very much seen as a *cause* of the problems facing countries in the early 1930s. Calls for the introduction of national governments or even dictator-ships were linked to the idea that it was class warfare which had to be eliminated and superseded by a political system which would be directed towards national salvation. The establishment of a national government in Britain in 1931 stimulated thinking along the same lines in Newfoundland, but it was the crisis of April 1932 which produced a flood of calls for an end to democracy.[135] Foremost amongst the voices was that of Sir William Coaker.

Coaker had been drawn back into politics in the late 1920s under Richard Squires as Prime Minister. But, with the crisis of

1931–32 and the ousting of the Squires government, his already weakened faith in democracy was totally undermined. He refused to run in the 1932 election and issued further calls for Government by Commission (*Fishermen's Advocate* 6 May 1932:4). Moreover, in the election he endorsed Alderdice's commitment to look into the possibilities of this type of government for Newfoundland. It was corruption and the need to control spending as well as the failure of the liberal-unionist forces to bring about substantial reforms in Newfoundland which had shattered Coaker's faith in democracy. As we can see from the case of Coaker, the movement for a new form of government was not in any simple sense a right wing movement.[136]

By mid-1932 Coaker was deeply pessimistic about the situation in Newfoundland and about world affairs generally:

> Will the large army of sufferers remain peaceful or will civilization disappear in a stupendous upheaval that will surpass the suffering and despair of the Great War?[137]

For Newfoundland he predicted excruciating hardship for the winter of 1932–33 and default before 1934. The *Fishermen's Advocate*, the official organ of the Fishermen's Protective Union, also urged an end to party politics, or, as it put it, the struggle between the "ins" and the "outs":

> The average, deep thinking man is not heart and soul in this election, as he feels that there is going to be very little difference, to the general good, whoever happens to hold office, under our present system of Party Government. Daily there is growing a conviction in the minds of the people, which we hear expressed by voice and correspondence, that Newfoundland ought to give Government by Commission a chance as long recommended by the *Advocate* (3 June 1932:6).

In line with this argument the *Advocate* encouraged its readers to vote for the "best man" in the 1932 election whether Liberal or Tory.

In trying to understand the movement for a form of exceptional state in Newfoundland in the early 1930s, it is important to focus attention on the way in which particular social groups experienced the economic crisis and the framework within which they interpreted events. Images of order and stability draw their power from images and experiences of chaos and instability. It was against the chaos and uncertainty of the events of 1931–32 that calls for dictatorship were made. In particular, it was the violent events of April 1932 which stimulated many calls for a new order. Riots are unsettling and sometimes profoundly frightening events for many people. They can rearrange the social kaleidoscope.[138] They invoke passionate responses. For this reason it is important to try to understand their significance while being careful not to overburden them with symbolic meaning. We project our fears onto the events around us. When we feel threatened we are likely to see dangers in every shadow.

As A.J. Toynbee (1932:13) makes clear in his article "Annus Terribilis 1931," a sense of apocalypse was widespread and deeply felt by the early 1930s.[139] Many feared the end of what they termed "civilization" by a process of "dilution and disintegration." The feeling is captured well by Mr. Hepburn, one of the directors of Baine Johnston Ltd., who was in regular contact with Spain and Scotland:

> Every country is labouring under the same difficulty, that is, unrest among the people, and it seems to me that the feeling of the people elsewhere is for a republican Government. Monarchy, to my mind, is being done away with, and if this sort of thing continues by and by there will be no gentlemen left. I mean gentlemen in the true sense of the word.[140]

With the Squires government of "political heelers" and "blood suckers" in power, Hepburn could not be optimistic about the situation in Newfoundland. In fact, he was less than enthusiastic about an offer from Newman's in London to handle Mumm's champagne given the circumstances.[141]

The riots of early 1932 greatly upset business and encouraged the idea that exceptional measures were needed to save the country from chaos. The violence was the final evidence that responsible government had become unworkable. Stability must be restored, this being seen as a prerequisite for industrial recovery. This might be achieved under an Imperial Tribunal, by a "bloodless revolution" by businessmen, or by Commission of Government. The aim was to save the country from the disgrace of poverty and bankruptcy, and from misery, internal strife and possibly bloodshed.

If those facing unemployment and hardship had expected a better deal under the Alderdice administration they were very quickly disillusioned. The cuts in relief and other spending announced in July might have been favourably received by many of a conservative persuasion, but those who were close to destitution must have had any remaining faith that they had in politics undermined. Based on the belief that "the first charge of this country is to see that nobody starves" the government's actions could be soundly condemned:

> Beri-Beri is rampant throughout certain sections of the country. It will take ten years to build up the physical deterioration of the people. Babies are born deformed and suffering from bone diseases, etc, due to malnutrition of the mothers. Even the rocks are crying out to high Heaven against such a crime as under nourishment—

and this is in the twentieth century. You cannot measure such a crime against humanity (*Evening Telegram* 27 July 1932:6).

Disillusioned with party politics and in the face of such devastation this writer cried "Oh, for a Mussolini," for a dictator who would act rather than fiddle, like "our modern Nero," while the country burned.

The attack on the party system was related to efforts to trim state spending in the crisis which started in 1931. The need to reduce pressures from below led many to advocate an end to politics altogether. Still others focused specifically on the dole question. The idea that those in receipt of the dole should be denied the vote was promoted as a means of limiting relief expenditures. In 1933 this idea was being seriously considered as part of the Alderdice government's war against relief. In November 1933 the Minister of Justice outlined his reasons for this. First, it might have the "psychological effect" of encouraging people to "struggle along" without the dole. Second, it might undermine the influence of "agitators" who were on the dole. And finally, but most importantly, it would deprive the destitute of a say in electing the government:

> A Government which is doing its best under distressing circumstances will necessarily be unpopular with those who are receiving less dole than they think they are entitled to and these will be by far the greater majority. This large number of disenfranchised dole recipients have it in their power to swing the electorate and deprive those who are paying the bill of the choice of Government.[142]

The question of politics and relief was also very much on the agenda for the Amulree Commission when it began its enquiry into Newfoundland's future in 1933. Appearing before the Commission, ex-Squires minister H. Mosdell offered a powerful indictment of voter irresponsibility in Newfoundland.[143] Relief had become a political issue. While he did not suggest the disenfranchisement of those in receipt of poor relief as a means of solving the problem of political influence in relief provision, he did argue that somehow "people must be made to realize their own personal responsibility" on the question of public spending. He thought that this might be achieved by means of a decentralised form of relief and health in which local committees were provided with a fixed grant.

The idea that government had become too close to the people and too sensitive to public pressure to effectively control spending was very characteristic of the inter-war period in Newfoundland and elsewhere. It followed from this that if effective controls over spending were to be introduced some means of lessening pressure from below would have to be introduced. In fact, all the means which were at the disposal of the government in Newfoundland in the early 1930s were directed towards limiting such pressure. That part of the solution to the problems of Newfoundland might lie in depriving the destitute of any say in electing the government was something the Amulree Commission explored in its interviews with a number of important individuals. Some were not sure about the positive effects of this, but others argued strongly for removing the franchise from paupers, including the Deputy Minister for Public Works and the influential L.C. Outerbridge.[144] Speaking for the larger merchants of St. John's, Outerbridge suggested that dole recipients should be deprived of their vote for four years and that their names be published in post offices in order to discourage them from becoming dependent on the state.

In advocating disenfranchisement for paupers, people like Outerbridge were following a powerful current of thought. In nineteenth century Newfoundland those in receipt of poor relief had been denied the vote. In Britain this disqualification persisted until the end of World War I. The standard argument used by people of such stature as John Stewart Mill and William Beveridge was that the vote was a reward for independence, self-sufficiency, and labour and those who were a drain on the public purse should have no say in how the contents of that purse were spent (Deacon and Briggs 1974; Brown 1978; Mill 1910:282).

In all events, by the time the disenfranchisement of paupers was under serious consideration in 1933 events were rapidly moving towards a temporary resolution in Newfoundland. When the Amulree Commission reported later in that year it recommended Commission of Government. The whole country was to be disenfranchised. After the storm and stress of 1932 Commission Government seemed to offer the kind of stability which would be required for capital investment and the work of reconstructing the shattered country.

In February 1934, Newfoundland moved from being a democracy with Dominion status to being governed by a Commission responsible to the Secretary of State for the Dominions in London. This Commission consisted of six persons, three from Britain and three from Newfoundland, with the governor of the colony acting as chairman. Exceptional times and circumstances had called for exceptional measures and what Thomas Lodge (one of the Commissioners) called a "bizarre experiment in dictatorship" was undertaken (Lodge 1939). It was hoped that the new government would quickly fulfil its task of bringing immediate and temporary relief to the country, while attention was also given to finding ways to strengthen the basic economic and social fabric of Newfoundland so that a speedy return to responsible government would be possible.

COMMISSION OF GOVERNMENT

Relief and Public Order

> Where were you born? How were you born?
> Are you sure you were born?
> Where do you live?
> How many children do have?
> What do you want to have children for?[145]

When the Commission came to power in 1934 it immediately faced the difficult question of what to do about relief. Widespread agitation against existing government policies continued along with raids and other more serious incidents.[146] The new government was under intense pressure to improve relief provision. At the same time others were calling for action to end what was called the "dole racket."[147] Many argued that the dole system was too lax and that those who were too lazy to work should be denied assistance. The *Fishermen's Advocate*, focused on the inequality of treatment between St. John's and the outports and more generally made the argument that the dole was a "canker" eating the heart out of Newfoundland (11 April 1934:5).[148] All this amounted to a plea for extensive reforms to systematize the distribution of relief and for the development of productive work to replace the dole ration.

The relief situation greatly troubled not only those responsible for administering the Department of Health and Welfare, but also the Commissioner responsible for Justice. In March 1934 he produced a major review of the dilemmas of policing the country, much of it focusing on the problem of relief. He noted that "repeated complaints" were reaching his department from magistrates and from the police of grave disturbances and breaches of the peace in many parts of the country. These were directly caused by the destitute condition of the people and the inadequacy of the dole allowance. It was the Justice Department's position that breaches of the law would "not be tolerated." However it was recognized that such a policy could only be enforced if there were "sufficient force to compel observance." Under existing conditions (the police force was now almost 300 men) this would be "practically impossible." To make matters worse the condition of the population was rapidly deteriorating. The Commissioner for Justice felt that the government had no alternative but to increase the dole ration even if it meant "the expenditure of additional moneys." Such spending, it was argued, could be justified because it would both "reduce the occurrence of breaches of the law" and "fit people physically for the undertaking of whatever schemes of employment that it is hoped will be developed during the early summer." The increased expenditure on the dole would also be offset by savings on "sending round sufficient police force to enforce authority" when violations of the law did occur. Police would also be freed up for any possible emergency:

> We have at the moment under the consideration of the Department at least three serious cases of flagrant defiance of the law, and several other cases which cannot be ignored, but which are not of the same importance. It is impossible under present conditions to provide sufficient force in these various places to deter agitators from further resistance; and in any case when weather and travelling conditions do permit our dealing with them we are faced first of all with considerable expenditure, and secondly with the distribution of our Police Force at a time when the public interests require that the major portion of that Force, if not all of it, should be available for instant emergency.[149]

The government also acknowledged that if disturbances increased then breaches of the law would either have to be ignored or further prison accommodation provided "at considerable expense." The increase in the dole ration which dates from 1934 was, therefore, made not on humanitarian grounds, but after a full consideration of the costs and benefits of not increasing relief. The costs of the increased ration were kept to a minimum by the bulk purchase of items such as flour, tea, and molasses and by more effective control of the distribution of relief and merchants' prices. Other changes in the dole system were made after similar consideration of their value. This is true of the decision to make the consumption of brown flour compulsory for dole recipients: The flour was intended to combat beri-beri and thus reduce pressure on the inadequate medical system, as well as fitting people for productive work.

Trouble in the Woods

While the government was deciding to increase relief, it was also making the decision to eliminate dole during the fishing season. All able-bodied relief was to be cut from June 1934 in fishing districts.[150] The government would thus try to force as many people as possible to support themselves through productive labour. Those unable to go fishing would be expected to work in the woods. Woods work was viewed "as a means of improving the lot of families who are on relief." However, the wages paid for cutting wood were too low to allow men with families to get off the dole. Already men being paid 40–50 cents a day were only continuing to work "until they are hopelessly beaten."[151] Declining wage rates made it harder and harder for even experienced cutters to cover expenses. For example, in Middle Brook it was reported that in 1933 some 4,000 cords of wood were cut at $1.40 per cord, but that in 1934 only 2,500 cords would be cut at $1.10.[152] In Goose Bay it was documented that men working six full days per week were only clearing $2.50 for this work.[153] When poor weather prevented these men from working they still had to pay 50 cents per day for board. Under such circumstances it is not surprising that many were returning home in debt. In spite of such evidence the government proceeded with its plan to cut the dole. Men would be forced to work on whatever terms were available. The idea was that even if they only earned a few dollars this would lessen the costs of relief. Meanwhile an enquiry into working conditions in the lumber woods was to be conducted by F.G. Bradley.[154]

Soon large numbers of men, including those with no logging experience and those who were not in the best of health, were flocking to the lumber woods to try to earn a dollar. Many were ill-equipped and in poor physical condition after a period on the dole.[155] A crisis situation quickly developed. The situation was described by the *Fishermen's Advocate* as "the dirty stuff from which revolutions are bred" (20 July 1934:4). This may have exaggerated the revolutionary potential of those engaged in woods work, but a flood of reports to the government in 1934 testified to the seriousness of the plight of the loggers. The government might force men to labour for practically nothing, or for enough to pay for their expenses, but this did nothing about the problem of supporting their families during the summer or getting them off the dole in the long term. Any real solution to the problem lay in raising the earning levels of workers by improving wages and fish prices and it was against this rock that the plans of the Commission foundered throughout the 1930s.

By the middle of 1934 many of those faced with the futility of trying to earn their keep in the lumber woods had decided to give up the unequal struggle and head for home. Soon destitute men were abandoning their jobs and trying to find a means of transportation to their places of residence. Forcing passage on trains was already an established practice for destitute loggers in Newfoundland by the early 1930s.[156] The problem of men abandoning woods work and stealing transportation came to a head in July 1934. In that month eighteen men from Avondale and Conception Harbour, who had gone to White Bay logging for William Dawe and Sons, abandoned work and boarded the *S.S. Prospero* at Pacquet (*Fishermen's Advocate* 20 July 1934:6). When the steamer arrived in St. John's they were arrested and charged under the Newfoundland Railway Act with boarding the steamer with the intent of being fraudulently carried without payment of fare. They all pleaded guilty and were fined $15 or in default given thirty days in prison. About the same time another seventy men appeared in the court charged with stealing rides on the train (*Fishermen's Advocate* 20 July 1936:6). These men, mainly from the southwest coast, had abandoned work and boarded the train in Grand Falls, Bishops Falls and Badger. Twenty policemen were sent from St. John's to Clarenville in a freight train to arrest the men. They were tried in St. John's and all fined $15 or thirty days in jail.

All eighty-eight loggers were unable to pay their fines and so had to be sent to jail. The spectacle of a large body of loggers being marched through St. John's first to the lockup and then to prison was one which brought home very forcefully the state of the crisis in the woods. Statements were taken from the men by F.G. Bradley and his assistant Bernard Summers as evidence in the Commission of Enquiry into logging and newspapers published several accounts of conditions in the woods.[157] The *Fishermen's Advocate* in particular took up the case of the "eighty-eight unfortunates" (3 August 1934:3). In an editorial, the *Advocate* provided a powerful indictment of the Commission's failure to act on "the rotten system of the employment of loggers which obtains in this country" (3 August 1934:3). The law might have been "satisfied" by the imprisonment of the men, but many questions about the government's action were raised. Forcing men to work "under such damnable conditions" by refusing them dole was little better than slavery.

The public outcry may have encouraged the Governor to pardon the men, but no doubt the problems of accommodation at the prison were also a major consideration in this regard.[158] However, there is no evidence that the government took a laxer position on woods work and the dole as a result of the outcry over the imprisonment of the eighty-eight men.[159] In August, one magistrate reported that men were returning to the Burin and Marystown area from woods work in a destitute condition, but that the relieving officer was refusing to provide them with relief.[160] Some of the men were even being remanded on charges of vagrancy. Reports from 1936 indicate that it was still standard practice to discourage men from abandoning woods work under any circumstances.

The summer of 1934 saw the government encouraging private schemes to provide employment for loggers as part of their efforts to cut the dole. In June and July men were shipped from Newfoundland to work in the Alexsis River area of Labrador. Trouble immediately erupted over terms and conditions of work and the men went on strike. The government responded quickly and on July 17, Inspector General Hutchings of the Newfoundland Constabulary was instructed to investigate the situation. He left St. John's on July 19 and arrived at Alexsis Bay at noon on July 21. He took with him aboard the S.S. *Imogene* forty-five other members of the constabulary. On arrival Hutchings reported that he "immediately landed with our party under arms" to find 500 men in logging camps. The first men had arrived at Alexsis River on June 23, having been contracted to cut wood for $2 per cord for rough wood at the stump and $3 per cord for peeled wood at the stump. On July 9, 225 men had stopped work and sent a letter to the Labrador Development Company requesting that they provide free board and transport or increase wages. The president of the company arrived on July 14 and indicated that he was prepared to provide the men with $2.30 per cord for rough wood plus free passage. Any men who indicated that they were not satisfied with the new rate would be returned to Newfoundland. About half the men refused this offer and were shipped back to Lewisporte.[161]

The incident passed without any violence or threat of violence on the part of the strikers. According to Hutchings "no real grievance was disclosed" which would account for the work stoppage. In fact, it seems that the problem had arisen because the company had landed 500 men in Alexsis Bay without being ready to take care of them. Many of the woodsmen were inexperienced and the promises made to the men by the sub-contractors who had been paid 25 cents per man for recruiting were not in line with the company's policy. In addition, when the men arrived they found work conditions very different to those which they had expected. This kind of incident revealed several distinct problems. First, make work schemes could not be put into operation hastily. If they were to succeed they had to be carefully planned and managed. Second, it was not possible to take inexperienced men and put them to woods work and expect them to be satisfied and make even a minimum wage without some kind of training. Such schemes might offer a way of blunting the edge of the unemployment problem, but without caution they could generate as many problems as they solved.

The completion of the Bradley Report on the woods industry in Newfoundland confirmed the worst fears of the government. The situation as regards employment and wages was revealed to be quite appalling. In the political climate of the day the Commission, with the backing of London, thought that it would be political dynamite to make the findings of the report public. Behind the scenes, however, they used the report to gain some concessions from the two major pulp and paper companies on the question of loggers' wages. Minimum wage rates of $25 per month, to be paid as of January 1, 1935 were negotiated with these companies (Neary 1985). Nothing was done, however, about the many small contractors who employed loggers, often in the most appalling conditions, and throughout the 1930s trouble continued to flare up in the woods. In the second half of the 1930s unionization spread quickly amongst loggers and efforts to improve conditions led to a spate of strikes in 1937, including one at Robert's Arm where the strikers boarded the S.S. *Argyle* and forced the company to concede to their demands "under duress."[162] Again, lack of action on the part of the government to make even limited improvements in working conditions in the woods left loggers with no choice but militant action.

Unemployment Struggles

The winter of 1934–35 saw the government's new relief system being put into action throughout Newfoundland. It very quickly became clear to the unemployed that, despite some changes in relief rations, they were to be offered very little by the new government.

Although the situation was very much quieter than it had been for some time, the government was concerned about the unemployed becoming a focus for political opposition. In the absence of any of the usual channels by which opposition to the government might be expressed (and managed and diffused) it was vital to have some way of keeping a finger on the pulse of the people. This was achieved, in part, by an improved system of magistrates, acting very much as district officers. They passed on information to the central authorities and implemented policy in a number of areas. However, increasingly after 1934 the police and, after its creation in 1935, the Ranger Force were used to monitor conditions.

The police received improved training. Some officers were sent to Scotland Yard, and, a small, but effective, security force was developed. The main task of this force was to keep an eye on the unemployed and the activities of those known to be in opposition to the government. From 1934 all the meetings of the unemployed in

St. John's were attended by the police who made notes on what was said at the meetings, who was there, and what was done. This helped the authorities to gauge the mood of the unemployed and to estimate the strength of opposition to its policies. It also provided information which might be used against the leaders of the unemployed in the courts, if required.

In the summer and fall of 1934 the unemployed in St. John's began serious efforts to build a campaign to bring about improvements in the relief system. They emerged as the first coherent body of opponents to Government by Commission. A meeting was held at the Parade grounds on August 9. The meeting attracted about 150 people and was apparently calm since the police saw "not the least sign of any future rioting."[163] Pierce Power, James Kelly, and Peter Tremblett were accepted as members of the Labour Committee which was instructed to make submissions to the government regarding the condition of those on the dole. Power was elected chairman of the committee and Kelly was made secretary.[164] The committee also included W.J. Rodgers of the Penny-a-Week Club and John Cadwell who had been involved in the Newfoundland Industrial Worker's Association in the 1920s. Soon other meetings were being held.

One of the main issues for the unemployed movement was the provision of relief work. Without this, it was argued, the unemployed would be unable to afford clothes and rent. The Unemployed Committee was particularly concerned about this last issue. Periods of relief work were one way of providing the cash which would prevent people being put "bag and baggage on the sidewalks" by bailiffs. The third unemployment meeting on August 10 attracted about 1,000 people and led to the passing of a resolution to be forwarded to the government calling for work, an increase in the dole ration, relief for every single unemployed man over eighteen years of age, and the replacement of relief officials with people selected from the unemployed. The unemployed were gathering momentum for a confrontation with the new government.[165] The police observers were of the opinion that the movement was a fragile one which would not last long. They urged caution but noted that assurances had been given that the movement would remain within the law. The leaders of the movement might "incite the illiterate class to a high state of excitement" and this might "lead to a repetition of the last disorders."[166] A close eye was needed to gauge the mood of the protesters and attention was also focused on the leaders of the unemployed in the hope that criminal activity might be uncovered. Within a short time the constant surveillance, the interviews with contacts of the unemployed group and the group itself, and the information received from recruited informants provided hints of shady activity on the part of one of the leaders of the unemployed.[167]

By mid-August the Unemployed Committee had obtained an office and issued a small paper under the name of the *Avalon Welfare and Protective Association Bulletin*. They had also met with the Commissioners. The results of this meeting were presented to the public in the Majestic Theatre on August 14 and published in the *AWPA Bulletin*. The Unemployed Committee's requests had been "flatly turned down." The meeting expressed a great deal of anti-Commission sentiment, the general feeling being that "poor old Newfoundland" had been "betrayed and sold into the hands of foreigners" who were ignorant of the needs of the working classes.[168] The Commissioners denied that any extensive unemployment existed in St. John's and, according to the *Bulletin*, Puddester had even suggested that St. John's men were too lazy to work and that when employed on public works they failed to give full value for money. According to the Commissioners, the fact that men had abandoned woods work in the summer of 1934 was clear proof that they were not really in need. Faced with such a position the unemployed had no choice but to fight. In the words of Pierce Power:

> It is now. . .a contest between Dictators and the masses of toiling Newfoundlanders trying to exist in their own country as decent human beings, a contest for right, justice and liberty between the proletariat and the Oligarchy sent across the Atlantic to rule us against our will.

> This movement will be conducted within the law. We know we are being watched, and we must not give the enemy an excuse to interfere in the name of "law and order." The slogan which autocracy always throws out to justify clubbing the masses into silence. . ..That is the badge of bureaucracy everywhere. We were misled into the belief that the Commission of Government was installed for our benefit, but we now know they are here chiefly in the interests of the country's bondholders. They are our creditors' bailiffs, and the sooner we get rid of them the better for this country. We are fools to pay our last dollar to money lenders while people are on the verge of starvation (*Avalon Welfare and Protective Association Bulletin* 1934).

Instead of aid, Newfoundland's population was being given "a dose of Prussionism." It was being "sacrificed" to pay "the Shylocks of finance. . .their pound of flesh."

The unemployed mobilized for a showdown which would test the Commission's resolve. That the trial of strength might lead to a violent confrontation was recognized by both the government and the unemployed. But the government made no great efforts to avoid a clash and it continued to maintain its position on relief and work. For their part, the unemployed, while mobilizing, constantly stressed the need for their movement to remain within the law and avoid violence. Through the *AWPA Bulletin* a great deal of effort was made to inform the public that:

> should our progress be marred by acts of disorder the blame will not be ours but will be the unfortunate consequences of those in authority closing their eyes to the misery and their ears to the pleadings of half-starved, half-naked, cold and hungry men, women and children (1934).

The Unemployed Committee had great plans for a large movement with representatives from every trade in the country. They also took up the issue of the Bradley Report on the logging industry. In late August problems developed. One of the Unemployed Committee was arrested under a warrant sworn by another member of the Committee.[169] He was charged with misappropriating funds. With the case still pending disagreement erupted in public meetings and internal tensions within the unemployed movement mounted. Soon the police were able to report that "such friction" existed that future activities would "no longer hold the co-operation of the public in general."[170] However, the unemployed were still considered to be a dangerous force and in October the Commissioner for Justice reported to the governor that:

> It is evident. . .that internal dissention amongst these people is affecting progress of their programme, but at the same time there appears to be a desire to have some open demonstration of hostility. I rather gather that some one other than the parties themselves, probably with more money and more prominence, is behind this measure and I have instructed the Chief of Police to spare no effort to try and locate this party (or parties).[171]

Within a week of this statement the committee had disbanded.[172]

Tensions within the leadership of the unemployed played a key role in the movement's temporary collapse. There were disagreements about tactics, a distinct lack of solidarity and some dishonesty. Pierce Power had come under attack because he was rather more radical than many of the other leaders.[173] The police were not slow to exploit this situation by recruiting those disenchanted with the unemployed movement as informers. For example, Pierce Power identified J.T. Meaney, Herman Archibald, and J.R. Smallwood as "Newspaper Men" having an interest in the unemployed. He identified Smallwood as the leader of the group.[174] However, Power's disenchantment with the unemployed movement was short-lived and soon he was again at the front of efforts to improve conditions.

Throughout the winter of 1934–35 the unemployed in St. John's mobilized to win concessions from the new government. They demanded the relaxation of the regulations concerning the introduction and use of brown flour ("cattle food") and a greater choice of relief rations. They requested action to prevent evictions for non-payment of rent.[175] But just as important as these requests for an improvement in the material condition of the unemployed was the issue of how the unemployed were to be treated by the authorities and the degree of control that was to be exercised over their lives.

Early in 1935 more issues (improved coal and clothes allowances) were taken up. Issues like the non-publication of the Bradley Report on logging continued to be talked about at the meetings and contrasts were regularly made between the conditions which the unemployed of Newfoundland were forced to live under and those enjoyed by the unemployed in Canada and Britain. The Commission was clearly identified as a "dictatorship" and, faced with its refusal to make any substantial improvements in the relief system, firm opposition to this form of government was widespread amongst the unemployed in early 1935. In fact, some minor concessions had been provided by the authorities, but on many issues there had been no movement. From the government's point of view the limit to which the dole could be increased had been reached. Further improvements would prove costly, but much more importantly they might make relief too attractive. The average income from fishing was approximately $130 per year and with few other opportunities to supplement this income, most of the population were little, if at all, better off than those on the dole. To increase dole under such circumstances without any substantial increase in industrial wages and incomes from fishing would be to undermine incentive to work and put at risk what remained of the shattered industrial base of the country. With any further improvements in relief, the country would risk wholesale pauperization.

Police surveillance of the movement's leaders was intensified in early 1935 because of the rising tension between the unemployed and the Commission. A riot or serious disturbance was anticipated and it was thought necessary to identify particular grievances which might lead to such a confrontation.[176] Friction between the unemployed and government relief officials was identified as a particular problem. The investigating police officer agreed that "the officials at the said office execute their duties in an officious manner."[177] He supported this observation with the example of a man being refused the dole because he was thought to have participated in an unemployed parade. Detective Constable Mahoney saw such "discrimination" as unjustified. He also argued that the use of "diplomacy and common courtesy" which would not "cost the Department one cent" would ease the dissatisfaction of the unemployed and lessen the risk of riot. The unemployed were also hostile to the police, a fact which is not surprising given their role as relief investigators, their surveillance activities, and their actions during parades and confrontations.

The unemployed movement gathered momentum during the winter of 1935. Pierce Power had emerged as the undisputed leader of the movement, meetings were heavily attended, and action was in the air. Most of the pressure from the unemployed was directed towards the Department of Public Health and Welfare. But, by and large, Commissioner Puddester resisted or ignored these representations. However, the Department of Justice also had a great interest in relief matters. They viewed the situation with some alarm because if a disturbance did occur they would have to deal with it. In view of this the Commissioner for Justice was more willing to meet with the leaders of the unemployed than the Commissioner for Public Health and Welfare:

> Both the Chief of Police and myself have had to be on the watch; and, on several occasions, we have been faced with the possibilities of a rather critical situation.

> I finally came to the conclusion that, after making allowances for the activities of professional agitators, there must be somewhere amongst the unemployed some grievance, real or imaginary, and I thought that it might be well if an attempt were made to discover what these grievances were.[178]

The unemployed organized parades to back up their demands. In January 1935 a parade to Government House protested the introduction of brown flour. However, the police prevented the committee from seeing the Governor. In late February the unemployed paraded to the Department of Public Health and Welfare to interview Mr. Puddester.[179] The parade was led by Pierce Power, but Puddester refused to meet with him. He did agree to meet with other members of the Unemployed Committee, however. At this time the situation was rather tense, but any serious confrontation was avoided as some minor concessions were granted (vegetables and a better coal allowance).

By the end of February the unemployed were being geared up for trouble by the use of inciting language. Those present at meetings were said to be carrying sticks and fishplate bolts. Threats were also being made against relief controllers. This explosive atmosphere coincided with a change in the character of the unemployed movement. According to Detective Constable Mahoney, the movement increasingly took on a distinct political flavour. The meetings became the focus of much "political propaganda," particularly by Pierce Power, and much of this was directly anti-Commission of Government.[180] Mahoney attributed this to the influence of J.T. Meaney, a newspaper correspondent, whom he described as "our greatest agitator." Considerable police effort was directed towards identifying the money and brains which were supposedly behind the activities of the unemployed.

If the unemployed faced great difficulties in trying to present their case to government and in gaining concessions, they also faced the difficult task of maintaining a strong and united organization. By the end of February tensions within the leadership were again in evidence. These were probably a result of the increasingly political and militant direction which the movement was taking under the leadership of Pierce Power. The majority of the unemployed, however, continued to support him.

Sets of demands continued to be presented to the government, but, with the exception of some minor concessions, nothing moved (*Daily News* 6 March 1935). The gradual broadening of the political orientation of the unemployed in this period led figures such as George Wilkinson, a night school teacher in the Battery who had trained as a United Church minister in Montreal, into the movement. The relief issue became a key element in what was developing as a small but broad-based attack on Commission of Government.

Efforts were also being made to extend the support of the unemployed movement by forging links outside St. John's. An opportunity to do this was afforded in March by the presence of outport sealers in town. A sealer's meeting of 1,000 people was addressed by Pierce Power and J.R. Smallwood in the Majestic Theatre.[181] Smallwood spoke for over one and a half hours, mainly dealing with the sealer's grievances. He then allowed Power to speak on the need for the working classes of St. John's to act together with the outports to improve conditions. Smallwood argued that the Commission of Government possessed "strong power and strong authority." They were backed by the British government and they had a "marvellous opportunity" to change things. But, according to Smallwood, the Commissioners lacked the "courage and determination and backbone" to challenge the merchants and "give the working man a square deal." Already the expectation that the new government would be a powerful reforming one had been shattered.

It was becoming increasingly obvious that the Commissioners intended to do very little for the working people of the country, not because they did not wish to improve conditions (Smallwood thought Hope Simpson and Thomas Lodge did), but because they had become aware of the powerful forces which limited their sphere of action.

With the approach of the Royal Jubilee on May 6, 1935, the police received information about a parade being arranged by the unemployed to take place on that day. Newspaper correspondent J.T. Meaney was working "hand-in-hand" with the Unemployed Committee to organize this protest. The intention was for a peaceful parade by the unemployed, under a banner carrying the slogan "God Save the King; but we want work."[182] Meaney, in his capacity as press correspondent, intended to photograph the parade and use this as a means to publicize the plight of Newfoundland.

With the Jubilee just a few days away and with the unemployed in a confrontational mood, the provision of a limited amount of relief work was announced on May 3 (*Daily News* 4 May 1935:1). This would provide employment for 250 men, week on and week off, for a total of twelve weeks. In all, 500 men would be provided with some employment. But already another issue connected with relief work was causing problems, that of the administrative structure for selecting those who would perform the work.

The Jubilee on May 6 passed quietly in St. John's. The planned parade had been made unnecessary by the promise of work. Meanwhile the Unemployed Committee was in contact with the police chief concerning the selection of men to be employed. The offer of work had temporarily eased the pressure on the government at a crucial time; however, the number of men registered as needing work was well above the number of jobs to be provided. There was also continuing uncertainty as to whether the promised jobs were going to materialize. At a time of great unease amongst the unemployed, the government were lax about their communications with the Unemployed Committee, and in this atmosphere of uncertainty the unease became anger. The police reported:

> There has been a great change in the unemployed, and they now figure that the promise of putting five hundred men to work was merely a ruse so that they would not parade on Jubilee day. Power says that as far as he can understand now, there will be one hundred men to go to work instead of the number that was promised.[183]

There was also considerable uncertainty about how to select those to be given work.

To clarify the situation Power and the Unemployed Committee called on the government engineer to discuss the proposed work and the way in which it would be distributed. If no satisfaction was obtained they planned to visit Commissioner Puddester and demand an interview. The police knew that trouble was brewing. They reported that Power had instructed the unemployed to "bring along tools, pickets, pokers, or whatever they can get" in order to defend themselves.[184]

When the unemployed assembled on May 8 in front of the Public Works Department they did so with a formal set of demands. Receiving no satisfaction, they later visited Mr. Puddester (*Evening Telegram* 8 May 1935).[185] In the meeting they requested that the committee be recognized as the official representative of the unemployed. Puddester claimed that such recognition would have to be given by the Commission. After this long meeting, the crowd, which had been watched by all the available police in St. John's as well as the force of special constables (plain clothed police had mingled with the crowd), dispersed peacefully. Later the same day a request was submitted to the Commission that the committee, consisting of Pierce Power, John Caldwell, Herbert Saunders, Joseph Milley, and George Wilkinson, be officially recognized as representing the unemployed of St. John's and that the government accept from the committee the list of 1,000–1,500 unemployed men that had been compiled (*Evening Telegram* 9 May 1935:4). The Commission met on May 9 and discussed the demands of the unemployed. They had the letter written by the committee in hand, but J.C. Puddester took on the task of explaining the unemployed's demands to the other Commissioners. According to Puddester, the unemployed were not only asking for official recognition of the committee but that they be given "complete control of the public works in the neighbourhood of St. John's" and that "recruitment of labour for those works be entirely divorced from the Relief Department" (*Evening Telegram* 9 May 1935:4). On the basis of this interpretation, the Commission felt obliged to reject all of the requests. There would be no recognition of the committee, control of work would be in the hands of the Department of Public Works, and selection of those who would be given work would be handled by the police for the Department of Public Health and Welfare. A list of 500 "deserving" applicants would be drawn up, but the city engineer would be at liberty to reject any person found unsuitable or who provided unsatisfactory work. The limit for the number of persons to be set to work was firmly set at 500.

A meeting on May 10 with the chief of police and Power confirmed that the Unemployed Committee was to have no say in the allocation of work. Power and the rest left after expressing their dissatisfaction with the situation. Later the same day the unemployed assembled to discuss their position. They had received a flat refusal of any kind of official recognition from the government, but there was also the feeling that Puddester had misrepresented their case and had thus contributed to their rejection. Feelings ran high at the meeting and after speeches by the committee a parade was started to carry the case of the unemployed to the government.[186]

About 1,000 people led by Pierce Power and Joseph Milley, who had literally wrapped themselves in the Union Jack, made their way to the Colonial Building. Police had been dispatched to protect the building, but the squad had not reached its destination when the crowd brushed aside the few policemen who were guarding the gates and entered the grounds. The parade lined up facing the police. The whole scene was overlooked by a large gathering of curious citizens. As soon as the leaders of the unemployed mounted the steps of the Colonial Building to present their case to the government, the police moved in. Soon stones were flying. A police baton charge followed. In short order they cleared the grounds in front of the building and pursued the scattering crowd into Bannerman Park, beating those they caught. They continued the attack until the park was cleared. Some of those being chased tried to rally. They showered the police with stones and engaged in hand-to-hand fighting with fence pickets, but they were quickly forced to retreat. In the initial police baton charge some of the leaders of the unemployed were quite severely beaten. Pierce Power was beaten around the head and was in such poor condition that he was unable to attend the meeting of the unemployed which was held late that evening. George Wilkinson was also beaten, subdued and handcuffed. He was taken inside the building, but later released. Others also received wounds as did several constables who were hit with stones. J.T. Meaney of the United Press, who was at the gate of the Colonial Building with his camera, was hit on the head with a police baton. The *Evening Telegram* staff photographer also had his camera smashed.

The crowd which had assembled at the Colonial Building soon dispersed. Meanwhile, a detachment of police who had been guarding the office of the Department of Public Health and Welfare, but were then marching towards Colonial Building were attacked with stones and responded with a baton charge (*Fishermen's Advocate* 17 May 1935:8).

Things remained quiet until the evening when the unemployed assembled again. Some efforts were made to calm the crowd, but there were calls for revenge and with the cry of "put her up" the crowd "stampeded" west along Water Street smashing windows in stores as they went (*Fishermen's Advocate* 17 May 1935:8). There was also a small amount of looting.

The violence did not last long and soon St. John's was quiet again. Several men were arrested and charged with disorderly conduct and obstructing the police. The following day they appeared in court and were remanded for trial. Bail was refused.

On Saturday, May 11, four members of the Unemployed Committee were also arrested. Power, Milley, Saunders, and Wilkinson appeared before a special night session of the court where they were asked not to plead to the charges and were remanded without bail to the penitentiary until a preliminary hearing before a magistrate could be arranged. The arrest of the leaders of the unemployed was the result of a political decision.[187] According to police officer Mahoney, there was no evidence that the committee had been "acting disorderly during the parade."[188] But clearly the government, acting on police advice, thought that they had enough evidence gleaned from records of meetings, to prove that the committee had been responsible for the riot. The government had decided to take the sting out of the unemployed movement.

The actions of the police were, however, not above reproach. Innocent citizens had been injured and some of those attacked had not really been in the immediate vicinity of the disturbance (*Fishermen's Advocate* 17 May 1935:8). There was the feeling that police discipline had been lax and that the behaviour of some officers had gotten out of hand. The *Fishermen's Advocate* called for an official enquiry into the affair to be undertaken by independent citizens.

Meanwhile the authorities decided that there was enough evidence to proceed with a charge of inciting riot and riotous assembly. The second court appearance was a preliminary one and it was then decided that there was sufficient evidence to proceed to a trial before the Grand Jury. This started on May 27 before Chief Justice Horwood and a special jury. The trial concluded on May 30 after the Crown had attempted to prove its case using mainly police witnesses. From the evidence presented it is not clear what part the four defendants played in the actual riot. Wilkinson, for example, was apparently tripped by the police while he was running away from the steps after the constabulary had advanced. He had then been arrested by several policemen while struggling to get free. None of the witnesses were able to say at what point he was beaten with batons. Similarly there was confusion amongst the police as to whether the stone throwing preceded the police charge or not. It was also not clear whether the unemployed had been instructed to leave the steps of the Colonial Building before the police moved into action.

At 11:20 on the evening of May 30 the jury returned a verdict of "not guilty" in the riot trial. Immediately "the crowd in the court room burst into cheering, which was taken up by a large crowd assembled outside the Court House." When they left the court the four acquitted men were surrounded by "immense crowds" which followed them to their homes cheering (*Fishermen's Advocate* 31 May 1935:5).

The situation was quiet in St. John's in the period after the riot and the trial of the leaders of the unemployed. The government had failed in its efforts to convict Power, Milley, Wilkinson, and Caldwell, but the confrontation had damaged the unemployed movement. Meanwhile the police continued to carefully monitor the activities of the unemployed and those they considered to be a threat to the government. Efforts were also made to lessen the tension in the capital city by removing some of the unemployed from St. John's.[189] But while speed was needed, so was caution. The government wanted to ease tension, not create new trouble spots:

> I do not suppose that Turner will be able to do more than get his advanced party out and arrange for the clothing of the first batch of unemployed young men, before I come back. I think it is essential that the Chief of Police should be very careful to vet the first batch, as they will doubtless set the standard, and, above all things, we must avoid the presence of agitators in these particular camps.

In order to further lessen the chance of trouble it was also decided to open a centre for the unemployed in St. John's during the winter of 1935–36.[190]

In the summer of 1935 the government followed its established policy of abolishing able-bodied public relief in fishing districts.[191] Any exceptions to this general policy were only made following evidence of destitution and an investigation by relief inspectors. However, support, even where there was good evidence of destitution, was not automatic and government's policy continued to cause serious problems for relieving officers and local merchants who were handling relief supplies.

The May riot in St. John's was very much a political event. The government had decided to refuse the demands of the unemployed in the full awareness that this would bring to a head the confrontation which had been building for some time. The Commission wanted to make it clear that pressure tactics would not yield concessions. But, more than this, it was felt that the unemployed were being manipulated by "professional agitators" and that a potentially dangerous movement of opposition to the Commission had to be stopped.[192] It was the "unanimous opinion" of the Commissioners that the unemployed movement be confronted and it was thought that the display of force by the police on May 10 would "have excellent sedative effect."

The use of force against the unemployed on May 10 and the arrest and trial of their leaders did indeed inflict a defeat on the movement to improve conditions for those on relief in St. John's. Meetings were temporarily abandoned and the momentum which had been built with great difficulty was lost. Pierce Power clearly recognized the negative effect of the events of May 1935 on efforts to improve conditions. While he remained convinced that "no progress" would be made in St. John's "without a riot," he found it hard to gather support for actions where the unemployed would stand a high risk of being beaten by the police.[193] By late 1935, however, efforts were being made to rekindle the unemployed organization in St. John's.[194] The issues continued to be those of relief work, inadequate rations, and the threat of eviction for non-payment of rent. By this time though, some of the previous leaders of the unemployed were out of action. Power himself was forced to leave St. John's for a while to obtain work (apparently in St. Lawrence) and George Wilkinson probably left Newfoundland in 1935, "his head beaten silly with billies."[195] The crackdown on the unemployed made new leaders reluctant to come forward and face the possibility of arrest and prosecution:

> I want to tell you this, that when you pick your committee, pick the best you know how, because they have no easy task. They may be heading for the PENITENTIARY, nevertheless someone has to make the sacrifice.[196]

Some of the old leaders did try to maintain the unemployed organization and a few new leaders did come forward, but they did not achieve much success. Also these efforts were closely watched by the police who were clearly pressing for a tough line against "born agitators" and the other dubious characters whom they felt were trying to lead the unemployed into bad ways.[197] One man speaking for the first time at an unemployed meeting was immediately investigated by the police:

> From what could be gathered it appears as though this man at one time was an inmate of the Asylum and which undoubtedly accounts for his radical remarks.[198]

The investigating officer even suggested that the man be arrested, arguing that this "would have a decided effect on future cases."[199] Preventative policing meant that the unemployed and those prepared to speak out against the government were subject to harassment. They were followed by the police. Questions were asked about them. Their remarks were recorded. Their friends and associates were encouraged to become police informers. The actions of the police obviously went far beyond any efforts to prevent crime and apprehend those breaking the law. Intimidation was a powerful weapon in the battle to prevent the unemployed from again becoming a well-organized force. Not surprisingly many of the unemployed were hostile to the police. This hostility is clearly expressed at their meetings in 1935 and 1936 and such feelings may go some way towards explaining an incident on New Years Eve, 1936 when Pierce Power attacked a constable with a razor. Power was sent to the penitentiary where he continued his organizing efforts and led at least one major protest.[200]

Political Undercurrents

After May 1935, the activities of the unemployed declined in importance but other political opposition groups started to emerge. By early 1937 a number of important individuals were involved in the move to restore independence. Richard Squires was making "politically inclined" speeches in St. John's and Conception Bay.[201] Reuben T. Vardy, a former resident of Hickman's Harbour, was busy trying to organize what was called the Newfoundland Independence Association.[202] In this he was working with "an agitator in the under current" who was "deadly opposed to Commission of Government."[203] According to police reports, the Newfoundland Independence Association received fairly broad support amongst a group of what the police clearly thought of as dubious individuals. Joseph R. Smallwood, another involved with the group, was described as "a mysterious man, getting along solely on his wits." Although Mahoney could not "say anything about him by way of a criminal nature" he did regard him as "a 'shady' character." The others involved with the N.I.A. were generally respectable citizens, lawyers, and businessmen, but there were less savory characters, including some connected to the unemployed movement in St. John's.

The main aim of the N.I.A. was to pressure the British government for a return to Responsible Government. To this end they planned a parade to bring their demands to the governor. It was hoped that he would then forward the petition to London. Meanwhile the police recruited informers to report on Vardy's activities. They also harassed the organization by making it difficult for them to obtain a meeting hall.[204] Outside St. John's the N.I.A. established some close contacts, in particular, with Ken Brown of the Fishermen's Protective Union.[205] It was rumoured that this organization had a membership of 9,000 in early 1937 and while this may be an exaggeration it is clear that the union had been gaining strength in rural Newfoundland, particularly among those involved in logging on the northeast coast. Constabulary reports indicate a union membership of 1,000 in the Valleyfield, Badger's Quay, and Greenspond area in 1937. Kenneth Brown, president of the union and Nathan Winsor, another ex-M.H.A., had largely been responsible for expanding the influence of the F.P.U. in northern Newfoundland. By the late 1930s both were making anti-Commission speeches; Winsor was described as "a man who is prepared to say anything that is detrimental to the Commission of Government."[206]

With the growth of unionism in rural Newfoundland there was evidence of a new mood taking hold of the people. The new belligerence was reflected in the difficulties that the local police had "regarding Dog Taxes."[207] Loggers were also taking industrial action to improve conditions. Those on relief in areas influenced by unionism also appeared less willing to accept conditions and more aggressive in their dealings with the authorities in the period after 1937. When economic conditions deteriorated in 1938 widespread opposition to the government developed on the northeast coast.

Even a small but vocal opposition was more than the Commission was willing to tolerate and from the mid-1930s various means by which this could be diffused were considered. Modifications to the existing political system were looked at closely, including the establishment of an elected advisory council. But this idea was finally abandoned as being potentially too dangerous.[208] What they most feared was that criticism would become focused and that opponents would forge themselves into a political movement capable of mobilizing support on a large scale. To prevent this they were willing to abandon all ideas of introducing even a limited measure of democracy. The Commission felt that it would be safer to continue the use of local magistrates to gauge public opinion. It was also thought prudent to use undercover police to keep a careful eye on the life of the "under current."

The Newfoundland Independence Association did not last long. It failed to attract the public support of "men of standing" and so the

Commission felt no compulsion to act on its petition.[209] Soon, however, a new group, the Newfoundland Public Welfare League, was on the scene.[210] In 1938 this group was headed by Bernard Lilly. It included "agitators," but also was supported by several merchants, particularly Chesley Crosbie. Like the N.I.A. this group pushed for a return to Responsible Government, but without success.

By late 1938, however, the opposition to the Commission was becoming quite widespread and extensive. It ranged from the unemployed and labour organizations to the St. John's Board of Trade. Much of this opposition was focused on the Commission's failure to secure the construction of a third paper mill on the Gander River. This failure, coming at a time when economic conditions were worsening and pressure for action was increasing, created political problems for the Commission which no doubt played a role in decisions to increase spending on reconstruction projects. Efforts to bring about constitutional change continued as the outbreak of war approached (Webb 1986). However, the character of the opposition to the Commission of Government was very different from that of the early days. It was merchant-led and elitist, but it had a populist-nationalist character.[211]

It is not surprising that the Commission of Government should have been sensitive to adverse publicity and criticism. All governments are so to a greater or lesser degree. What is perhaps surprising is the Commission's absolute abhorrence of any critical commentary on its actions or on the state of Newfoundland. The Commission was also prepared to go to quite extreme lengths in order to protect itself, a situation which presumably reflected its feelings of vulnerability and weakness.

Attempts were made to control potentially embarrassing information from the Commission's first days in power. That task was a relatively easy one. Unless something very dramatic happened in the country it was unlikely to be reported in the British press and lead to awkward questions being raised in the House of Commons. In addition, the main newspapers in Newfoundland were, at least initially, rather supportive of the new government. A critical line was taken by the *Fishermen's Advocate*, but this does not seem to have posed much of a problem for the Commission.

What information the Commission did allow to circulate about the situation in Newfoundland was carefully vetted before release. Early in 1935 a report on the economic situation which had been requested by the British parliament was published, but not before the Dominions Office had omitted certain passages "which seemed to be either of doubtful accuracy or of dangerous import."[212] This careful attention to detail was symptomatic of both the Commission's and the British government's concern with the potential dangers of adverse publicity. From the very first there was a clear awareness of the potential power of the press and of public opinion. As Hope Simpson put it in 1936:

> When I came out to this country I had no conception of the low standard of life of the mass of the people and of the destitution prevailing in very many of the outports, especially in the smaller settlements. If an enterprising journal were to send out a correspondent to publish the true facts concerning conditions in many of the outports there would be a serious outcry in Britain.[213]

Some St. John's newspapermen were correspondents for the British papers and the Commission believed their actions required careful monitoring. Jeffrey of the *Evening Telegram* did provide articles to the *Times*, but that newspaper took advice from the Dominion's Office on his submissions, at least from 1935.[214]

The authorities could exert less control over the actions of J.T. Meaney. In his capacity as foreign correspondent for British United Press, Meaney was forwarding articles to London from 1934. He started a paper, *The Newfoundlander*, dedicated "solely to a policy of a restoration of Self-Government," in the fall of 1934, but it did not last long. He was also closely involved in the unemployed movement in St. John's. Meaney was carefully watched by the police in the fall of 1934 when serious efforts to organize the unemployed commenced.[215] An astute politician, he was aware of the Commission's potential vulnerability to press criticism. By early 1935 Meaney had become a major thorn in the side of the Commission. In February his despatches about the confrontation between the unemployed and the Department of Health and Welfare triggered questions and debate in the House of Commons about the Newfoundland situation.[216] The Secretary of State for Dominion Affairs was forced to speak on the matter and the Government of Newfoundland was required to issue a refutation of Meaney's claims. The awkward moment passed.

Meaney continued his campaign to bring the plight of Newfoundland to the notice of the British people. In 1935 the *Daily Herald* of London carried an article with the title "Dominion of Despair" (*Fishermen's Advocate* 3 May 1935:3). Part of the object of the Jubilee protest plans of the unemployed was to create something which would be worthy of reporting in the foreign press, as was the riot of May 10. The question of Meaney was important enough for the governor to be presented with a seven page confidential memorandum on his activities at the end of August 1935. Its comments on Meaney and the unemployed are revealing:

> The so-called unemployed demonstrations were really not demonstrations of the unemployed at all. We have in the City of St. John's a small number of what you might call professional agitators, and these people have been foremost in all the attempts at demonstration referred to by Mr. Meaney. Some of them have been at this business for years. Some of them relieve the monotony of their occupation by serving terms in the Penitentiary for various offenses.[217]

Meaney, it was claimed, had been interested in the unemployed "from the very beginning," this interest being "prompted" by "a desire to embarrass the government as far as possible," by "his natural inclination to intrigue and to defiance of authority" and "by his desire to collect or create material of a sensational nature to form the subject of a despatch, which would be remunerative to him." The authorities clearly saw the protests of the unemployed as simply the result of the activities of agitators. In doing so they conveniently relieved themselves of any responsibility for acting to improve conditions:

> Any demonstrations that occurred were entirely the work of the above named professional agitators, fomented and encouraged and helped by J.T. Meaney. It is true these agitators are unemployed, but they are always unemployed and they cannot be taken as a fair representation of the mass of the people, either employed or unemployed.[218]

Meaney continued to irritate the Commission. He may even have been connected with the visit of Morley Richards, the *Daily Express* reporter who caused such embarrassment to the government later in the decade.

Efforts by the Commission and the British government to control criticism of what was happening in Newfoundland also extended to such key figures as Thomas Lodge. One of the original Commissioners, Lodge was replaced in 1937. As early as 1935 a speech he had made to the Institute of International Affairs in London had been censored. Another controversy arose over a BBC broadcast early in 1936. Lodge was not prepared "to talk drivel" so "the official censorship operated" and he did not broadcast.[219] As an ex-Commissioner, Lodge was treated with caution and in the volatile climate of 1938 serious consideration was given to preventing him from visiting Newfoundland (to collect information for his book *Dictatorship in Newfoundland*) unless some assurance was given that he would not prove an embarrassment to the Commission.[220] In the end it was decided not to interfere with his visit.

What the above examples show with great force is the extreme sensitivity of those responsible for managing Newfoundland's affairs to any criticism whatsoever. The line was drawn very starkly even if its violation could not be prevented on occasion. Given the poverty of Newfoundland, the lack of political representation, and the absence of any channels by which complaint and criticism could be made and diffused, the government was particularly anxious lest any radical doctrine should catch hold of Newfoundland's people. As we have seen from the Commission's dealings with the unemployed, there was a tendency for the government to view *any* signs of opposition with grave misgivings. It seems as if, in the minds of those responsible for law and order, even relatively innocent and not particularly critical opposition assumed the shape of a major threat. The spectre which haunted the Commission was that of "agitation." The police and those responsible for justice, with the assistance of the church, gave this spectre material form.

Anxiety about socialist, unionist, and communist ideas was a persistent, if relatively minor, theme in Newfoundland in the 1930s. During 1936, the son of a Water Street tailor returned to St. John's from Edinburgh where he was a medical student. During his two-month vacation he talked to officials of the labour unions in the city and discussed arranging for William Gallagher of West Fife, Scotland to visit Newfoundland.[221] The initiative was immediately reported to the police by the unions and Police Chief O'Neill informed the Secretary for Justice of the incident, adding that in Britain Gallagher was "classed" as a "communist":

> I have no doubt about it that an effort is being made to introduce Communistic ideas into this country. Reports would indicate that this is the only country apparently free from Communists at present.[222]

By 1937 the undercover police had placed the Water Street tailor (the father of the medical student) at the centre of Newfoundland's own Jewish-communist conspiracy. Communist "plants" who were working to take over Newfoundland had also been discovered. One was even working for Bowring Brothers and sending messages in code.[223]

Unfamiliar ideas were abroad and this was profoundly upsetting for some. As the archbishop of Harbour Grace noted in September 1936, "literature of a gravely objectional nature" was circulating in his area. It was:

Irreligious, openly or insidiously propagating the principles of communism; and. . .immoral, dangerous to the morals of our people (*Evening Telegram* 14 September 1936).

What was it which had produced such a reaction?

By May 1937 the Jehovah's Witnesses were attempting to gain a foothold in Newfoundland. Three people had arrived from the United States and were distributing literature in St. John's. There was a strong reaction from many residents and the police.[224] From 1937 a systematic campaign against the Jehovah's Witnesses was conducted by the Newfoundland government and the Newfoundland constabulary. Their literature was confiscated, their mail intercepted, and their members harassed. The government seriously considered prosecuting them for sedition.[225] Some of the opposition to the Jehovah's Witnesses was generated by the established religious denominations in Newfoundland; but beyond this, the state was concerned that the teachings of the Witnesses might encourage disaffection:

> This literature. . .is very offensive to a large number of our citizens; it has a bad social effect in that it predicts the coming of revolution and anarchy, and it is particularly noticeable also that the British Empire comes in for constant criticism.[226]

In fact, much of the commentary touched a raw nerve in Newfoundland:

> All the NATIONS are sick unto death. Distress of mind and body is upon all peoples.

> Some of the human remedies offered as a cure for national ills are there, to wit: Fascism, Communism, rule by dictators, and the League of Nations. Fascism and Nazism, which are one and the same, regiment the people, take away their liberty of thought and action, overburden them with taxation, destroy real manhood, and turn men into infidelity.[227]

The Witnesses were critical of all established religions, especially the Church of Rome, as well as money grubbers, politicians, and all earthly governments. According to Police Chief O'Neill, they were "out-and-out communists" who were propagating subversive ideas.[228]

Already in the 1930s "communism" was an emotive word in Newfoundland. It could be used in a wildly inaccurate manner to condemn any unsettling activities. Thus both the Jehovah's Witnesses and the land settlement scheme at Markland could be described as "communist."[229] Labour agitation could be thought of as communist at the same time as the growing labour movement in Newfoundland was expressing a strong anti-communist ideology.[230]

Discontent in the late 1930s

In 1936, the government felt that it was necessary to relax somewhat
its policy of cutting the dole in the productive season. However, the
summer of 1936 saw 20,000 more people receive relief than in the
summer of 1934.[231] This caused alarm. The fear grew that the
country was becoming pauperized and so in late 1936 attention
began to be devoted to the problems of rehabilitation in Newfoundland.[232] Attempts were made to limit relief spending in the
summer of 1937 and related to this an upsurge of protest and some
violence occurred.[233] In most cases this was dealt with by issuing
relief. The problem faced by the government was that, in the absence
of any general improvement in trade, the cutting of relief could only
be achieved by providing work for the unemployed or by subsidizing
them to fish. Both of these were costly and inefficient. Nevertheless,
the government did undertake some such schemes in 1937. These,
together with woods work and a slight improvement in fish prices,
took some of the edge off unemployment in that year.[234]

Much of the pressure to keep spending down in Newfoundland
came from the British Treasury. In October 1937, for example, the
Treasury noted that the costs of maintaining public order in Newfoundland had doubled since 1931.[235] It was suggested that the
Dominions Office give serious attention to cutting costs in this area.
In 1938, however, the political situation became tense. By January
1939, the Dominions Office was defending existing expenditures,
arguing that any cuts in spending on law and order would be
inadvisable:

> Having regard to the serious economic stress through which New-
> foundland is passing and to the discontent caused by the recent
> set-back, which is bound to increase the risk of local disturban-
> ces.[236]

Reports indicated that there was an "ugly spirit" abroad in the
country. Newfoundland became very volatile in the late spring of
1938 as the economic situation deteriorated. By the middle of the
year it was clear that the police force might actually have to be
strengthened to deal with any trouble.[237]

The government had been moving slowly and hesitatingly
towards the implementation of schemes for the permanent
rehabilitation of the unemployed in Newfoundland, when in May and
June 1938 the economic situation deteriorated with "embarrassing
suddenness." The fishery experienced difficulties due to import
restrictions in South America; many loggers were unable to find
work because of the "unfavourable industrial prospects" in the pulp

and paper sector and the "final disappointment of the country's hopes in regard to a mill on the Gander;" and a recession in the United States cast further shadows on Newfoundland economic prospects. Although the numbers on public relief had not risen dramatically, the outlook of the people had become "tinged with a feeling of depression."[238] Those without work had no alternative but to pressure the government for action.

In early June well-organized protests developed in the Bonavista area. The *Daily News* (6 June 1938) reported that between 1,200 and 1,600 men singing the national anthem demonstrated against the dole ration, the lack of seed potatoes, and the system of road works. The seriousness of the situation was quickly reported to London. Immediate "ad hoc measures" were called for to deal with the "growing spirit of despondency" since:

> Public relief is sufficient to maintain life but it is not sufficient to and cannot safely be made sufficient to relieve its recipients from their mood of hopelessness.[239]

Public works had been introduced to deal with the situation, but this had been the source of more trouble, and the mood of hopelessness was giving way to militant action:

> At Bonavista parades of between 1,000 and 1,500 men have taken place, threats of violent action have been uttered and the crowd have compelled men employed in public works to quit their work with the object of enforcing upon the officials in charge the fantastic ideas of equal distribution of available work among all who are unemployed.[240]

The authorities found themselves "compelled to recognize" this as "a warning that unless economic conditions improved" they might "have to deal before long with serious disturbances of the public peace by large numbers of men." In alarm they "most reluctantly" began to spend funds "not provided for in the Budget," arguing that:

> If we are to forestall developments at Bonavista which could be damaging to our work, embarrassing to His Majesty's Government and perhaps impossible to deal with effectively by the ordinary methods of enforcement of the law we must in this particular case provide some measure of employment which will enable the people to meet at least a few of their most pressing necessities outside the limits of public relief.[241]

Public works which would fit well with the Long Range Reconstruction Plan were to be used to ease the situation, but this was recognized as an *ad hoc* measure.

In fact, the evidence suggested that the "working classes" were "becoming restive" in many areas.[242] Reports of serious destitution soon reached the government from many places along the northeast coast. Those in difficulty were not passively accepting their fate. Unemployed committees had been formed in many communities and they were demanding sufficient work on roads, bridges, and wharves to provide food. Protests were also coming from those not engaged in the fishery. Some of the committees represented destitute fishermen. Others, including the Trinity Committee, represented men who had worked at industrial centres and who were not equipped for fishing. At that place some 800 labourers wanted work. As "signs of discontent" mounted so did the government's anxiety. Nor did the provision of work always calm the situation. Work had been started at Bonavista, but it had been stopped by men from Elliston "with the object of extracting a promise of employment for themselves." In all, the situation was proving very volatile and "all eyes, from all directions" were "focused on Bonavista."[243]

As the government had always feared, the provision of assistance was triggering the spread of demands for equal treatment. By late June the situation was most alarming:

> In a number of settlements on the Northern Shore of Trinity Bay meetings have been held during the past fortnight which have elected representatives to attend a central meeting at Trinity. A letter has been received from the central committee containing thinly veiled threats of disturbance if employment on roads, bridges and wharves is not found shortly. There have been further signs of trouble at Corner Brook in connection with a dispute between two unions in regard to selection of men for loading ships. . . .In the city of St. John's itself there are signs of some unrest owing to the lack of employment at a season when the hopes of the unemployed are normally revived. It is extremely difficult to gauge the real temper of the people from these reactions on their part to the depressed outlook that now confronts them for next Fall and Winter.[244]

Reports might have overestimated the dangers of a breakdown of law and order, but the government was aware of its vulnerability:

> Some allowance must, of course, be made for the tactical considerations which are no doubt fully realized by a naturally shrewd people and for the possibility that they have deliberately imparted a tone of exaggeration to expressions of both their sufferings and their anger. On the other hand we are in the presence of conditions very favourable to the spread of inflammatory influences and we apprehend that one example of serious violence would be swiftly followed by others. We are advised by the Commissioner for Justice that the combined strength of the Constabulary and the Rangers

would be insufficient to deal efficiently with a disturbance involving any considerable number of able-bodied men in two places at the same time.[245]

Under the circumstances, the government was "forced to rethink its strategy:"

Our policy has been to adhere to a system of sound administration, long range reconstruction and public relief for the unemployed. In [the] present temper of people we are uncertain whether we may not have in places to go further than this unless we are prepared for agitation and disturbances which may spread rapidly and which we have not sufficient force at our command to control.[246]

August saw a serious incident at Bonne Bay involving a Commissioner, and in early October the government was informed by telegram from Hodge's Cove that the "whole arm" was organized to "defend themselves" and that "serious trouble" was "pending" over the issue of work.[247] Those who were making efforts to challenge the Commission and drum up support for a return to Responsible Government were also involved in the protests, including R.T. Vardy of the Newfoundland Independence Association:

Monstrous demonstration headed chiefly by ex-servicemen all sections met here today invited Mr. Vardy demanding work start immediately whole Arm organized proceeding St. John's. Thousands guarantee follow unless relieving officer charged Destitution relieved and work start promptly prepared and determined face consequences All motions unanimous Its work is on our mind It is our just demand May God stand by we all shall die to save our Newfoundland.[248]

The Government of Newfoundland had been forced into *ad hoc* spending on public works in order to try to quieten the protests which had developed from May 1938 onward. However, there were strong pressures from London to pay for this by both increasing customs revenue and by "savings on able-bodied relief."[249] Given such constraints, the government found itself trapped. Raising customs revenue and cutting relief would increase hardship and the likelihood of unrest. With an inadequate police force this could not be risked and so spending on public works was required to manage the situation. The political problem called for some adroit handling.

The seriousness of the events of the early summer led the government to look closely at the question of policing the country. In June they reviewed the forces at their command and assessed the problems which might have to be faced in the event of outbreaks of unrest. The constabulary consisted of 249 men, excluding non-combatants, and there were 15 vacancies for constables and non-commissioned officers. There were also 62 rangers scattered throughout 31 centres in rural areas, all of whom were armed with rifles and revolvers. In St. John's there was a small force of 25 special constables who could be called on in emergencies.[250]

Of the constabulary force, 75 men were stationed outside St. John's, with the largest contingent of 15 in Corner Brook. The capital city, with over 170 members of the constabulary, was the "general reserve" for the country, but of this figure usually about 25 men were absent due to sickness or other causes. Of the approximately 150 available men, 60 were used day and night in patrol and other routine work. This left a relatively small force which could be used in the event of a serious problem. The 25 specials were the remnant of the special force of 100 which had been created in 1932 during the civil disturbances, but this group was regarded as being of "little potential value."

In terms of armaments and equipment, the force was not well situated. A mounted force of 7 existed in St. John's. All the members of this force were armed with batons, but they had at their disposal only 190 steel helmets, 23 tear gas hand grenades, 19 tear gas batons with 214 cartridges, 49 assorted revolvers, and 110 rifles fitted with bayonets of the "old long type." Ammunition was limited and 50 percent of the rifles were in bad condition and in need of replacement. The steel helmets and the tear gas bombs had been purchased in 1932–33. The former were still in "good condition," but the tear gas was "out of guarantee."[251] The assistant chief of police was instructed by the Commissioner for Justice to "make an experiment" with it to determine if it was still effective.[252] In reviewing the situation the Secretary of Justice identified several possible areas where disturbances might occur:[253]

(1) The St. John's Area
(2) Conception Bay from Topsail to Bay de Verde
(3) Bonavista from Keels to King's Cove
(4) Buchans-Grand Falls-Botwood
(5) Corner Brook-Deer Lake
(6) Twillingate Island and Fogo
(7) Any logging operations

It might be possible to send "a posse" of about 90 men to any disturbance. But while "mob action" in one area was being dealt with, trouble might erupt in another area. The problems of policing were made more difficult by the fact that only the St. John's area and Conception Bay were "within effective striking distance" of the reserve force based in the city. Also, bearing in mind the events of 1932, even Conception Bay might be difficult to reach quickly:

It would. . .be relatively easy for any determined body of rioters to block the road and railway running round the Bay, in which case, except in the season of ice, transportation of forces to these areas from St. John's would have to be carried out by sea, and if the Bay was full of ice it could not be carried out at all, except by marching on foot.

Access to more distant places was even more problematic. Bonavista could be reached in 12 hours by rail or in 7 hours by sea and Grand Falls and Corner Brook were 13 1/2 and 19 1/2 hours respectively from St. John's. Some areas were all but inaccessible in winter. Consequently:

> It is obvious that any determined force of rioters could have finished its work in these areas before any force arrived, [and] unless a complete censorship of telegraphic and wireless messages was put into force the movements of the Constabulary Force would be fully known to agitators.

Another possibility to be faced in the event of an outbreak of violence outside St. John's was that the police posse of 75 or even more might prove inadequate to control "really determined rioting" and that while this reserve force was away from the city the "St. John's agitators might take the opportunity to create disturbances."

In light of these considerations the country was thought to be inadequately policed. It had only one officer per 1,000 population, a very low figure compared with the 5 per 1,000 in London and the 4 per 1,000 which it was argued was common elsewhere. In addition, unlike most other countries, Newfoundland had no standing army which could be called upon in an emergency. Even so the authorities showed great reluctance to increase the police force. First, there was the financial consideration. Second, it was argued that an increase in the force, say by 100 men stationed in St. John's, "would be found embarrassing" and the "psychological effect" of the police presence "would be bad."

An increase in the regular police force was rejected but it was decided to make the existing force more formidable by re-arming the constabulary with modern rifles.[254] The police were also trained in the effective use of these weapons. Consideration was given to other means of policing the country. The support of the British navy might be called on as it had been in the early 1920s and early 1930s, but this measure was not favoured. The alternative was to use a body of special constables or a defence force for policing. However, there were arguments against this:

> In both cases it must be remembered that during the prevalence of well founded economic discontent, forces other than professional

police forces may be expected to sympathize with the public, unless serious violence occurs, in which case the sympathies of non-professional forces, like those of the respectable portion of the population, may be against those perpetrating the violence.[255]

After full consideration of the problems of policing the country in 1938, the government concluded that the "only effective way of dealing with the situation" was to remove the causes of the existing discontent.[256] Aware that this might prove difficult, an auxiliary force consisting of 150 part-time policemen was set up at a cost of $1,000 a month. (It was disbanded in July 1939 when the situation in Newfoundland became calmer.)[257]

The growth of unrest had again revealed the fragility of the government's position. The unemployed by this time knew how to exploit the government's vulnerability in an effort to gain concessions. In 1938, for example, the "Voice of the Unemployed" column in the *Labour Herald* skilfully used a variety of images of social breakdown (crime, suicide, madness, revolt) to pressure the government:

> Just what is wrong with the Government? Is it that they are dissatisfied with the shortage of criminals and that they have to increase the list by pressure of poverty and hunger? Or is it that there are not enough suicides and they'd like to see the local papers headlined with such happenings, or maybe they would like a bit of excitement by the way of Newfoundland being swept in a wave of anarchism not unlike the French Revolution. How the people have endured it so long is beyond human understanding. I would not be at all surprised if such a thing as a proletarian revolution materialized in Newfoundland soon, if the Government doesn't change its policy (23 December 1938:3).

Newfoundland and the Colonial Question

The vulnerability of the Commission to public pressure in the late 1930s cannot be understood without a brief discussion of the shifting political climate in the world at large. In Newfoundland dissatisfaction was fairly widespread as many people, who had originally welcomed the Commission, were disillusioned. This opposition became adept at exploiting the weaknesses of the Commission. Also, in a political climate where democracy and the condition of colonial peoples were particularly contentious issues, both the Commission and the British government became more sensitive to criticism. Germany's request for the return of former colonies focused attention on what became known as the "colonial question" (Morgan 1980:14–22). In 1937 the colonial question was debated eleven times in the House of Commons in Britain. Influential individuals such as Lord Rothermere of the *Daily Mail* campaigned for the restoration of Germany's colonies. Italy and Japan also had "colonial ambitions." And it was clear that the "complete fulfilment" of these would "require a redistribution of colonial territory, including mandates. . .under the British flag." As a consequence it was increasingly felt that "if demands in the colonial sphere" were "directly and openly made upon the British Empire by the 'dissatisfied' Powers," then Britain would have to "return a reasoned answer" to those demands. Thus, it was argued that any refusal to accede to the demands of the "expansionist" countries and any defence of British "trusteeship" would have to be based on "a sound moral case." What this meant was that Britain would have to be above reproach on colonial matters. This, in turn, would rest on the social, economic, and political condition of the colonies and on the degree of satisfaction with British rule in the dependent territories (Royal Institute of International Affairs 1938).

It was clear to many that Britain would not easily pass the test in such matters. The Depression had seriously affected most parts of the Empire. There were serious disturbances in some countries and "widespread manifestation of dissatisfaction" from the West Indies to the Rhodesian Copper Belt (Morgan 1980:23–27). In addition, appalling social conditions existed in many areas, as was made clear in 1939 in the important report on the problem of nutrition (HMSO 1939). Growing nationalist agitation from within the colonies was matched by the British public's keen interest in their affairs, fostered to some extent, by the news media (Morgan 1980:81). As Morgan notes, it was the interest of the popular press in colonial matters which "helped to change the political atmosphere in which colonial development was approached in Westminster and Whitehall."

However, Britain's increasing sensitivity to the colonial question and willingness to seriously consider funding reconstruction projects to improve conditions and buy stability, was not simply a defence against expansionism. In the late 1930s it was becoming clear that Britain might have to fight a war in the near future. If that happened then the question of the internal stability and the welfare of the various parts of the Empire would become crucial. It was in this climate that attention was directed towards identifying measures which would improve the welfare of the colonies and undermine the position of those who might use dissatisfaction with existing conditions for political ends.

An incident in Bonne Bay illustrates the vulnerability of the Commission to public pressures. In August 1938, as part of his tour of the island, Commissioner Sir Wilfred Woods visited Bonne Bay on the revenue cutter *Shulamite*.[258] On arriving at Woody Point he was met by a large crowd of people demanding work. He interviewed representatives from the surrounding settlements who asked him for a definite promise of employment. Sir Wilfred declined to give such an undertaking and explained to the crowd assembled outside the Court House that it was impossible for the government to provide work as an alternative to relief. Not satisfied with this answer, the crowd tried to board the cutter to prevent Woods from leaving the settlement. However, the *Shulamite* managed to leave with Woods aboard, accompanied by six youths who were taken to Corner Brook and arrested. The following day a party of twenty policemen landed at Woody Point to find the situation calm.

The incident at Bonne Bay was not particularly serious, but a Commissioner had been involved and it was reported in the United States (*Time* 12 September 1938) and in Britain. In fact, the *Daily Herald* in Britain claimed that Sir Wilfred Woods had been "seized by the unemployed." This triggered a request from the Dominions Office for "an early and prompt enquiry into the matter" by the Newfoundland government, it being argued that:

> With European Countries demanding colonies the trouble in some parts of the British Empire is disconcerting to say the least.[259]

Although the investigation found that the press reports were "exaggerated," the incident does reveal just how sensitive the British government had become to the issue of law and order in the various parts of its Empire.[260]

Throughout 1938 there had been a growing uneasiness about the Newfoundland problem in London stimulated by the economic setbacks of that year. Representations had been made to the Dominions Office concerning the need for a visit to the country by some responsible person in order to investigate conditions there. After various names had been discussed in this connection, including J.L. Paton, ex-Head of Memorial College, and L.S. Amery, late in 1938 a ministerial visit by Lord Stanley was put on the agenda for 1939.[261]

Another visit to Newfoundland was also being planned in 1938. Beaverbrook's *Daily Express* decided to send Morley Richards, an investigative reporter, to examine the plight of the country. J.L. Paton heard of this and issued a warning to Malcolm MacDonald of the Dominions Office:

Things are, as you are aware pretty serious out there and the *Daily Express* is not likely to make things better. There is very serious poverty and in the next 4 months, the poverty will be felt more acutely and any untoward incident might start a flare up. There are clever people who are ready to turn such an incident to their own selfish aims.[262]

The slump of 1938 had proved the stimulus for an outbreak of dissatisfaction. Even some civil servants were expressing criticism of the Commission and the fact that there had been no visible improvement in conditions after five years.[263] It was precisely this situation which had attracted Beaverbrook's *Daily Express*, and by March 1939 Morley Richards' observations on Newfoundland were being given front page exposure.[264]

"The truth has not been told about Newfoundland," wrote Richards in the first of his reports on his seven week intensive investigation of Newfoundland (*Daily Express* 1939). Visiting the country was, according to the reporter, "like stepping back into the Middle Ages." He had found the country of "300,000 pure-bred Britons" to be "sunk in misery" with about a quarter of them living on the dole of 3d a day. A full half of the population was on the starvation line, there was "bitter and open discontent," and the government was "apprehensive of riots and disorder." Richards also pointed to the inadequacy of government action to improve the situation. Specifically, he charged that even the government admitted that the dole "was not enough alone to keep body and soul together." Many people were almost naked and unable to leave their homes in winter because of this. A portion of the population also lived hundreds of miles from the nearest doctor, and the transportation system was chronically bad. Education was not compulsory nor was it free. Children of ten and upwards were sent to prison, there existed at least 20,000 active cases of tuberculosis, and malnutrition was "widespread and increasing." In spite of government assistance, cod fishing, the mainstay of half the country, was declining in size and value. Tens of thousands of fishermen were unable to fish because they had no equipment. No systematic rural reconstruction had been attempted, and the five land settlement schemes which did exist were at best an indifferent success. In political terms "democracy had been stultified" and "public opinion . . .seldom consulted."

Richards went beyond documenting the appalling situation in Newfoundland and suggested a program to "put the colony on its feet." He called for capital loans of £20 million to aid industrial development. This would be a massive increase on the existing grants-in-aid scheme which provided less than £2.5 million over a five year period. The money would be spent on roads, ships, agriculture, and tourism. A move away from the production of unprofitable salt cod was also advised. The production of fresh fish was the wave of the future and associated with this, the population of the smaller outports would have to be centralised in the vicinity of the new processing plants. The reintroduction of an elected House of Assembly was also advised as the first step towards a return to Responsible Government. This would, however, be on a "non-party, national, not district" basis and outside experts with cabinet status would be used. Financial control would remain in British hands.

The "cruelly parsimonious" dole should be "substantially increased," especially for children, and those on relief should be provided with clothes and kitchen utensils. Close supervision of the system would ensure that the undeserving did not benefit from these changes. A determined attack should be launched on disease. More doctors should be employed, at least ten sanatoria built and education in health hygiene introduced.

As far as possible, a system of free and compulsory education should be established and vocational instruction provided. The system of denominational education should be modified. Revenues from income tax and death duties should be substantially increased and customs duties (which hit the poor) should be reduced. Town councils with the power of local taxation should be set up on a compulsory basis.

Finally a naval reserve with a training ship and a territorial regiment should be established and facilities provided for young men and women to move to Britain, the former for enlistment and the latter for domestic service.

Thus, the horrifying details of the destitute and depressed country of Newfoundland and the widespread dissatisfaction with Commission of Government were reported to the over two million readers of the *Daily Express*.[265] Questions were asked in the British parliament, the telegraph wires began to hum, and Commission of Government was called to account. Internal pressure and a changing world situation had combined to produce a situation in which greater attention was directed towards reconstruction and in which there was a greater willingness to spend money to buy stability.[266] There were moves to increase spending on employment schemes and to proceed rapidly with rehabilitation schemes such as that started in the Placentia Bay Special Area.[267] Efforts to contain political dissatisfaction and to mobilize patriotic sentiment were made by means of a Royal Visit in 1939. However, the declaration of war in late 1939 changed everything. In particular, the whole political climate shifted, and by 1941 the growth of independence sentiment in Newfoundland had been blunted as patriotism was rekindled.[268]

World War II

Recruitment for the armed forces eased the unemployment problem in Newfoundland, but despite the pressures, low recruitment in some areas indicated that there were many who were not anxious to join the military. Nevertheless, by August 1940 some 7,090 men had enlisted and this represented about 10 percent of the male labour force of 73,000 between the ages of 18 and 60. Many of those who did join up were on the dole. This was particularly true of rural areas in the Bonavista District where 160 of the 255 men *accepted* by 6 May 1940, were on relief.[269] It was the construction and servicing of the American and Canadian military bases during the war, however, which gave the country close to full employment.

Fear that unemployment and social unrest would return to Newfoundland haunted thinking throughout World War II and the immediate post-war period:

> The. . .fear is that which we have known only too well in the past, and which we are told we shall know again in the future, the fear of poverty and destitution, the desperation of the able-bodied man who tramps the water-front vainly for employment which he knew from the start did not exist, and finally turns his fear-ridden steps homeward, where wife and children wait in cold, patient hunger for the bread and warmth that an ill-ordered economic system denies them. There are those who say that this day may come again. . .
> (*Newfoundland Quarterly* 1943).

In 1943 Cold War thinking was already in evidence. Would a return to poverty and destitution open the gate to the "Red Menace?"

> Newfoundlanders, having tasted to the full this type of fear in the past, will refuse to accept a like condition of things in the future, and if it comes, it will surely lead, not to subservience, but to anarchy, to crime, to the adoption of communistic philosophies of living, and it will tend, far more than the present unprecedented struggle between fundamental principles, to wipe individual and communal freedom from the face of the world (*Newfoundland Quarterly* 1943).

CONCLUSION

> Men aim at projecting their own inward unease on to as large a screen as possible. When they tremble, the universe must; when

their great ones die, the elements must register disturbance (Muggeridge 1971).[270]

This essay is concerned with the forces which produced certain kinds of violence in the 1930s. The economic and political crisis of the period, with its unemployment, destitution, and loss of Responsible Government provides the general context in which the riots and raids must be understood. However, a glance at the crises of the 1930s shows that there is no straightforward connection between economic and political events, unemployment, poverty, and loss of political rights, and protest and violence.

It was government policy regarding public relief and unemployment which triggered much of the violence of the 1930s. Protest resulted from efforts to restrict relief. But, it was also just as likely to result from the state's inadequate and bumbling efforts to manage these protests and provide work for the destitute. Changes which occurred in public relief provision were intimately associated with the story of civil disturbance and protest and in particular with the organized efforts of the unemployed to improve their conditions of life.

Public relief policy was not determined by a rational assessment of needs nor very much influenced by evidence of distress. In a country with a very low standard of living for the majority of the population, and at a time when incomes from productive employment were falling, the government tried to ensure that the provision of relief would not undermine the will to work. The fiscal problems caused by falling state revenues and increasing expenditures were also dealt with by massive retrenchment in many areas.

Poverty weakens people and renders them submissive. It deepens people's sense of inferiority. Poverty means not only material impoverishment, but also the shrinking of needs and expectations. The poor police themselves. What can be fought for, or even hoped for, is circumscribed. Time is suspended and movement is halted. The future shrinks to the next crust of bread. The story of poverty is that of squandered lives. Poverty is not something to be tolerated and accepted, albeit forcibly. It is, under certain circumstances, something to be protested. Such action is never simply a response to poverty, however, it is as much related to the possibilities inherent in social organization. Protest and collective action to, in Pierce Power's words, "sweep poverty away" are not spontaneous. They must be organized. The possibilities for this depend on people's experience and attitudes as well as social organization. They also depend on having a group of people with a set of ideas to capture the hearts and minds of the unemployed.

The limits to which the state was able to cut spending on relief in Newfoundland in the 1930s were set by the organized resistance to government policy which was mounted by the unemployed. In the final analysis the level of support to be given to the unemployed was determined by what they could squeeze out of the government, by political means, by protest, and by raids and riots. In this context the issue of law and order was a loaded one in class terms. Maintaining law and order, expanding the police force, and arming them more effectively, was about defending property and enforcing the government's decisions. To give in to the demands of the unemployed would have been to threaten the basic class structure of the country and the power and privilege of the propertied. In a situation where the government for the most part refused to respond to requests and protests, the police were used to impose unpopular decisions on the population. The unemployed clearly saw that they were fighting a triple force: capital, the government and the police. Pierce Power's claim that it was necessary to "make a Police Force out of the working classes" in order to gain concessions from the government may have been made while he was "under the influence of liquor," and while the beating that he received in the May 1935 riot was still fresh in his memory, but it is perhaps a realistic assessment of the kind of action needed to fight the battle to survive in Newfoundland in the 1930s.[271]

This essay documents the struggles of the unemployed and the destitute. It provides details of the situations in which serious violence occurred, and it shows precisely the way in which the authorities employed force as a part of economic and social policy. The essay is also very much concerned with how the raids and riots of the 1930s were perceived, interpreted, and acted on by the authorities. When considering responses to violence we are in difficult terrain. Did the decision to increase the police force in Newfoundland in 1932 represent a reasonable response to fears that there would be a major breakdown in law and order? Was the undercover work of the police under Commission of Government necessary to maintain law and order? Or did both of these actions have something of the "moral panic" about them? Did they represent a situation in which public and official anxieties, expressed and amplified in part through the press and heightened by violent clashes, called forth powerful responses on the part of the institutions concerned with law and order? The concern here has not been with trying to answer the question of whether or not the actions of the authorities were justified given the threat they faced, or whether they represented an exaggerated reaction to problems which were not very serious, rather an attempt has been made to piece together evidence to explain why the state did what it did.

Fear and anxiety shape actions.[272] As Malcolm Muggeridge suggests, people do tend to project their anxieties onto a large screen and there is evidence that, in projecting our fears, we may, to a degree, create the objects of our fear. Nye's work on France shows that there are whole areas in which public awareness of security issues seems to be heightened and that the feeling that new and dangerous forms of deviance are taking shape is common (Nye 1984). There may also be fear that existing mechanisms of social control will be unable to deal with the situation. During such periods a "vague sense of public disquiet" can easily be turned into "a fully-fledged movement of ideas" in which certain problems and social groups become the focus of anxiety. In such periods, vagrants, anarchists, or a number of other "deviants" can become the symptom of social breakdown. Jennifer Davis' study on the "London garotting panic of 1862" shows how "English ruling class" anxiety about crime and the penal system in the 1850s and 1860s gave rise to a moral panic about one particular form of crime (1980). This moral panic led to greater public awareness of the problem and an increase in police activity. This led to more arrests, and there is evidence that the courts began to "define criminal actions of alleged offenders more seriously during the panic." Davis concludes that the moral panic about garotting actually preceded the rise in the incidence of this crime in 1862 (1980:204). The garotting wave of 1862 was a product of the panic but once it had occurred it led to a "considerable extension of police powers."

Another example of the way in which official anxiety can affect policing is provided by Robert Tombs' study of the "repression of the Paris Commune of 1871" (1980:214–37). In the wake of the commune, the police and the authorities, armed with a set of prejudices and ideas about the "dangerous classes" and those most likely to participate in revolution, undertook intense repression in which men and women were condemned "merely because they looked like criminals," and those not at work were sentenced to transportation because they were suspected of being Communards (1980:4).

The work of Stuart Hall and others on the mugging panic in Britain which developed in the 1970s goes a long way towards identifying the complex way in which a social fear is constructed (Hall *et al.* 1978). Recent work on the British riots of the early 1980s has begun to explore the manner in which the disturbances were appropriated by a variety of observers in order to express concerns about unemployment, bad housing, immigration and racial inequality, and youth. Commentaries on the riots seem to "reflect as much the wishes and anxieties" of those writing about the riots as anything about "the nature of the riots themselves," according to Field (1982).[273]

In the 1930s, according to John Saville, there was a widespread view on the left which linked economic crisis and mass unemployment with potential and actual social unrest and even revolution (1977:232–284). The crisis then, as now, deeply penetrated social consciousness and many saw signs of breakdown and pathology or resistance and revolution everywhere. This mechanistic, vulgar theory was widely subscribed to, even though it represented a rather inaccurate view of what actually happened in most countries during the 1930s. But like the fear of communism in the Cold War period, it greatly influenced action.

In Newfoundland, the most serious social unrest of the Depression occurred in 1932. One of the riots had a distinct political flavour, but most other violent incidents were specifically related to government attempts to restrict relief. The use of force by the state can be regarded as part of an effort to impose austerity on an already destitute population. In the battle for food and work one of the few relatively effective weapons wielded by the unemployed was the threat or use of force. In justifying their policy of retrenchment the governments of the day did so by citing the need to balance the budget and avoid bankruptcy, but they also operated with the clear assumption that destitution was much less severe than indicated by the numbers on relief, that there was widespread abuse of the dole, and that much of the pressure for improvements in rations was the result of the work of agitators. In the language of the time: many of the destitute were undeserving.

The riots of the early 1930s set the tone for the whole decade and influenced the Commission's attitude to the question of law and order after 1934. The fear that further extensive violence might occur and that the government would be both unable to cope with this and embarrassed by it, haunted the Commission right up to the outbreak of World War II. Was this fear reasonable? Could it justify the close surveillance of the unemployed and of figures like Smallwood? What of the flagrant violation of the rights of the Jehovah's Witnesses? Did their persecution represent the reasonable actions of reasonable men or was it a rather unpleasant case of paranoia?

After 1934 the retreat from politics in Newfoundland was complete in the sense that the formal and informal structures of a representative democracy had ceased to operate. If Sir Percy Thompson had complained in the fall of 1932 that the government was too close to the people to be able to govern, after 1934 there existed a yawning gulf between those responsible for government and the people. Throughout the 1930s the Commission rejected any effective mechanism for bridging or closing the chasm which had been created. The radio, the press, and the magistracy were used to disseminate selected information, but there was no real way in which dissatisfaction could be expressed through established channels. Organized interest groups like the Board of Trade could communicate with the government, but many were left voiceless. In theory, the new arrangement allowed the government to act quickly and even make far-reaching changes without lengthy public debate and discussion and without the need to pander to existing interest groups. In actual fact, the interest groups did find effective ways of presenting their arguments. The mood of such groups could be easily monitored and to a degree accommodated, if necessary, but from the government's point of view the greatest threat to their power came from the "undercurrent" of ex-politicians, agitators, and "shady-types."[274] These people represented an unknown number of Newfoundlanders who might under the correct circumstances be forged into a powerful political force in opposition to the Commission. Without a system by which the energy and dissatisfaction of the population could be channelled and diffused, the situation must have proved quite threatening for the lonely and uncertain men given the responsibility of governing the poverty-stricken country.

The end of democracy in Newfoundland had broken any meagre hold which the destitute and poor had on politics and the purse strings of the country. But the fear that the lower orders might resort to other methods of making their will felt led the Commission to instruct the police to keep careful observation of those who might be the sources of any possible unrest and dissent. Patterns of policing and surveillance both at the level of policy and at the level of the everyday activities of the Newfoundland Constabulary were shaped by prevailing ideas and fears regarding those likely to participate in opposition to the government. If the government believed that the mass of the people represented a potential pool of grievance and opposition, it was, however, left to the police to confirm the existence of this reservoir and map out the contours of this dangerous class. It is perhaps understandable that particular attention was directed to the unemployed. They had already demonstrated their power as an organized force and an essential part of the Commission's project was to keep relief to the minimum possible without causing severe political problems. It was thought that political agitators might seize upon this issue to cause difficulties for the Commission.

The unemployed and political dissidents did, then, represent a threat to those concerned with the government of the country. But, through their reports, the police also populated the Commissioners' universe with a variety of more or less dangerous agitators, with communists, shady characters, and swimmers in the undercurrent. From a perusal of police reports it is hard to avoid the conclusion that any attempts to weld the unemployed into a force for the improvement of conditions, and indeed any criticism of the government *at all* were seen as the equivalent of criminal activity. Agitation was even equated with mental disease. Just as men were "born criminals," they were also "born agitators."[275] In this context the issues of public order and of political opposition shades into that of criminality.

Respectable fears of the dangerous classes have a long history. Very often this anxiety has taken the form of concern that an alliance between political agitators, the unemployed, and criminals would develop—an ever-present fear in Newfoundland in the 1930s. Political agitators and criminals might, for their own ends, stir up an otherwise accepting and quiescent population. They might lead the unemployed in violent opposition to the government. This theory of opposition, while it served to focus the fears of the government, also relieved the Commissioners of responsibility for the plight of the unemployed and from the necessity of improving conditions. It assumed that, by and large, conditions for the unemployed were not that bad. It assumed that in the absence of agitation the population would have accepted their poverty in silence and their loss of political rights without complaint. In the same way that the violence of April 1932 could be dismissed as the responsibility of the hooligan element, so the riot of May 1935 was the result of manipulation by self-seeking and unscrupulous agitators. This theory also provided a justification for attempts to limit or break the hold of the agitators on the minds of the unemployed. Finally, if relatively subtle ways of doing this did not succeed, the masses could be clubbed into temporary silence.

Notes

1. See for example, Szwed (1966), Firestone (1967), Cohen (1975). Much of this work has been summarized by Felt (1987). Felt argues that outport social controls continue to affect the behaviour of those who move to small urban settlements—they are an extension of ourport culture—and he uses this idea to try to explain why there has been no

explosion of interpersonal violence (wife beating) in small towns. He does exclude St. John's from this rule, however, and finds evidence of a very small (but, he argues, *significant*) difference in the incidence of domestic violence between the capital city and the rest of the province. He thus finds *some* support for his assertion that as people become distanced from outport life, and as traditional conflict avoidance mechanisms weaken, then more interpersonal violence occurs. Felt presents a rather complex argument, but the evidence used to support his view is very slim.

2. I am exploring different aspects of this view in my current research on culture and development. See, for example, Overton (1980, 1988). The myth of a non-violent past is by no means unique to Newfoundland. It is dealt with by Pearson (1985, 1983) and Torrance (1986). Williams (1975) is also useful here.

3. A number of good attempts to establish long-term trends in patterns of crime and violence exist. A glance at some of this work will provide a clear picture of the possibilities and limits of this type of analysis. See, for example, Beattie (1974:47–95) and Gatrell (1980:238–337).

4. See Miles and Irvine (eds.) (1979:113–129), Box (1981). There has been a tremendous expansion of interest in deviance, crime, and violence since the 1960s. This interest parallels the expansion of the welfare state and the greater expanded role given to "experts" who have some social science or related training in planning, lobbying and administration. Unfortunately, it is clear that many of those who are responsible for making pronouncements about deviance and related problems are armed with a few rather mundane and not very useful theories which guide their actions. There is very little evidence that the new perspectives on crime and related problems discussed above, or an awareness of the many problems which exist with traditional social theory in this area, have penetrated the thinking of many of these experts, let alone popular consciousness. In fact, it seems likely that interest groups armed with social science have played a key role in shaping a greater public awareness of deviance, crime, and violence. They have also fostered the impression that these problems are growing.

5. The concept of a "moral panic" is due to Cohen (1972).

6. Some of the best work has been published in the *Journal of Law and Society* and in *Contemporary Crises*. In 1985 the former journal published a special issue dealing with the miners' strike.

7. The phrase "the jungle of history" is taken from Jacques Leonard and is found in Nye (1984).

8. See Hay (1982:302), Stevenson (1979). I have challenged the usefulness of Piven and Cloward's influential social control perspective on the relationship between public relief policy and protest in Overton (1988).

9. Davis' interpretation has been challenged, however, by Bartrip in Bailey (1981:150–181).

10. PANL GN 13/1, Box 171, File 15C: Alex Parsons, Superintendent of the Penitentiary to Hon. W.J. Higgins, Minister of Justice, "Report of Superintendent of H.M.P. for the Year 1926," January 1927.

11. Pierce Power was one of the leaders of St. John's unemployed in the mid-1930s. His words are taken from police reports: PANL GN 13/1, Box 172, File: "Unemployed Meetings 1936." Constable Leo Cochrane to P.J. O'Neill, "Re Public Meeting Tonight in Beck's Cove," June 10, 1936.

12. There is no history of Newfoundland which focuses specifically on poverty. Useful background information is, however, to be found in Alexander (1974, 1976), Noel (1971), Hiller and Neary (eds.) (1980). Godfrey (1985) provides a history of social policy but treats this "as distinct from economic policy or politics."

13. PANL GN 13/1, Box 172, File 2. Constable Mahoney to P.J. O'Neill, "Re Unemployed Meeting held Tonight," January 14, 1935.

14. PANL GN 14/1/A, File 304.2, Statistical Report, 1936–7, p. 123. In 1929 cod averaged $9.14 per quintal and the exports of $16,301,735 represented 44.22 percent of total exports. By 1936 the price per quintal was $4.00 and exports were valued at $7,338,271, a mere 25.79 percent of all exports.

15. The financial crisis is dealt with in the Amulree Report, see, *Newfoundland Royal Commission Report, 1933*, sections 121–195. Valuable background material is also provided in Noel (1971:186–203).

16. Grenfell claimed that Labrador would have starved in the Winter of 1930–31 if assistance had not been provided from outside the country. See, PANL GN 1/3A, 1931, File 1271 and the *Daily News* (St. John's), 28 November 1931.

17. PANL GN 1/3A, 1931, File 842, Squires' telegram to Governor Middleton and the subsequent request for a British Navy ship to assist in dealing with the unemployment situation on July 22, 1931; PANL GN 1/3A, 1932, File 349, Governor Middleton's Secret Memorandum of the Disturbances in St. John's, 1932:7.

18. Cuts in the pensions of war veterans were made and the *Evening Telegram* 2 March 1932:5 estimated that the budget had increased the cost of living by 30 percent. The budget led to a political crisis for the Liberals. Dr. Mosdell accused the Government of "grinding the faces of the poor," *Evening Telegram* 16 March 1932:5. In fact, Mosdell along with Sir William Coaker and F.G. Bradley had been appointed to a Retrenchment Committee in 1931.

19. PANL GN 14/1/A, Finance, File 304.2, Statistical Record 1935.

20. The *Evening Telegram* 2 October 1931:15 reported 487 cases of beri-beri on the south coast in 1930.

21. The International Pulp and Paper Co. announced a 10 percent reduction in wages and salaries effective 15 September 1931, see *Evening Telegram* 5 September 1931:6. *Evening Telegram* 8 September 1931:4, reported that the Longshoreman's Protective Union in St. John's was meeting to discuss a proposed 15 percent wage cut. They decided to refuse the cut and eventually a strike resulted. On 12 September 1931:4 the *Telegram* also announced that working hours for miners on Bell Island had been cut.

22. See for example the poem "A Rally Call" by "Voter" in *The Liberal Press* (St. John's), 26 October 1928:3:

    Sons and daughters of this Island,
    Tories call you "simple folk,"
    You're the masses, they're the classes
    Who have put you on the yoke.

23. Figures on relief spending differ. This is not surprising because of the lack of any systematic accounting procedures in the period before Commission of Government. Also many relief bills were not paid until months after they were incurred. Newfoundland Royal Commission, 1933, Section 138 provides one set of figures for relief spending and estimates this at 15 percent of the government's revenue in the early 1930s. A different set of figures is presented in PANL GN 14/1/A Finance, File 304.2, Statistical Record 1935. According to this source, spending on relief rose to over $4.00 per capita in 1932, falling off slightly in 1933, but then rising to well over $5.00 in 1934.

24. *Evening Telegram* 31 October 1931:4, argued that those handling relief orders were "profiteering on a tremendous scale."

25. See, for example, the editorial in the *Fishermen's Advocate* 5 February 1932:4. The most sustained campaign was mounted in the *Evening Telegram* in the fall of 1931 and throughout 1932. For an example of the kind of material used, see the editorial of 11 January 1932:6 and the article "Ignorance of Crime" by "Topic of the Times" on the same date. The churches also played a key role in creating a fear of pauperism, or dependence on the state for support, at the same time as they were willing to offer limited charity to those whom they considered deserving of aid. See also the sermon of the Rev. C.H. Johnson on "Poor Relief" preached in the Queen's Road Congregational Church on 8 November 1931, *Evening Telegram* 14 November 1931:8.

26. The attempt to reorganize relief had been announced in the *Evening Telegram* 14 November 1931:4. Detail of Magor's scheme were presented in the *Evening Telegram* 19 November 1931:4 and in the *Fishermen's Advocate* 27 November 1931:2, 5.

27. Reports of starvation were common throughout the winter of 1931–32. They came from all parts of Newfoundland. For Spaniard's Bay see, *Evening Telegram* 2 January 1932:4.

28. For Mr. Taylor's "Memo on Able-Bodied Relief," presented to the Amulree Commission, see C.A. MacGrath Papers, MG 30 E82, Vol. 12. P9/61, B-2-1, 352.5, Reel 1:3 of memo. These papers are deposited in the Public Archives of Canada in Ottawa. A microfilm copy of the papers is available in the Public Archives of Newfoundland and Labrador.

29. This was launched by the mayor in December 1931. The "Mayor's Appeal" appeared in the *Evening Telegram* 30 December 1931:11.

30. See also, *Fishermen's Advocate* 12 February 1932:1.

31. The strike had been called on January 23 by the LSPU in an attempt to resist efforts by the Employers' Association to cut wages. The strike was called off February 5 on the union's terms. See *Evening Telegram* 6 February 1932:6 and the *Fishermen's Advocate* 12 February 1932:1.

32. John C. Hepburn was born in Scotland and had come to Newfoundland in 1885. PANL P7/A/2 Baine Johnston, J.C. Hepburn, Box 2C; Hepburn to M. Campos, February 12, 1932.

33. PANL P7/A/2 Baine Johnston, J.C. Hepburn, Box 2C; Hepburn to R.L. Newman, London, 18 February 1932.

34. PANL P7/A/2 Baine Johnston, J.C. Hepburn, Box 2C; Hepburn to Mr. Dick, Scotland, 8 June 1931.

35. Details of the new ration system were published in the *Evening Telegram* 20 February 1932:6.

36. The Editor suggested adopting the maxim "If any would not work, neither shall he eat."

37. See, for example, the *Evening Telegram's* editorial, 23 February 1932:6 and a letter by W.H. Frost published the same day (p. 7). Various churches also played a key role in encouraging the restoration of simple living and a return to the soil. Adult educators such as W.W. Blackall promoted this "solution" to the crisis. During the second week in March a "patriotic rally" was organized by Blackall to promote the idea that the "soil is our salvation," *Evening Telegram* 10 March 1932:1.

38. PANL GN 2/5, File 541 F: Magistrate Casey to Secretary of State A. Barnes, 28 February 1932.

39. PANL GN 2/5, File 554, Retrenchment: Percy Thompson to A. Barnes, 3 December 1931. In this letter Thompson suggested severe cuts in public relief. For 1931–32 he argued that $100,000 be made available for widows, orphans, and dependants and $50,000 for salaries, etc. in the Charities Department. Able Bodied Relief was to be provided out of "what can be spared."

40. There was considerable public outcry against the cuts in war veterans' pensions. A letter signed by S.G. accused the government of "plundering" the G.W.V.'s repatriation fund (*Evening Telegram* 4 March 1932:6). The G.W.V. *demanded* that there be no cuts and organized a mass meeting in the second week of March (*Evening Telegram* 10 March 1932:1).

41. PANL P7/A/2, Baine Johnston, Box 2C, H. Collingwood, Private Letters, 1932: H. Collingwood to R.L. Newman, 23 March 1932.

42. PANL P7/A/2, Baine Johnston, Box 2C, H. Collingwood, Private Letters, 1932: H. Collingwood to Newman, 23 March 1932.

43. PANL P7/A/2, Baine Johnston, Box 2C, H. Collingwood, Private Letters, 1932: H. Collingwood to Mr. Dick, 23 March 1932.

44. Dr. Mosdell was Minister Without Portfolio.

45. PANL GN 2/5, File 541F, 1931–32: Unemployed petition dated 31 March 1932.

46. PANL GN 2/5, File 541F, 1931–32: Squires to Cadwell and Foley.

47. PANL GN 2/5, File 541F, 1931–32: C.H. Hutchings to Mr. Mews, 4 April 1932.

48. PANL GN 2/5, File 541F, 1931–32: C.H. Hutchings to A. Barnes, 7 April 1932.

49. PANL GN 2/5, File 541F, 1931–32: Deputy Secretary of State to R.P. Horwood of the Charity Bureau Organization, 8 April 1932.

50. PANL GN 2/5, File 541F, 1931–32: Penson to Mews, 8 April 1932.

51. Most of what follows is based on the account of the riot given in the *Evening Telegram* 6 April 1932:4.

52. PANL GN 1/3A, File 349, 1932: Inspector General of Constabulary to the Governor, 9 April 1932.

53. PANL GN 14/4, 1934, Finance: Memorandum by the Board of Liquor Control for the information of Commission of Government, n.d. Liquor was only available to those possessing permits. These permits set a limit on what could be purchased on a daily basis.

54. PANL GN 1/3A, File 349, 1932: Inspector General of Constabulary to the Governor, 9 April 1932.

55. According to the *Daily News* 11 April 1932:1, some 2,000 men registered at the Armoury for use as Specials. The Specials by this account, were paid $1.60 per day plus food.

56. PANL GN 1/3A, File 349, 1932: Deputy Minister of Justice to the Governor, 9 April 1932.

57. PANL GN 1/3A, File 349, 1932: Governor Middleton's "Secret Despatch" to London, 5 May 1932:8, 21.

58. PANL GN 1/3A, File 349, 1932: Deputy Minister of Justice to the Governor, 9 April 1932.

59. PANL P7/A/2, Baine Johnston, Box 2C, J.C. Hepburn, 1932: Hepburn to Mr. Dick, 18 April 1932.

60. PANL P7/A/2, Baine Johnston, Box 2C, H. Collingwood, Private Letters, 1932: H. Collingwood to Dick, 22 April 1932.

61. PANL P7/A/2, Baine Johnston, Box 2C, J.C. Hepburn, 1932: J.C. Hepburn to R.C. Newman, 18 February 1932.

62. Coaker's resignation was announced in the *Fishermen's Advocate* 6 May 1932:4. At that time he restated his support for Government by Commission.

63. PANL GN 2/5, File 541F, 1931–32: Deputy Secretary of State to Mr. Taylor, 30 April 1932.

64. PANL GN 2/5, File 541F, 1931–32: Assistant Relief Controller Taylor to A.J. Walsh, 21 May 1932.

65. PANL GN 2/5, File 541F, 1931–32: Mr. Mews to J.C. Puddester, 9 July 1932.

66. PANL GN 2/5, File 541F, 1931–32: "Memorandum: Able-Bodied Relief and Economics," Mr. Penson, Deputy Minister of Finance, 11 July 1932.

67. PANL GN 2/5, File 541F, 1931–32: Mr. Penson's "Memo on Able-Bodied Relief."

68. MG 30E 82, Vol. 12. P9/61, B-2-1, 352.5, Reel 1:6 MacGrath Papers, "Memorandum re City Relief" compiled by the Secretary of the Charity Organization Bureau (Mrs. Muir).

69. The phrase came from a letter written by Alderdice to Jackson Dodds of the Bank of Montreal, 27 September 1932.

70. See also a letter by G.W.B. Ayre, "The St. John's Unemployment Situation," *Bay Roberts Guardian* 12 August 1932:2.

71. Ayre, *Bay Roberts Guardian* 12 August 1932:2. Apparently Cadwell was pushed aside by "hotheads" after having himself led a coup against the leadership of Mr. Ayre.

72. Smallwood had been the secretary of the Unemployed Committee in St. John's in the late 1920s.

73. PANL GN 2/5, File 541F: Telegram to J.C. Puddester from Carbonear, 16 July 1932.

74. PANL GN 2/5, File 541F: Secretary of State to Mr. Taylor, 23 July 1932.

75. PANL GN 2/5, File 541F: Mr. Puddester to W.G. Bowring and Others, 20 July 1932.

76. PANL GN 2/5, File 541F: Relieving Officer Bartlett, Trinity to Acting Prime Minister, 30 July 1932.

77. PANL GN 2/5, File 541G: Telegraph from Britannia, 18 August 1932.

78. PANL GN 2/5, File 541G: Unemployed Committee to Mr. Puddester, 23 August 1932.

79. PANL GN 2/5, File 541G: Various communications.

80. PANL GN 2/5, File 541G: Rev. Ivany to Mr. Stone, 12 October 1932.

81. PANL GN 2/5, File 600.4: B. Moss to J.C. Puddester, 23 February 1933. Moss described himself as "a sheep amongst wolves" (GN 2/5, File 600.2: March 29, 1933) in a letter to Puddester. He refers to being rough-handled several times in his reports.

82. PANL GN 2/5, File 541H: Cross to Hutchings, 15 October 1932.

83. PANL GN 2/5, File 541H: Secretary of State to Mr. Emerson, 27 October 1932.

84. PANL GN 2/5, File 541H: Various items.

85. PANL GN 2/5, File 541G: Secretary of State to Mr. Taylor, September, 1932.

86. PANL GN 2/5, File 541G: Secretary of State to R.O. Wicks of Wesleyville, 26 September 1932.

87. PANL GN 2/5, File 541G: Secretary of State to Magistrate Jones, Nipper's Harbour, 24 September 1932.

88. PANL GN 2/5, File 541G: Circular to Stipendiary Magistrates and Justice of the Peace, 6 September 1932. The New declaration form was included.

89. PANL GN 2/5, File 541G: Deputy Secretary of State to Mr. Emerson, 27 September 1932. On September 26, 1932, Mr. Emerson reported to the Secretary of State that nine arrests had been made since the new declaration had come into force.

90. PANL GN 13/2, Newfoundland Constabulary, Trinity Police Diary, 1 August 1932.

91. PANL GN 13/1, Box 239, File 15, Poor Relief matters: "Circular to Persons Receiving Government Relief or Free Medical Treatment and to the Public Generally," September, 1932.

92. PANL GN 2/5, File 541G, 1932: George Winsor to J.C. Puddester, 18 August 1932.

93. PANL GN 2/5, File 541G, 1932: Secretary of State to George Winsor, 19 August 1932.

94. *Fishermen's Advocate* 12 October 1932:1. PANL GN 1/3A, 1932, File 1091: Report of Sgt. Bussey to C.H. Hutchings, 7 October 1932.

95. PANL GN 1/3A, 1932, File 1091: Report of Sgt. Bussey to C.H. Hutchings, 7 October 1932.

96. PANL GN 2/5, File 541G, 1932: I.G. Hutchings to Mr. Puddester, 10 October 1932. This letter enclosed the undertaking signed by the representatives of the Spaniard's Bay rioters.

97. PANL GN 1/3A, 1932, File 1091: A. Dwyer to C.H. Hutchings, 8 October 1932.

98. The comment was made by James Moore during the trial of the rioters in St. John's, *Evening Telegram* 14 December 1932:6. Other accounts of evidence given were published in the *Evening Telegram* on December 13:4; 14:6; 15:12; 16:6.

99. MG 30E 82, Vol. 12, P9/61, B-2-1, 352.5, Reel 1:6. MacGrath Papers, Report on the Charity Organization Bureau, 4.

100. Alderdice to Mr. Dodds, 27 September 1932. See also, PANL GN 2/5, File 582.1, Correspondence with the Bank of Montreal.

101. A loan of $100,000 was used to pay off 25 percent of the debts in early October. The *Fishermen's Advocate* announced another loan on 26 October 1932:4.

102. Dodds to Bennett, 13 October 1932, R.B. Bennett Papers, cited in Neary 1985:46.

103. For details of cuts, see, PANL GN 2/5, File 559.2, Retrenchment. On September 6, 1932 the Deputy Secretary of State wrote Mr. Taylor concerning a further cut of 10 percent in government salaries and civil pensions, PANL GN 2/5, File 541G, 1932.

104. PANL GN 2/5, File 582.7: Report of the Newfoundland Government Financial Position, 7 March 1933.

105. PANL GN 13/1, Box 69, File 25: Hutchings to Squires, 1 December 1921.

106. PANL GN 13/1, Constabulary Files, 1932: I.G. Hutchings to W.J. Higgins, Minister of Justice, 30 July 1925.

107. PANL GN 13/1, Constabulary Files, 1932: I.G. Hutchings to Richard Squires, 22 June 1929.

108. PANL GN 1/3A, 1932, File 349, Governor Middleton's Secret Memo, 5 May 1932.

109. PANL GN 1/3A, 1932, File 349, Governor Middleton's Secret Memo, 5 May 1932:21.

110. PANL GN 1/3A, 1932, File 349, Governor Middleton's Secret Memo, 5 May 1932:7.

111. PANL GN 1/13, Box 236, File 96: 29 March 1932.

112. The problems of policing in the period before Commission of Government are discussed in a report drawn up for the Amulree Commission: PANL GN 13/1, Box 161, File 62: Report on the Department of Justice, Its Staff, Work and Finances, For the Consideration of the Royal Commission, February 21, 1933. A Report of February 1, 1934 updated this information (*ibid*)..

113. PANL GN 13/1, Constabulary Files, 1932: Newfoundland High Commissioner in London to Mr. Emerson, 19 October 1932.

114. PANL GN 1/3A, File 102.

115. PANL GN 13/1, Constabulary Files, 1932: Report of the Newfoundland Constabulary 1933, July 1934.

116. PANL GN 13/1, Box 239, File 15: Minister of Justice to Secretary of State, 26 September 1932.

117. PANL GN 13/1, Box 285, File 2: Magistrate Small to Minister of Justice, 24 August 24, 1921; Minister of Justice to Small, 6 September 1921; Deputy Minister of Justice to Small, 21 November 1921.

118. PANL GN 1/3A, File 98: Secretary for Justice to Private Secretary, Government House, 19 December 1934. William Nixon was committed to the Harbour Grace jail on November 10, 1934. He was sentenced to six months for vagrancy, living on the street. The maximum charge for this was ten days.

119. PANL GN 1/3A, 1931, File 836.

120. PANL GN 1/3A, 1933, File 102: Petition for the Release of the Carbonear Rioters, 10 February 1932.

121. PANL GN 2/5, File 547, Petitions 1931–32: Minister of Justice to Secretary of State, 4 March 1933.

122. PANL GN 13/1, Box 73, File 10: Report of the Grand Jury on the Penitentiary, 20 March 1934.

123. PANL GN 13/1, Box 161, File 62: Memo re Justice, 22 February 1936:4.

124. PANL GN 1/3A, 1937, File 323A, Report by Magistrate Quinton.

125. PANL GN 2/5, File 600.4: Magistrate's Reports for February and March 1933. The comment was made about a resident of Curling who had recently returned from the U.S.A.

126. PANL GN 2/5, Files 579A–579C.

127. PANL GN 2/5, File 600.2: Constable Wellon to I.G. Hutchingson, 4 April 1933.

128. PANL GN 2/5, File 600.6: Constable King to Hutchingson, 12 June 1933; Magistrate Rowsell to Mr. Puddester, 16 June 1933; Secretary of State to Magistrate Quinlan, 15 June 1933; Secretary of State to Magistrate Wornell, 20 June 1933.

129. PANL GN 2/5, File 600.6: Expenditure Report for Able-Bodied Relief, June 1933.

130. PANL GN 2/5, File 600.7: Mr. Taylor to Mr. Mews, 17 July 1933.

131. PANL GN 2/5, File 600.8: Documents re Reorganization of the Dole, 16 November 1933.

132. PANL GN 1/3A, 1934, File 566: Report on the Journey to Hebron and the Investigation of the Trouble Among the Eskimos of that District by E.H.B. Baker, 17 February 1934. Renatus Tuglivina had swayed the

population into believing that they had a right to break into the store if they were hungry. He was sent to jail in Twillingate.

133. This article was reprinted from the Bay Roberts *Guardian*. It was noted that the use of tear gas was "deeply resented by all classes of our citizens" and that "Bay Roberts is not like New York or Chicago." The public meeting was reported in the *Evening Telegram* 24 October 1933:4. The arrests were the result of an incident in which Sergeant Russell was assaulted.

134. The events leading up to the introduction of government by Commission are dealt with in more detail in Overton (1990).

135. See, for example, the call for a dictatorship to be installed by a "bloodless revolution" made by E.J. Neary in the *Evening Telegram* 12 April 1932:5.

136. Hence one "workingman" urged those of his class to "get aboard the S.S. Royal Commission" in order to save the country and put "some nourishment in the[ir] bodies and put some clothes on their backs," *Evening Telegram* 28 November 1932:8.

137. Coaker's apocalyptic vision was outlined in his farewell speech to the voters of Bonavista South, *Fishermen's Advocate* 6 May 1932:4.

138. The metaphor was used by Lord Scarman in discussing the urban riots of the early 1980s in Britain (Unsworth 1982:63).

139. The widespread sense of fear in the United States in the early 1930s is discussed in Baskerville and Willett (1985:1–12).

140. PANL P7/A/2, Baine Johnston, Box 2C, J.C. Hepburn 1932: Hepburn to Mr. Campos, 4 May 1931.

141. PANL P7/A/2, Baine Johnston, Box 1C, J.C. Hepburn, Private Letters 1930: Hepburn to Newman, 26 March 1930.

142. PANL GN 13/1, Box 239, File 15: Minister of Justice of Mosdell, November, 1933.

143. MG 30E 82, Vol. 12, P9/61, B-2-1, 352.5, Reel 1:6. MacGrath Papers. Mr. Mosdell provided evidence to the Commission on 31 May 1933 (Number 82).

144. L. C. Outerbridge made his comments to the Amulree Commission on 9 June 1933 when he appeared as a representative of "The Merchant's Committee," Evidence (Number 101); James Harris gave evidence on 6 April 1933 (Number), and Mrs. Muir on 10 March 10 1933 (Number 39).

145. PANL GN 13/1, Box, 172, File 2: Constable Mahoney to P.J. O'Neil, 11 January 1935:4.

146. The *Fishermen's Advocate* 9 February 1934:4 reported "begging from door to door, by people without enough food" in Catalina. The *Advocate* argued that the dole of $1.20 to $1.60 was not enough to "keep the heart of a man beating for a month, to say nothing of giving him

strength to work." Slight dole trouble was reported by the *Advocate* at Carbonear on 31 March 1934:1. Later a petition was sent to the Commission of Government from that area in an effort to improve relief, *Fishermen's Advocate* 4 May 1934:6.

147. See the letter published in the *Fishermen's Advocate* 11 April 1934:4 which suggested that the dole was undermining the work ethic.

148. This editorial was part of a campaign to get the government to provide work not dole.

149. PANL GN 38, S4–4–1, File 1: Memorandum circulated at the request of the Commissioner for Justice for the consideration of the Commission of Government, W.R. Howley, 14 March 1934.

150. This intention was announced in the *Fishermen's Advocate* 4 May 1934:6. Able Bodied Relief was to be cut between June 1 and July 1, depending on the district.

151. PANL GN 38, S6–6–1, Box 1, File 5; Dr. Mosdell to the Commissioner for Public Health & Welfare, 1 March 1934.

152. PANL GN 38, S6–6–1, Box 1, File 5: Report of R.O. Pritchett, 1 March 1934.

153. PANL GN 38, S6–6–1, Box 1, File 3: Reported by Sergeant Humber, 16 May 1934.

154. The decision to set up an enquiry under F.G. Bradley was taken in early April. The report was never made public. It has recently been published with a commentary (Neary 1985:193-232).

155. "What About the Aged Poor?" *Fishermen's Advocate* 11 May 1934:2. This letter noted that men of 65–70 were being sent to the woods. The government was accused of "cold-blooded murder" on this account.

156. For similar problems in the early 1920s, see PANL GN 13/1, Box 285, File 2: Arthur Mews to the Deputy Minister of Justice, 15 August 1922; Deputy Minister of Justice to Inspector General Hutchings, 17 August 1922. Instructions were issued to Judge W.A. Oke by the Minister of Justice to prosecute the ringleaders on 21 August 1922.

157. "A Logger Sums it up," *Observer's Weekly*, 21 July 1934:11–12; "Out of the Woods," *Observer's Weekly*, 21 July 1934:2; "The Logging Problem," *Observer's Weekly*, 28 July 1934:9; "Those Eighty-Eight Unfortunates," *Fishermen's Advocate*, 3 August 1934:6; "Loggers Wages," *Fishermen's Advocate*, 19 October 1934:4.

158. Ramsay MacDonald also arrived on the H.M.S. *Dragon* for a visit to Newfoundland in early August.

159. Towards the end of August it was announced that more loggers had been jailed, *Fishermen's Advocate* 31 August 1934:6.

160. PANL GN 13/1, Box 239, File 16: Report from Magistrate Sinnott, Placentia, 7 August 1934.

161. DO/35/489/N1003/12: Report on Labrador to Chas. H. Hutchings, Inspector General, Newfoundland Constabulary by Superintendent O'Neill, July 1934.

162. The background to the events at Robert's Arm is provided in "Nfld. Lumberman's Association Organizer States his Case," *Evening Telegram*, 23 October 1937:4. For an account of the violence, see "Striking Loggers Threaten to Haul S.S. *Argyle* Ashore," *Evening Telegram*, 29 October 1937:4. The *Argyle* had arrived at Robert's Arm with the Managing Director of Bowater-Lloyd and Mr. H.A. Winter, the solicitor for the company, aboard. The ship also carried Sir. Richard Squires who was acting as solicitor for the Newfoundland Lumbermen's Association. The loggers were demanding $2.50 at the stump for cutting wood. When their demands were rejected 300-400 men attacked the *Argyle* and threatened to haul the boat ashore and "make a flower garden of her." The Rangers present were unable to control the men, and Mr. Winter agreed to their demands in order to prevent injury.

163. PANL GN 13/1, Box 238, File 45: Detective Constable Mahoney to O'Neil, August 9, 1934.

164. Information about the committee members is scanty. Pierce Power had recently been deported from Canada. The Penny-a-Week Club's activities were well summed up in a letter to the *Daily News*, 25 March 1935:10. The aim of the club was to provide the unemployed with a free meal "which would be in the nature of nourishment that he may not be able to obtain on his relief order." Books of meal tickets were issued to the club's donors and these tickets were handed to those in need of food. The club also acted as a kind of advocacy agency for the unemployed, assisting in cases of eviction and providing some clothing. Those running the club complained that subscriptions had fallen since 1934.

165. PANL GN 13/1, Box 238, File 45: Mahoney to O'Neill, 10 August 1934. This was the third meeting of the unemployed.

166. PANL GN 13/1, Box 238, File 45: Mahoney to O'Neill, 9 August 1934.

167. PANL GN 13/1, Box 238, File 45: Head Constable Whalen to O'Neill, 12 August 1934.

168. Vol. 1, No. 1, was published on 17 August 1934. This appears to have been the only issue of the Bulletin. A copy is in the above file.

169. PANL GN 13/1, Box 238, File 45: Mahoney to O'Neill, 27 August 1934.

170. PANL GN 13/1, Box 238, File 45: Mahoney to O'Neill, 6 and 27 September 1934. At the meeting on September 6 all the Unemployed Committee had resigned and new elections were held.

171. PANL GN 13/1, Box 238, File 45: Commissioner for Justice to Governor Murray Anderson, 5 October 1934.

172. PANL GN 13/1, Box 238, File 45: Constable Bennett to O'Neill, 10 October 1934.

173. PANL GN 13/1, Box 238, File 45: Mahoney to O'Neill, 15 August 1934. An informer had already told the police chief that Power had recently been deported from Canada "because the Canadian Police believed him to be an agitator." PANL GN 13/1, Box 238, File 45: Fred McGinn to O'Neill, 15 August 1934.

174. PANL GN 13/1, Box 238, File 45: Mahoney to O'Neill, 3, 4 October 1934. J.T. Meaney was the publisher of *The Newfoundlander*, which first appeared on the streets of St. John's on 7 October 1934. This newspaper was explicitly *against* Commission of Government.

175. PANL GN 13/1, Box 172, Files 1 and 2.

176. PANL GN 38, S6-1-1, File 4: Mahoney to O'Neill, 16 January 1935.

177. PANL GN 13/1, Box 172, File 2: Mahoney to O'Neill, 16 January 1935.

178. PANL GN 13/1, Box 166, File 70: Commissioner for Justice to Mr. Puddester, 14 February 1935.

179. PANL GN 13/1, Box 172, File 2: Mahoney to O'Neill, 10 January and 26 February 1935.

180. PANL GN 13/1, Box 155, File 3: Mahoney to O'Neill, 26 February 1935.

181. PANL GN 13/1, Box 155, File 14: Mahoney to O'Neill, 5 March 1935.

182. PANL GN 13/1, Box 155, File 3: Mahoney to O'Neill, 31 March and 30 April 1935.

183. PANL GN 13/1, Box 155, File 3: Mahoney to O'Neill, 7 May 1935.

184. PANL GN 13/1, Box 155, File 3: "Meeting at 11 a.m. at Beck's Cove," 8 May 1935.

185. The events of early May are reviewed in police reports and the sworn statements of police and other witnesses. For accounts, see: PANL GN 13/1, Box 282, File "Re Riot (May 1935)"; PANL GN 13/1, Box 155, File 3. Most of what follows is based on these accounts.

186. There are a number of accounts of the events of 10 May 1935. Police files (cited above) provide many statements. Also useful are newspaper reports such as those published in the *Fishermen's Advocate*, 17 May 1935:8 and in the *Evening Telegram*, 11 May 1935:4. The report of the trial of the leaders of the unemployed was published in the *Evening Telegram*, May 27:6; May 28:5; May 29:6, 7; May 30:6, 13; May 31:6.

187. PANL GN 38, S1-1, Minutes of Special meeting of Commission of Government, May 11, 1935 re disturbance on 10th. At this meeting the Commissioners consulted with the Secretary of Justice and the Chief of Police and it was decided that Wilkinson, Power, Milley, and Saunders should be arrested.

188. PANL GN 13/1, Box 155, File 3: Mahoney to O'Neill, 12 May 1935.

189. PANL GN 38, S6-1-1, File 17: Hope Simpson to Puddester, 18 May 1935.

190. PANL GN 1/3A, 1935, File 33: Governor to Secretary of State for Dominion Affairs, 24 December 1935.

191. The decision was taken on May 17, 1935 to discontinue able-bodied relief progressively in various parts of the country from May 31. This was announced in the *Evening Telegram*, 18 May 1935:12.

192. PANL GN 1/3A, 1934, File 353: Telegram from Governor to Secretary of State for Dominion Affairs, 11 May 1935.

193. PANL GN 13/1, Box 135 File 74: Mahoney to O'Neill, 25 March 1936.

194. PANL GN 13/1, Box 155, File 3.

195. PANL GN 13/1, Box 155, File 3: Mahoney to O'Neill, 19 August 1935:11.

196. PANL GN 13/1, Box 155, File 3: Mahoney to O'Neill, 19 August 1935:7. When Joseph Milley was asked to speak at a meeting in August he declined with the words "What? and get the Billy used on my head again. . .Nothin 'cookin'. . . I thank you," see PANL GN 13/1, Box 155, File 3: Mahoney to O'Neill, 12 August 1935.

197. PANL GN 13/1, Box 155, File 3: Mahoney to O'Neil, 19 August 1935:16.

198. PANL GN 13/1, Box 155, File 3: Mahoney to O'Neil, 26 August 1935:7.

199. PANL GN 13/1, Box 155, File 3: Mahoney to O'Neill, 26 August 1935:9.

200. Pierce Power was sent to prison for five years for wounding with intent. During the 1930s conditions in the penitentiary were very poor and Power became involved in attempts to improve conditions. In 1938 he was involved in a protest in which prisoners refused to leave their cells and also in a hunger strike. According to the superintendent of the penitentiary Pierce Power and George Roberts were the leaders of the protest. Power was also accused of brewing beer in the penitentiary. See PANL GN 13/1, Box 9, File 97: Superintendent of the Penitentiary to Commissioner for Justice, 7 November 1938.

201. PANL GN 13/1, Box 135, File 74: Mahoney to O'Neill, 8 February 1937.

202. Reuben Vardy's manifesto was issued in 1937. It carried the title "Comrades: 'Shun.'" See PANL GN 13/1, Box 135, File 74. The association was dedicated to the restoration of Responsible Government. The character of this movement of opposition to Commission of Government can be gauged by the fact that some of its meetings were held in the Board of Trade rooms. It did, however, attract individuals who had been already involved in the unemployed movement, including J.R. Smallwood and J.T. Meaney.

203. PANL GN 13/1, Box 135, File 74: Mahoney to O'Neill, 4 February 1937.

204. PANL GN 13/1, Box 135, File 74: Sgt. J. Walsh to O'Neill, 28 February 1937; J. Walsh to O'Neill, 1 March 1937; District Inspector Whalen to O'Neill, 3 March 1937.

205. PANL GN 13/1, Box 135, File 74: Walsh to O'Neill, 28 February 1937.

206. PANL GN 13/1, Box 135, File 74: Constable George Wellon to O'Neill, 4 January 1937.

207. PANL GN 13/1, Box 135, File 74: Constable George Wellon to O'Neill, 4 January 1937.

208. PANL, GN 38 S1-1-1-2, Minutes of Commission of Government, 7 December 1936.

209. DO 35/723/N2/7: Governor Walwyn to Secretary of State for Dominion Affairs, Malcolm MacDonald, 15 March 1937.

210. PANL GN 13/1, Box 233, Newfoundland Affairs.

211. PANL P6/A/12, Box 1, File 3. *The Leader* was not above using the threat of the "devils' doctrine," communism, to agitate against Newfoundland's situation, while at the same time being anti-communist. "It is the treatment such as we are receiving that breeds Communism and begets Revolutions," *The Leader*, 17 July 1937:3. See also, "A John Lewis Man to Visit Here," *The Leader*, 1 May 1937:3.

212. *Newfoundland: Report by the Commission of Government on the Economic Situation, December 1934* (London: HMSO, 1935), Cmd. 5788. For comments on the report: DO/35/504/N1051/3: 18 December 1934.

213. DO/35/499/N1002/91: Hope Simpson to Harding, 26 March 1936.

214. DO/35/504/N1051/11: Comments on economic situation in Newfoundland, 1 October 1935. In this *The Times* passed a copy of a letter from their correspondent in Newfoundland to A. Ridgeway of the Colonial Office for comment. *The Times* also requested permission to embody some of Ridgeway's comments in their reply to their correspondent. See also, DO/35/504/N1051/18: *The Times* to A. Ridgeway, 15 April 1936. Mr. Jeffrey's "rather assertive line" was causing concern in 1936.

215. PANL GN 13/1, Box 155, File 3: Mahoney to O'Neill, 26 February 1935. The first issue of *The Newfoundlander* was published to 6 October 1934. It continued publication at least until 13 December 1934.

216. PANL GN 13/1, Box 155, File 3: Mahoney to O'Neill 26 February 1935. See also, the *Evening Telegram*, 16 March 1935:10. On 16 March 1934:6, the *Evening Telegram* described Meaney's despatches as "Fouling the Nest." This editorial attacked the "revolting" way in which Newfoundland was being represented "to strangers." Conditions in the country, while acknowledged to be far from satisfactory, were, it was argued not serious enough "to warrant such sensational accounts." Such bad publicity would do nothing to help the country, according to the *Telegram*. Mr. Thomas' remarks were made in the House of

Commons on March 5, 1935. Also relevant is PANL GN 1/3A, 1934, File 353: Meaney to Horwood, 19 March 1935; *Fishermen's Advocate*, 30 August 1935:2–3. The Government's refusal to deal with Meaney's criticism should be contrasted with their detailed reply to criticism of the Commission's relief program made by the Rev. J.T. Richards of Flowers Cove. The Rural Dean of the Straits of Belle Isle published his remarks in the *Evening Telegram*, 10 January 1938. A 14-page, 28-point reply was prepared by the Commissioner for Public Health and Welfare, Mr. Puddester on January 13, 1938 for circulation to the Commission of Government. See PANL GN 38 S6-1-6, File 2.

217. PANL GN 13/1, Box 282, Confidential Memo re J.T. Meaney, 26 August 1935:1, 2.

218. PANL GN 13/1, Box 282, Confidential Memo re J.T. Meaney, 26 August 1935:5.

219. DO/35/723/N2/26: T. Lodge's memo, September 1937. Lodge's memo was written because he wanted there to be a "contemporary record" of his reaction to what was happening. It sets out the details of his dealings with the Dominions Office.

220. DO/35/737/N111/33: Notes on Mr. Lodge's visit, 10 June 1938. There was some concern expressed by Mr. Penson because Lodge was going to stay with his friend Mr. Pippy in Newfoundland. Lodge had apparently entered into a business arrangement with Pippy (The Island Timber Company). This arrangement was considered improper and it was thought that the "traditions of the British Public Service" were not being "enhanced" by Lodge's conduct.

221. Gallagher was the author of *Revolt on the Clyde*, published in London in 1936.

222. PANL GN 13/1, Box 9, File 119: O'Neill to Secretary for Justice, 19 September 1936.

223. PANL GN 13/1, Box 135, File 74: Freake to O'Neill, 3 March and 15 April 1937.

224. PANL GN 13/1, Box 137, File 88: Whalen to O'Neill, 30 October 1986; O'Neill to Secretary for Justice, 5 November 1936; Assistant Secretary for Justice to O'Neill, 6 November 1936; O'Neill to Assistant Secretary for Justice, 9 November 1936.

225. PANL GN 13/1, Box 137, File 88: O'Neill to Acting Secretary for Justice, 21 May 1937; O'Neill to Acting Secretary for Justice, 31 May 1937. An order to deport the Witnesses was signed in May 1938.

226. PANL GN 13/1, Box 137, File 88: O'Neill to the Commissioner for Justice, 28 March 1938.

227. PANL GN 1/3A, 1938, File 58. The quotation comes from a pamphlet, *The Cure* (Brooklyn, New York: Watchtower Bible Society, 1938). This was one of the over 4,000 pamphlets seized in a police raid on Pennywell road in St. John's on May 23, 1938.

228. PANL GN 13/1, Box 137, File 88: O'Neill to the Commissioner for Justice, 21 June 1939.

229. Markland was labelled a "communist" settlement by the *Fishermen's Advocate*, 22 May 1936 in an editorial.

230. For the anti-communist flavour of the labour movement, see the legal affidavit sworn by the leaders of the Newfoundland Trades and Labour Council on May 28, 1938 and published in the press (Gillespie 1986:70). Gillespie argues that this anti-communist stance reflected the weakness of the union movement at the time and the belief of their leaders that it was necessary "to make a strong moral argument for unions to the public." The unionists, he suggests, were following a policy of "conciliation not confrontation" and in doing so were attempting to distance themselves from "any hint of confrontational tactics, foreign radicalism, of violence" and of "deliberate disruption." There is obviously a great deal of truth in this explanation, but I think it fails to capture and explain the strength of the anti-communist current (it was not simply expedient to be thus) in the labour movement. The view of some labour leaders was "let Christians christianize the unions, or the communists will certainly communize them," see the *Labour Herald*, 7 October 1938:3. In fact, unions were weak and they did seek the protection of the state. Their vision was very much a corporatist one. Some unionists very clearly preached the gospel of co-operation between labour and capital in the late 1930s in the pages of the *Labour Herald*. "Michael," for example, emphasized that "trade unions reduce the worry of employers by putting an end to industrial disputes," *Labour Herald*, 10 November 1938:6.

231. Part of the reason for the serious state of affairs was the failure of merchants to issue supplies. Their action in this regard was the result of "the unfortunate experience of the previous season," *Newfoundland: Annual Report of the Commission of Government, 1936* (London: HMSO 1937:13). Merchants had found it difficult to dispose of their fish due to the closure of the Italian and Spanish markets. Able-bodied relief funds were drawn upon to provide some of those denied credit with food supplies so that they could fish, but many were forced to remain idle. The summer of 1936 was possibly the worst of the 1930s and the winter of 1936–7 was a bad one because lack of earnings during the fishing season forced many people onto the dole early.

232. In the budget speech of July 1937, the government announced the inauguration of a comprehensive reconstruction programme. This programme was to involve spending on health, education, and public works as well as economic reorganization. A sum of $8 million was tentatively sugggested for this work, the spending to take place over a number of years. In the budget speech of 1938, spending on reconstruction was given a separate head for the first time. Just under $1.5 million was allocated for this purpose. See *Newfoundland: Annual*

Report by the Commission of Government on the Work of the Commission during 1938 (London: HMSO 1939:7).

233. Government officials made a great effort to "check abuses," according to the Commission's report: *Newfoundland: Annual Report of the Commission of Government, 1937* (London: HMSO 1938:12). One confrontation over relief took place at Burin in the autumn of 1937. Serious trouble was prevented by local merchants issuing relief. Local law officials were instructed to arrest the leaders of the protest and make "an example of these men." (See PANL GN 38 S6-1-2, File 4.)

234. Fish producers were provided with a salt subsidy of one cent per hogshead. Given the low earnings of those engaged in fishing, many were "quite unable to maintain their equipment and premises in proper repair." Late in 1937 the government did provide some employment in the construction of the airport at Gander and on road works. An extension of the paper plant at Grand Falls provided work for about 800 men and woods operations expanded in the fall. A variety of other schemes, including berry picking, also provided opportunities for wage-earning. This kept the numbers on relief down.

235. DO/35/739/N33/3: James Roe of the Treasury to the Under Secretary of State for Dominion Affairs, 20 October 1937. The letter was in response to a request for an increased lodging allowance for the constabulary. In fact, the constabulary had been allowed to run down somewhat in the mid-1930s as a result of the establishment of the Newfoundland Ranger Force. In February 1936 the constabulary consisted of 266 men, excluding support staff (PANL GN 13/1, Box 166, File 62: Supplementary Memo re Justice Changes). The Ranger Force reached its full complement of 52 officers in 1937 (Horwood 1986:163).

236. DO/35/729/N33/17: Clutterbuck to Inch, 7 January 1939.

237. PANL GN 1/3A, 1938, File 89: Draft Telegram to the Secretary of State for Dominion Affairs, 3 June 1938.

238. PANL GN 38 S6-1-2, File 27: Telegram to the Secretary of State for Dominion Affairs, 7 June 1938.

239. PANL GN S6-1-2, File 27: Telegram to the Secretary of State for Dominion Affairs, 7 June 1938.

240. PANL GN S6-1-2, File 27: Telegram to the Secretary of State for Dominion Affairs, 7 June 1938.

241. PANL GN S6-1-2, File 27: Telegram to the Secretary of State for Dominion Affairs, 7 June 1938.

242. PANL GN 1/3A, 1938, File 89: Draft Telegram to the Secretary of State for Dominion Affairs, 3 June 1938.

243. PANL GN 1/3A, 1938, File 89: Relieving Officer J.S. Rowsell to Commissioner Puddester, 24 June 1938.

244. PANL GN 1/3A, 1938, File 89: Telegram to Secretary of State for Dominion Affairs, 29 June 1938.

245. PANL GN 1/3A, 1938, File 89: Telegram to Secretary of State for Dominion Affairs, 29 June 1938.

246. PANL GN 1/3A, 1938, File 89: Draft Telegram to the S.S.D.A., 7 June 1938.

247. PANL GN 1/3A, 1938, File 639: Telegram to Governor Walwyn from A. Peddle and others at Hodge's Cove, 7 October 1938.

248. PANL GN 1/3A, 1938, File 639: Telegram to Governor Walwyn from R.T. Vardy and others at Little Hearts Ease, 7 October 1938.

249. PANL GN 1/3A, 1938, File 89: S.S.D.A. to Walwyn, 2 July 1938.

250. PANL GN 38 S4-4-3, File 3: Memo on the Police Situation in Relation to the Possibility of Civil Disturbance, Prepared for the Commission of Government by the Secretary for Justice, 24 June 1938.

251. PANL GN 13/1, Box 69: File "Re Police Situation in Case of Civil Disturbance, June 1938": Report on "Forces at our Command," 14 June 1938.

252. PANL GN 13/1, Box 69: To Assistant Chief of Police from Commissioner for Justice, 10 June 1938.

253. PANL GN 38 S4-4-3, File 3: Memo on Police Situation in Relation to the Possibility of Civil Disturbance, Prepared for the Commission of Government by the Secretary for Justice, 24 June 1938.

254. Some efforts to improve the armaments of the constabulary had been made earlier in the decade and some new rifles had been acquired in 1937. In 1938, however, the old Lee Enfield rifles which had been in general use were replaced with modern rifles. See PANL GN 13/1, Box 76, File 28: Report of the Newfoundland Constabulary, 1938. By early 1939 extensive changes had been made in the constabulary by the Commission of Government. Administration, recruitment, training, and equipment were all improved and new facilities were provided. Modern police methods were introduced in the 1930s as a result of contacts with Scotland Yard. In the late 1930s, fingerprinting and photography were being used and record keeping had been improved. The officers of the constabulary were encouraged to practise their shooting skills at an improved shooting range. In 1937 a system of numbers for the identification of officers was introduced.

255. PANL GN 38 S4-4-3, File 3: Memo on Police Situation in Relation to the Possibility of Civil Disturbance, Prepared for the Commission of Government by the Secretary for Justice, 24 June 1938.

256. PANL GN 38 S4-4-3, File 3: Memo on Police Situation in Relation to the Possibility of Civil Disturbance, Prepared for the Commission of Government by the Secretary for Justice, 24 June 1938.

257. PANL GN 13/1, Box 69: "Special Police."

258. PANL GN 1/3A, 1938, File 639, "Civil Disturbances."

259. PANL GN 1/3A, 1938, File 639, Civil Disturbances: Kempster to W.C. Hankinson, 30 August 1938.

260. PANL GN 1/3A, 1938, File 639, Civil Disturbances: Kempster to W.C. Hankinson, Reply, 7 September 1938.

261. DO/35/723/N2/39: A. Mansbridge to M. MacDonald, 30 October 1938. In this letter Mansbridge hints that he would have agreed to be a Newfoundland Commissioner if asked; DO/35/723/N2/26: Report of a Meeting between the Duke of Devonshire and Mr. Christiansen of the *Daily Express* 12 December 1938.

262. DO/35/729/N31/25: J.L. Paton to M. MacDonald, 7 September 1938.

263. DO/35/729/N31/25: Clutterbuck's notes on Legal and Judicial Staff, 8 December 1938. The "focus of discontent" seems to have been Brian Dunfield, Dr. Mosdell and Mr. Emerson.

264. Evidence suggests that Richards was in contact with Meaney while in St. John's. They probably attended a meeting of the Newfoundland Welfare League in St. John's in January 1939. PANL GN 13/1, Box 70, File 25.

265. During this period the *Express* claimed to have the world's largest daily sales of almost 2.5 million copies (see Gannon 1971:34).

266. The Morley Richards articles stimulated discussion of the situation in Newfoundland and action was soon forthcoming. It was the outbreak of war in September 1939 which put an end to reconstruction efforts in Newfoundland.

267. The Placentia Bay Special Area was an early experiment in what would now be called regional development. Its aim was the comprehensive rehabilitation of the area based on the development of a craft industry, agriculture and other small industries.

268. DO/35/723/N2/74: Reports by Mr. Shakespear and Mr. Gardener on their visits to Newfoundland, September 1941.

269. These statistics are taken from documents to be found in PANL GN 14/1/A, File 307.01.

270. See Muggeridge (1971:19). From the writings of the columnist Walter Lippman in 1931, to F.D. Roosevelt's statement that "the only thing we have to fear is fear itself" (borrowed from Thoreau) made in March 1933, it is clear that fear gripped many in the early 1930s. This is discussed in Baskerville and Willett (1985:1–12).

271. PANL GN 13/1, Box 135, File 74, "Secret Observations": Mahoney to O'Neill, 25 March 1936.

272. The concept of a "moral panic" is due to S. Cohen (1972). It was taken in by S. Hall, *et al.* (1978). It is, however, a concept which should not be used without caution. A recent critique of *Policing the Crisis* by Waddington (1986) is essential reading in this regard.

273. See also Rock (1981), Unsworth (1982).

274. The phrases are taken from police reports. See PANL GN 13/1, Box 135, File 74.

275. These phrases are common in police reports.

Part IV

Conclusion

The origins of this book are tied up with the widespread expression of concern about increases in violence in Newfoundland. The specific aim of the book is to shed some light on whether or not there has been a noticeable shift in patterns of violent behaviour in Newfoundland in recent years. More broadly, the book begins an exploration of the complex of issues and problems involved in trying to examine violence and public anxiety.

This is achieved by means of three pieces of original research; each piece is distinctive, yet informed by the same concerns and questions.

The work of O'Grady addressed the important question of whether or not an examination of official crime statistics can help provide a clear picture of the incidence and character of violent crime in Newfoundland in recent years. O'Grady moved from an examination of the use of statistics in commentary on violence, to a detailed investigation of the social processes involved in the generation and use of statistics on violence. He has argued that there is no evidence of a significant shift in patterns of violence in the official statistics. Changes in levels of recorded crime can be explained quite readily in terms of changes in police recording procedures and other police practices and changes in public reporting habits. O'Grady's findings support those of an increasing body of researchers in that the importance of disentangling the complex of practices involved in producing official statistics is stressed. O'Grady examined statistics, but also went behind them to look at how they are compiled. He found that many of those who use official statistics show little awareness of the nature of the data they are using. He also raised the issue of why it is that so many people have been willing to accept wholeheartedly statistical and other evidence that violence is on the increase.

Elliott Leyton took up the issue of the manufacture of popular concern about violence. Although all the essays have explored the social meaning of violence, Leyton has done so by means of a detailed look at the role of the press in generating, shaping, amplifying, and sustaining concern about violence in Newfoundland. However, a year-by-year content analysis of the St. John's *Evening Telegram* has revealed that the paper was more than anything a vehicle for the ideas, concerns, and arguments of a variety of social interest groups which all took up the issue of violence in the period studied. These groups linked their arguments for attention, funds, and government action to the issue of violence in many different ways, but the overall impact was to generate a great deal of anxiety over the supposed increasingly violent nature of Newfoundland society. Leyton's work has thus raised important questions concerning why interest groups have taken up the violence issue at this time.

Beyond the announcement of crime waves lies the widespread acceptance of explanations for crime and violence which link the level of these problems to social breakdown caused by urbanization, modernization, and/or unemployment. Such "explanations" seem to set people's expectations and frame their observations in a way which generates anxiety about violence during periods of change and economic difficulty. Evidence suggests, however, that such theories are not particularly valuable in explaining violence.

Overton's essay suggests that much current concern about violence rests on the assumption that in the past Newfoundland was a non-violent place. The "myth" of the peaceful past was confronted with the realities of collective violence and protest in the 1930s in his account of "raids and riots." Using archival and other sources, Overton has offered a history of the 1930s in Newfoundland, which focuses on public relief, unemployment, and policing. But Overton's aim has not simply been to point out that in certain periods Newfoundlanders have been violent. Rather, in his narrative he has examined the complex relationship which existed in the 1930s between economic and political crisis, state policy regarding public relief, prisons and policing, and public protest and collective violence. He has thus explored the whole question of law and order during a period of acute crisis in Newfoundland in order to trace the connections between this and the events and circumstances which shaped thinking about the question. As a result, the research has drawn attention to the great complexity of the issue of violence and emphasized the importance of understanding the meaning which groups of people give to violent acts in specific, but changing, sets of circumstances. In Newfoundland in the 1930s much thinking about violence was informed by the sense of crisis which existed in the country and by the vulnerability felt by those who were concerned with maintaining law and order. This finding has an obvious significance for understanding the broad questions raised by O'Grady and Leyton concerning public anxiety.

The historical and contemporary analyses presented here challenge many of the assumptions which relate crime and violence to processes of social and economic change in a simple, one dimensional fashion. The analyses also reveal the extreme complexity of the relationships between social and economic forces, agencies of political and social control, and the perception and reality of crime and violence. What we offer is not a simplistic and reductive resolution to the question of whether or not Newfoundland is becoming more violent, but an awareness of some of the problems and difficulties of coming to terms with the meaning of this question. We offer some ways to begin thinking about the broad issues involved in the problem of violence.

In the course of this research we became convinced that what was needed was not an explanation for the present crime-ridden state of Newfoundland—we are not convinced that crime and violence are on the increase. What is needed is an explanation for why so many people are currently preoccupied with violence. We hope the research goes some way towards providing an answer.

Interesting questions still remain. How much influence does the press have over public opinion? Does the press shape opinion or reflect it? Or does it do both? Why have various interest groups picked on the violence issue to give weight to their arguments *at this time*? Why have their pronouncements been so willingly accepted? Why are people *at this time* so willing to believe we are in the midst of a crisis of crime and violence? How have these various interest groups appropriated and used expert knowledge to make their arguments? How much is the end outlined by Elliott Leyton the natural outcome of a certain style of pressure group politics which evolved in the 1960s and which in the 1980s finds a myriad of different groups competing for dwindling state funds? Is the rhetoric escalating as the competition increases?

References

Alexander, David 1974 "Development and Dependence in Newfoundland 1880–1870." *Acadiensis*, 4(1):3–31.

_____ 1976 "Newfoundland's Traditional Economy and Development to 1934." *Acadiensis*, 5(2):56–78.

Anderson, Olive 1980 "Did Suicide Increase with Industrialization in Victorian England?" *Past and Present*, 86:149–173.

Armstrong, Pat 1984 *Labour Pains: Women's Work in Crisis*. Toronto: The Women's Press.

Bailey, Victor 1981 "The Metropolitan Police, the Home Office and the Threat of Outcast London." In V. Bailey (ed.), *Policing and Punishment in Nineteenth Century Britain*. New Brunswick, N.J.: Rutgers University Press.

Bartrip, Peter 1981 "Public Opinion and Law Enforcement: The Ticket-of-Leave Scares in mid-Victorian Britain." In V. Bailey (ed.), *Policing and Punishment in Nineteenth Century Britain*. New Brunswick, N.J.: Rutgers University Press.

Baskerville, Stephen W. and Ralph Willett (eds.) 1985 "Introduction." *Nothing Else to Fear: New Perspectives on America in the Thirties*. Manchester: Manchester University Press.

Beattie, John 1974 "The Pattern of Crime in England, 1660–1800." *Past and Present*, 62:47–95.

Benjamin, Walter 1978 "Critique of Violence." In *Reflections*. New York: Harcourt Brace Jovanovitch.

Berger, John 1984 "Once Through a Lense." In J. Berger (ed.), *And Our Faces, My Heart, Brief as Photos*. London: Writers and Readers.

Black, Donald 1970 "Production of Crime Rates." *American Sociological Review*, 35:733–47.

Bottomley, Keith and Clive Coleman 1981 *Understanding Crime Rates.* Westmead: Gower.

_____ and Ken Pease 1986 *Crime and Punishment: Interpreting the Data.* Milton Keynes: Open University Press.

Box, Stephen 1981 *Deviance, Reality and Society.* London: Holt, Rinehart and Winston.

_____ 1983 *Power, Crime and Mystification.* London: Tavistock.

_____ and Chris Hale 1982 "Economic Crisis and Rising Prisoner Population in England and Wales." *Crime and Social Justice,* 17:20.

_____ 1985 "Unemployment, Imprisonment and Overcrowding." *Contemporary Crisis,* 9:209–228.

Brantingham, Paul and Patricia 1984 *Patterns in Crime.* New York: Macmillan.

Brewer, J. and J. Styles 1980 *An Ungovernable People: The English and their Law in the 17th and 18th Centuries.* London: Hutchinson.

Brown, J. 1978 "Social Control and the Modernization of Social Policy." In P. Thane (ed.), *The Origins of British Social Policy.* London: Croom Helm.

Butler, Michael A. 1986 "Our Newfoundland Way of Life." *Encore,* 2(5):5.

Cake, Gary 1986 "Energy Development and Social Problems: A Critical Review of the Literature." Newfoundland and Labrador Petroleum Directorate, Unpublished paper.

Carr, E.H. 1944 *Conditions of Peace.* New York: Macmillan.

_____ 1986 *What is History?* London: Macmillan.

Carr-Hill, Roy A. 1985 "Whither (research on) Unemployment?" In Bryan Roberts, Ruth Finnegan and Duncan Gallie (eds.), *New Approaches to Economic Life.* Manchester: Manchester University Press.

_____ and N.H. Stern 1979 *Crime, the Police and Criminal Statistics.* London: Academic Press.

Chappell, Duncan 1983 "Violent Crime in Canada: Trends and Comparisons." Paper presented at the IXth International Congress on Criminology, Vienna, Austria, September 27, 1983.

Chibnall, Steven 1977 *Law and Order News.* London: Tavistock.

Clark, Lorenne and Debra Lewis 1977 *Rape: The Price of Coercive Sexuality.* Toronto: The Women's Press.

Clarke, Annett M. 1986 "Placentia Public Hearings." *Summary-Public Hearing Proceedings.* Background Report, Royal Commission on Employment and Unemployment, Newfoundland and Labrador. St. John's: Queen's Printer.

_____ 1986 "Rocky Harbour Public Hearings." *Summary-Public Hearing Proceedings.* Background Report, Royal Commission on Employment and Unemployment, Newfoundland and Labrador. St. John's: Queen's Printer.

Cohen, A.P. 1975 *The Management of Myths*. Manchester: Manchester University Press and St. John's: Institute of Social and Economic Research, Memorial University of Newfoundland.

Cohen, Stanley 1972 *Folk Devils and Moral Panics: The Creation of the Mods and Rockers* London: MacGibbon and Kee.

_____ 1983 *Folk Devils and Moral Panics*. St. Alban's: Paladin.

_____ 1985 *Visions of Social Control.* Cambridge: UK Polity Press.

Community Services Council 1986 *A Blueprint for Action: The Report of the Working Group on Child Sexual Abuse & Background Papers*. St. John's: Newfoundland.

Cutler, Ebbitt 1969 "Introduction." In George Allan England, *The Greatest Hunt in the World*. Montreal: Tundra Books.

Dahrendorf, Rolf 1959 *Class and Class Conflict in Industrial Society*. Stanford: Stanford University Press.

Davis, Jennifer 1980 "The London Garotting Panic of 1862: A Moral Panic and the Creation of a Criminal Class in mid-Victorian England." In Gatrell et al. (eds.), *Crime and the Law: The Social History of Crime in Western Europe since 1500*. London: Europa.

Deacon, A. and E. Briggs 1974 "Local Democracy and Central Policy: The Issue of Pauper Votes in the 1920s." *Policy and Politics*, 2(4):347–364.

Dominion Bureau of Statistics 1960–1962 *Annual Reports*.

Duggan, Diane 1986 "Dealing With Violence Against Women." *Newfoundland Herald*, January 11–17, pp. 19–20.

Dussuyer, Inez 1979 *Crime News: A Study of 40 Ontario Newspapers*. Toronto: Centre of Criminology.

Dyer, Geoff 1984 "Ways of Witnessing." *Marxism Today*, 36–38.

Economic Council of Canada 1980 *Newfoundland: From Dependency to Self-Reliance*. Hull: Minister of Supply and Services.

Elias, N. 1983 *Power and Civility: The Civilizing Process, Vol. 2*. New York: Pantheon.

Elliott, R.M. 1980 "Newfoundland Politics in the 1920s: The Genesis and Significance of the Hollis Walker Enquiry." In J. Hiller and P. Neary (eds.), *Newfoundland in the Nineteenth and Twentieth Centuries: Essays in Interpretation*. Toronto: University of Toronto Press.

Ericson, R.V., P.M. Baranek, and V.B.L. Chan 1987 *Visualizing Deviance: A Study of News Organization*. Toronto: University of Toronto Press.

Fairfield, F. 1912 *Newfoundland*. London: Black.

Faris, James 1972 *Cat Harbour: A Newfoundland Fishing Settlement*. St.

John's: Institute of Social and Economic Research, Memorial University of Newfoundland.

Farrington, D. P. and E. A. Dowds 1985 "Disentangling Criminal Behaviour and Police Reaction." In D. P. Farrington and J. Gunn (eds.), *Reactions to Crime: the Public, the Police, Courts and Prisons*. New York: John Wiley.

Felt, L. 1987 *Take the Bloods of Bitches to the Gallows: The Rhetoric and Reality of Interpersonal Violence in Rural Newfoundland*. St. John's: Institute of Social and Economic Research Policy Paper No. 6, Memorial University of Newfoundland.

Field, S. 1982 "Urban Disorders in Britain and America." In S. Field and P. Southgate (eds.), *Public Disorder: A Review of Research and a Study in One Inner City Area*. Home Office Research Study Number 72. London: HMSO.

Firestone, Melvin 1967 *Brothers and Rivals: Patrilocality in Savage Cove*. St. John's: Institute of Social and Economic Research, Memorial University of Newfoundland.

Fishman, Mark 1978 "Crime Waves as Ideology." *Social Problems*, 25(5):531–543.

Fitzpatrick, Peter 1980 "Really Rather Like Slavery: Law and Labour in the Colonial Economy in Papua New Guinea." *Contemporary Crises*, 4:77–95.

Foucault, Michel (ed.) 1975 *I, Pierre Riviere, Having Slaughtered My Mother, My Sister and My Brother. . .A Case of Parricide in the Nineteenth Century*. Trans. Frank Jellinek. New York: Pantheon.

_____ 1977 *Discipline and Punish: The Birth of the Prison*. Trans. Alan Sheridan. New York: Pantheon.

Friedland, Roger 1983 *Power and Crisis in the City*. New York: Shocken Books.

Fuchs, R. and M. Shrimpton 1977 "Crime, Vandalism Increasing? Policy-Makers Wise to Seek Economic and Social Solutions." *Evening Telegram*, October 29.

Gannon, F.R. 1971 *The British Press and Germany, 1936–1939*. Oxford: Clarendon Press.

Gatrell, V.A.C., B. Lenman and G. Parker (eds.) 1980 *Crime and the Law: The Social History of Crime in Western Europe since 1500*. London: Europa.

Giffen, P.J. 1976 "Official Rates of Crime and Delinquency." In W.T. McGrath (ed.), *Crime and its Treatment in Canada*. Toronto: Macmillan.

Gillespie, B. 1980 "A History of the Newfoundland Federation of Labour, 1936–1963." Unpublished Masters Thesis, Memorial University.

_____ 1986 *A Class Act: An Illustrated History of the Labour Move-*

ment in *Newfoundland and Labrador*. St. John's: Newfoundland and Labrador Federation of Labour.

Godfrey, Stuart 1985 *Human Rights and Social Policy in Newfoundland 1832-1982*. St. John's: Harry Cuff.

Goldstein, Jeffrey *et al.* 1975 *Aggression and Crimes of Violence*. New York: Oxford University Press.

Griffiths, R. 1983 *Fellow Travellers of the Right: British Enthusiasts for Nazi Germany, 1933-39*. Oxford: Oxford University Press.

Gunn, Gertrude 1966 *The Political History of Newfoundland 1832-64*. Toronto: University of Toronto Press.

Gurr, T.R. 1981 "Historical Trends in Violent Crime: A Critical Review of the Evidence." *Crime and Justice: Annual Review of Research*, (3)295–353.

Gusfield, J.R. 1981 *The Culture of Public Problems: Drinking, Driving and the Symbolic Order*. Chicago: University of Chicago Press.

Haldane, L., Elliott, D. and P. Whitehead 1972 "Particularism of Sentencing Juvenile Delinquents." In C. Boydell *et al.* (eds.), *Deviant Behaviour and Societal Reaction*. Toronto: Holt, Rinehart and Winston of Canada.

Hall, Stuart, Chas Critcher, Tony Jefferson, John Clarke and Brian Roberts 1978 *Policing the Crisis: Mugging, the State and Law and Order*. London: Macmillan.

Harris, Marvin 1981 "Why It's not the Same Old American." *Psychology Today*, 15(8):23–51.

Hay, Douglas 1982 "War, Death and Theft in the Eighteenth Century: The Record of the English Courts." *Past and Present*, 95:118.

_____ *et al.* 1975 *Albion's Fatal Tree: Crime and Society in Eighteenth-Century England*. London: Allen Lane.

Herbert, A. P. 1987 "What Charming Folk." In D.W.S. Ryan and T.P. Rossiter (eds.), *The Newfoundland Character*. St. John's: Jesperson Press.

Hill, R.H. 1983 *The Meaning of Work and the Reality of Unemployment in the Newfoundland Context*. St. John's: Community Services Council.

Hiller, James and Peter Neary (eds.) 1980 *Newfoundland in the Nineteenth and Twentieth Centuries: Essays in Interpretation*. Toronto: University of Toronto Press.

Hobsbawm, E.J. 1982 "Political Violence and Political Murder: Comments on Franklin Ford's Essay." In W.J. Mommsen and G. Hirshfeld (eds.), *Social Protest, Violence and Terror in Nineteenth- and Twentieth-Century Europe*. New York: St. Martin's Press.

Horwood, Harold 1986 *A History of the Newfoundland Ranger Force*. St. John's: Breakwater Books.

Hurka, Thomas 1990 "Statistics: Time to Update our Brains." *Globe and Mail*.

Jones, B. (ed.) 1985 *Political Issues in Britain Today.* Manchester: Manchester University Press.

Jones, Trevor, Brian MacLean and Jock Young 1986 *The Islington Crime Survey: Crime, Victimization and Policing in Inner-City London.* London: Gower.

Kaill, Robert and Paul Smith 1984 *Atlantic Crime Profile.* Halifax: Atlantic Institute of Criminology.

Keith, A.B. 1935 *Letters on Imperial Relations, Indian Reform, Constitutional and International Law, 1916–1935.* Oxford: Oxford University Press.

Kinsey, Richard 1986 "Crime in the City." *Marxism Today,* May, pp. 6–10.

_____ John Lea and Jock Young 1986 *Losing the Fight against Crime.* Oxford: Basil Blackwell.

Kirwin, W.J. (ed.) 1982 "Twenty-One Years on the 'Meigle'." *John White's Collection of Johnny Burke Songs.* St. John's: Harry Cuff.

Kitsuse, J. and A. Cicourel 1963 "A Note on the Uses of Official Statistics." *Social Problems,* 11:131–139.

Lea, John and J. Young 1984 *What is to be Done about Law and Order? Crisis in the Eighties.* Harmondsworth: Penguin Books.

_____ Robert Matthews and Jock Young 1988 *Law and Order: Five Years On.* Centre for Criminology: Middlesex Polytechnic.

Leyton, Elliott 1975 *Dying Hard: The Ravages of Industrial Carnage.* Toronto: McClelland and Stewart.

_____ 1979 *The Myth of Delinquency: an Anatomy of Juvenile Nihilism.* Toronto: McClelland and Stewart.

_____ 1983 "A Social Profile of Sexual Mass Murderers." In Thomas Fleming and L.A. Visano (eds.), *Deviant Designations: Crime, Law and Deviance in Canada.* Toronto: Butterworths.

_____ 1986 "Drunk and Disorderly: Changing Crime in Newfoundland." In Rex Clark (ed.), *Contrary Winds: Essays on Newfoundland Society in Crisis.* St. John's: Breakwater Books.

_____ 1986 *Hunting Humans: The Rise of the Modern Multiple Murderer.* Toronto: McClelland and Stewart. Published simultaneously in the U.S.A., under the title *Compulsive Killers,* by New York University Press.

_____ and Don Handelman 1979 *Bureaucracy and World View: Studies in the Logic of Official Interpretation.* St. John's: Institute of Social and Economic Research, Memorial University of Newfoundland.

Lodge, Thomas 1939 *Dictatorship in Newfoundland.* London: Cassell.

MacDonald, M. 1986 "The Secularization of Suicide in England 1660–1800." *Past and Present,* 111:51.

MacKay, H. 1983 "Social Impact of Unemployment." *Perception,* 6(5):32–34.

MacLean, Brian 1986 "State Expenditures on Canadian Criminal Justice." In B. MacLean (ed.), *The Political Economy of Crime: Readings for a Critical Criminology in Canada.* Scarborough: Prentice-Hall.

Malwaka, E. J. 1983 "The Price of Youth Unemployment." *Social Perspectives*, 2(3):2.

Manwaring-White, S. 1983 *The Policing Revolution.* Brighton: Harvester.

Matthews, Ralph 1976 *'There's No Better Place Than Here': Social Change in Three Newfoundland Communities.* Toronto: Peter Martin.

Matthews, R. and J. Young (eds.) 1986 *Confronting Crime.* London: Sage.

McCabe, Sarah and Frank Sutcliffe 1978 *Defining Crime.* Oxford University Centre for Criminological Research, Occasional Paper Number 9. Oxford: Basil Blackwell.

McDonald, Ian 1980 "W.F. Coaker and the Balance of Power Strategy: The Fishermen's Protective Union in Newfoundland Politics." In J. Hiller and P. Neary (eds.), *Newfoundland in the Nineteenth and Twentieth Centuries: Essays in Interpretation.* Toronto: University of Toronto Press.

McDonald, L. 1976 "Crime and Punishment in Canada: a test of the 'Conventional Wisdom.'" *The Canadian Review of Sociology and Anthropology*, 6:212–236.

McGahan, Peter 1984 *Police Images of a City.* New York: Peter Lang.

McGrath, P.T. 1911 *Newfoundland in 1911.* London: Whitehead, Morris and Co.

Mckie, C. and Paul Reed 1979 "The Repercussions of Criminal Statistics on Public Attitudes." Research Study Number 6. Ottawa: Statistics Canada.

Miles, Ian and John Irvine 1979 "The Critique of Official Statistics." In John Irvine, Ian Miles and Jeff Evans, *Demystifying Social Statistics*. London: Pluto Press.

Mill, J.S. 1910 *Representative Government.* London: J.M. Dent.

Milliband, Ralph 1982 *Capitalist Democracy in Britain.* Oxford: Oxford University Press.

Morgan, D.J. 1980 *The Origins of British Aid Policy, 1924–1945.* London: Macmillan.

Muggeridge, M. 1971 *The Thirties.* London: Collins-Fontana.

Murdock, Graham 1982 "Mass Communication and Social Violence: A Critical Review of Recent Research Trends." In Peter Marsh and Anne Campbell (eds.), *Aggression and Violence.* Oxford: Blackwells.

Neary, Peter 1985 "The Bradley Report on Logging Operations in Newfoundland, 1934: A Suppressed Document." *Labour/Le Travail*, (16):193–232.

_____ 1988 *Newfoundland in the North Atlantic world 1929–1949.* Kingston: Queen's University Press.

Nelson, B.J. 1984 *Making an Issue of Child Abuse: Political Agenda Setting for Social Problems.* Chicago: University of Chicago Press.

Newfoundland: Annual Reports of the Commission of Government 1934–1939 London: HMSO.

Newfoundland Department of Justice, Adult Corrections Division 1971–1985 Annual Reports. St. John's, Newfoundland.

Newfoundland Department of Rural, Agricultural and Northern Development 1983 "Persistence and Change: The Social and Economic Development of Rural Newfoundland and Labrador, 1971 to 1981." Research and Analysis Division.

Newfoundland and Labrador Federation of Labour 1978 "Now That We've Burned Our Boats..." The Report of the People's Commission on Unemployment. St. John's: Creative Printers.

_____ 1983 "Unemployment Isn't Working." Report on the Provincial Economic Conference, June 13 and 14.

Newfoundland Royal Commission Report 1933.

Newfoundland Status of Women's Council 1982 "A History of Celebration: 10 Years of Feminism (1972–1982)." St. John's.

Noel, S.J.R. 1971 *Politics in Newfoundland.* Toronto: University of Toronto Press.

Nye, Robert A. 1984 *Crime, Madness, and Politics in Modern France.* Princeton: Princeton University Press.

O'Grady, Bill and Jim Overton 1986 "Popular Anxiety, Armed Robbery and Sentencing in Newfoundland." St. John's, unpublished paper.

Overton, James 1980 "Promoting the 'Real' Newfoundland: Culture as a Tourist Commodity." *Studies In Political Economy,* 4:115–137.

_____ 1985 "A Newfoundland Culture?" Unpublished paper presented at the Political Economy sessions of the Canadian Political Science Association in Montreal, May 31.

_____ 1986 "Beyond a Cost-Benefit Approach to the Problem of Unemployment." Unpublished paper prepared for the Sixth Conference on Workers and their Communities held at the University of Ottawa, May 11.

_____ 1987 "Politics of Culture and Ecology." *Journal of Canadian Studies,* 22(1):84–103.

_____ 1988 "A Newfoundland Culture?" *Journal of Canadian Studies,* 23(1):5–22.

_____ 1988 "Public Relief and Social Unrest in Newfoundland in the 1930s: An Evaluation of the Ideas of Piven and Cloward." *Canadian Journal of Sociology,* 3(1/2):143–169.

_____ 1990 "Economic Crisis and the End of Democracy: Politics in Newfoundland in the Great Depression." *Labour/Le Travail*, 26:85-124.

Pearson, Geoffrey 1983 *Hooliganism: A History of Respectable Fears.* London: Macmillan.

_____ 1985 "Lawlessness, Modernity and Social Change: A Historical Appraisal." *Theory, Culture and Society*, 2(3):15-33.

Pepinsky, H. 1980 *Crime Control Strategies.* New York: Oxford University Press.

Petty, Sir William 1967 *The Petty Papers; Some Unpublished Writings of Sir William Petty.* Edited from the Bowood Papers by the Marquis of Lansdowne. New York: A.M. Kelley.

Phipps, A. 1986 "Radical Criminology and Criminal Victimization: Proposals for the Development of Theory and Intervention." In R. Matthews and J. Young (eds.), *Confronting Crime.* London: Sage.

Pick, Daniel 1986 "The Faces of Anarchy: Lombroso and the Politics of Criminal Science in Post-Unification Italy." *History Workshop Journal*, 21:61.

Powell, George H. 1981 "The Impact of Offshore Gas and Oil Development on Policing Requirements in Newfoundland." Royal Canadian Mounted Police.

Prowse, Judge 1900 *Newfoundland in 1900.* New York: The South Publishing Co.

Roberts, Barbara 1983 "No Safe Place: The War Against Women." *Our Generation*, 15(4):7-26.

Rock, P. 1981 "Rioting." *London Review of Books*, 17(30):3-4.

Royal Canadian Mounted Police-"B" Division Various information was obtained from criminal files ranging from 1953-1984.

Royal Newfoundland Constabulary Various information was obtained from annual reports ranging from 1933-1985 and criminal files, ranging from 1950-1984.

St. John's Board of Trade 1985 "A Case Study of Retail Crime." St. John's, Newfoundland.

St. John's Status of Women Council 1986 "Report on the Child Sexual Abuse Workshop." *The Web*, March-April, pp. 36-37. St. John's.

Saville, J. 1977 "May Day 1937." In A. Briggs and J. Saville (eds.), *Essays in Labour History, 1918-1939.* London: Croom-Helm.

Schacter, Eric 1986 "The James Duke Story." Unpublished essay. St. John's.

Schechter, Susan 1982 *Women and Male Violence.* Boston:, South End Press.

Sewell, John 1985 *Police: Urban Policing in Canada.* Toronto: James Lorimer & Company.

Sharpe, J.A. 1985 "The History of Violence in England: Some Observations." *Past and Present*, 108:212.

Sherizen, Sanford 1978 "Social Creation of Crime News: All the News Fitted to Print." In Charles Winick (ed.), *Deviance and Mass Media*. Beverly Hills: Sage.

Solicitor General Canada 1984 *Preliminary Findings of the Canadian Victimization Survey*. Ottawa: Ministry of the Solicitor General of Canada.

Statistics Canada/Dominion Bureau of Statistics 1947–1984 *Crime and Traffic Statistics*. Ottawa: Queen's Printer.

Statistics Canada 1981 *Future of National Justice Statistcs Information in Canada: Report from the Work Group on Resource and Coordination for Justice Statistics and Information*. Ottawa: Supply and Services.

Sharpe, J.A. 1985 "The History of Violence in England: Some Observations." *Past and Present*, 108:206–215.

Snyder, Francis 1980 "Law and Development in the Light of Dependency Theory." *Law and Society Review*, 14(3):723–802.

Spitz, D. 1949 *Patterns of Anti-Democratic Thought*. New York: The Free Press.

Stevenson, John 1979 *Popular Disturbances in England 1700–1870*. London: Longman.

Stone, Lawrence 1983 "Interpersonal Violence in English Society 1300–1980." *Past and Present*, 101:22–33.

_____ 1985 "A Rejoinder." *Past and Present*, 108:216–224.

Sumner, Colin (ed.) 1982 *Crime, Justice and Underdevelopment*. London: Heineman.

Swigert, V.L. and Ronald A. Farrell 1976 *Murder, Inequality, and the Law*. Toronto: Lexington Books.

Szwed, J. 1966 *Private Cultures and Public Imagery*. St. John's: Institute of Social and Economic Research, Memorial University of Newfoundland.

Taylor, Ian 1981 "Crime Waves in Post-War Britain." *Contemporary Crises*, 5:43–62.

_____ 1983 *Crime, Capitalism and Community*. Toronto: Butterworths.

_____ 1984 "'Taking the Side of the People' in Canada." *Perception*, 7(4):12–14.

_____ 1985 "Criminology, the Unemployment Crisis and the Liberal Tradition in Canada." In T. Fleming (ed.), *The New Criminologies in Canada: State, Crime and Control*. Toronto: Oxford University Press.

Tepperman, Lorne 1977 *Crime Control*. Toronto: McGraw-Hill Ryerson Limited.

Thompson, E.P. 1971 "The Moral Economy of the English Crowd in the Eighteenth Century." *Past and Present*, (50):76–79.

_____ 1975 *Whigs and Hunters: The Origin of the Black Act.* London: Allen Lane.

Tombs, Robert 1980 "Crime and Security of the State: the 'Dangerous Classes' and Insurrection in Nineteenth-century Paris." In V.A.C. Gatrell, B. Lenman and G. Parker (eds.), *Crime and the Law: The Social History of Crime in Western Europe since 1500.* London: Europa.

Torrance, Judy M. 1986 *Public Violence in Canada, 1867–1982.* Kingston: McGill-Queen's University Press.

Toynbee, A.J. 1932 *Survey of International Affairs, 1931.* Oxford: Oxford University Press.

Unsworth, Clive 1982 "The Riots of 1981: Popular Violence and the Politics of Law and Order." *Journal of Law and Society*, 9(1):63–85.

Voumvakis, Sophia and Richard Ericson 1984 *News Accounts of Attacks on Women: A Comparison of Three Toronto Newspapers.* Toronto: Centre of Criminology.

Waddington, P.A.J. 1986 "Mugging as a Moral Panic: A Question of Proportion." *The British Journal of Sociology*, XXXVII(2):245–259.

Webb, J.A. 1986 "British Policy in Newfoundland and the Quest for a Constitutional Solution, 1934–1945." Unpublished paper, Department of History, Memorial University of Newfoundland.

Williams, Raymond 1975 *The Country and the City.* London: Palladin.

_____ 1976 *Keywords.* London: Fontana.

Wilson, Elizabeth 1983 *What is to be Done about Violence Against Women?* Middlesex: Penguin Press.

Wright, Kevin N. 1985 *The Great American Crime Myth.* Westport, Conn.: Greenwood Press.

Young, Jock 1986 "The Failure of Criminology: The Need for a Radical-Realism." In Roger Matthews and Jock Young (eds.), *Confronting Crime.* London: Sage.

_____ 1987 "The Tasks Facing a Realist Criminology." *Contemporary Crisis*, 11:337–355.

Newspapers

Avalon Welfare and Protective Association Bulletin 1934.
Bay Roberts Guardian 1932
Daily Express 1938–1939
Daily Globe 1925
Daily News 1931–1938, 1978
Evening Telegram 1931–1937, 1975–1986
Fishermen's Advocate 1931–1936

Labour Herald 1938
Leader, The 1937
Liberal Press 1928
Metro, The 1986
Montreal Gazette 1983
Newfoundland Herald 1986
Newfoundland Quarterly 1943
Observer's Weekly 1934

Archival Sources

Provincial Archives of Newfoundland and Labrador (PANL) 1930–1938
Correspondence, Memoranda, Reports and Telegrams

Dominions Office (DO) 1934–1941 various reports

ISER BOOKS

Papers

19 **Living in a Material World: Canadian and American Approaches to Material Culture**—Gerald L. Pocius (ed.)

18 **To Work and to Weep: Women in Fishing Economies**—Jane Nadel-Klein and Dona Lee Davis (eds.)

17 **A Question of Survival: The Fisheries and Newfoundland Society**—Peter R. Sinclair (ed.)

16 **Fish Versus Oil: Resources and Rural Development in North Atlantic Societies**—J.D. House (ed.)

15 **Advocacy and Anthropology: First Encounters**—Robert Paine (ed.)

14 **Indigenous Peoples and the Nation-State: Fourth World Politics in Canada, Australia and Norway**—Noel Dyck (ed.)

13 **Minorities and Mother Country Imagery**—Gerald Gold (ed.)

12 **The Politics of Indianness: Case Studies of Native Ethnopolitics in Canada**—Adrian Tanner (ed.)

11 **Belonging: Identity and Social Organisation in British Rural Cultures**—Anthony P. Cohen (ed.) (in North America only)

10 **Politically Speaking: Cross-Cultural Studies of Rhetoric**—Robert Paine (ed.)

9 **A House Divided? Anthropological Studies of Factionalism**—M. Silverman and R.F. Salisbury (eds.)

8 **The Peopling of Newfoundland: Essays in Historical Geography**—John J. Mannion (ed.)

7 **The White Arctic: Anthropological Essays on Tutelage and Ethnicity**—Robert Paine (ed.)

6 **Consequences of Offshore Oil and Gas—Norway, Scotland and Newfoundland**—M.J. Scarlett (ed.)

5 **North Atlantic Fishermen: Anthropological Essays on Modern Fishing**—Raoul Andersen and Cato Wadel (eds.)

4 **Intermediate Adaptation in Newfoundland and the Arctic: A Strategy of Social and Economic Development**—Milton M.R. Freeman (ed.)

3 **The Compact: Selected Dimensions of Friendship**—Elliott Leyton (ed.)

2 **Patrons and Brokers in the East Arctic**—Robert Paine (ed.)

1 **Viewpoints on Communities in Crisis**—Michael L. Skolnik (ed.)

Mailing Address:
    ISER Books (Institute of Social and Economic Research)
    Memorial University of Newfoundland
    St. John's, Newfoundland, Canada, A1C 5S7